Economic Growth and Development in Africa

In recent years Africa has undergone the longest period of sustained economic growth in the continent's history, drawing the attention of the international media and academics alike. This book analyses the Africa Rising narrative (ARN) from multidisciplinary perspectives, offering a critical assessment of the explanations given for the poor economic growth and development performance in Africa prior to the millennium, and the dramatic shift towards the new Africa.

Bringing in perspectives from African intellectuals and scholars, many of whom have previously been overlooked in this debate, the book examines the construction of Africa's economic growth and development portraits over the years. It looks at two institutions that play a vital role in African development, providing a detailed explanation of how the World Bank and the International Monetary Fund (IMF) have interpreted and dealt with the African challenges and experiences. The insightful analysis reveals that if Africa is rising, only 20–30 per cent of Africans are aboard the rising ship, and the main challenge facing the continent today is to bring on board the majority of Africans who have been excluded from growth.

This book makes the complex, and sometimes confusing, debates on Africa's economic growth experience more accessible to a wide range of readers interested in the Africa story. It is essential reading for students and researchers in African Studies, and will be of great interest to scholars in Development Studies, Political Economy, and Development Economics.

Horman Chitonge is a senior researcher at the Centre for African Studies, University of Cape Town, South Africa. He holds a PhD in Development Studies from the University of KwaZulu-Natal and has taught development theory and policy on Africa at various African universities. His research interests include access to water and land, poverty, and alternatives for Africa's economic growth and transformation.

Routledge Studies in African Development

**Self-Determination and Secession
in Africa**
The post-colonial state
Edited by Redie Bereketeab

**Economic Growth and Development
in Africa**
Understanding trends and prospects
Horman Chitonge

Economic Growth and Development in Africa

Understanding trends and prospects

Horman Chitonge

Routledge
Taylor & Francis Group

LONDON AND NEW YORK

First published 2015
by Routledge
2 Park Square, Milton Park, Abingdon, Oxfordshire OX14 4RN

and by Routledge
711 Third Avenue, New York, NY 10017

First issued in paperback 2016

Routledge is an imprint of the Taylor & Francis Group, an informa business

© 2015 Horman Chitonge

The right of Horman Chitonge to be identified as author of this work has been asserted by him in accordance with sections 77 and 78 of the Copyright, Designs and Patents Act 1988.

British Library Cataloguing in Publication Data
A catalogue record for this book is available from the British Library

Library of Congress Cataloguing in Publication data
Chitonge, Horman, author.
  Economic growth and development in Africa: understanding trends
  and prospects / Horman Chitonge.
    pages cm
  1. Economic development–Africa. 2. Africa–Economic conditions. I. Title.
  HC800.C494 2015
  338.96–dc23
  2014029397

ISBN 13: 978-1-138-22602-9 (pbk)
ISBN 13: 978-1-138-82680-9 (hbk)

Typeset in Goudy
by Out of House Publishing

Contents

Figures

Tables

Foreword

This book is the product of an extended period of reflecting on Africa's economic growth and development performance over the past six decades. Although this reflection started a long time back, it was a 2000 World Bank publication entitled *Can Africa Claim the 21st Century?* which stirred my interest in the topic more poignantly. What caught my attention in this publication was the report that, excluding South Africa, the total output for all 47 countries that constituted Sub-Saharan Africa in 2000 was slightly less than Belgium's Gross Domestic Product (GDP) – and that the median GDP for countries in the sub-continent was just US$2 billion, "about the output of a town of 60000 in a rich country" (World Bank, 2000: 7).

When I read this, I stopped for a while to think about the various implications of this comparison, and my mind could not accommodate well the idea that Sub-Saharan Africa, with its 616.1 million people (excluding South Africa's population of 42.8 million), produced fewer goods and services (valued at US$196.8 billion in 2000) than Belgium (US$222.7 billion) with its population of just 9.8 million people. One way of looking at this is that in 2000 there were 63 Africans for every Belgian, and assuming that all the people contributed to producing the respective outputs, this means that, on average, one Belgian produced more than what 63 Sub-Saharan Africans produced. These proportions, despite the challenges associated with the data on which these estimates are derived[1], are astounding, and should make the curious reader pause to reflect a little more on the meaning beyond just the naked numbers. Of course this comparison becomes even more staggering if we look at Sub-Saharan Africa in comparison to big countries and economies such as the USA, Germany, France, Japan and Italy.

For the many people who read the report, both within and outside Africa, there was nothing unusual about the numbers; it was common knowledge that Sub-Saharan Africa's economies had been declining since the 1970s, and therefore it was not surprising that the combined output of the more than 600 million Sub-Saharan Africans was actually less than that of Belgium's ten million people. Analysts and lay people alike have become so used to the idea of an African economic tragedy, failure and crisis that nothing appears unusual as far as Africa is concerned. When it comes to Africa, many people perform a super 'normalisation' act without the slightest probe. Such attitudes are often reinforced by long-surviving media articles and popular stories about Africa being a weird place where only disorder, hopelessness and instability reign.

This image of Africa has been so embedded in our thinking that even startling statistics seem not to cause any disturbance to many people. Since time series data became readily available it has become fashionable to make comparisons between Africa and other regions; though not to reflect upon what the proportions actually mean but rather just as a way of showing how badly Africa fares. No effort is dedicated to understanding *why* Africa has fared this way. Few people stop to think about what such comparisons mean; critics of these statistics simply dismiss them as meaningless aggregates used as a propaganda tool by the World Bank and the International Monetary Fund (IMF), while others simply see nothing really unusual. To many there is nothing bizarre about the fact that in 2000, 63 Sub-Saharan Africans produced less than what one Belgian produced; neither does it raise curiosity that Belgium, with just 30,500 km^2 of land, produced more than Sub-Saharan Africa with its 23 million km^2 of land (excluding South Africa's 1,221,037 km^2).We are not sure what lies beneath Belgian soil, but we know for sure that African soil is endowed with various kinds of minerals, oil, natural gas, forests, surface and underground water, wildlife, etc. A curious mind should be unsettled by the fact that less is actually produced in the land of plenty. Even if one were to believe, as many do, that most people in Africa are unproductive, equipped with crude tools and a smaller impetus for greater achievement, the mere scale of the proportions involved in the equation should make a curious mind ask the prime question – why?

The many who have grappled with this question have produced diverse and sometimes contradictory explanations. As elaborated in this book, some commentators have blamed the weak economic growth performance in Africa on the fact that almost two-thirds of the continent is located in the tropics; others have pointed to the lack of adept leaders, poor policies, and the stunted nature of capitalism which has developed in Africa; while yet others have put the blame on the fundamental nature of capitalism itself – which gave rise to the slave trade, colonialism, and now multilateral imperialism. Some have explained the African economic performance in terms of Africa's failure to emulate countries in Europe – and now Asia – in their quest for growth and development. All these different explanations have different starting points and areas of focus in their attempts to understand the economic growth and development experience in Africa over the past six decades. This book looks at these different explanations from different perspectives and scholarly traditions, thereby presenting a wider window through which Africa's economic growth and development experience – past and present – can be viewed. By looking critically at the various accounts offered for this performance, this work also highlights some of the unresolved puzzles.

Since 2000, many countries in Africa have been experiencing sustained growth, and this experience is slowly giving rise to a new optimism, an optimism that is captured widely in the Africa Rising narrative (ARN). However, as with the past experience, it is important to understand the sources and drivers of the current growth spurt in order to respond appropriately to the challenges and opportunities that this momentum brings. Judging by the initial curiosity and reflection that inspired the writing of this book, there has been little progress. Eleven years after the World Bank's 2000 publication, the comparison between Belgium and 47 Sub-Saharan African countries should still make the critical reader pause to think. In 2011, the now 11 million Belgians produced goods and services valued at US$506.2 billion – compared to the US$748 billion produced by the 824 million Sub-Saharan Africans (excluding South Africa). If we now take Nigeria out of the equation, we are back at those 2000 proportions.

To some people, seeking to understand Africa's economic growth and development experience is a futile exercise given the continent's history of disorder and instability. But for those of us in the continent, understanding this experience should be a starting point for re-imaging and rewriting Africa. Our understanding of this condition should draw from the lived experience in-continent, and be driven by the enduring challenges that we face, as well as by the possibility of a better prospect for the future. Such a discussion is all the more appropriate today, at a time when the debate about Africa's past and future economic growth and development performance is rising to the top of the agenda, in different forums, both within and outside Africa – be they media, business, academic, donors, non-governmental organisations (NGOs), politicians or investors. It is my hope that the reflection in this book on past trends and future prospects for Africa's growth and development performance will contribute towards efforts aimed at understanding these dynamics and managing them better in an African context.

Notes

1 For a detailed discussion on the quality of the System of National Accounts (SNA) data from which GDP estimates are derived, see Jerven (2013), Deverajan (2013), Srinivasan (1994) and Wade (2004).

Acknowledgements

This work was made possible by contributions from different people. Writing the book required sacrificing hundreds of hours away from family and friends, and I would like to thank Dr Millicent. A. Chitonge and the children for their understanding and support. I would also like to thank Millicent for taking the time to read through the entire draft manuscript and for the constructive comments and suggestions.

The final manuscript of the book was prepared while I was travelling around Africa, particularly during my research fellowship visits at the University of Zambia (UNZA) and the Makerere University in Uganda. I would therefore like to express my sincere gratitude to my hosts (the Department of Geography and Environmental Studies at UNZA, and the School of Distance and Life Long Learning at Makerere). I would also like to thank the two anonymous reviewers for their useful comments and suggestions which have helped reshape the book. My sincere thanks to the Commissioning Editor, *Environment and Sustainability*, the *Routledge Studies in African Development Series*, Khanam Virjee, for taking keen interest in this work; and also the Assistant Editor, Bethany Wright, and the entire editorial team for their patience and unwavering assistance during the preparation of the final manuscript.

Chapter 7 of the book was written during my visiting fellowship at Keele University, and I would like to thank Emeritus Professor Peter Lawrence for inviting me, and for all the assistance and encouragement he provided while I was at Keele. I would also like to acknowledge the SOC5010F class of 2012 at the University of Cape Town (UCT) with whom I discussed some of the draft chapters during the seminars. I wish to acknowledge financial support in the form of a Research Development Grant awarded by UCT's research office, which provided financial support during the time I was working on Chapter 7 of this book. I would also like to express my sincere gratitude to the UCT inter-library loan staff for their unwavering support in sourcing some of the material I used in this book which could not be found in the UCT main library.

Acronyms

AERC	African Economic Research Consortium
AGOA	African Growth Opportunity Act
ANC	African National Congress
APPP	African Power and Politics Programme
APR	Africa Progress Report
ARN	Africa Rising narrative
AU	African Union
BoP	Balance of Payments
BWI	Bretton Woods Institutions
CCLs	Contingent Credit Lines
CE	Common Era
CODESRIA	Council for the Development of Social Research in Africa
CBOs	Community-based Organisations
CPIA	Country Policy and Institutional Assessment
DRC	Democratic Republic of the Congo
EAS	Emergence Assistance
EEIT	East and South-Eastern Investment Trust
EFF	Extended Fund Facility
EPAs	Economic Partnerships Agreements
ESAF	Enhanced Structural Adjustment Facility
EU	European Union
FDI	Foreign Direct Investments
FED	Federal Reserve
GDP	Gross Domestic Product
GNP/I	Gross National Product/Income
HDR	Human Development Report
HIPC	Highly Indebted Poor Countries
IBRD	International Bank for Reconstruction and Development
ICSID	International Centre for the Settlement of Investment Disputes
ICT	Information and Communications Technology
IDA	International Development Association
IFC	International Finance Corporation

IFI	International Financial Institution
ILO	International Labour Organisation
IMF	International Monetary Fund
INGOs	International Non-Governmental Organisations
ISI	Import Substitution Industrialisation
LDCs	Less Developed Countries
LPA	Lagos Plan of Action
MDRI	Multilateral Debt Relief Initiative
MGI	McKinsey Global Institute
MIGA	Multilateral Investment Guarantee Agency
MITI	Ministry of International Trade and Industry
MOA	Market-oriented Approaches
NEPAD	New Partnership for African Development
NGO	non-governmental organisation
NICs	Newly Industrialised Countries
NIE	New Institutional Economics
NIIP	Negative Net International Investment Position
NPE	New Political Economy
NPV	Net Present Value
OAU	Organisation of African Unity
ODA	Official Development Assistance
OECD	Organisation for Economic Cooperation and Development
OIE	Old Institutional Economics
OLS	Ordinary Least Square
PE	Political Economy
PEA	Political Economy Approaches
PPP	Purchasing Power Parity
PRGF	Poverty Reduction and Growth Facility
PRSP	Poverty Reduction Strategy Papers
R&D	Research and Development
RAL	Report on Adjustment Lending
RECs	Regional Economic Communities
RPE	Radical Political Economy
SAF	Structural Adjustment Facility
SAL	Structural Adjustment Lending
SALs	Structural Adjustment Loans
SAPs	Structural Adjustment Programmes
SBA	Stand-By Arrangement
SDRs	Special Drawing Rights
SECAL	Sectoral Adjustment Loans
SOA	State-oriented Approaches
SRF	Supplementary Reserve Facility
SSA	Sub-Saharan Africa
SSBG	Steady-state Balanced Growth
TFP	Total Factor Productivity

UNCTAD	United Nations Conference on Trade and Development
UNECA	(United Nations) Economic Commission for Africa
UNDP	United Nations Development Programme
UNICEF	United Nations Children's Fund
WDI	*World Development Indicators*
WDR	*World Development Report*
WWGI	World Wide Governance Indicators

1 Introduction: in search of the 'Africa dummy'

Introduction

In a book, compiled from a collection of Ohlin lecturers,[1] Paul Krugman (1996) starts with a story about how European knowledge of Africa has evolved over the last 500 years. Krugman cites a paper by Craig Murphy, entitled "The Evolution of Ignorance in European Mapping of Africa, 1500–1800". The main point made by Krugman in telling this story is that as European knowledge of Africa advanced – as a result of progress in map-making technology and communications – the map of Africa, and primarily the stories about Africa, remained sensationally inaccurate, often distorted by design. For instance, even as late as the eighteenth century, there were popular myths about certain regions in Africa "inhabited by men with their mouths in their stomachs". Adam Hochschild talks about a "Benedictine monk who mapped the world about 1350 [AD] and claimed that Africa contained one-eyed people who used their feet to cover their heads". He also reports that a geographer, during the fifteenth century, "announced that the continent held people with one leg, three faces, and heads of lions" (cited in Fredland, 2001: 26).

Of course, prior to the map-making endeavours of the fifteenth century, Europeans had been making contact with coastal communities in West and North Africa over a long time (see Iliffe, 1983; Davidson, 1992) – but the interior remained largely unknown until the time of the European explorers towards the end of the eighteenth century. Seemingly, most of the stories and maps about Africa's interior were based on third-hand reports of people visiting Africa's coastline (see Coetzee, 1988). In most of these undertakings,

> Cartographic vagueness had been the hallmark of Africa's depiction from the first attempt – by Ptolemy – to map part of the continent in Anno Domini 150. Some 1,300 years later the seafarers of Portugal began to plot the coastline but [the] African interior remained a mystery to the rest of the world and a field for the imagination of map makers drawing upon hearsay, in the words of Dean Swift:

'So geographers, in Afric-maps,
With savage-pictures fill their gaps,
And o'er unhabitable downs,
Place elephants for want of towns'
(Mackay, 2008: 243)

As Europeans penetrated the African interior, not only did they replace the flourishing African civilisations with their stories of 'savages', but also the "achievements of states that had manufactured in iron and gold and carried on lucrative international trade were expunged from memory … It does not require a very perceptive mind to appreciate the disastrous consequences [this] has had upon African development" (Nkrumah, 1963: 5).

Reading these eighteenth and nineteenth century stories about Africa today, makes them seem gawkily fictitious – though it is clear that the denigrated portraits of the African continent and its peoples have stoutly populated the 'invented' history, economy, politics and cultural representation of Africa and its inherent discourse of what has been referred to as the "ideology of 'otherness'" (see Mazrui, 2005: 69).

Given that the dominant representation of Africa and its peoples was one of 'negative difference' – leading to the popular notion of a barbarous, inferior, backward people – it is not surprising that as knowledge about the continent and its people increased, the negative difference mode of representation persisted well beyond the European exploration of the African interior, serving as the foundation stone of the colonial project (Hill, 2005). Eighteenth and nineteenth century explorers such as James Bruce, Mungo Park, David Livingstone, Richard and John Lander, Richard Burton, John Hanning Speke, and the naturalised American journalist, Henry Stanley Morton – during the first half of the nineteenth century – added new layers to the ideology of otherness.[2] While these explorers played an important role in opening the African interior to European interests, it has been observed that apart from creating myths about 'beastly savages' and 'barbaric splendours', the explorer stories "speak about neither Africa nor Africans, but rather justify the process of inventing and conquering a continent and naming its 'primitiveness' or 'disorder' as well as the subsequent means of its exploitation and methods for its 'regeneration'"(Mudimbe, 1988: 20). Radical critics have argued that the main drivers behind these adventures, including the colonial enterprise that followed, were

> neither evangelization, nor a philanthropic enterprise, nor a desire to push back the frontiers of ignorance, disease, and tyranny, nor a project undertaken for the greater glory of God … the decisive actors here are the adventurers and the pirates, the wholesale grocer and the ship owner, the gold digger and the merchant … and behind them, the baleful projected shadow of a form of civilisation.
>
> (Cesaire, 2000: 33)

Notably, the encounter between Africa, and mainly Western European culture(s), has produced exceptional forms of mystification which have served as the justification for several projects. Examples of this mystification include claims such as: Africans had no history prior to the encounter with the West; Africa is incomprehensible, irrational and disorderly by nature, with no ability for self-government; that African societies are inherently undemocratic; that Africans have not contributed to world progress (Leakey, 1961, cited in Nkrumah, 1963). Historical accounts by authors such as Basil Davidson about a rich tradition of democratic practices – obliterated by the imperial and colonial projects – have done little to sway popular beliefs, even among Africans (Brown, 1995).

In a way, the fourteenth century stories and maps – with their depictions of monster-like beings in Africa – are not just myths produced by angelic innocence or a sheer lack of knowledge about the continent; they are part of a strategic narrative upon which the conquering and domination of Africa and African peoples has been built, refined into ideologies that serve specific interests of the subsequent social, political and economic architects. This negative portrait of Africa, through stories and maps, fed and nurtured the colonial attitude of treating anything different as inferior, barbaric, uncultured, uncivilised, pagan, undeveloped, pre-capitalist, pre-industrial, and pre-modern; hence the self-appointed mission of evangelising, civilising and developing – *Pax Romana*, *Pax Britanica*, *Pax Americana*. To justify these grand missions it was necessary to depict Africa in vague and belittling terms right from the start.

This ideology of subordinating anything that is different (or other) was so profound that some European and American thinkers and commentators perceived themselves as not just superior beings, but as gods or deities in relation to Africans. Joseph Conrad, in his biographical novel about the Congo, reflects upon the dominance of such beliefs among senior staff at the Belgium Congo Company: "we whites, from the point of development we had arrived at, must necessarily appear to them [savages] in the nature of supernatural beings – we approach them with the might of a deity". A similar view is expressed by an American senator, Albert Beveridge, who in 1903 is reported to have argued that God "has made us ['English speaking and Teutonic peoples'] the master organisers of the world to establish systems where chaos reigns. He has made us adept in governance that we may administer government among savage and servile peoples" (cited in Alavi and Shanin, 1982: 74–6).

Subsequent hegemonic projects in the economic, social, political and cultural spheres have been justified not only through the creation of 'paradigmatic opposites' such as tradition versus modern, pagan versus Christian, 'savage' versus civilised, pre-capitalist versus capitalist, underdeveloped versus developed, rural versus urban, agrarian versus industrial, but also through open denial of the African humanness. A typical example of this is a description of indigenous South Africans by a Dutch publisher (apparently based on the traveller's reports during the seventeenth century):

> The local natives have everything in common with the dumb cattle, barring their human nature... [They] are handicapped in their speech, clucking like turkey-cocks or like the people of Alpine Germany who have developed goitre by drinking the hard snow-water.
>
> (cited in Coetzee, 1988: 12)

Influential thinkers and writers – including Immanuel Kant, Georg F.W. Hegel, David Hume, the famous Historian Arnold Toynbee, and the renowned American statesman Thomas Jefferson – earlier cast doubt on the ability of Africans to think (see Asante n.d.; Mamdani, 1996: 4). This has often generated a tacit reluctance among non-Africans to accept Africans as equals. One example of this is evidently clear in John Cecil Rhodes' 1898 submission to the Cape Parliament, where he argued that:

> I have made up my mind ... that we have got to treat natives in a different way to ourselves. We are to be lords over them. These are my politics on the native affair, and these are the politics of South Africa.
>
> (cited in Alavi and Shanin, 1982: 72–3).

A renowned French historian and writer expressed a similar view, albeit in more explicit terms, when he argued that:

> nature has made a race of workers ... a race of tillers of the soil, the Negro ... a race of masters and soldiers, the European race. Let each one do what he is made for, and all will be well.
>
> (cited in Hill, 2005: 142)

Such views have not just been restricted to politics and international relations; they have permeated every sector of interaction between Africa and the West, including the intellectual sphere. In 1906 Mary H. Kingsley is reported to have complained that "the African has never made an even fourteenth-rate piece of cloth or pottery" (cited in Mudimbe, 1988: 10). Centuries of cultural, educational, political, architectural, musical and economic hegemony have had a deleterious impact on the perception of Africa and Africans, a situation that has been highlighted by critical African thinkers including Aime Cesaire, Franz Fanon, Leopold Senghor, Amical Cabra, Kwame Nkrumah, etc. This sneering about the African continent and its peoples has been carried out in many areas of life, including the way Africa is studied and knowledge produced on Africa and Africans. The study of Africa, even in many African universities (and there are few universities which offer African Studies as part of the curriculum), is consigned to 'area studies' that are largely reserved for emotional or sensational exploration rather than rational inquiry – which is the reserve of the 'disciplines'. And the key distinction here is that the 'disciplines' teach *Western* experience – regarded as the "universal human experience" – whereas area studies are taught as "the experience of people of colour as an ethnic experience" (Mamdani, 1998: 104).

Those fourteenth century (and later) stories about Africa and its peoples have continued to evolve, giving rise to new layers of 'otherness', such that though more information is available today about the continent, there are still ways in which our understanding and image of Africa (and Africans) has been largely meditated through the negative mode of representation – the ideology of otherness. A particular way of writing and imagining Africa has been entrenched through physical interaction as well as through the production and dissemination of knowledge and popular culture. At both levels, Africa does not produce for its own consumption; African economies are set to produce primary commodities for export, leading to the extroversion of both knowledge and economic production structures (see Hountondji, 2002). In view of this, some analysts contend that because of this extroversion of "African knowledge production and economic activity, … Africa lost the independence to produce its own knowledge to serve its own economy", resulting in a vicious circle that perpetuates the view of Africa as a continent that is less intelligible, less rational (Nabudere, 2006: 37).

Aware of the continued scheme of defining Africa from outside, some authors have attributed this phenomenon to the ironic role of education in Africa, arguing that education – which might have been expected to produce enlightened African citizens – has in fact been a means through which the extroversion of Africa has been perpetuated (see Armah, 2010; Brown, 1995). Scholars who see this as one of the biggest challenges facing Africa, have suggested that "African scholars will have to purge themselves of the infection of Eurocentrism (which has continued to claim the right to know Africa) if Africa is to be retrieved from the Curse of Ham" (Nabudere, 2006: 47). Delo Oluwe, a prominent Nigerian political science professor, makes a similar point – arguing that what will make Africa find itself is not copying organisational and production systems from others, but rather harnessing the organisational and problem-solving capacity of local communities (see Brown, 1995). It is in this context that the idea of an 'African epistemology' has been proposed as the only path towards an understanding of African challenges, as well as towards finding effective ways of responding to these challenges.

This book does not focus on the Eurocentric-Afrocentric debate (which has already been discussed extensively in the literature); instead the book seeks to draw attention to the apparent deficit in understanding economic growth and development experiences in Africa as part of the broader challenge of the constructive re-imagining and decolonising of Africa (Davidson, 1992). With particular reference to economic growth and development, there has been some kind of double deficit (with the exception of the last decade or so) – a deficit in economic growth performance (which is widely acknowledged from different perspectives), but, more fundamentally, a deficit in understanding the growth deficit itself. While the economic growth deficiencies have been popularly (and sometimes triumphantly) proclaimed, understanding and explaining this experience has not gone beyond the popular images of Africa as a continent which is inherently flawed and unintelligible, with some analysts suggesting that it is probably a waste of time trying to make sense of the African chaos (Kitching, 2000). In economic explanations of the African economic growth experience, as Peter Lawrence (2010) has noted, often the explanatory variables offered are in serious need of explanation themselves. As elaborated in Chapter 3, it took the World Bank and the International Monetary Fund (IMF) 30 years to begin to realise that their understanding of the African continent was lacking, a fact that had led to misguided and disastrous policy prescriptions. In view of this, one would be justified in arguing that "adjustments [SAPs] were needed more in the Bank's policies than in those of the African governments" (Brown, 1995: 5).

The main focus of this book is to critically examine the different perspectives from which African economic challenges and opportunities – including the current Africa Rising narrative (ARN, see Chapter 7) – have been explained. While there has been an enormous amount of literature written on this topic, it still remains one of the least researched areas of study, even at a time when the world is experiencing an information and communications revolution. Apart from the post-2009 financial and economic crisis literature – which has been influenced by the ARN – the larger part of the discourse on Africa's growth experience has been expressed in the negative terminology of tragedy, crisis, false starts, endemic failure, erratic growth, etc. Although several accounts about the African economic growth and development experience have been written over the last 60 years (see Ndulu *et al.*, 2008; Severino and Ray, 2011) there has been no critical assessment of these accounts, which are often taken as *the* true reflection of Africa's economic growth experience. Most analysts who have written on the topic have taken pleasure in demonstrating just how tragic the African growth and development experience has been, often avoiding the tough task of explaining why economic growth has been deficient in Africa since the mid-1970s. Thus, a critical look at the different explanations provided for Africa's economic growth and development experience is important, especially given that different accounts provide different and often contradictory explanations – as will become evident in subsequent chapters.

However, this book does not claim to offer counter explanations for Africa's growth and development experience; what it does seek to do is to highlight some of the gaps in the existing explanations, and to identify areas needing further research and, perhaps, different approaches. In highlighting some of the inadequacies and gaps this book does not imply that current explanations are entirely incorrect. What is intended is the initiation of a robust debate and the search for liberating ways of imagining, thinking and writing about Africa. In looking critically at how economic growth in Africa has been explained – from various perspectives – this book provides an opportunity for readers to independently assess whether such accounts capture the actual African growth experience. While it is clear that an adequate understanding of the economic growth and development experience in Africa requires going beyond pure economic analysis – to include the broader forces that influence economic processes – the focus in this book is on the economic and political aspects of this experience. Other dimensions – such as cultural, religious and environmental aspects – are beyond the scope of this work.

'Africa bashing'

Interestingly, ever since the age of the invention of Africa, the world has never stopped to look for something peculiar to Africa, for accolades or patents of failure, something that the editor of *The Economist*, at the beginning of this century, called an "inherent flawed character" which inclines Africa "towards chaos" (*The Economist*, 2000). Recent growth – which has been described by the same magazine as "Africa's impressive growth" – that has transformed Africa from a 'hopeless' to a 'hopeful' continent in less than five years (*The Economist*, 2011) – does little to sway public opinion: "To be frank, no matter how fast the economy of some of these African countries will grow in the coming future, I still do not put much hope on this pathetic continent", writes one of the Twitter followers of *The Economist* magazine. During the 1990s many analysts described the African economic crisis as the worst tragedy of the twentieth century, with one American diplomat predicting that the crisis was going to get so bad that in "five years' time Africans will be begging to be recolonized" (see Michaels, 1993).

'Africa bashing', as these ideas are often referred to (see Versi, 2000), has not only been attractive to the major international media houses, but has also infiltrated and influenced academic work, as well as the actions of policymakers. For instance, the Report of the Commission for Africa (2005), an initiative of former British Prime Minister Tony Blair, argues that "Africa's history over the last fifty years has been blighted by two areas of weakness. These have been *capacity* – the ability to design and deliver policies; and *accountability* – how well a state answers to its people" (2005: 13, emphasis in original). While lack of capacity may appear to be a genuine concern with regard to Africa's governance performance, such views reinforce the mystification of African peoples as lacking ability to do things on their own. This has often led to the belief that development has to be done on behalf of Africa – that Africa has to be somehow 'taught' to do development (see Nabudere, 2006; Davidson, 1992) – a belief which, regrettably, many African leaders have strongly espoused for a long time. Even now, when most economies are experiencing modest economic growth, it is common to hear African politicians argue that there are no medicines in hospitals because donors have not given us money. The politicians assume that only donor money can advance development in Africa; that local money sources are bound to be inadequate and therefore fail. As a result, many African leaders beg donors to come and help; and, for sure, donors have been coming for over 60 years now, albeit with the ever growing need for more of them. It is like an addiction.

The other example of the tendency to attribute poor economic performance in Africa to something intrinsically African is the widespread notion within the empirical growth literature of what is known as the *Africa dummy*, the unique African *features* which purportedly account for what some analysts have referred to as 'Africa's growth tragedy' (See Easterly and Levine, 1995, 1997). Since Robert Baro's (1991) seminal work on cross-country growth regression, a whole 'industry' has sprung up in search of the Africa dummy, as we shall see later in Chapter 4 (see also Jerven, 2009), though the search seems to have lost steam in the last couple of years. But two decades of sifting through the statistical databases has only produced more controversy and circular arguments, with little insight into understanding what is going on (see Severino and Ray, 2011).

Nonetheless, this book is not a historical account of the mystification and the subsequent inferiorisation or bashing of Africa, although that historical pedigree forms an indispensable part of the African challenge which should not be ignored in the attempt to 'de-exoticise' – on the one hand – and 'banalise' Africa, on the other (see Mamdani, 1996). What this book focuses on is the apparent theoretical, as well as empirical, impasse in accounting for Africa's economic growth and development experience in the post-colonial period. Arguably, the different perspectives presented in this book form part of the narrative that seeks to contextualise the many explanations offered for the observed economic growth and development patterns in Africa. It must, however, be noted that although on the policy side the impasse of understanding Africa's growth and development experience has been rendered invisible by the hegemonic nature of the policy space created – especially since the 1980s – the theoretical side has been characterised by a hodgepodge of explanations and proposed remedies, making Africa look even more disoriented.

For instance, the Economic Commission for Africa (UNECA) reports nine competing economic growth and development approaches which have been proposed in Africa since 1960 (UNECA, 2010). To avoid duplicating these approaches here, the various strands of these explanations have been grouped in three broad categories: the market-oriented approaches (MOA, Chapter 2, Chapter 3 and Chapter 4) which have been championed by the multilateral and bilateral development institutions, relying mainly on neoclassical economic principles and explanations; the state-oriented approaches (SOA, Chapter 5) which have largely relied on notions of the absence of a bureaucratic or developmental state in Africa as the main reason for the observed growth pattern; and the political economy approaches (PEA, Chapter 6), which mainly employ a structural analysis, borrowing from different traditions of political economy (PE), emphasising the imbalance in power relations.

As it will become clearer in subsequent chapters, these three broad approaches are not mutually exclusive in their account of the African growth experience, neither is each approach homogeneous. However, each tends to emphasise particular aspects when explaining the African growth and development experience. For instance, while the PEA emphasises the external factors relating to the structure of the global economic system, the SOA emphasises the nature and character of the state and state institutions in Africa (internal factors) as critical in explaining this experience. In this book the debates are organised around these broad approaches to highlight the unique strength, but also the deficiencies, as far as explaining Africa's growth and development challenges is concerned. In other words, each of these approaches needs to be problematised within the complex condition of Africa's economic growth and development experience.

Notably there has been, even within the academic community, a tendency to treat these perspectives as irreconcilable streams of thought, to the extent that operating in one of these approaches implies dismissing the others as mere ideolo-gies or, sometimes, hegemonic propaganda or even conspiracy to undermine Africa's development. For instance, those vested in the neoclassical mainstream (particularly the professional, not necessarily academic, economists) dismiss other approaches as ideology-based explanations devoid of scientific evidence, discipline and rigour, while those vested in what I refer to as the radical political economy (RPE) traditions, dismiss the neoclassical adherents as 'marginalists', whose approaches are 'economistic' and narrow. When it comes to explaining Africa's economic growth and development experience, as will be seen in subse-quent chapters, there is sometimes a hostile idolisation of these perspectives, a reality which has certainly contributed to the 'double deficit'.

The politics of nomenclature

A discussion on economic growth and development needs to make a clear dis-tinction between the two terms. Economic growth is used here to refer to the increase in various economic indicators – mainly Gross National Product/Income (GNP/I) or Gross Domestic Product (GDP), and GNP/I or GDP per capita. These indicators are popularly viewed as preconditions for the broader process of development – which includes economic, social, political and cultural trans-formation. Thus, it is important from the start to note that economic growth is not synonymous with development. As the first *Human Development Report* (1990) argues, this basic idea is "often forgotten in the immediate concern with the accumulation of commodities and financial wealth" (UNDP, 1990: 9). The social, political, economic and cultural transformation which the term 'develop-ment' embraces is not limited to how many kilometres of roads or railway have been built, or how many people have access to clean water – it also includes changes relating to how many people are able to live lives which they value (see Sen, 1988). Development in this broader sense includes changes in the way people perceive themselves; improvements in self-confidence in the general population; overcoming a general feeling of despondency and despair in the gen-eral population. A good example of this, in recent times, is the Chinese story. The society-wide transformation that the rapid and sustained economic growth experienced in China over the last three decades has occasioned, increased self-confidence, self-belief and self-assertion among most Chinese nationals, especially the younger generations. Certainly economic growth has played an important role in this transformation, but it has also led to a broader process of social, cultural and political transformation.

This is the sort of rounded transformation that the concept of development entails – and goes way beyond the mere counting of apples, smartphones or tons of copper produced in a country. Development in this broader sense goes beyond the physical changes in society to include non-physical aspects of life such as the ability and opportunity to choose among available options; the ability for people to see themselves as repositories of inestimable value and not just as objects of charity and aid. Clearly,

> Development in human society is a many-sided process. At the level of the individual, it implies increased skill and capacity, greater freedom, creativity, self-discipline, responsibility and material well-being. Some of these are virtually moral categories and are difficult to evaluate – depending as they do on the age in which one lives, one's class origins, and one's personal code of what is right and what is wrong. However, what is indisputable is that the achievement of any of those aspects of personal development is very much tied in with the state of the society as a whole.
>
> (Rodney, 1972: 1–2)

From this perspective it can be argued that while economic growth is essential for development, economic growth does not automatically translate into development. As has become evident over the years, it is "possible for a country to have an expansion of GNP/I per head, while its distribution becomes more unequal, possibly even the poorest groups going down absolutely in terms of their own real incomes" (Sen, 1988: 13). Today it is a well-known fact that a country's GDP per capita can increase without an increase in the number of people having access to basic education or clean water, for instance. Chapter 7 of this book shows that a sustained economic growth averaging more than 5 per cent per year in Africa over the last 15 years has not resulted in a significant reduction in poverty and, much less, the narrowing of the inequality gap. Thus, while economic growth is essential for the broader transformation of society, it does not automatically translate into the broader social transformation implied by the term *development*.

Further, notions of transformation implied by the term development are here not given the unilinear evolutionary meaning as in the post-World War Two modernisation paradigm; the transformation processes are understood to be non-linear, and as such need not follow any deterministic paths that are moulded on any particular historical trajectory. Therefore, the African growth and development experience need not conform to any growth and development norm; the continent can develop in unique ways. Appreciating this basic point requires a lot of unlearning among Africans and non-Africans alike. This kind of fresh break from the theoretical straitjacket – imposed by what some critics have called the *ideologies of legitimation* – is indeed necessary if the understanding of Africa's growth and development experience is to be advanced beyond the limiting binaries of the modernisation paradigm (see Ekeh, 1975; Mamdani, 1996).

What is 'Africa'?

Since, for some reason, there are unsettled debates about what, exactly, constitutes Africa, it is essential to clarify the usage of the term 'Africa'[3] in this discussion. While aware of the debates about whether Africa should be taken as a single continent or a multitude of dissimilar nations, Africa here is used to refer to all those 54 countries which are member-states of the African Union (AU).[4] However, the 54 countries do not constitute an 'African economy', or an 'African state', as some analysts lazily assume. Conversely, some analysts see

African countries to be so diverse that even to talk about Africa as a single continent does not seem to make any sense. This debate is not only at the theoretical level; it is common practice in some institutions to treat countries south of the Sahara separately from the countries to the north of it (see any edition of the *World Development Indicators*). Even today, many international data sets, for reasons of convenience presumably, report the North African countries as part of the Middle East. From the beginning, the World Bank's *World Development Indicators* have been reporting the five North African countries as part of the Middle East, citing the reason that these countries have little in common with Sub-Saharan Africa (SSA) countries, and that they have a more common cultural, social, economic and political heritage with the Arab states of the Middle East. The IMF sometimes includes Djibouti, Sudan and Mauritania as part of North Africa (see IMF, 2013). In this book the five North African countries are examined as part of Africa, unless stated otherwise (see Appendices I, II and III).

Using commonality (cultural, political, social, economic, etc.) as the basis for asserting African unity may prove to be an impossible mission, for the simple reason that it is often difficult to find sufficient levels of social or cultural commonality among the different African countries which might justify treating them as a homogeneous entity. If geography alone fails to adequately define Africa, then cultural, linguistic, economic, political and social similarities – which the so-called 'scientific definition' of Africa uses – are far from being adequately convincing grounds for imposing uniformity on African countries, even those south of the Sahara. To avoid imposing arbitrary definitions of what Africa is, the political consensus – which Ankie Hoogvelt *et al.* (1992) refer to as the "unity of purpose" expressed as a collective aspiration of the peoples of Africa through the Organisation of African Unity (OAU) and its successor the African Union (AU) – is used here as the basis for defining what constitutes 'Africa'. The advantage of using the expressed unity of purpose is that Africa is then defined by the self-conscious collective acts of those who have *deliberately* chosen to be identified with it, as such; it is not something imposed by some rational or scientifically determined formula, which may not actually be an adequately reasonable ground.

The other advantage of taking the collective aspiration approach is that Africa then becomes a self-defined entity to the extent that the African leaders who choose to belong to the OAU/AU have made a deliberate and conscious choice, whether out of consideration of a common past, culture, geography or for economic reasons. Here the importance of using the expressed common aspiration of African leaders lies in the fact that Africa is not something externally defined or 'invented', something which in the case of Africa can be quite liberating (Hoogvelt *et al.*, 1992: 93). Under this approach, Algeria is very much part of Africa, just as Malawi, Madagascar or Cape Verde are. Even if Algeria decides to join the European Union (EU), as long as it identifies its collective aspirations with the rest of the African continent – via its AU membership – it still remains very much part of Africa. In this case, geography need not be destiny.

In the past, there has been a tendency to isolate not just North Africa, but also South Africa from the 'African' continent, the argument being that South Africa is unique, different from the rest of the continent – leading to what Mahmood Mamdani (1996) calls the *South African exceptionalism*. While the apartheid government may have seen South Africa as a unique country which had nothing in common with the rest of the African countries, and opted for an official *de facto* policy of *splendid isolation* – while at the same time maintaining a policy of *subversive intervention* on the ground – the expressed aspirations of the African National Congress (ANC)-led government points in the opposite direction towards a notion of a South Africa set apart from Africa. This was clearly expressed at the OAU Summit in Tunis in 1994, which Nelson Mandela attended as the first majority-elected president of the Republic of South Africa:

> The total liberation of Africa from foreign and white minority-rule has now been achieved .... Finally ... we shall remove from our agenda ... the question of Apartheid South Africa. Where South Africa appears on the agenda ... let it be because we want to discuss what its contribution shall be to ... African renaissance.
>
> (cited in Mbeki, 2010)

Speaking at the opening session of the OAU Conference of the African Ministers of Information in Sun City (South Africa), the then ANC deputy president, Thabo Mbeki, confirmed South Africa's commitment to the African aspiration and unity of purpose when he stated: "Within the broader plane, we would also like to reaffirm the commitment of this democratic republic to participate fully in the efforts of the OAU and our continent to confront the challenges that face us all" (Chikane *et al.*, 1998: 198). Thus, unless otherwise stated, Africa here is used to refer to the 54 countries which have expressed the unity of *purpose* (maybe not so much the unity of *minds* and *actions*) through their collective political commitments.

The African growth crisis and the deficit of understanding: the double deficit

A close look at the analysts from the different economic growth and development perspectives on Africa discussed in this book highlights the fact that they explicitly or implicitly argue that scholars operating in the other perspectives have failed to comprehend the African growth challenge; that the basic assumptions are foreign to the African context, and therefore irrelevant. In this way, the understanding of Africa's economic growth and development experience remains a contested terrain. Although there have been a monumental number of studies and literature on Africa (Severino and Ray, 2011), this wealth of information has not led to a fuller understanding of the African growth and development experience. To the contrary, it has sometimes rendered Africa unintelligible and incomprehensible, with some authors suggesting that this incomprehensibility is itself part of the nature of things in Africa; that this unintelligibility is what works in Africa (Chabal and Daloz, 1999). In this sense, the abundance of information and interpretations have not made it easy to explain and understand Africa. It appears as though the more information is generated the more difficult it becomes to explain clearly Africa's growth and development experience.

Like the nineteenth century map of Africa, it seems that our understanding of Africa's economic growth and development experiences, in particular, is increasingly becoming deficient, despite the exponential growth in information available. Many analysts have, of course, doubted the credibility of the data on Africa (especially GDP data) (Jerven, 2013; Deverajan, 2013), and there are valid reasons for this. But on the whole more information on Africa exists today than, say, in 1980. Like it was for map-making, as map-making techniques improved, the map of Africa became more blurred than before,[5] especially with regard to the interior. Clearly, the creatures with their mouths in their stomachs disappeared – but so did the 'cities', the civilisations, cultures and the real people of the interior who were rendered invisible, uncivilised, uncultured (Nkrumah, 1963).

This apparent irony is acknowledged less in the literature on Africa's economic growth and development. A common tendency has been to blame the available data for being scanty, outdated and less credible. The strategy of blaming the data has, in very subtle ways, often reinforced various forms of 'Africa bashing', with some analysts giving up on trying to make sense of what they see as 'unintelligible' Africa (see Kitching, 2000). Among those who seek to make sense of Africa's growth experience, it is common practice not to raise questions if the 'tools' used to explain this experience are actually appropriate; it is often the observed phenomenon which is characterised as 'deviant', unintelligible, underdeveloped, tragic, hopeless, divergent, pathetic, and sometimes irredeemable (Hill, 2005). This, in a fundamental way, reveals the hidden tendency to make data fit a particular paradigm, and whatever data fail to fit are either ignored or simply explained away; it seems as if the more data one has, the more difficult it becomes to account for it all. For instance, the ARN is now seeking to explain the current economic growth episode in terms of such narrow views as Nigeria's Nollywood now producing more movies each year than Hollywood, and Nigerian business tycoon, Aliko Dangote, being the richest black man on the planet, having overtaken Oprah Winfrey in 2012. While these two stories might be true, they tell us little about whether Africa is indeed rising (or not), or, more importantly, how we should understand Africa's growth experience over time.

Apparently an area where this irony is more evident is Africa's economic growth experience. Prior to the early 1980s, when time series data on most African countries were not readily available, factors accounting for the low human, economic and social development in Africa could be summarised in a single sentence. Kamarck (1967: 4) identified nature as the main factor:

> the obstacles nature placed in the way of economic development in Africa south of the Sahara were so great that they could be overcome only after the rest of the world had progressed sufficiently to have invented self-propelled

machine transport (the railway and then the automobile and airplanes) and to have sufficient surplus of wealth to aid Africans to acquire these necessary means to break out of their isolation.

Crude, simplistic and reductionistic as this may sound today (just like the fourteenth century stories of people in Africa with their mouths in their stomachs), geography and climate *are* widely accepted explanations for Africa's weak economic performance, especially within the growth regression studies. In current literature this has been expressed in terms of its climate, disease burden, poor soil, being landlocked and resources curse – all related to the fact that Africa is situated almost entirely within the tropics (see Ndulu *et al.*, 2008). But geography alone, as with many other time insensitive variables, falls short of explaining why countries such as Indonesia, which are wholly located in the tropics, have developed at a staggering pace since the 1980s (see Calderisi, 2006).

The compilation of the Penn World Tables,[6] which have made available time series data on many African countries since the1960s, instead of helping clarify the nature and causes of Africa's growth and development challenges, have in fact occasioned the 'big hunt' for something unique to explain in Africa. As more and more data become available, the search for understanding Africa's apparently poor economic growth performance has resulted in myriad explanations, which leave both the devout student of Africa – as well as the secular observer – muddled. In this regard, the most intriguing observation is that Africa's developmental challenges increase "in an inverse proportion to the increase in explanations, theories and strategies meant to tame the situation" (Murunga, 2005: 8). This raises the question of whether the explanations, theories and strategies are out of tune with the challenges on the ground.

Just a couple of years ago, in a book that claimed to "make Africa comprehensible", the author offered the following explanation:

> Many Africans, however, have little and see themselves potentially acquiring even less. Needing so much, they cannot think about being efficient. They want to garner what they can – in this sense they are certainly materialists – but they cannot and will not risk the little that they have on the chance of creating more. The image that comes to my mind is of a market woman alongside a road with her small stack of fruits or vegetables. I have often seen, across African cultures, such women stack and restack a few lemons, groundnuts, or green pepper, apparently savouring the value of the inventory and the prospect of garnering a few coins. This vendor is usually seated only a few feet from another woman who is selling the same lemons, doing the same rearranging. There is no apparent sense of competition – that is not the African way. And so African society avoids both the unpleasantness of competition and confrontation, and the attendant savings account! That African societies have developed in this way is easily understood, but such understanding does not make life more productive.
>
> (Fredland, 2001: 9–10)

From colonial anthropology through to development economics, in political studies and public finance, and in international development aid literature, it is not uncommon to come across such satirical accounts. Even if one were to accept the observation that "many Africans ... cannot think about being efficient", or that they "avoid both the unpleasantness of competition and confrontation", this does not explain why these practices are more prevalent in Africa and seemingly have such a huge impact on Africa's growth. If women stacking and restacking small heaps of lemons or mangos, or people who are afraid of taking risks are only to be found in Africa, then focusing on such occurrences may help "make Africa comprehensible". But if the tendency towards risk aversion – even at the cost of potentially higher returns on investment – is a widespread trait among low-income communities generally (as James Scott asserts in his book the *Moral Economy of the Peasant*, 1976), then avoiding risk in itself fails to explain why such a practice should be proving so decisive in *Africa*. In other words, if these traits are found in other parts of the world which have achieved a different growth trajectory, it is somewhat opportunistic to use such practices to account for Africa's weak economic performance.

Certainly, there have been no shortage of theories and explanations surrounding Africa's development challenges. In a recent book that tries to answer the question of why Africa is poor, the author argues that "the primary reason ... is because their leaders make this choice ... they do not make such choices because they lack examples of successful development to observe and learn from"; it is also attributed to African leaders "pursuing too many other agendas, whether personal or political" (Mills, 2011: 163, 174). In a more recent article on this topic, the authors argue that "the main reasons that African nations are poor today is that their citizens have very bad interlocking economic and political incentives" (Acemoglu and Robinson, 2010: 22). Of course this explanation begs the following questions: why have African leaders chosen to make their people poor, and why do they have bad incentives? While the *how* has been explained in such accounts, the *why* remains a challenge. As the chapters in this book show, the current challenge lies in understanding the challenge itself. In a fundamental way, "Africa's most important development challenge is the lack of understanding of the social struggles of the poor majority" (Murunga, 2005: 8).

Although the notion of an 'African crisis', or 'tragedy', was publicised during the 1980s and 1990s from different perspectives – see, for example, World Bank, 1983 (banking perspective), Richard Sandbrook, 1986 (political perspective) and Sandbrook (1993), Thomas Callaghy and John Ravenhill (1993), Giovanni Arrighi (2002) (PE perspective) – the competing accounts of the crisis have largely explained it in terms of the failure to catch up with Western Europe's GDP per capita: the so-called 'convergence controversy' (see Romer, 1994). In both the market-oriented and political economy approaches, the African crisis has been seen through the prism of conventional modernisation theories: failure to industrialise, underemployment in the subsistence sector, low savings, lack of backward and forward linkages, an underdeveloped agricultural sector, missing markets, lack of financial depth, and the diminutive nature of capitalism on the continent – leading to disarticulation of the production structure as well as of social formation, which in turn blocks the transformation of both social and economic structures within society. But as Bade Onimode argues,

> The crisis is not merely an economic crisis in the bourgeois or Marxian sense. It is much more than a bourgeois economic crisis of threatened starvation, massive unemployment, growing deficits and debts, disequilibria in different markets and sluggish economic growth. These are merely the surface manifestations of the crisis. Neither is the … crisis in Africa just a Marxian crisis arising from under consumption, disproportionality and related factors, which are commonly associated with contradictions of industrial capitalism.
>
> (Onimode, 1988: 1)

In a sense there seems to be a double deficit: at one level there has been a deficit in economic growth performance (especially before 2000) which is widely acknowledged; on another level there is inadequate understanding of this deficient growth. Some analysts have suggested that the reason for this double deficit is that the wrong paradigms have been used to understand the African condition (see Onimode, 1988; Nabudere, 2006; Brown, 1995).

The inappropriateness of the paradigms used in trying to explain Africa's growth experience is attributed to the idea that all the explanations are conceptualised within a modernisation paradigm which was constructed to understand the process of economic growth and social transformation in the *now-industrialised* (or post-industrial) societies (Nabudere, 1997). The assumption underlying the modernisation paradigm that all countries would have to go through an evolutionary process of economic and social transformation similar to what the industrialised countries went through (Broadberry and Gardner, 2013) is challenged by many African scholars on the basis that it is hard to justify such assumptions outside of Western Europe (see Nabudere, 2006; Hountondji, 2002; Mamdani, 1996; Mudimbe, 1988). Although analysis of the African crisis, as will become evident in subsequent chapters, has not gone far beyond the modernisation thesis, the conclusion which has been highlighted is that

> the African crisis is neither a crisis of institutions per se nor a bourgeois business cycle. Bourgeois economic theory, whether Keynesian or neoclassical is also useless for understanding the crisis. The Marxist theories of crisis such as the falling rate of profit, under-consumption or over-production and disproportionality do not explain the African crisis either.
>
> (Onimode, 1988: 13)

Here the contention is not just against economic modernisation, but also against political and cultural modernisation approaches which see the postcolonial African political institutions as imperfect replicas of countries in Western Europe (see Chabal and Daloz, 1999). This inability to move beyond the modernisation paradigm has been seen by some analysts as a crisis of development theory (see Mudimbe, 1988). In all the multifarious analyses of the African crisis there has been a slow realisation that "it is not possible to separate the African crisis from the crisis in the understanding of Africa" (Chabal, 1991: 530).

The larger part of this crisis of understanding Africa revolves around the impasse of development theory itself (see Hirschman, 1981), and in particular the conception of development as an evolutionary, unilinear process that every country has to go through. In the case of Africa the crisis of understanding is in fact a product of the disenchantment resulting from the failure to mimic Western Europe's experience of economic growth and development. And the argument has been that if one tries to explain Africa's economic growth and development experience within the mordernisation paradigm, the resulting understanding is bound to be deficient. Common concepts such as full employment, perfectly competitive markets, bureaucratic and meritocratic states, the proletariat, and surplus labour, need serious adjustment to capture African realities. If they are merely lifted into African conditions, they impose a certain epistemological straitjacket on something that may not fit perfectly (Brown, 1995).

In a fundamental way, the campaign that Africa needs to absorb, assimilate and imitate the European (and now the East Asian, see Morrissey, 2001) models of economic growth and development in order to 'catch up' with everybody else, has almost turned into mission impossible – for the simple reason that imitating what others have done has never worked well for anyone. The long-term consequences of trying to replicate the colonial master's economic, education, social security and even cultural models – in Africa – has led to what some have referred to as a 'development trap' (Nabudere, 1997: 204). In this way, the crisis is seen not in terms of the challenges that people in Africa face – such as hunger, lack of medicine, and poor educational facilities – but more in terms of Africa's failure to replicate the social, political and economic institutions of Western Europe and other developed regions.

Here the crucial issue is not that Africa needs improvements in living conditions, but what the nature of those improvements should be, and how they can be achieved. From the experience of the past half century, the impossibility of reproducing Europe in Africa – even with the brutal imperial technique of discrediting and later subjugating the African worldview (Mangubane, 1972) – has been painfully evident. While there has been some discernible success in trying to create "Oxbridge and Sorbonne" in Africa (see *State of Academic Freedom in Africa*, 1996), this has not been a solution, but part of the problem. The imagination which has shaped the definition and understanding of Africa's development experience has always been from an angle of what Africa "ought to be", which has resulted in reflecting on alien problems (Armah, 2010). Sure, one can learn from others, but one must know oneself before learning from another, otherwise the learning will be a process of replacing 'oneself' with the 'other'. Understanding Africa is a complex process that requires a great deal of unlearning. For this process of unlearning and learning to take root, it has been argued that "Africa must reclaim the right to its own knowledge production, self-

direction and self-determination. This implies developing an African epistemology through which we can sharpen our own self-perception and that of others"
(Nabudere, 2006: 48).

Scope of the challenge

An honest admission on the part of those responsible for formulating development policy and strategy (be it the World Bank and its allies, or African
bureaucrats) that the challenge is indeed a complex one, and as such requires
a broad-based strategy, would have been a lot more productive in this regard.
Development challenges in Africa are not just economic in nature, able to be
understood and addressed only by the most eminent international development economists (if there are any left),[7] international development agencies,
donors, and innovatively charged international non-governmental organisations
(INGOs). Acknowledging that the nature and scope of economic growth and
development challenges in Africa is complex is a first step to accepting that a
clearer understanding of the challenges requires more than just the endeavours
of international experts or local academics and intellectual celebrities. The crucial point is to understand the challenges more broadly, which requires moving
away from a purely economistic conception of Africa's growth and development
experience.

Growth trends in Africa

For quite some time now it has become a standard approach to explain economic
change through the dominant neoclassical economic model, relying solely on
time series data. From this angle, the African crisis has been largely formulated
as a crisis of failure to achieve sustained balanced economic growth, often conceived in terms of GDP and GDP per capita. The popular opinion on Africa's
long-term economic growth and development challenge is that the continent
experienced episodic or highly volatile growth between 1960 and 2000 (see
World Bank, 2007; Ndulu et al., 2008). Volatility in Africa's growth experience
is illustrated by examining real GDP per capita growth rates over this period. A
long-term analysis of GDP per capita trends across the continent does suggest
that most countries have been in and out of the growth grove; recording alternating episodes of moderate growth followed by usually prolonged periods of decline
(Ndulu and O'Connell, 2008). As Table 1.1 shows, a large number of countries which recorded positive growth during the 1960–1970 period experienced
declining output per capita during the following three decades, with almost half
of the countries in the continent experiencing declining income per capita in
the 1980–1990 and 1990–2000 periods – though output per capita growth has
broadly rebounded in the 2000–2010 period. In terms of GDP per capita trends
over the past six decades, it is interesting to note that only a few countries – such
as Benin, Botswana, Burkina Faso, Egypt, Lesotho, Morocco and Tunisia – maintained sustained growth throughout the entire period (see Appendix I).

Table 1.1. GDP per capita and GDP growth dynamics in Africa (1960–2010)

	1961–1970	1971–1980	1981–1990	1991–2000	2001–2010
GDP per capita growth rate		Number of countries			
Greater than 5%	4	4	3	2	8
Between 2–5%	10	11	6	12	21
Between 0–2%	16	9	13	17	16
With negative growth	4	13	25	21	7
Missing (no data)	20	17	7	2	2
GDP growth rates		Number of countries			
Great than 5%	12	17	8	9	21
Between 2–5%	19	8	26	26	27
Between 0–2%	4	21	12	11	3
With negative growth	0	1	2	4	1
Missing (no data)	17	7	6	4	2

Source: author, based on World Bank data (http://databank.worldbank.org/data). For the decadal average GDP and GDP per capita growth rates, as well as the actual GDP per capita in current US$ prices for each African country, see Appendices I, II and III.

Most of those countries that started off the first post-independence decade with strong per capita growth – such as Algeria, the Democratic Republic of Congo, the Cote d'Ivoire, Liberia, Malawi, Nigeria, Sierra Leone, South Africa and Zimbabwe (most of them growing at an average of above 2 per cent for the entire decade) – experienced declining per capita growth in at least one of the next three decades (see Appendix I). There is another set of countries – including Comoros, Cote d'Ivoire, Eritrea, Gabon, Madagascar, Togo and Zimbabwe – that have experienced declining income per capita in the last decade (2001–2010), a time when most economies on the continent have experienced modest GDP per capita growth.

However, it is important to note that the episodic scenario revealed by GDP per capita growth does not mean that these economies have been decelerating during this period – as some analysts who talk about the 'African tragedy' often imply. In fact, most of these economies have been recording positive GDP growth for the past six decades (see Table 1.1). The crucial issue is that this growth has been weak relative to population growth; hence, the negative GDP per capita growth rates. It is also evident from Table 1.1 and Appendices I and II that the 1980s and 1990s were the worst years for most countries, with 25 and 21 countries, respectively, reporting declining GDP per capita.

When we consider the actual GDP in US$ dollars, it is also apparent that most countries started off from very low initial levels, such that in 2012 almost half of the countries have GDP per capita of less than US$1,000, while ten countries still have a GDP per capita of less than US$500 (see Appendix II). Nonetheless, what has dragged down Africa's growth trajectory is rather prolonged periods of slow growth. It is from this angle that the African economic growth and development challenge becomes more evident, especially when compared to other developing regions. Growth for most countries in the region has been irregular, and this has affected the overall performance of real income per head, averaging just 0.5 per cent per annum in the period 1960–2000 compared to an average of 2.5 per cent per annum for other developing regions over the same period (World Bank, 2007).

Erratic growth in real per capita income is evident when we consider the performance of individual countries as illustrated in Table 1.2.

For the continent as a whole, the real income per capita in 2013 has just recovered to the peak level reported in 1976 (see World Bank, 2014), though most countries have *real* income per capital way below what they had in 1976.

Though it is common practice for analysts to look at the performance of a country using GDP per capita data, there has been widespread criticism of the seeming obsession with such aggregate measures. The main criticism is that income per capita, though better than the GDP data alone, does not represent the actual conditions in which people live and work. Analysts critical of using GDP per capita as a measure of well-being argue that this indicator is an inaccurate reflection of the actual living conditions experienced by most people (see Reddy and Pogge, 2005). Other than the serious problems associated with the compilation of the data (see Srinivasan, 1994; Deverajan, 2013; Jerven, 2013), there are concerns around the fact that per capita income figures often fail to capture the real struggles of people on the ground, especially in situations where income distribution is highly skewed, a trend that has been reported in Africa in the last decade (see AfDB, 2013).[8] Relying on real GDP per capita growth often leaves a critical observer with the question, "where did all the growth go?"(see Rodrik, 1998). As the United Nations Development Programme (UNDP) Human Development Index suggests, there is no clear correlation between broader development and GDP per capita.

Overall trends

In terms of overall trends in economic growth, it is apparent that there has been great heterogeneity in the performance of African countries – with a few countries maintaining relatively sustained growth over the past six decades, while the majority of countries have been alternating between short periods of growth followed by prolonged periods of stagnation and decline in terms of real income per capita. However, the real income per capita growth rates for the continent as a whole have improved significantly in the last decade since 2001 – reaching the average of 2.6 per cent per annum for the period 2001–2012 – and this rate is projected to reach 3 per cent in 2014 (see Figure 7.1). One unique trend in the current growth spurt in Africa is that sustained growth has been experienced by a broad range of countries including resource rich and non-resource rich countries (World Bank, 2014). Nevertheless, this robust growth, in most countries, is threatened by the lack of depth in most economies, most evident in the failure

Table 1.2. Average per capita growth rates and coefficient of variation

Less than 0%	Between 0–1%	Between 1–2%	Above 2%
C.A. Rep (-1.0) 4.4	Cameroon (0.8) 6.6	Tanzania (1.5) 2.8	Botswana (5.5) 1.1
DRC (-2.6) 3.4	Comoros (0.7) 6.5	South Africa (1.5) 1.5	Cape Verde (3.2) 2.0
Somalia (-1.6) 4.7	Cote d'Ivoire (0.7) 7.5	Benin (1.2) 3.7	Egypt (3.2) 1.6
Djibouti (-1.5) 6.5	Kenya (0.4) 9.7	Burkina Faso (1.2) 5.1	Equat. Guinea (8.4) 2.8
Niger (-0.7) 7.8	Uganda (0.6) 8.2	Mali (1.3) 4.9	Lesotho (2.9) 2.5
Senegal (-0.4) 9.7	Burundi (0.3) 20.7	Mozambique (1.7) 3.7	Mauritius (3.2) 2.1
Liberia (-1.6) 13.8	Gambia (0.2) 34.1	Namibia (1.1) 4.0	Morocco (2.8) 2.1
Libya (-1.1) 10.7	Guinea (0.2) 17.2	Nigeria (1.8) 4.9	Seychelles (4.0) 2.1
Madagascar (-0.2) 57.6	Rwanda (0.5) 26.0	Sudan (1.9) 4.3	Swaziland(3.5) 2.8
Sao T. and Prin (-0.3) 27.0	Sierra Leone (0.4) 19.3	Algeria (1.2) 7.0	Tunisia (3.4) 1.2
Zimbabwe (-0.5) 20.6	Togo (0.2) 24.1	Chad (1.2) 8.0	Angola (2.1) 5.3
	Zambia (0.2) 69.7	Eritrea (1.3) 6.3	Congo (2.8) 3.9
		Ethiopia (1.0) 7.1	Gabon (2.2) 4.0
		Guinea-Bissau (1.6) 7.9	Ghana (2.9) 5.4
			Malawi (2.0) 4.4
			Mauritania (2.6) 4.2

Source: author, based on data from UNECA (2011: 79).

Note: the figures in brackets are average annual per capita growth rates for the period 1960–2007. The figures outside the brackets are the coefficient of variation for each of these countries over the same period. Coefficient of variation is the ratio of the standard deviation to the absolute value of mean per capita growth rates. It measures the level of volatility of growth over the reference period. Low volatility is indicated by a coefficient of variation of between 0.1 and less than 3; moderate volatility falls within the 3–6 per cent range, while high volatility is anything above 6 but less than 10 per cent, and extreme volatility is any figure above 10 per cent. By this measure, real GNP per capita growth in 11 African countries falls within the low volatility range, while the rest are spread between moderate to very high volatility.

to transform the production structures so as to improve productivity and competitiveness (ACET, 2014).[9] Lack of economic transformation is a challenge that has been acknowledged widely in the literature on Africa's growth trends and prospects, with some analysts observing that "economic transformation characterised by a reallocation of resources from low-productivity activities such as agriculture into a modern, high productivity sector has not taken place in Sub-Saharan Africa's growth boom" (World Bank, 2014: 32). This has led to some critics dismissing the current growth spurt as something of a 'false start', similar to that seen in the 1960s. However, there are different vantage points from which the economic growth experience in Africa has been explained; here we focus on three dominant approaches.

The market-oriented approach (MOA)

One of the dominant approaches used to explain Africa's growth experience is a set of neoclassical growth theories, here referred to broadly as the market-oriented approach (MOA). Empirical growth studies form the backbone of MOA, and most of the explanations and findings from these studies are used as a basis for policy prescription by international donors and the development community. Though not all of the studies are conducted by the World Bank's or the IMF's staff, a majority of the studies are commissioned by these two institutions.

Findings of these studies and the resulting literature have "had a large impact in academia and on policymakers and public opinion. Its conclusions have to some extent been coherent with the policy agenda as set by the Bretton Woods institutions" (Jerven, 2009: 289). As discussed in Chapter 4, Africa's growth and development experiences have been evaluated primarily through this approach by mainstream economists and policy advisors.

Empirical growth studies have been largely built around the belief that cross-national time series data can reveal some unique African characteristics, which can in turn account for the puny economic growth and development trends observed in Africa. This seemingly 'intrinsically unique African' growth feature is widely referred to in the literature as the *Africa dummy*, especially during the 1990s (see Baro, 1991; Sachs and Warner, 1997; Easterly and Levine, 1997; Collier and Gunning, 1999a; 1999b; Ndulu *et al.*, 2008).

The idea behind the Africa dummy is that if the difference in growth experienced in Africa and other regions cannot be entirely accounted for through the standard growth regressors,[10] then part of what explains the observed difference in growth performance between Africa and other regions can be attributed to the mere fact of "being in Africa" (Baro, 1991: 419). In other words, the Africa dummy hypothesis seeks to identify unique African characteristics or variables which have adverse effects on growth (ibid.: 436). What this entails is that even if you provide the same level and quality of physical and human capital – and technology – to an average African economy and to an average economy outside Africa, the growth rates of the two would ultimately differ if the Africa dummy is significant – suggesting that growth would be affected by virtue of "being in Africa".[11]

The assumption has been that these growth models, since they have helped to explain much of the growth experience in Canada or Norway, should have the same explanatory power in Africa. On the basis of this logic, an entire industry[12] emerged, especially during the 1990s (the momentum around the search for the Africa dummy has waned, currently, perhaps dampened by the current growth episode). But although controversy rages about the significance of the Africa dummy variable in explaining Africa's growth and development challenges (see Chapter 4), a lot of hours have been spent by some of the most prominent men/women in the profession on this topic.

In a sense, the notion of the Africa dummy is another way of coming close to saying that the realities in Africa may be so different from conditions in other parts of the world that conventional growth theories and models that apply elsewhere may not be adequate to capture the core dynamics of the African continent.[13] As some analysts have noted, a "significant coefficient on a regional dummy indicates that some regularities are missing from the model to explain the difference in regional growth, i.e., these regressions are not able to explain *why* these regions' growth rates have been different" (Hoeffler, 2000: 29, emphasis in original). But what the Africa dummy literature has meant for most researchers is that Africa's development challenges should be explained using conventional neoclassical models and tools, arguing that a significant Africa dummy is a sure sign that an average African economy can be predicted and explained by the neoclassical model.

However, while the Africa dummy serves as a heuristic tool for analysts, this idea has often been used to feed into deep rooted stereotypes on Africa. This is a popular view that justified the implementation of Structural Adjustment Programmes (SAPs) during the 1980s, based as it was on the thinking that if the problems were largely caused by internal factors, then we should restructure and fix those internal conditions. One example of this logic is evident in Paul Collier's argument that "in much of Africa, although there have been a multiplicity of policy failures, the overriding errors have been macroeconomic" – such as trade policy, exchange rates, interest rates and inflation (Collier, 1991: 113). Within MOA, although external factors are acknowledged, emphasis has been placed on the internal causes of the crisis – hence its policy recommendations are focused on restructuring African economies and states (Brown, 1995).

The political economy approach (PEA)

Apart from the empirical growth studies, other analysts have explained Africa's economic growth and development experience in terms of the way Africa relates with the rest of the world. In this view, external factors such as terms of trade – unequal exchange, imperialism (old and new) – are seen as decisive factors in understanding Africa's growth and development challenges (see Chapter 6). A number of African scholars have used this approach. Onimode, for instance, argues that the African crisis is anchored primarily in the "relations of exploitation, domestic class structures, prostrate external dependency and the distortion of the dominant neo-colonial social formations in Africa" (Onimode, 1988: 1). Other African scholars argue that it is Africa's relations with the capitalist world which explain the former's underdevelopment and growth crisis (see Amin, 1974, 1990; Rodney, 1972; Arrighi, 2002; Nabudere, 2006). According to this view, the disarticulate nature of African economies requires an analysis which includes domestic (internal) factors – as well as external ones deeply rooted in colonial rule and neo-colonialism – to understand Africa's growth and development experience. Broadly, within PEA, although there is an acknowledgement of domestic factors that contribute to an economic and development malaise in Africa, the emphasis is directed towards the external forces which undermine the continent's ability to recover and embark on sustainable growth. In this view, factors such as high inflation, a balance of payment (BoP) deficit, fiscal deficit, escalating debt, low productivity, overvalued currencies, high interest rates, failure to diversify the production structure, low physical and human capital, and low technology, are seen as inescapable outcomes of Africa's position in the global economy.

Within the PEA framework, Africa has experienced weak growth not because of the existence of any features unique to Africa, as suggested by the idea of the Africa dummy, but mainly because of the asymmetrical power relations between the 'core' (industrialised) countries and the periphery (less developed) countries). Samir Amin, one of the main proponents of this view, in his recent book *Beyond US Hegemony*, has argued that since the beginning of the Industrial Revolution in Britain – which resulted in the division of the world into core and periphery – the two are "synonymous with industrialised and non-industrialised countries" respectively (Amin, 2006: 3–4). This division of the world "involves a hierarchy of occupational tasks, in which tasks requiring higher levels of skill and greater capitalization are reserved for higher-ranking areas" resulting in the uneven distribution of global income, wealth and power (Wallerstein, 1974).

According to the PEA view, international division of labour in the global economy was organised in such a way that

> Africans were to dig minerals out of the sub-soil, grow agricultural crops, collect natural products and perform a number of other odds and ends such as bicycle repairing. Inside Europe, North America and Japan, workers would refine the minerals and the raw materials and make bicycles
>
> (Rodney, 1972)

Most analysts using this framework argue that the economic structures set up during colonial times – which have continued up to the present day – ensure that this asymmetrical distribution of reward for labour and natural resources inherent in the current process of value addition or creation, is maintained through 'normal economics', though sometimes by extra economic measures.

Thus, in the view of most analysts operating within PEA, Africa's development and growth experience is not a mystery that one should look for in the thicket of national accounts data, or time series survey data; they are a direct consequence of the operation of a capitalist system – which gave birth to imperialism, colonialism and neo-colonialism, and now multilateral imperialism (Shivji, 1990). Though most analysts who use this framework to explain Africa's underdevelopment admit that in post-colonial Africa internal issues of leadership, corruption, class formation, elitism, greed and ethnic manipulation have contributed to the problems of underdevelopment, they argue that these are inevitable consequences of the capitalist system:

> The global context loomed large in our view of the situation … we attributed a key role to world capitalism in constraining and shaping development

efforts and outcomes at the national level. The patterns of surplus absorption undermined the long-term growth potential of African economies.

(Arrighi, 2002: 12)

The state-oriented approach (SOA)

The third dominant approach to explaining Africa's growth and development challenges is the analysis of the nature of states, public institutions and leadership in Africa. In this approach, the African crisis is largely seen as a crisis of leadership and inadequate state institutionalisation – the poor development of an effective bureaucratic state in the Weberian sense of the term. This approach is here referred to as the state-oriented approach (SOA). Since the early days of independence there have been warning bells rung – mostly by Africanist scholars who have been critical of the nature of post-independence African states and leadership. Rene Dumont's *False Start in Africa* (1966) is one of the earliest accounts. Other authors who have focused on the nature of state formation in Africa include Jean-Francois Bayart (1993), Crawford Young (1976),[14] Patrick Chabal and Jean-Pascal Daloz (1999), as well as Richard Sandbrook (1993) and, more recently, Robert Rotberg (2013). Dumont's book, which mostly discusses post-colonial francophone Africa, raises concerns about the new administrations in the newly independent African states, arguing that new African leaders simply took over colonial administrative arrangements and continued with business-as-usual: "The situation is largely a hold-over from colonial times" (Dumont, 1966: 81). The tendency among post-independent African elites to emulate the attitudes and lifestyle of the former colonial elites has attracted attention among some Africa scholars. Franz Fanon, for example, is critical of the African elites at the dawn of independence:

> The national bourgeoisie steps into the shoes of the former European settlement ... It considers that the dignity of the country and its own welfare require that it should occupy all these posts ... its mission has nothing to do with transforming the nation; it consists, prosaically, of being the transmission line between the nation and capitalism, rampant though camouflaged, which today puts on the masks of neo-colonialism.
>
> (Fanon, 1963: 152)

For analysts who operate with the SOA framework, the key point is that this new bourgeoisie is selfish and elitist, but mostly corrupt and inefficient, and has captured the state for its personal enrichment. This has led to the failure to *formalise* the state, a situation which has resulted in patrimony being the dominant form of interaction within the state. According to this view the resulting patrimonial state in Africa is not interested in the business of promoting economic growth and broad-based development; it is only interested in preserving the patron's and his (or maybe her) network's hold on power at any cost. The networks of the political elites are not just cascades of corruption, they are also corridors of lavish consumption with little or no concern about production, in such a way that "African leaders and foreign donors alike placed the cart before the horse. There was nobody to pull the cart and the horse soon proved unable to push the cart from behind". As the economic decline continued, Africa's policymaking tools and spaces were taken over by what has been referred to as the "supply-side economist" (Hyden, 1983: 2).

The capture of the state by elite networks, it is argued, has led to a situation in which most decisions are mediated through informal rather than formal state structures. For instance, Chabal, while acknowledging that there have been positive political developments on the continent during the 1990s, argues that these changes have not transformed most African states in ways that promote complete formalisation:

> Contemporary politics in Africa is best understood as the exercise of patrimonial power. What this means ... is that, despite formal political structures in place, power is exercised essentially through [the] informal sector. This form of government rests on the well-understood ... forms of political reciprocity which link patrons with their clients.
>
> (Chabal, 2002: 450)

Other analysts within this framework have argued that the state in Africa has not been *developed* enough to implement even the most basic reforms essential for economic growth and development (Ravenhill, 1993).

While African states are often demonised for being largely responsible for the poor economic growth and development performance, it has been observed that

> most of the analyses about the African states that have led to so much despondency about the prospect of development are based on invidious comparison between African states in crisis and idealised and tendentiously characterised states elsewhere. This invidious comparison has occulted African states.
>
> (Mkandawire, 2001: 290)

Chapter 5 illustrates that not only have African states been compared with the 'ideal type' Weberian states, but that the analyses are largely based on anecdotal evidence – often third-hand stories about corruption, neopatrimonialism and the inefficiency of African states. While one cannot deny the existence of this alleged political and social malaise, the lack of systematic analysis of the concrete situations in which these states operate has rendered most of these assertions as malicious comments meant to feed and maintain the 'old myths'. Unfortunately, the

> ultimate result of this misreading of experience in Africa and elsewhere is not only to throw the proverbial baby out with the bath water, but also

to nourish deep-seated prejudice that makes the understanding of Africa's strengths and weaknesses practically difficult.

(ibid.)

As noted earlier, the three approaches outlined above (MOA, SOA and PEA) are not mutually exclusive. What is common to all three is the idea that internal problems of leadership, governance and exercise of power have contributed to Africa's growth and development crisis since the 1960s. However, although all of them offer a critique of the African states, they take different standpoints. In all three approaches African states have been viewed as cancerous, evoking feelings of pessimism, disappointment, repugnance, contempt, outrage and desolation, such that:

> By the 1990s, the African state had become the most demonised social institution in Africa, vilified for its weakness, its over-extension, its interference with the smooth functioning of markets, its repressive character, its dependence on foreign powers, its ubiquity, its absence etc.
>
> (Mkandawire, 2001: 293)

The dual consensus

While some have damned – and continue to 'bash' – the African state for being predatory and overly patrimonial, there has been a realisation among many analysts (including the World Bank and the IMF) that the state is a critical institution around which economic growth and development revolves. This realisation, driven mainly by the new institutional economists, has crystallised into some kind of dual consensus – framed around good governance with emphasis on accountability, transparency, efficiency, respect for the rule of law (and private property) and human rights, but also around notions of a developmental state – and stresses the importance of effective and autonomous state institutions that are capable of intervening and directing the economic growth and development process (see UNECA, 2010).

Nonetheless, close analysis of debates concerning the role of the state in development in Africa suggests that these have evolved in ways which reflect the shifts in dominant developmental thinking. During the 1940s the state was seen as the main actor, planning for and delivering development. The 'big push' strategy – for instance the "big D-development" (Hart, 2001) – advocated for the state playing a decisive role in ensuring that plans are laid out, resources (human, financial and physical capital) are mobilised, and programmes are implemented. Paul Rosenstein-Rodan (1943) – who is often acclaimed as one of the pioneers of development economics (see Krugman, 1996; Martinussen, 1997) – saw the state as the main player in the game of development.

But generally, during the 1980s, the state was seen as the stumbling block. The 'good governance' drive of the mid-1990s did little to restore state capacity, self-confidence, or a sense of direction. As Mkandawire argues, this shift in attitude towards the state cannot only be attributed to the dismal performance of African states, but mainly to the shifting ideological and economic paradigms:

> First at the ideological level, there was a dramatic ascendancy of neoliberalism – partly as a result of the rise and triumph of neo-conservatism movements riding on the discontent with [the] welfare state and [the] inflationary impact of Keynesian solutions and the collapse of central planning in socialist countries.
>
> (Mkandawire, 2001: 294)

In more recent years the role of the state in development is slowly being re-emphasised as being evident in a number of national development plans or visions (Vision 2020 or 2030) in a diverse set of countries that includes Ghana, Malawi, Nigeria, Namibia, Kenya, Zambia and South Africa.

African intellectuals and Africa's development

The role of African intellectuals and academics in shaping the understanding of African experiences requires some assessment. Here there are two points that need to be disentangled in order to appreciate the key issues. The first is that understanding Africa's growth and development experiences has always been an exercise largely operated from outside (Brown, 1995).

The second point, which needs to be understood more fully (and related to the first), is that the very structure through which Africa is interpreted and imagined is constructed with scaffolds that do not pay much attention to knowledge and views from within the continent. The entire structure of knowledge production is controlled by a system in which African knowledge systems have little influence (Mamdani, 1994). This debate touches on critical questions about the role of African intellectuals – and scholarship – in understanding, shaping and writing about African experiences more broadly. Literature on Africa's economic growth and development creates an impression that there have been very few African scholars who have provided their understanding of the crisis. In actual fact many scholars on the continent have expressed their views, in a number of ways, about the economic and development crisis. These are illustrated in Chapter 8. Claims that there are no scholars on the continent who one can look to for guidance or robust discussion, reflect the nature and structure of knowledge production about Africa. For this reason it is essential to engage with debates about the role of African scholarship around the broad theme of economic growth and development.

Outline

The book is organised into eight chapters. The next three chapters discuss the market-oriented approach (MOA). Chapter 2 looks at the World Bank's understanding of, and its role in, Africa's economic and development experience. Although the World Bank's involvement in Africa dates back to the 1950s – when countries such as Ethiopia and South Africa became members – it was during the 1980s and 1990s that the Bank's views influenced not just economic policy, but also the entire production of knowledge about Africa. Chapter 3 focuses on the Bank and the Fund's engagement in Africa's development challenges, and the strategies designed to respond to them. Chapter 4 discusses the empirical growth studies on Africa. Focus here is on empirical growth studies and the various explanations offered for the observed economic growth performance. Issues related to the state and development in Africa are discussed in Chapter 5. Chapter 6 discusses the views which I have broadly referred to as the political economy approach. Here, contrast with the other two approaches in understanding and explaining the African development crisis is drawn, focusing on the differences in the identified causes of the crisis. Chapters 5 and 6 also discuss SOA and PEA respectively. Chapter 7 looks at the current narrative of Africa Rising in the context of the broader and longer term economic growth and development experience. This chapter attempts to bridge the old and new narrative on Africa's growth portraits. The main focus of the chapter is to discuss what the ARN means in terms of understanding Africa's growth experience. The last chapter focuses on African intellectuals and how they have contributed, or failed to contribute, to shaping the understanding of Africa's economic growth and development experience.

Notes

1 These series of lectures were presented at the Stockholm School of Economics (Sweden) in 1992, in honour of Swedish economist Bertil Ohlin, who together with fellow Swedish economist Eli Hecksher was central in formulating the factor price theorem (the famous Hecksher-Ohlin factor proportion theory).

2 In a sense, the works of these explorers initiated another layer of myths, like: David Livingstone discovered the Victoria Falls; Mungo Park discovered the River Niger; James Bruce discovered the source of the River Nile; Samuel Barker discovered Lake Albert. In actual fact these European explorers were guided to such sites by local people.

3 Mazrui (2005) briefly discusses the origins of the term 'Africa', noting that the name itself has been traced to different narratives including those of the Berbers, the Romans and the Greeks, who used the name to refer to present day Tunisia or Algeria, and sometimes Egypt. See also Mbeki (2010).

4 The 54 countries include South Sudan, which became an independent state in July 2011, though for purposes of analysis the separate data may not be available for this country. Though Morocco is not a member of the AU, its leaders have decided to participate in many AU activities.

5 Even as late as 1964 Toynbee is reported to have argued that "Africa is by and large a plateau, with rivers falling over the escarpment in a series of falls or rapids near the coast" (cited in Kamarck, 1967).

6 The Penn World Tables (PWT) compile standardised (that is, different currencies are converted into a single comparable currency) economic time series data on national accounts of various countries in the world. The data set was first compiled by Summers, Kravis and Heston in 1980, and has been published ever since in subsequent versions (PWT1, PWT2, etc.) with the current one being PWT7.

7 Krugman talks of a counter-revolution that swept development economics away: "Once upon a time, there was a field called development economics – a branch of

economics concerned with explaining why some countries are so much poorer than others, and with prescribing ways for poor countries to get rich. In the field's glory days in the 1950s, the ideas of development economics were regarded as revolutionary and important … That field no longer exists. And very few economists would now presume to offer grand hypotheses about why poor countries are poor or what they can do about it. In effect, a counterrevolution swept away development economics" (Krugman, 1996: 7).

8 For a critical analysis of the inadequacy of per capita income see Wade (2004) and Reddy and Pogge (2005). For problems related to the quality and credibility of the data used, see Srinivasan (1994), as well as Heston (1994).

9 Depth is an acronym for the five indicators of structural transformation; namely, diversification, export growth, increased productivity, technological advances and improved human well-being (see ACET, 2014).

10 There is actually no approved list of 'standard growth regressors'; different researchers regress a combination of different variables – usually on GDP per capita. But there are certain variables which are common in most regressions, starting with Baro's (1991). See Sachs and Warner (1997), for a sample list.

11 Regional dummies are used to examine whether different regions grow significantly differently. But so far it has been the Sub-Saharan and Latin American dummies which have been significant. Here we focus on the Africa dummy.

12 Stein (2004) refers to the upsurge in empirical growth studies since 1991 as the "growth regression industry", while Jerven (2009) calls the empirical growth focused on Africa the "quest for the African Dummy".

13 This realisation was articulated in the 1950s and 1960s by a number of economists, and formed the basis for the emergence of a sub-discipline of development economics (see Chapter 5)

14 This pair have been described as the "two most prominent Africanists in the world" (see Englebert, 2000: 16).

References

Acemoglu, D. and Robinson, J. (2010). "Why is Africa Poor?" *Economic History of Development Regions*, Vol. 25, No. 1: 21–50.

Africa Centre for Economic Transformation (ACET) (2014). *2014 African Transformation Report: Growth with Depth*. Accra: ACET.

African Development Bank (AfDB) (2013). "Annual Development Effectiveness Review 2013: Towards Sustainable Growth for Africa". Online, available at www.afdb.org, accessed 23 October 2013.

Alavi, Hamza and Shanin, Teodor (1982). "Colonialism in the Words of its Contemporaries: Cecil Rhodes, Jules Harmand, Albert Beveridge, Jospeh Conrad, James Connolly" in H. Alavi and T. Shanin (eds) *Introduction to the Sociology of Development Societies*. New York: Monthly Review Press: 72–7.

Amin, Samir (1974). "Accumulation and Development: A Theoretical Model." *Review of African Political Economy*, No. 1: 9–26.

Amin, Samir (1990). *Delinking: Towards a Polycentric World*. London: Zed Books.

Amin, Samir (2006). *Beyond US Hegemony: Assessing the Prospects for a Multi-Polar World*. London: Zed Books.

Armah, A. Kwei (2010). "Remembering the Dismembered Continent." *New African*, 1 March.

Arrighi, G. (2002). "The African Crisis: World Systemic and Regional Aspects." *New Left Review*, No. 15 (May–June): 5–32.

Asante, K. Molefi (n.d.). "Locating a Text: Implications of Afrocentric Theory." Online, available at: http://multiworldindia.org/wp-content/uploads/2010/05/Locating-a-Text.pdf, accessed 17 September 2011.

Baro, Robert (1991). "Economic Growth in a Cross Section of Countries." *The Quarterly Journal of Economics*, Vol. 106, No. 2: 407–43.

Bayart, Francois (1993). *The State in Africa: The Politics of the Belly*. London: Longman.

Broadberry, Stephen and Gardner, Leigh (2013). "Africa's Growth Prospect in a European Mirror: A Historical Perspective." Competitive Advantage in the Global Economy (CAGE), Chatham House Paper Series No. 5. Online, available at: www.warwick.ac.uk/go/cage, accessed 15 December 2013.

Brown, B. Michael (1995). *Africa's Choices: After Thirty Years of the World Bank*. London: Pluto Press.

Calderisi, Robert (2006). *The Trouble With Africa: Why Foreign Aid Isn't Working*. New Haven/London: Yale University Press.

Callaghy, Thomas and Ravenhill, John (1993). "How Hemmed In? Lessons and Prospects of Africa's Response to Decline" in T. Callaghy and J. Ravenhill (eds) *Hemmed In? Responses to Africa's Economic Decline*. New York: Columbia University Press.

Cesaire, Amie [1955] (2000). *Discourse on Colonialism: A Poetics of Anticolonialism.* (translated by Jaon Pinkham). New York: Monthly Review Press.

Chabal, Patrick (1991). "African, Africanist and the African Crisis." *African Journal of International African Institute*, Vol. 61, No. 4: 530–2.

Chabal, Patrick (2002). "The Quest for Good Governance in Africa. Is NEPAD the Answer?" *International Affairs*, Vol. 78, No. 3: 447–65.

Chabal, Patrick and Daloz, Jean-Pascal (1999). *Africa Works: Disorder as Political Instrument.* London: James Currey.

Chikane, F.W., Esterhuyse, M., Langa, V., Mavimbela, V. and Pahad, E. (1998). *Africa: The Time Has Come – Selected Speeches of Thabo Mbeki*. Cape Town/Johannesburg: Tafelberg & Mafube.

Coetzee, J.M. (1988). *White Writing: On the Culture of Letters in Southern Africa*. New Haven: Yale University Press.

Collier, P. (1991). "African External Economic Relations 1960–90." *African Affairs*, Vol. 90, No. 360: 339–56.

Collier, Paul and James W. Gunning (1999a). "Explaining African Economic Performance." *Journal of Economic Literature*, No. 37: 64–111.

Collier, Paul and James W. Gunning (1999b). "Why Has Africa Grown Slowly?" *Journal of Economic Perspectives*, No. 13: 3–22.

Commission for Africa (2005). "Our Common Interest: Report of the Commission on Africa." Online, available at http://www.commissionforafrica.info/wp-content/uploads/2005-report/11-03-05_cr_report.pdf, accessed 30 March 2014.

Davidson, Basil (1992). *The Black Man's Burden: Africa and the Curse of the Nation States*. New York: Three Rivers Press.

Deverajan, S. (2013). "Africa's Statistical Tragedy." *Review of Income and Wealth*, DOI: 10.1111/roiw.12013, 2013. Accessed 3 November 2013.

Dumont, Rene (1966). *False Start in Africa* (translated by Phylis Nauts Ott). London: Andre Deutsch.

Easterly, William and Levine, Ross (1995). "Africa's Growth Tragedy: Retrospective, 1960–89." *Policy Research Working Paper No. 1503*, World Bank.

Easterly, William and Levine, Ross (1997). "Africa's Growth Tragedy: Policies and Ethnic Divisions." *The Quarterly Journal of Economics*, Vol. 112, No. 4: 1203–50.

The Economist (2000). "Hopeless Africa." 11 May.

The Economist (2011). "Africa's Impressive Growth." 6 January.

Ekeh, Peter (1975). "Colonialism and the Two Publics in Africa: A Theoretical Statement." *Comparative Studies in Society and History*, Vol. 17, No. 1: 91–112.

Englebert, Pierre (2000). "Pre-colonial Institutions, Post-colonial States and Economic Development in Tropical Africa." *Political Research Quarterly*, Vol. 53, No. 1: 7–36.

Fanon, Franz (1963). *Wretched of the Earth*. New York: Groves Press.

Fredland, Richard A. (2001). *Understanding Africa: A Political Economy Perspective*. Chicago: Burnham Inc.

Hart, Gillian (2001). "Development Critiques in the 1990s: Culs de Sac and Promising Paths." *Progress in Human Geography*, Vol. 25, No. 4: 649–58.

Heston, Alan (1994). "National Accounts: A Brief Review of Some Problems in Using National Accounts Data in Level of Output Comparisons and Growth Studies." *Journal of Development Economics*, Vol. 44: 29–52.

Hill, Jonathan (2005). "Beyond the Other? A Postcolonial Critique of the Failed State Thesis." *African Identities*, Vol. 3, No. 2: 139–54.

Hirschman, Albert (1981). *Essays in Trespassing: Economics to Politics and Beyond*. Cambridge: Cambridge University Press.

Hoeffler, A.E. (2000). "The Augmented Solow Model and the Africa Growth Debates." *Centre for International Development (CID) Working Paper No.36*, Cambridge, MA: Harvard University.

Hoogvelt, Ankie, Phillips, David and Taylor, Phil (1992). "The World Bank and Africa: A Case of Mistaken Identity." *Review of African Political Economy*, No. 54: 92–6.

Hountondji, Paulin (2002). "Introduction" in P. Hountondji (ed.) *Endogenous Knowledge: Research Trails*. Dakar: CODESRIA Book Series.

Hyden, Goran (1980). *Beyond Ujamaa in Tanzania: Underdevelopment and Uncaptured Peasantry*. London: Heinemann.

Hyden, Goran (1983). *No Shortcuts to Progress: African Development Management in Perspectives*. London/Nairobi: Heinemann.

Hyden, Goran (1986). "The Anomaly of the African Peasantry." *Development and Change*, Vol. 17, No. 3: 677–705.

Iliffe, John (1983). *The Emergence of African Capitalism*. Minneapolis: University of Minnesota Press.

International Monetary Fund (IMF) (2013). *Regional Economic Outlook May 2013: Sub-Saharan Africa – Building Momentum in a Multi-speed World*. Washington DC: IMF.

Jerven, M. (2009). "The Quest for African Dummy: Explaining African Post-colonial Economic Performance Revisited." *Journal of International Development*, DOI: 10.1002/jid.1603.

Jerven, Morten (2013). "Comparability of GDP Estimates in Sub-Saharan Africa: The Effect of Revision in Sources and Methods Since Structural Adjustment." *Review of Income and Wealth*, Vol. DOI: 10.1111/roiw. 12006: 201.

Kamarck, Andrew (1967). *The Economics of African Development*. New York: Praeger.

Kitching, Gavin (2000). "Why I Gave up African Studies." *African Studies Review & Newsletter*, Vol. 22, No. 1: 21–6.

Krugman, Paul (1996). *Development, Geography and Economic Theory*. Cambridge, MA: MIT Press.

Lawrence, Peter (2010). "The African Tragedy: International and National Roots" in V. Padayachee (ed.) *The Political Economy of Africa*. London/New York: Routledge: 19–38.

Mackay, Peter (2008). *We Have Tomorrow: Stirrings in Africa 1959–1967*. Norwich: Michael Russell.

Mamdani, Mahmood (1994). "The Intelligentsia, the State and Social Movements in Africa" in M. Diouf and M. Mamdani (eds) *Academic Freedom in Africa*. Dakar: CODESRIA: 247–60.

Mamdani, Mahmood (1996). *Citizen and Subject: Contemporary Africa and the Legacy of Late Colonialism*. Princeton, NJ: Princeton University Press.

Mamdani, Mahmood (1998). "Is African Studies to be Turned into a New Home for Bantu Education at UCT?" Text of remarks by Professor Mahmood Mamdani at the Seminar on the Africa Core of the Foundation Course for the Faculty of Social Sciences and Humanities, University of Cape Town, 22 April 1998. Online, available at: http://www.hartford-hwp.com/archives/30/136.html, accessed 17 March 2011.

Mangubane, Bernard (1972). "A Critical Look at Indices Used in the Study of Social Change in Colonial Africa." *Current Anthropology*, Vol. 12, No. 4/5: 419–45.

Martinussen, John (1997). *Society, State and Market: A Guide to Contemporary Theories of Development*. London: Zed Books.

Mazrui, Ali (2005). "The Re-Invention of Africa: Edward Said, V.Y. Mudimbe and Beyond." *Research in African Literatures*, Vol. 36, No. 3: 680–82.

Mbeki, Thabo (2010). "The Role of Africa's Student Leaders in Developing the African Continent." Address by former President of South Africa, Thabo Mbeki, at the African Student Leaders' summit meeting held at the University of Cape Town, 6 September 2010.

Michaels, Marguerite (1993). "Retreat from Africa." *Foreign Affairs*, Vol. 72, No. 1: 93–108.

Mills, Greg (2011). *Why Africa is Poor: And What Africans Can Do About It*. Johannesburg: Penguin Books.

Mkandawire, Thandika (2001). "Thinking About the Developmental States in Africa." *Cambridge Journal of Economics*, Vol. 25, No. 3: 289–313.

Morrissey, Oliver (2001). "Lessons for Africa from East Asian Economic Policy" in P. Lawrence and C. Thirtle (eds) *Africa and Asia in Comparative Economics*. London: Palgrave: 34–48.

Mudimbe, V.Y. (1988). *The Invention of Africa, Gnosis, Philosophy and the Order of Knowledge*. Bloomington and Indianapolis: Indiana University Press.

Murunga, Godwin (2005). "A Note on the Knowledge Question in Africa's Development." *CODESRIA Bulletin*, Nos 3–4: 8–10.

Nabudere, Dani (1997). "Beyond Modernisation and Development, or Why the Poor Reject Development." *Human Geography*, Vol. 79, No. 4: 205–15.

Nabudere, Dani (2006). "Development Theories, Knowledge Production and Emancipatory Practice" in V. Padayach (ed.) *The Development Decade? Economic and Social Change in South Africa 1994–2004*. Pretoria: HSRC Press: 33–52.

Ndulu, Benno and O'Connell, Stephen (2008). "Policy Plus: African Growth Performance" in B. Ndulu, S. O'Connell, R. Bates, P. Coulier and C. Soludo (eds) *The Political Economy of Economic Growth in Africa: 1960–2000*. Cambridge: Cambridge University Press: 3–75.

Ndulu, B., O'Connell, S., Azam, J.P., Bates, R.H., Fosu, A.K., Gunning, J.W. and Njinkeu, D. (2008). *The Political Economy of Economic Growth in Africa 1960–2000* (Vols 1 and 2, Country Case Studies). Cambridge: Cambridge University Press.

Nkrumah, Kwame (1963). *Africa Must Unite*. London: Panaf.

Onimode, Bade (1988). *A Political Economy of the African Crisis*. London: Zed Books.

Ravenhill (1993). "A Second Decade of Adjustment: Greater Complexity, Greater Uncertainty" in T. Callaghy and J. Ravenhill (eds) *Hemmed In? Responses to Africa's Economic Decline*. New York: Columbia University Press.

Reddy, Sanjay and Pogge, Thomas (2005). "How Not to Count the Poor", Version 6.2. Online, available at: http://www.columbia.edu/~sr793/count.pdf, accessed 2 February 2012.

Rodney, Walter (1972). *How Europe Underdeveloped Africa*. Washington DC: Howard University Press.

Rodrik, Dani (1998). "Where did All the Growth Go? External Shocks, Social Conflict and Growth Collapses." Online, available at: http://www.ksg.harvard.edu/rodrik, accessed 13 July 2008.

Romer, Paul (1994). "The Origins of Endogenous Growth." *The Journal of Economic Perspectives*, Vol. 8, No. 1: 3–22.

Rosenstein-Rodan, Paul (1943). "Problems of Industrialisation of Eastern and South-Eastern Europe." *Economic Journal*, Vol. 53, Nos 210/211: 202–11.

Rotberg, Robert (2013). *Africa Emerges*. Cambridge: Polity Press.

Sachs, Jeffrey and Warner, Andrew (1997). "Sources of Slow Growth in African Economies." *Journal of African Economies*, Vol. 6, No. 3: 335–76.

Sall, Ebraima (1996). "Introduction" in E. Sall (ed.) *The State of Academic Freedom in Africa*. Dakar: CODESRIA: 1–21

Sandbrook, Richard (1986). "The State and Economic Stagnation in Tropical Africa." *World Development*, Vol. 14, No. 3: 319–32.

Sandbrook, Richard (1993). *The Politics of Africa's Economic Recovery*. Cambridge: Cambridge University Press.

Saul, J. and Leys, C. (1999). "Sub-Saharan Africa in Global Capitalism." *Monthly Review*, Vol. 51, No. 3: 5–19.

Scott, James (1976). *The Moral Economy of the Peasant*. New Haven: Yale University Press.

Sen, Amartya (1988). "The Concept of Development" in H. Chenery, T. Srinivasan and P. Streeten (eds) *Handbook of Development Economics Volume 1*. Hague: Elsevier: 9–26.

Severino, Jean-Michel and Ray, Oliver (2011). *Africa's Moment*. Cambridge: Polity Press.

Shivji, Issa (1990). "Tanzania: The Debate on Delinking" in Mahjoub, A. (ed.) *Adjustment or Delinking? The African Experience*. London: Zed Books.

Srinivasan, T.N. (1994). "Data Base for Development Analysis." *Journal of Development Economics*, Vol. 44: 3–27.

Stein, Howard (2004). "The World Bank and the IMF in Africa: Strategy and Routine in the Generation of a Failed Agenda." Centre for Afro-American and African Studies (CAAS), University of Michigan. Online, available at: http://www.macua.org/Howard_Stein.pdf, accessed 29 April 2009.

Summers, Robert and Heston, Alan (1981). "The Penn World Table (Mark 5): An Expanded Set of International Comparisons, 1950–1988." *Quarterly Journal of Economics*, Vol. 106, No. 2: 327–68.

United Nations Development Programme (UNDP, 1990). *Human Development Report 1990*. New York: Oxford University Press.

United Nations Economic Commission for Africa (UNECA) (2011). *Economic Report on Africa 2011: Governing Development in Africa: the Role of the State in Economic Transformation*. Addis Ababa: UNECA.

Versi, Anver (2000). "The Heart of Darkness." Editorial, *African Business*, June.

Wade, Robert (2004). "On the Causes of Increasing World Poverty and Inequality, or Why the Matthew Effect Prevails." *New Political Economy*, Vol. 9. No. 2: 163–88.

Wallerstein, Immanuel (1974). *The Modern World System: Capitalist Agriculture and the Origins of the European World-Economy in the Sixteenth Century*. New York: Academic Press.

World Bank (1983). *Sub-Saharan Africa: Progress Report on Development Prospects and Programs*. New York: World Bank.

World Bank (2000). *Can Africa Claim the 21st Century?* [The Gelb Report]. New York: IBRD/World Bank.

World Bank (2007). *Challenges of African Growth: Opportunities, Constraints and Strategic Directions*. New York: IBRD/World Bank.

World Bank (2014). "Africa Pulse Rate: An Analysis of Issues Shaping Africa's Economic Future." April, Vol. 9. Online, available at: http://www.worldbank.org/content/dam/Worldbank/document/Africa/Report/Africas-Pulse-brochure_Vol9.pdf, accessed 14 June 2014.

Young, Crawford (1976). *The Politics of Cultural Pluralism*. Maidson: University of Wisconsin Press.

2 The World Bank and the IMF in Africa: the project-lending era

The early years

Engagements between the Bretton Woods institutions (BWI: World Bank and International Monetary Fund, IMF) and Africa have a long history, dating back to just a few years after the institutions were first established. Although the Bank and the Fund's involvement in Africa increased significantly from the late 1970s onwards, the Bank, in particular, had been engaging different African countries prior to the first oil crisis of the mid-1970s – mainly through project lending for infrastructure developments such as energy, transportation (road and rail), telecommunications, water supply and education. Often, discussions of the operation of the Bank and the Fund in Africa focus on the Structural Adjustment Programmes (SAPs) and their associated instruments – the Structural Adjustment Loans (SALs) and Sectoral Adjustment Loans (SECALs) for the Bank, and the various financing facilities for the Fund – and overlook the Bank and the Fund's earlier activities. While the range, intensity, and level of their involvement increased during the 1980s, Africa's relationship with the World Bank and the IMF did not start with SAPs. The Bank, in particular, had been providing project loans to different African countries prior to the policy-based lending of the 1980s. After country missions to two of its first African member countries (Ethiopia and South Africa) in 1950, the Bank approved the first loan in Africa: to Ethiopia.[1]

Nonetheless, prior to the 1980s the Bank and the Fund had limited activities and influence in Africa, with most of the work focusing largely on providing technical assistance related to the projects which they funded. During this period several countries – chiefly Cameroon, Cote d'Ivoire, Kenya, Nigeria, Tanzania, Zambia, Ethiopia and Sudan – were the Bank's biggest clients, accounting for more than 60 per cent of total lending to Sub-Saharan Africa (SSA) (Kapur et al., 1997). In the case of the Fund, it had limited business in African countries prior to the first oil shock of 1973. The Fund's main form of engagement was the Stand-by Arrangement (SBA), a short-term balance of payments (BoP) support facility initiated during the 1960s. The Extended Fund Facility (EFF), which was a medium-term lending mechanism, was only introduced in 1974 to provide support to countries affected by the first oil shock. However, despite these low-key engagements, it is possible to discern the Bank and Fund's understanding and explanation of Africa's economic growth and development challenges at this time.

Although the focus in this chapter is on the World Bank, IMF activities and views are also discussed, especially with regard to issues over which the two institutions had different views and approaches. But before discussing the approach and programmes of the BWIs in Africa, it is essential to look at the general operational arrangement and mandate of the two institutions. A more detailed historical account of the World Bank and the IMF can be found in Edward Manson and Robert Asher (1973) as well as Devesh Kapur *et al.* (1997).

The World Bank Group

What is commonly referred to as the World Bank is in fact a conglomeration of five different entities that together form the World Bank Group. The five divisions that make up the World Bank Group are: The International Bank for Reconstruction and Development (IBRD, the main organ of the World Bank Group which started operations in 1946), the International Development Association (IDA, the development aid department of the Bank, which started operations in 1960), the International Finance Corporation (IFC, which focuses on promoting private sector investment, and was established in 1956), the Multilateral Investment Guarantee Agency (MIGA, established in 1988), and the International Centre for the Settlement of Investment Disputes (ICSID, an autonomous division set up by the Bank in 1965 to arbitrate investment disputes between member states and private investors). The IBRD and the IDA constitute the core of the Bank's development activities, and these two divisions are what this chapter will focus on. The IFC and the MIGA are the private sector arms of the World Bank Group that are devoted to promoting private investment in member countries.

The IBRD, from the beginning, was mandated with providing development loans at market or near-market interest rates. As the name suggests, the IBRD had two main objectives at the beginning: first, to provide resources to finance the *reconstruction* of war-torn European countries at the end of World War Two;[2] second, to provide resources for economic development to less developed member countries. It is important here to note that the initial draft proposal to establish the Bank did not have a developmental component to it; the Bank was initially thought of as a revolving fund meant to assist European countries emerging from the war to reconstruct their economies and societies broadly. Concerns about what to do with the Bank after the reconstruction[3] of Europe was over prompted some founding members to include the *development* component as a long-term vision for addressing underdevelopment challenges in less developed member countries. Development at that time was understood in terms of increasing "productivity and hence the standard of living of the peoples of member countries" (Kapur *et al.*, 1997: 57). The primacy of the reconstruction of Europe is evident in Article I (ii) of the Bank's *Articles of Agreement* which defines the Bank's mission as:

To assist in the reconstruction and development of territories of members by facilitating the investment of capital for productive purposes, including the restoration of economies destroyed or disrupted by war, the reconversion of productive facilities to peacetime needs and the encouragement of the development of productive facilities and resources in less developed countries.

(IBRD *Articles of Agreement*, 1944)

It is also important to remember that very few less developed countries (LDCs) were represented (except Mexico, Argentina, Colombia and Brazil) at the 1944 Bretton Woods conference, where discussions to establish the IMF and World Bank were finalised. In the case of Africa, no country was present; all were 'represented' by their colonising countries. Most importantly, at this moment many participants at the conference were thinking about European countries destroyed by war,[4] and the emphasis was on setting up a reconstruction fund, and not necessarily a development bank (Kapur *et al.*, 1997: 61). The addition of the IDA (14 years after the BWIs started operating) may be another indication of the fact that development of LDCs was largely an afterthought, coming into the spotlight only after the reconstruction of Europe was completed. Over the years the Bank has made available its resources for development purposes through two main instruments: the IBRD and IDA loans.

The International Bank for Reconstruction and Development (IBRD) resources

IBRD loans are usually provided to middle-income countries with sufficient creditworthiness to repay the loans at near-market interest rates. Creditworthiness is defined by the bank as the "ability to service new external debt at market interest rates over the long term" (World Bank, 2001: 3). A member country's creditworthiness is determined by the Bank based on its assessment of several factors, including a country's Gross National Product (GNP) per capita, but crucially the export earnings to debt service ratio and implementation of prescribed policy reforms. Though the Bank considers a number of factors in determining a country's creditworthiness, some observers have argued that it has adopted narrow and conservative assessment criteria which mainly focus on debt service ratio[5] (Ayres, 1983). However, there is no clear-cut ratio at which a country is deemed creditworthy or not. As for the GNP per capita criterion, the 2008 IBRD eligibility range was set at a GNP per capita of between US$936 and US$11,455 (at current dollar prices), which is in fact the Bank's definition of the middle-income country status. The 2013 classification of a middle-income country ranged between US$1,025 to US$12,475. In 1964 the ceiling for middle-income status was set at a GNP per capita of more than US$250. Although countries with a GNP per capita outside the middle-income band *have* accessed IBRD loans, most, in practice, have gone to the upper middle-income countries. For example, in the 2008 fiscal year, 56 per cent of IBRD loans went to four middle-income countries: China, Argentina, India and Turkey. Using the middle-income country classification in the past meant that very few SSA countries could borrow through IBRD instruments; only a handful of countries fell within the middle-income band. In 2008 only 11 SSA countries had a per capita income within the middle-income range.[6] A number of countries – such as Cote d'Ivoire, Cameroon, Ghana and Zambia – have been falling in and out of the middle-income category since the 1960s. Recently, a number of African countries – including Nigeria, Ghana, Zambia, Djibouti, Sao Tome and Principe, and Sudan – have technically graduated to middle-income status, but they still do not borrow from IBRD resources. Up to this point, almost 99 per cent of the World Bank's resources committed to Africa are IDA resources (see Table 2.4).

Why borrow from the Bank?

There are three main reasons which make IBRD loans more attractive than commercial bank loans. First, the period of repayment for IBRD loans is longer, usually 15–20 years. Second, IBRD loans have a three to five year grace period before the repayment of the principal loan begins. Third, rescheduling under the IBRD loans is often more open than with commercial banks. However, during the late 1970s up to the present, most African countries, because of their low credit rating,[7] could not borrow from the commercial banks, and even from the IBRD. The only source of development finance available to them has been through the IDA resources, which provide loans at zero or near-zero interest rates (concessional loans). Currently, many African countries do not have sovereign credit rating status and many have low ratings, and as such would find it more expensive to borrow from international capital markets. Low, or lack of, sovereign credit rating means that a country's borrowing will be more expensive since the interest rates are largely correlated with the risk for a particular client, such that the lower the rating (high risk), the higher the interest rate. In other words, a country rated AAA+ can borrow at lower interest rates when compared to a country with a C- rating.

The rating process itself has become controversial, especially in the wake of the Eurozone debt crisis which saw many countries' sovereign credit rating down-graded – resulting in higher interest rates on government bonds and borrowing costs in general.[8] While a wide range of factors such as growth prospects, size of public debt, structure and size of the tax base, depth of the financial markets, independence of the central bank, public debt threshold, employment levels, political and social stability, and prospects of the state's revenues against expenditure are taken into account, some countries have begun to question the international credit rating agencies' (Standard and Poors, Moody's, and Fitch) credibility, arguing that they are colluding with the speculators to engineer high profits for financial kingpins, and there have been some suggestions to ignore them altogether. For example, the former governor of the Bank of England, Mervyn King, argues that there is unjustified credence given to the credit rating agencies, suggesting that it is probably better to base one's investment decision on the yields on government bonds than follow these agencies. "We need to move to a point, and I think markets have gone some way towards that, where they pay less attention to the verdicts of the rating agencies" (cited in Davie, 2012: 5). However, there are many government officials who idolise these credit rating agencies, and are ready do anything in their power to comply with their verdict. A good example is the reaction of former French president, Nikola Sarkozy, following the early 2012 down-grading of France's credit outlook. Sarkozy wasted no time complaining about the down-grade; instead he immediately swung into action, negotiating with labour unions on how to get the notch back (see Bishop, 2012: 7).

In the case of SSA, most countries are not rated (see endnote 7), and most of those that are rated have BB+ or lower, except South Africa and Botswana which have BBB+.[9] In this sense, credit rating down-grade has little impact on many African countries which are not able to borrow from international capital markets, including the IBRD facilities. As shown below, most African countries rely on concessional loans from the IDA, IMF, Africa Development Bank (AfDB) and other bilateral lenders, though there are a number of countries that are now borrowing from commercial markets through the Euro Bond – including Zambia (2012), Ghana, Angola, Nigeria and Rwanda (see IMF, 2013).

The International Development Association (IDA) resources

One of the widely used instruments by the Bank to lend to African countries is the IDA, which provides loans at concessional interest rates of close to zero (the soft lending window). The IDA resources are referred to by the Bank as the "Fund for the Poorest" (World Bank, 2014). IDA offers loans and grants which are different from the IBRD loans in the sense that a country with low creditworthiness is eligible to borrow as long as it meets the three IDA eligibility criteria: income below the IDA threshold, lack of creditworthiness to borrow from financial markets, and a track record of "good policy performance" (see www.worldbank.org/ida). In 1964 the ceiling for countries to qualify for IDA loans was a Gross Domestic Product (GDP) per capita income below US$250, while in 2010 the threshold was set at a GDP per capita income below US$1,135. Table 2.1 provides a list of African countries eligible for IDA in 2010, with corresponding ranges of per capita income in which they fall. Classification and eligibility of countries to access IDA resources has not been a transparent and consistent process, and has exhibited double standards at times (see Moss *et al.*, 2004).

The World Bank sees the IDA as a "transitional instrument of concessional support, from which most countries should over time graduate" (World Bank, 2001: 1). Graduation from IDA is triggered when a country's GNP per capita exceeds the set eligibility threshold, although there are a number of blend countries (see Table 2.1).

Of interest here is the fact that the 2014 IDA list has SSA members who have been on the list since the 1960s, with few exceptions, suggesting that there have been fewer SSA countries graduating from the IDA. Countries such as Cameroon,

Table 2.1. SSA countries eligible for IDA and GNP per capita (2010)

US$100–500	US$501–900	US$901–1,200	Mixed
Burundi	Ghana	Cameroon	Angola[A][L]
Burkina Faso	Kenya	Cote d'Ivoire	Somalia[B]
Central African Republic	Chad	Lesotho	Zimbabwe[B][L]
DR Congo	Mali	Nigeria[L]	Sudan[B]
Eritrea[B]	Mauritania	Senegal	Djibouti[K]
Ethiopia	Benin	Zambia	Cape Verde[K][L]
Gambia			Comoros[K]
Guinea			Congo Republic[L]
Guinea-Bissau			
Liberia			
Madagascar			
Malawi			
Mozambique			
Niger			
Rwanda			
Tanzania			
Togo			
Uganda			

Source: compiled by author, based on data from the Africa Development Bank website (www.afdb. org) and data from the *World Development Indicators* (2010).

Note: [A] = in the process of graduating from IDA (see *IDA Funding Cycle* on page 42). [B] = under sanctions (inactive members). [L] = blend countries (countries able to borrow from IBRD and IDA). [K] = no GNP per capita data available.

Congo Republic, Cote d'Ivoire and Zimbabwe have graduated from IDA at one time, but have reaccessed the IDA resources in recent years.[10] The fact that many countries have remained on the IDA client list may be an indication that the loans they have been receiving for the past 40 years have not achieved the envisioned objective, otherwise we should have seen more 'graduates' from Africa by now. Out of the nine SSA countries reported in 2010 to have graduated from the IDA during the 1970s, four have reaccessed the IDA resources,[11] and currently 42 SSA African countries are IDA clients – 55 per cent of the total number of IDA countries. In 2000 there were 39 SSA countries on the IDA client list out of a total of 68 countries.

Clearly, SSA remains a leading client base for the IDA, and it has been argued by the donor countries during IDA15 that priority should be given to Africa as far as access to IDA resources is concerned. Even if there are suggestions that by the year 2025 (when the IDA turns 65) the IDA client base would shrink to only 31 countries from the current 79 countries – since a majority of the countries would have 'graduated' – the observation that 81 per cent of the post-2025 IDA clients will be African countries suggests that these loans are having insignificant developmental impact in Africa (Moss and Leo, 2011). While within the Africa Rising narrative (ARN) there have been suggestions that debt relief (most of which is

IDA money) has contributed to sustained growth in Africa over the past decade, some critics argue that aid, in its various forms, has been the barrier to Africa's growth (Calderisi, 2006; Moyo, 2009).

This not only raises the question of what IDA loans have achieved in the recipient countries over the past 50 years, it also touches on the long-term interests of IDA operations in Africa. Arguably, this situation makes the work of the IDA seem paradoxical in that, if its objectives are achieved, it would have no clients, therefore rendering itself jobless! Just how much interest the IDA has in making itself redundant is an interesting question.

IDA funding cycle

To understand the politics of the IDA it is important to look at where the resources come from. IDA resources come mainly from three sources: replenishments, reflows and IBRD transfers. The largest share of IDA resources comes from richer member countries who contribute resources on a three-year cycle called the *IDA replenishment cycle*, with IDA1 (the initial IDA) negotiated and completed in 1964. From 1960 up to the present day, 16 IDAs (three-year replenishments) have been negotiated, with the latest replenishment (IDA16) having been concluded towards the end of 2010. The next replenishment (IDA17) will be finalised towards the end of 2014. The second largest source of IDA resources are the reflows – the repayment of loans from borrowers, though this is always a small portion since most loans have longer repayment periods of between 20–40 years. The third source is transfers from the profits made from IBRD loans. For the IDA16, which had a total value of US$49.3 billion, US$31.7 billion (63 per cent) came from replenishment, US$14.6 billion (31 per cent) from reflows and US$3 billion (6 per cent) from IBRD transfers (see IDA/World Bank, 2010).

Given this resource structure, the IDA has to justify to donors, every three years, that the resources are helping to meet intended objectives – otherwise donors[12] will not replenish the resources. In a way this amounts to the IDA justifying its own existence. Although there is a service charge of only 0.75 per cent on IDA loans, the IDA's existence can only be justified if there are clients willing to borrow money, and its credibility lies in showing that the poorest countries are actually accessing these resources. Unlike the IBRD resources, which charges near-market interest rates on its loans and raises money through the international capital markets, the IDA has to convince donors, in every replenishment round, that their money is being spent in poor countries to promote growth and poverty reduction.

In general, the World Bank provides development assistance through these two mechanisms (IBRD and IDA) to developing countries, and the resources can be accessed as project loans or policy-based loans – though since the 1980s there has been a mix of project and policy-based lending, with the latter dominating (Mosley *et al.*, 1995a). In later years, most of the loans have been policy-based (conditional programme lending), which ties their disbursement to institutional and policy reform performance. For the World Bank there are two main types of lending instruments: Structural Adjustment Lending (SAL) and the Sectoral Adjustment Loans (SECAL). The former supports economy-wide reforms, including institutional capacity building, while the latter focuses on particular sectors which are identified as strategic sectors linked to economic growth and development. These instruments have been used by the Bank in its engagement with African countries.

The International Monetary Fund

As noted earlier, the IMF also provides loans to member countries using various financial instruments such as the Stand-By Arrangement (SBA, which are short-term loans meant to assist member countries experiencing BoP problems), the Extended Fund Facility (EFF, medium-term loans of up to five years to support macroeconomic stabilisation), the Poverty Reduction and Growth Facility (PRGF, low interest loans to poor member countries to support poverty reduction policies and programmes), Supplementary Reserve Facility (SRF, short-term loans to member countries experiencing sudden capital outflows), Contingent Credit Lines (CCLs, short-term loans to support countries experiencing negative 'contagion' from other countries) and Emergence Assistance Support (EAS, support provided to member countries experiencing natural disaster and sometimes military conflict). The focus of the IMF as specified in its *Articles of Agreement* is to stabilise the international financial system by providing support to member countries experiencing financial problems, mainly BoP shortfalls.

The rationale behind IMF loans is that a single country that is having problems meeting its international financial obligations poses a threat to the *entire* global financial system. As such, the point of interest is not so much the struggling individual country, but the health of the global financial system. Although the IMF has repeatedly stated that it is not a development agency, and therefore does not support project funding, it does however provide loans to member countries at below-market rates, including project funding. The primary concern of the IMF, however, is providing short-term loans to eligible member countries experiencing problems with meeting international financial obligations, and this was initially based on the understanding that BoP problems are a short-term phenomenon. But what happens when you come to dealing with countries that face perpetual BoP problems, as many countries in Africa (mainly SSA) during the 1980s and 1990s did? Somehow the experience of the late 1970s and early 1980s forced the IMF to expand its horizons, and worldview, to accommodate the fact that BoP shortfalls can, in fact, be a prolonged condition such that the stabilisation instruments have to respond to a situation of perpetual BoP problems. To deal with countries in such situations, the Fund created the EFF in 1974, which provided medium-term loans to countries whose BoP problems could not be resolved in the short term. Similar measures such as the Structural Adjustment Facility (SAF, created in 1986) and the Enhanced Structural Adjustment Facility (ESAF, created in 1987) – which disbursed loans at close-to-zero interest rates with a longer repayment period of up to ten years – have been introduced over the years, pushing the Fund towards medium-term lending similar to the Bank's IDA loans. In a way, this change in approach to lending forced the IMF to extend its realm of operation beyond BoP concerns, a situation that at times resulted in a strained relationship with the Bank, especially during the mid-1980s (see Polak, 1997; Mosley *et al.*, 1995b).

To access the Fund's resources, a member country has to comply with the conditionality attached to a loan; failure to comply can result in the suspension or withholding of future resource disbursement. Most countries in Africa, though they did not engage much with the IMF until towards the end of the 1970s, have often found themselves without any other option but to seek IMF resources and endure the conditionality. When compared to the Bank, the IMF has had very stringent conditionalities, and has taken a conservative economistic approach to the challenges of economic growth and development in Africa.

The World Bank and the IMF in Africa

In discussing the Bank and the Fund's involvement in Africa, the crucial point is that while countries eligible for IDA, IBRD and IMF loans are able to access funds at concessional rates and/or on flexible terms, accessing these resources comes at a cost; namely, that a benefiting country has to comply with policy and other reforms prescribed by the lending institutions. Generally, "the main factor that determines the allocation of IDA resources among eligible countries is each country's performance in implementing policies that promote economic growth and poverty reduction" (IDA/World Bank, 2010). This is what constitutes the infamous 'conditionality' – which started from the early days of the Bank's work in Africa, but became more pronounced during the SAL era, and right through its descendants – the PRSPs-HIPC, and the Multilateral Debt Relief Initiatives (MDRIs) – which are discussed in the next chapter. Tying development assistance resources to performance in the implementation of policy reforms has effectively led to a situation where the Bank and the IMF have had significant leverage over the policies of poorer countries, to a point where policymaking has been completely hijacked (Peet, 2003). Some analysts have even argued that, starting in the 1980s, "SAPs effectively replaced any form of development planning in Africa … and African leaders surrendered their right to design and implement policies for their countries" (Owusu, 2003: 1660).

In a fundamental way it is the provision of these flexible loans which has given the World Bank and the IMF great influence over policies in developing countries, and the more dependent a country is on these 'soft loans' the more leverage the Bank and the Fund exercise on that country's policies. By imposing conditionality under the policy-based lending programmes, the Bank, in particular, intended to kill "two birds with one stone; more generous financial flows and more effective economic policy combined in the same package" (Mosley *et al.*, 1995b: 65). Although conditionality of some sort is a way of increasing the probability of loan repayment (the collateral component), in the Bank's operations conditionality has mainly focused on forcing borrowing countries to remove what the Bank sees as policy distortions that make sustained economic growth very hard to achieve – which in turn reduces the probability of repaying the loans. By emphasising the need for economic structural reform to its clients, the Bank has traded collateral for leverage, such that concerns about repayment are indirectly addressed through the suggested economic reforms. This, however, does not amount to abandoning the collateral component of the loans; the idea behind this approach is that once the economic policy and structures are configured, achieving economic growth will be easier and therefore the probability of repayment of loans will increase. A critical question is whether this strategy has worked or not. In general, conditionalities are also imposed on borrowing countries as a way of dealing with the 'moral hazard' of lending.

In the case of SSA, as noted above, the fact that several countries have rescheduled their debts while others have entered non-accrual status,[13] suggests that there have been less than modest outcomes. As noted earlier, the influence of the Bank and the Fund has been greatest in SSA since the 1980s, mainly because of the region's increasing dependence on the Bank's resources – which is the case even today. In comparative terms, SSA is the region most dependent on the Bank and the Fund's resources, thus giving more leverage to the Fund and to the Bank not just over economic policy, but also the broader policy space. In the context of this analysis, the key point is that prescribing reforms entails a certain understanding of the challenges which the prescription seeks to respond to. Before the Bank can prescribe any reform, it first of all has to have some understanding and explanation of the economic growth and development challenges that it seeks to address, and this is where the Bank and the Fund become important in the African development story.

Policy convergence between the Bank and the Fund?

Though there are fundamental differences in the way the Bank and the Fund operate and how they have dealt with the challenge of development in Africa, starting from the mid-1980s, their approaches have largely converged, and broad agreements were reached on many issues, especially during the 1980s. In later periods, as we shall see in the next chapter, the two institutions started implementing jointly designed programmes, as in the case of the Highly Indebted Poor Countries (HIPC) initiative launched in 1996. The trend in later days has led to the blurring of the line dividing the Bank and the Fund's operations such that the two institutions have largely prescribed the same policies, conditionalities and loan terms. Clearly, the "conditionality applied by the two institutions in [their] lending operations, while not becoming identical, has converged into a large common area, and in general the countries borrowing under these conditions have been the same" (Polak, 1997: 483). Prior to the 1980s, the Fund and the Bank had distinct approaches, areas of operation, and, most importantly, economic policy and development orientation.

In the beginning the IMF's mandate, as noted earlier, was to provide short-term loans aimed at stabilising the macroeconomic conditions in member countries; while the Bank's mandate was a broader one, relating to both social and economic issues. In this sense the IMF has not been in the business of development since the beginning; its mandate has been to look after the health of the global financial system through surveillance of exchange rates (mainly), inflation, interest rates and price imbalances. However, as time went by this became an artificial separation: there has been an uneasy tension between the two BWIs as far as separating their mandates is concerned. Although Richard Feinburg (cited in Mosley *et al.*, 1995a) argues that the creation of two separate institutions was to prevent a concentration of power and the danger of putting all the eggs in one basket, "Bank-IMF tensions arose, however, from time to time about how far the responsibilities of each extended, where overlaps occurred, and who was entitled to do what" (cited in Mosley *et al.*, 1995a: 36).

Responsibility overlap and duplication of roles surfaced during the 1980s, with the Bank extending its lending arm to include policy reforms, while the Fund extended its operations into the sort of medium-term lending that had been the Bank's mandate. As mentioned earlier, the Bank's lending operations prior to the introduction of SALs at the end of the 1970s was predominantly project lending that did not necessarily require compliance with policy reforms as a condition for approving a loan. With the introduction of SALs, the Bank's policy conditionalities extended its operations into the Fund's mandate. Similarly, the introduction of the EFF by the IMF in 1974, and later SAF and ESAF in 1986 and 1987 respectively – which provided medium-term loans – has been seen as the IMF's incursion into the Bank's mandate. Ordinarily, conflicts over mandates are diplomatically resolved by referring to the articles of agreement which define the parameters for these two institutions, but sometimes this requires the introduction of new agreements – as was the case with the 1989 'concordat' (see Polak, 1997). While programmes such as the PRSP under the Highly Indebted Poor Country Initiatives are jointly designed and implemented, there are indications of serious differences on policy issues and approaches between these two institutions, with the World Bank's views often ignored by the IMF – which often works in tandem with the US Treasury Department (Stiglitz, 2000).

The Bank and Fund's understanding of Africa's growth challenge

From the early days of the Bank and the Fund's involvement in Africa, the Bank's understanding of Africa's growth and development challenge was not significantly different from the IMF's. Although the two institutions had, in principle, clearly differentiated mandates, as noted above, the similarity of policies and approaches adopted – especially during the mid-1980s – suggests a common understanding of the African challenges and how they were to be addressed. Some analysts have observed that while the monetarist views have been strong within the Fund (given its role of policing the international financial system), the dominant ideological position in the Bank, over the years, has shifted from Keynesian to neo-Keynesian, and then in the 1980s to neoliberalism (see Stein, 2004). Reasons for this shift are many and varied. Some have argued that the ideological orientation of staff at the Bank has often determined which side of the divide the pendulum swung, while other analysts note that global economic conditions make certain positions untenable and therefore a shift in the dominant ideology is inevitable (Brown, 1995). Whatever accounts for this shift, it is evident that since the 1980s there has been convergence between the BWIs, at least at policy and programme levels. Though cross-conditionality and cross-membership has been part of the Bank and the Fund's policy from the beginning, this has evolved into a monochrome development policy environment and a higher concentration of power and a higher exercise of leverage. It is even argued that

> The Fund's power does not depend on its net lending (drawings), which has been quite low over 1980–88 … It arises because a highly conditional agreement with the Fund is a precondition for the Bank's structural adjustment program, a Paris Club … debt rescheduling and for enhanced bilateral assistance.
>
> (Green, 1993: 48)

Arguably, the Bank and the Fund's approach has been, to varying degrees, market-oriented. Although the Bank entertained state-led approaches to development during the 1950s and 1960s, it has always emphasised the importance of markets as the engine for sustained economic growth and development. Even during the 1950s and 1960s, when its funding of development projects such as communications and education infrastructure were mainly through grants and loans to member countries, it continued to emphasise the importance of private investment (Ayres, 1983). However, it must be remembered that the Bank's lending to African countries prior to the 1980s was not determined by the ideological orientation of the client state; the Bank provided project loans to self-styled Marxist, socialist and mixed economy states alike. In this sense, the "Bank chose practical considerations such as the country's ability to organise and execute projects over ideology as the principal determinant of lending levels" (Kapur *et al.*, 1997: 699). Within the Bank itself, right from the start, many staff members had a strong leaning towards market liberalism, and most of them perceived the Bank as one concerned with market conditions – including interest rates and creditworthiness – in client states. Many officials at the Bank see the institution, first and foremost, as a bank (Brown, 1995). "Like any other bank it does not give things away. It does not subsidise undertakings" (Ayres, 1983: 10).

As for the IMF, the pre-eminence of the market – with a heavy leaning towards monetarist (supply-side) economic theory in its theoretical orientation and approach to development and growth – is beyond question. Fiscal austerity and 'shock therapy' (balanced budgets, low inflation, public expenditure cuts) are synonymous with the IMF's identity (Stiglitz, 2000). Although other approaches considered in this book have a place for markets in their frameworks, the priority of markets distinguishes the Bank and the Fund's approach from other approaches. As such, much of the market-oriented approach (MOA) discussions in this book focus on these two institutions. Even though during the 1990s, when it became apparent that SAPs did not deliver the anticipated outcomes, the Bank, in particular, was compelled to recognise the state as an important factor in the African crisis; markets still reigned large.

Notwithstanding the recent pronouncement that "the Bank is supporting development models that allow different mixes of government and market interventions" (World Bank, 2011: 7), the core of its approach has been market-based, with markets seen as the best arbiter of the complex interconnections between incentives, rewards and economic growth. Bringing in the state through the good governance and democracy door during the 1990s did not displace the centrality of markets in the Bank and Fund's approach to Africa's economic growth and development challenges. "At the heart of the Bank's agenda was [and still is] the desire to reshape the role of the state in Africa, giving greater scope to markets and the private sector" (Kapur *et al.*, 1997: 734). In this way the state became important only to the extent that it enhanced the functioning of markets.

As elaborated in the next chapter, the Bank's role in Africa's economic growth and development has been evolving, although its approach has remained conservative on core issues, particularly the emphasis on markets as the main driver of economic growth and development. In this sense, mainstream economic theories and strategies have had a strong influence on both the Bank and, more especially, the Fund's approach to issues of growth and development. With particular reference to the African case, despite the strong tendencies towards conservativism, the Bank and the Fund have been going through a steep learning curve in their engagement with African countries and economies. Part of this evolving knowledge of the African challenge is the natural outcome of growth and development in Africa. Changes in the Bank's understanding and approaches have been part of the changing conditions of African economic, political and social conditions, induced by the changing dynamics in the global economic and geopolitical environment.

The Bank's engagements in Africa

As noted earlier, prior to the 1980s the Bank's activities in Africa were largely restricted to project lending in a few countries. Even with more African countries becoming independent during the 1960s, and members in their own right of the Bank and the Fund (see Table 2.2), the Bank's involvement in Africa was limited in scale, concentrating on technical assistance and research linked to specific projects funded by the Bank.

Membership of African countries at the Bank grew from two in the 1950s to 34 at the end of the 1960s, and by the end of the 1980s almost all countries except

Table 2.2. World Bank memberships for African countries (1947–1996)

Period	Member countries	Cumulative total
1947–1957	Ethiopia and South Africa	2
1958–1962	Egypt, Ghana, Liberia, Sudan, Morocco, Tunisia, Libya, Nigeria, Togo, Somalia, Sierra Leone, Tanzania, Gambia, Senegal	16
1963–1967	Benin, Chad, Cameroon, Central African Republic, Congo Republic, DRC (Zaire), Cote d'Ivoire, Algeria, Uganda, Burundi, Rwanda, Guinea, Benin, Burkina Faso, Mali, Kenya, Niger, Malawi, Zambia, Botswana, Lesotho, Mauritius, Mauritania	39
1968–1971	Swaziland, Equatorial Guinea	41
1972–1980	Cape Verde, Comoros, Seychelles, Djibouti, Zimbabwe	46
1981–1996	Mozambique, Angola, Namibia, Eritrea	50

Source: World Bank (Chronological History, www.worldbank.org).

Note (1): the Reunion, Western Sahara, South Sudan and Sao Tome are not included due to lack of data.

Note (2): Bank membership refers to a country's signing the International Bank for Reconstruction and Development (IBRD) agreement. Membership to subsidiaries of the World Bank Group (the International Development Association (IDA), International Finance Corporation (IFC), International Centre for the Settlement of Investment Disputes (ICSID) and the Multilateral Investment Guarantee Agency (MIGA)), is only open once a country becomes a member of the IBRD. Being a member of the Bank requires a country to be a member of the Fund at the same time. The reason for this cross-membership is that linking the membership between the two institutions ensures that there are no 'free riders' in the sense that every member country contributes to the global stability goal by following the prescribed rules.

Note (3): though South Africa was placed under sanctions within the United Nations (UN) system in the 1960s, it continued to be courted by the Bank and by the Fund.

Namibia, Angola and Mozambique were members.[14] At present all members of the World Bank Group are also members of the IMF (cross-membership), and a country that is ineligible to borrow from one institution cannot borrow from the other (cross-conditionality).

Notably, the Bank's commitment and disbursement to Africa increased sharply during the early days of its Robert McNamara presidency, especially after the famous 1973 *Nairobi Speech*, which led to the launching of the 'Rural Development Strategy' (Ayres, 1983). As for the IMF, its engagement with Africa remained in low gear over the 1960s and 1970s.

The Bank's engagement with Africa took shape in 1961 when the Africa Department was created to look into the continent's development issues separately from other regions, and in 1962 Pierre Moussa was appointed the first director of the Africa Department at the World Bank. In the following year a special section within the Africa Department called the 'technical assistance' division was established to assist African countries on technical matters related to agriculture and social services such as education, housing, health and water supply. Project loans could only be approved based on recommendations from the technical experts. Ever since, the Africa Department has had its own members of staff who have studied and analysed the African economic and social challenges, providing a diagnosis as well as a prescription for the challenges. Though in the early days the majority of staff within the Africa Department were non-Africans, criticism from Africans resulted in the recruitment of more African staff during the 1980s (see Lancaster, 1997), and the African presence in the department has increased substantially. There are, however, doubts as to how well these staff members are acquainted with African conditions (Stiglitz, 2000).

In the early days of engagement between the Bank and African countries, lack of trust surfaced as early as 1971 and this started to shape the Bank's relationship with borrower countries. Mistrust on the part of African governments was for four main reasons. First, there was suspicion among African leaders that the economic and technical advice provided by the Bank's staff would only benefit the developed, Western, countries. This is captured in a 1971 memorandum from William Clark (the then senior vice president for Africa) to McNamara, in which Clark argued that there was "an extreme touchiness about sovereignty in most [African countries] and a strong suspicion that the economic advice is for the benefit of the metropolitan country rather than the ex-colony" (cited in Kapur *et al.*, 1997: 694). This suspicion was part of the African leader's militancy against new forms of control from former colonial masters in the name of technical assistance and aid. Ironically, although the suspicion was openly expressed, most African governments continued to rely on their former colonial master's technical assistance via 'seconded experts', aid, and policy advice.

Second, the intrusive nature of economic advice and loan conditionality impinged on matters of national sovereignty. Most African leaders perceived this as undermining their autonomy, seeing such moves as part of the neo-colonial, neo-imperial strategy. Third, the arrogant and heavy-handed manner in which most Bank staff conducted themselves during the 1970s reinforced some of the deep-seated suspicions of African leaders about the Bank being an agent of domination and neo-imperialism (see Lancaster, 1997). Fourth, within the general African public, most observers, especially intellectuals and academics, were critical of the fact that policy directives were being formulated by people who had little understanding of African conditions. This criticism became widespread and intensified during the years of SAPs. A former chief economist at the Bank argues that BWI officials who formulate policy for developing countries often "have [more] first-hand knowledge of the ... five star hotels than the villages that dot the countryside" (Stiglitz, 2000).

Thus, while the Bank was not involved in policy-based lending before the 1980s, there was uneasiness in the relationship, and the biggest challenge for the Bank was to win the trust of African leaders. However, this uneasy relationship remained largely calm over the 1960s and 1970s due to the fact that the Bank's activities in Africa did not intrude so much into most countries' policy spaces. One of the reasons for this lack of intrusiveness is that project lending did not require prescription of macroeconomic policy for the borrowing country. Most borrowing countries were left to design their own policies and development strategies, even if the Bank did not agree with these. A Bank review of its lending approaches in Zambia, for example, criticised the lending policy arguing that the "programmatic approach" (focusing on a particular programme) adopted by the Bank did not provide incentives for the country to "respect" the macroeconomic advice provided by the Bank (see Kapur *et al.*, 1997). Further, because the majority of African countries during the 1960s had positive economic prospects, there was little concern about the problem of countries failing to repay their loans.

Humble beginnings

The Bank's understanding of African economies grew from a very rudimentary level during the 1950s – informed only by a few country missions[15] – to a more complex understanding gained through studies carried out in the 1980s and 1990s. During the 1960s the Bank had very limited knowledge of conditions in many African countries, often relying on the isolated country reports compiled after country missions. "Thus, despite the upsurge in analytical work and the degree of involvement it would soon get into, the Bank – and indeed scholars outside the Bank – had limited understanding of African institutions and society" (Kapur *et al.*,1997: 688).

In a way, the Bank's limited knowledge of Africa prior to the 1980s is probably commensurate with the low stakes it had in Africa. Increased resources committed[16] to the continent during the 1980s may account for the significant surge in the interest and effort the Bank directed towards Africa – as evidenced by the number of regional reports, studies, working papers and analyses that were conducted almost every year after the *Berg Report* of 1981 (World Bank, 1981).

Though country missions quadrupled during the 1960s, as more African countries joined the Bank, the Bank's knowledge of African economies remained relatively weak. Influential sources of information on African economies during the 1960s include a study report on Africa's agriculture, led by John de Wilde (1967) – *Experience with Agricultural Development in Tropical Africa* (Volumes 1 and 2),[17] and a monologue by the Bank's director of the Economics Department at the time, Andrew Kamarck (1967) – *The Economics of African Development*. These two publications, supplemented by the mission reports, shaped the Bank's knowledge of Africa's economic conditions, challenges and prospects. Though in the two publications it is admitted that African economies are so diverse that it is difficult to talk about an 'African' economic situation, they both refer to an African economy in the singular. From an agricultural perspective, de Wilde describes the African situation as follows:

> We must recognize, however, that probably 90 percent of the population of tropical Africa is still rural, that agriculture and livestock husbandry employ about 80 percent of the people and are the major earners of foreign exchange. Experience with industrial development in most of the less developed world would indicate that even on the most sanguine assumptions about the rate of industrial growth it may well be long before industry absorbs all of the

increase in population quite apart from any significant proportion of those now obtaining their livelihood from the land. The profitable employment of people on the land will therefore need to remain a central preoccupation of government policy.

(de Wilde, 1967: 3)

This view, most probably, influenced McNamara's decision to focus on agriculture and integrated rural development as the key policy area for the Bank's engagement with Africa during the 1970s. In his *Nairobi Speech*, on top of pledging to treble the size of loans to Africa, the then World Bank president, Robert McNamara, identified rural development as the main priority for his second five-year period (1974–1979) – emphasising expansion of extension services, applied research, water availability, access to credit and accelerated land reform as the key policy pillars for the Bank. Africa's (and indeed the entire developing world's) growth and development constraints at this time were understood largely in terms of low productivity of the subsistence sector. Thus, in the Bank's view, in order to initiate economic growth and development in Africa, increasing the productivity of people engaged in subsistence agriculture so that they could contribute meaningfully to the economy was the central issue. It was thus argued that,

> very little has been done over the past two decades specifically designed to increase the productivity of subsistence agriculture. Neither political programs, nor economic plans, nor international assistance – bilateral or multilateral – have given the problem serious and sustained attention. The World Bank is no exception. In our more than a quarter century of operations, less than $1 billion out of our $25 billion of lending has been devoted directly to this problem. It is time for all of us to confront this issue head-on.
>
> (McNamara, 1973)

The understanding behind the focus on subsistence agriculture was that since a majority of the population in Africa lived in rural areas and practised subsistence agriculture, economic growth could be ignited and sustained by increasing the productivity of people in that sector. Increasing productivity in this sector had two crucial spin-offs: first, it was anticipated that improved productivity would produce surplus resources which could be taxed or saved to finance industrialisation. Second, it was also assumed that once productivity among the peasant households improved, fewer people would be required to grow the food needed to feed the urban population; as a result, more people would flock to the newly established industries to prevent labour shortages in urban sectors. This view can be located within the broader theoretical framework of the "two sector" model developed in the 1950s by W. Arthur Lewis (1954) and later refined by Gustav Ranis and John Fei (1961). Within this model, economic development entails "the re-allocation of surplus agricultural workers, whose contribution to output may have been zero or negligible, to industry where they become productive members of the labour force at wages equal (or tied) to the institutional wage in agriculture" (Ranis and Fei, 1961: 534).

In an African context, the two sector model faced many conceptual and practical hurdles, for the simple reason that underdeveloped commercial agriculture and the small size of the industrial sector made such a strategy difficult to operationalise. During the 1960s the size of industrial activities was tiny, in fact non-existent in most countries, with industry's contribution to GDP for most countries (except South Africa) being less than 5 per cent (see Kamarck, 1967).

Although modest expansion of the manufacturing sector was recorded during this period (Bates, 1982), most countries' share of industry in GNP was below 15 per cent. As illustrated in the next chapter (see Table 7.5), figures for the period 2000–2010 have remained very low, with some countries still having as low as 5 per cent share of manufacturing in GNP. As such, the two sector model had little relevancy to the African context, and the Bank was aware of this.[18] For this reason the Bank and other development agencies focused on improving productivity in the subsistence sector rather than promoting the relocation of labour to urban sectors. The Bank's objective in the 1970s was

> to increase production on small farms so that by 1985 their output will be growing at the rate of 5% per year. If the goal is met, and smallholders maintain that momentum, they can double their annual output between 1985 and the end of the century.
>
> (McNamara, 1973)

The other, earlier, work that shaped the Bank's understanding of Africa during the 1960s and 1970s was the one written by Kamarck (who is described as someone "who knows Africa very well – from north to south and from east to west").[19] Kamarck provides an overview of various sectoral issues from population, structure of the economy, foreign investment and aid. According to Kamarck, during the 1960s, "Economically and financially, the African nations [were] more like a series of islands lying off the coast of Western Europe than like parts of a single continent" (Kamarck, 1967: 21). This relationship between African countries and their colonial masters had prevented the establishment of closer economic ties between African countries, and formed an important factor in explaining Africa's economic growth and development experience.

Seen from this vantage point, the implications for economic growth and development from this set-up are clear: African countries' continued dependence – not just on assistance from former imperial powers but also in terms of exports, technology, and even development strategies – implied a certain level of control by the former colonial powers. Not surprisingly, Kamarck's conclusion was that without European aid it was impossible for Africa to gather the necessary investment capital needed to initiate economic growth and development:

it appears clear that there will have to be drastic changes in existing trends – certainly including the lifting of the whole aid and technical assistance effort … and planning and coordinating it through some new international effort – if they are to be able to move ahead at a proper pace.

(Kamarck, 1967: 247)

However, Kamarck's forecast for economic growth during the 1960s was positive, and he observed that economic growth for countries such as Congo, Rhodesia, Kenya and Gabon would be "among the highest in the world" (1967: 17). A similar optimism is evident in the Bank's reports on various African countries during the 1960s, concluding that the "overall growth in the region was at par with that in Asia" (cited in Kapur *et al.*, 1997: 689).

The Bank's lending policy prior to SAPs

For the Bank, as noted above, most of the loans prior to the late 1970s were long-term project loans, focusing on infrastructure development such as hydro-electric power, irrigation, road and rail transport, and telecommunications. It should, however, be noted that the Bank (and more so the Fund) has never lent money without conditions. World Bank loans prior to the SAL era often carried policy conditionality, though this was always a relaxed requirement. A loan for a hydro-electric power station, for instance, was made on condition that the borrowing country revised its electricity tariff, mainly so as to facilitate the success of the project (see Mosley *et al.*, 1995b) and thereby ensure that the borrower would be able to pay back the loan.

With the introduction of SALs, the Bank's nature and rules of engagement with African countries changed dramatically, though some analysts have suggested that the shift to more policy-based conditional lending was palpable even before the second oil crisis of 1979. Paul Mosley *et al.* (1995b) and Morten Boas and Desmond McNeill (2003) argue that the performance-based lending approach was evident from the 1960s and 1970s. Examples given are loans to Zambia in 1974, Tanzania in 1975 and Kenya, also in 1975, which carried policy reform conditionality, requiring changes to agriculture marketing and pricing policies (Mosley *et al.*, 1995b: 32).

While there are many factors which precipitated the transition from project lending to policy-based lending, the changing global political environment (the coming to power of conservative governments in the UK (Thatcher, May 1979) and the USA (Reagan, November 1981), together with the ideological disposition of the Bank's senior staff, significantly influenced both the reorientation as well as the tone of its engagement with African governments. Arguably, this shift in lending policy reflects the Bank's evolving understanding of the African economic challenges and how these were to be addressed. Prior to the 1980s, though the anti-state sentiments were there, state intervention in the economy was tolerated, especially in those African countries where the underdeveloped nature of markets justified strong state action to create an attractive environment for private sector involvement. The rationale for this approach was that Africa's underdevelopment was largely a result of low private sector investment, and the only way to attract such investment was to allow the state to create conditions amenable to it (see Kamarck, 1967). In the initial stages, this mainly entailed building physical infrastructure such as roads, rail networks, telecommunications networks and a pool of skilled manpower (Ayres, 1983). These tasks were envisioned to be the responsibility of the state, with support from the Bank. Interestingly, lack of private investment appears to dominate many of the Bank's reports on Africa during the 1980s and 1990s, although the explanation for low private investment is blamed on low returns on investment (see World Bank, 1986, 1989, 2007).

The simultaneous coming to power of conservative governments in the UK, USA and Germany, together with the apparent failures of the state-led development strategies in many African states during the 1970s, led to the surfacing of strong anti-state views within the Bank – which came to see state intervention in Africa as the problem and not the solution (see Chapter 5 for details). SAPs were particularly designed to curb incursion by the state into activities which the market was presumably more suitable to efficiently handle. Thus, policy-based lending became a central tool for achieving the necessary structural and policy changes, since there were no natural incentives to push African countries in the direction of reform of the economy and of the state. But, as Kapur *et al.* (1997: 734) have argued, although conditionality was an important tool for the Bank, "it was less potent than initially expected".

The Bank and socialism in Africa

Even if, in the beginning, the Bank tolerated (and sometimes encouraged) the heavy involvement of the state in the economy of many African countries, and did not worry much about the slogan of African socialism[20] (Kapur *et al.*, 1997), the hope was that as the government developed infrastructure, the private sector would begin to move in and supplement – and eventually undercut – state involvement in the economy. Writing about the newly independent African states, Kamarck (1967), while acknowledging the important role states play in development, makes it clear that "It is … of prime importance for government to maintain policies that encourage private investment. It helps greatly too, if a government provides the environment for growth: … political and legal security for private investors and producers".

As far as development is concerned, the dominant view at the Bank has always revolved around active participation of the private sector, though a strong emphasis towards private sector strategies became more pronounced from the 1980s onwards. The centrality of the private sector in the development process is clearly stated in the IBRD's Article I (ii) of the Bank's *Articles of Agreement*, which sees one of the objectives of the Bank as:

> To promote private foreign investment by means of guarantees or participations in loans and other investments made by private investors; and when

private capital is not available on reasonable terms, to supplement private investment by providing, on suitable conditions, finance for productive purposes out of its own capital.

(IBRD, *Articles of Agreement*, 1944)

In view of this, it is probably incorrect to argue that prior to the 1980s the Bank's view was ideologically neutral on the grounds that it approved loans even to self-proclaimed socialist states in Africa. Even if loans were approved to socialist and non-socialist states, the conviction within the Bank was that its lending would pave the way for more private sector involvement, a move which was expected to reduce the state's role in the economy.

The IMF's engagements with Africa prior to SAPs

The Fund's dealings with African countries in the early independence days was limited to SBAs (established in 1962) aimed at providing short-term bridging funds for countries facing BoP problems (with a maturation period initially limited to between 12 and 18 months but later extended to up to four years). During the 1960–1972 period, only 12 African countries signed SBAs; the first ones being Egypt in 1962, Liberia in 1963, and Mali, Somalia and Tunisia in 1964, and most of these were small loans of not more than 10 million SDR[21] (Kapur *et al.*, 1997; Stein, 2004: 13). Interestingly, despite requests from African ministers of finance (who during the 1960s met annually), to increase lending to Africa on more favourable terms, these requests were largely turned down by the IMF.

One of the reasons that explains the limited engagement between African countries and the IMF prior to the 1980s is the fact that most of them did not experience the sort of BoP problems which might have necessitated seeking assistance from the Fund. During this period, most African countries had healthy foreign currency reserves accumulated from the period when the price of commodities were favourable on the global market. It was during the late 1970s that the activity and influence of the IMF increased, though modestly compared to the 1980s. The other reason is that the IMF, unlike the Bank's IDA loans, had no concessional lending instruments prior to 1974, and most African countries in need of loans accessed money through the commercial banks and other international financial lenders. It was only in 1976, when the IMF created a trust fund amounting to US$2.9 billion SDRs to provide concessional loans to low-income countries over the next five years, that its lending to Africa increased.

Pre-SAPs World Bank and IMF lending in Africa

World Bank loans approved during the 1970s focused largely on agriculture, education and infrastructure projects – mainly in transportation and communications – as part of the strategy to create an environment attractive to private investment.

Table 2.3. Mean annual IBRD and IDA lending to SSA (1960–1994, %)

Sector	1960–1964	1965–1969	1970–1974	1975–1979	1980–1984	1985–1989	1990–1994
Agriculture	17	13	24	35	31	29	18
Mining	15	4	2	2	1	0	0
Energy[a]	46	10	14	6	16	8	15
Telecommunication	1	3	4	2	2	3	3
Transportation	20	52	38	25	21	22	20
Water Supply	0	1	2	6	4	6	8
Education	1	12	11	8	7	7	10
Industrial	0	0	0	5	3	2	2
Urban development	0	0	0	3	3	10	8
Population	0	0	0	0	1	5	10

Source: author, based on data from Lancaster (1997: 164).

Note: the column percentages may not add up to 100 because sectors with smaller amounts such as finance, public sector, tourism and non-sectors have been omitted.

[a]: refers to the total for 'power' plus 'energy' sectors.

The first World Bank Loan (US$5 million) in Africa went, in 1950, to Ethiopia[22] for the rehabilitation of its road network. For the IMF, Egypt was the first African country to sign an SBA,[23] in 1962. By the fiscal year 1970, total Bank lending to SSA reached US$2.18 billion. As Table 2.3 shows, a large proportion of Bank resources between 1960 and 1975 went to agriculture and transport infrastructure, with the two sectors accounting for almost half of the Bank loans to SSA during this period.

It is interesting to note here that the percentage share of agriculture increased sharply during the 1970–1974 period, and remained high until the 1990–1994 period. This is confirmed by other sources which report that during the 1960s and 1970s, "Loans for agriculture and rural development, many of them packaged as integrated rural development projects, together with transportation, and lending for other infrastructure-related loans, accounted for 70 per cent of all lending in this period" (Kapur *et al.*, 1997: 695). One of the probable justifications for the large share of the Bank's lending to the agricultural sector is that agriculture and rural development occupied a central role in the Bank's understanding of Africa's development challenge during the 1970s; the figures above could be a reflection of the Bank's commitment to the agricultural sector, though further detail of how these funds were used would provide some indication of where exactly the emphasis in the sector was placed. Although in the early days focus was on providing agricultural infrastructure as part of the McNamara vision of integrated rural development, the Bank's studies and reports on the region during the 1980s suggest that focus has been on reforming the pricing and marketing system for the agriculture sector, with little emphasis directed towards developing agricultural infrastructure, technology and skills.

Overall, the large share of loans going to agriculture, transportation and energy since the 1960s reflects the dominant thinking within the Bank and the

Table 2.4. World Bank lending to SSA by sector (2004–2009, US$ million)

Sector	2004	2005	2006	2007	2008	2009
Agriculture	268.5	215.3	585.5	369.7	367.6	1,249.3
% of total	7	6	12	6	6	15
Education	362.9	369.0	339.3	706.6	373.0	719.7
% of total	9	9	7	12	7	9
Energy and Mining	365.8	509.5	524.5	773.0	939.4	1,417.7
% of total	9	13	11	13	17	18
Finance	165.7	68.6	142.3	26.3	129.7	75.4
% of total	4	2	3	0	2	1
Health and Social Services	723.1	590.3	614.0	687.3	467.5	1,004.3
% of total	18	15	13	12	8	12
Industry and Trade	95.4	253.8	348.4	144.2	196.2	289.9
% of total	2	7	7	2	3	4
ICT	52.9	20.0	5.0	146.0	0.8	144.3
% of total	1	1	0	3	0	2
Law and Public Administration	1,004.2	1,077.5	1,263.0	1,352.5	1,748.0	1,602.3
% of total	24	28	26	23	31	20
Transportation	716.6	507.2	602.7	870.8	986.5	1,146.5
% of total	17	13	13	15	17	14
Water, Sanitation, and Social Protection	360.8	276.2	361.9	720.5	477.9	553.6
% of total	9	7	8	12	8	7
Total	4,115.9	3,887.5	4,786.6	5,796.9	5,686.5	8,202.9
IDA as % of total	100	100	99	99	99	96
IDA total	4,115.9	3,887.5	4,746.6	5,759.4	5,656.5	7,841.4

Source: author, based on data from the World Bank Databank.

Western donor community that financing of "investments in physical and human infrastructure … were necessary to encourage private investments and growth" (Lancaster, 1997: 163). From the beginning it was hoped that building modern social and economic infrastructure would make Africa more attractive to private investment and that this would lead to massive capital inflows, initiating, in turn, the sort of industrialisation, growth of employment and productivity that would be the bedrock for development in the broad sense. Though there has been shifting focus, over the years, as is evident in Table 2.4, the role of the private sector has always been central to the development strategy envisioned by the Bank in Africa.

Compared to the 1960–1980 period, it is clear from Table 2.4 that the Bank's resources in recent years are concentrated in public administration, which takes, on average, up to a quarter of the resources. This may be a reflection of the Bank's emphasis on good governance and building state capacity, a campaign prioritised since the 1990s. The declining share of agriculture could be a reflection of the reduced attention given to the rural development agenda in recent years, a process that started in the late 1980s. Although agriculture, as evidenced in the Bank's reports since the early 1980s, remained a crucial sector in explaining the African economic and development experience, the emphasis seems to have shifted from the more direct poverty reduction and basic needs approach of the 1970s towards providing the right incentives in agriculture through agricultural commodity pricing and marketing reforms. Interestingly, transport and education have received a fairly constant share of the Bank's resources in Africa since the 1980s, which may be an indication of the importance the Bank has attached to human capital formation and infrastructure. It is also interesting to note that the Bank's entire resources committed to Africa over this period have been IDA and not IBRD resources. This also reflects the fact that African countries have had negligible access to IBRD resources, reinforcing the view mentioned earlier that there have been few IDA 'graduates' in Africa. Broadly, the involvement of the Bank in Africa during the 1970s and earlier was dominated by what has been referred to as "enclave projects" which entailed lower financial risk and relied on foreign experts to carry out much of the project appraisal (Kapur *et al.*, 1997: 688).

Africa and the McNamara era

Many analysts attribute increased Bank activities in Africa during the 1970s to the McNamara vision, interest and emphasis on rural development and poverty (Ayres, 1983; Lancaster, 1997; Kapur *et al.*, 1997; Stein, 2004). However, although McNamara committed himself to prioritising Africa with his emphasis on agriculture, education and integrated rural development, it was probably the changing economic conditions in which many African countries found themselves – especially from the mid-1970s – which provided an opportunity for the Bank to expand its activities and influence. In fact, in line with the observation that "as the crisis in Sub-Saharan Africa deepened, so did the Bank's involvement" (Kapur *et al.*, 1997: 720), it can be argued that the Bank's involvement and leverage in Africa has been proportional to the level of the crisis. By any measure, the 1980s – when the Bank and the Fund's work in Africa intensified – were the worst years in terms of per capita incomes and other social indicators (see UNECA, 1989).

The major factor which triggered increased involvement of the Bank and the Fund in Africa was the declining price and demand for those commodities that most African countries exported – a situation that resulted in a shortage of foreign currency, and a prolonged and growing deficit on the external account of many countries. Prior to the global recession of 1981–1982, most African countries managed to cope well. Although most countries – particularly the non-oil exporting ones – were destabilised by the 1973–1974 crisis, for most countries,

> terms of trade improved as industrial economies and world trade returned to
> rapid growth; and guaranteed export credits and commercial finance became

available on an unprecedented scale (albeit unequally by country). As a result, 1976–79 were years of rapid (on average over 5%) output growth.

(Green, 1993: 48)

Countries such as Zambia, Cote d'Ivoire, Tanzania, Ghana, Togo and Madagascar suffered severe foreign currency constraints during this period, which necessitated going to the Bank and the IMF (especially) for short-term loans. However, the structural problems of African economies were soon to be exposed. The slight price shock of 1981–1982 caused multiple problems for most non-oil exporting countries such that they needed external help to meet their foreign payments obligations.

Conditionality prior to SAPs

As noted earlier, unlike the World Bank, the IMF has always imposed stringent lending conditionality, and there has been little change from this position. In fact, the more desperate a country's fiscal conditions become, the more stringent the IMF's conditionality – leading to a situation where there was "too much shock" but "too little therapy" (Stiglitz, 2000). Conditionality varied widely, from fiscal discipline through price adjustment, to concealed conditionality such as choosing the company that a client government can procure its presidential jet from. In the case of the World Bank, Kapur *et al.* (1997) make the observation that the most influential member countries contributing to the IDA resources used the World Bank lending programme to increase their influence over borrowing countries. While the Bank and the Fund's activities in Africa prior to the 1980s could be described as modest, and the two institutions' engagement with African countries came largely in the form of unassertive partnerships, towards the end of the 1970s, even before the second oil crisis of 1979, there were already signs of profound changes in the Bank and Fund's relationship with Africa.

> by the end of the 1970s, in the realm of economic development, the Bank had emerged as the dominant external actor in Africa. Its share in lending had not grown, and in Francophone Africa France was still preeminent, but the Bank had become the leading aid coordinator, analyst and source of technical assistance. Where once bilateral aid agencies would have assisted the Bank in projects, the roles were almost reversed.

(Kapur *et al.*, 1997: 712)

Evolution of the Bank's engagement with Africa from modest partner during the 1960s and 1970s, to dominant partner during the 1980s, may have had little to do with the change in personalities of the leadership at the Bank. While McNamara is largely seen as someone disposed towards, and passionate about, Africa's economic development, the circumstances in which he operated made it possible for a less intrusive relationship – subsequently, most African countries were left in charge of steering their own ships. The ideological shifts that occurred around 1980 – particularly among those countries who were the major shareholders of the Bank and the IMF – largely influenced and set the mood for Africa's relationship with the Bank in the decades that followed (Brown, 1995).

Consequently, the interpretation of Africa's economic challenges took a radical shift, following the counter-revolution (see Krugman, 1996), which saw the resurgence of a radical form of liberal economic fundamentalism. The emergence of economic liberalism, together with the weakening economic performance of most African countries, set the scene for the turbulent years of the 1980s and 1990s – not just for African countries, but also for the Bank and the Fund as they battled to prove themselves as international finance and development institutions of integrity.

Notes

1 Some analysts have commented that it is not by coincidence that the Bank's first client in Africa has become one of the poorest countries in the continent (Lancaster, 1997).
2 The Bank's first four loans, approved in 1947, went to France, Denmark, Luxembourg and the Netherlands – for reconstruction projects.
3 In fact the Bank did not have enough resources to finance the reconstruction needs of Europe; the US treasury stepped in through the Marshall Plan (which in 1948 approved loans amounting to US$5 billion to Europe) and provided the bulk of the funding. It has been suggested that "as the Marshall Plan gained momentum, the Bank moved out of the reconstruction field" (see Kapur *et al.*, 1997: 74).
4 It is interesting to note that while World War Two was also fought in many countries *outside* Europe – including North Africa, South Africa, Tanzania and others – the reconstruction project focused only on the rebuilding of Western Europe.
5 Debt service ratio is the percentage share of a country's interest and amortised payments in export earnings. If a country's total debt payment due is higher than, or close to, its export earnings, its creditworthiness is likely to be low and the country concerned may not be allowed to borrow from the IBRD.
6 The countries with middle-income status in 2008 were Angola (US$3,340), Botswana (US$6,640), Congo Republic (US$1,790), Equatorial Guinea (US$27,877), Gabon (US$7,320), Mauritius (US$6,700), Namibia (US$4,210), Seychelles (US$11,327), South Africa (US$5,820) and Swaziland (US$2,600); this is in addition to the five North African countries. Countries such as Cote d'Ivoire, Cameroon, Cape Verde, Nigeria, Lesotho, Sudan and Zimbabwe, though they have income falling within the middle-income band, are also eligible to access IDA resources, and are classified as "blend countries" borrowing on blend terms.
7 For instance, in 2009 only nine countries were rated by at least one credit rating agency. As of March 2013, a total of 20 SSA countries were rated, with Botswana having the highest rating: A2 by Moody's and A- by Standard and Poors (see IMF, 2013: 53).
8 During the course of 2010 and 2011 this problem affected the so-called GIIPS countries (Greece, Italy, Ireland, Portugal and Spain), but between the end of 2011 and the beginning of 2013 credit ratings for bigger economies such as France and the USA were also down-graded.
9 As of March 2013 Standard and Poors and Fitch rated South Africa as BBB+, while Moody's rated the country one notch higher (BAA1), though the credit rating outlook has been down-graded from stable to negative (see IMF, 2013: 53).

10 Out of the 42 IDA eligible countries, four – as at June 2014 – have non-accrual status and therefore are not receiving any IDA funding: Zimbabwe, Sudan, Eritrea and Somalia (see World Bank, 2014).

11 The nine countries are Botswana (1974), Cameroon (1981), Congo Republic (1982), Cote d'Ivoire (1973), Equatorial Guinea (1999), Mauritius (1975), Nigeria (1965), Swaziland (1975) and Zimbabwe (1983). Cameroon, Cote d'Ivoire, Nigeria and Zimbabwe were readmitted to IDA during the 1990s though Zimbabwe is suspended because of its arrears with the IMF. Only four countries have actually graduated since the 1960s: Botswana (1974), Equatorial Guinea (1999), Mauritius (1975) and Swaziland (1975).

12 In the case of IDA16, the USA (12.08 per cent), UK (12 per cent) and Japan (10 per cent) were the major donors, accounting together for more than a third of the contributions (IDA/World Bank, 2010).

13 This refers to a condition where a country is in arrears of debt servicing and is declared ineligible for further loans from the IMF, the Bank or other bilateral lenders. However, in some cases (e.g., Cote d'Ivoire and Cameroon) lenders continue to provide loans to countries that have arrears – just to enable them to clear those arrears. This is sometimes referred to as 'defensive lending'.

14 During the colonial period no loans to a colony were approved without the guarantee of the colonial master.

15 General survey missions (as they were called) included missions to Ethiopia and South Africa (1950), Nigeria (1953), Somaliland (1956), Tanganyika (now Tanzania, 1959), Kenya (1961) (World Bank Historical Chronology website: http://web.worldbank.org/ WBSITE/EXTERNAL/EXTABOUTUS/EXTARCHIVES/0,,contentMDK:20035657 ~menuPK:56307~pagePK:36726~piPK:437378~theSitePK:29506,00.html, accessed 28 February 2010).

16 Although the percentage share of SSA in the Bank's total lending did not rise dramatically (with the Africa share rising from 12 per cent during the 1960s, to 14 per cent during the 1970s and 15 per cent during the 1980s), the absolute size of loans rose from US$53 million in the 1960s to US$485 million in the 1978–1981 period (see Kapur *et al.*, 1997: 713–14). The Bank also increased the number of field offices in Africa from two (East African office in Nairobi and the West African office in Abidjan) during the 1960s, to more than 27 (resident representatives) in the 1980s.

17 This was based on case studies from Kenya, Uganda, Tanzania, Mali, Burkina Faso, Chad and Cote d'Ivoire, and research team visits to Rwanda, Burundi and Malawi (see de Wilde, 1967 (Vol. 1: 8–11).

18 Arrighi and Saul (1973) offer a detailed critique of the two sector model using the example of what was then Southern Rhodesia.

19 See the preface to Kamarck's (1967) book by Pierre Moussa.

20 Although the Bank did not agree with the socialist elements in the strategies of African leaders such as Leopold Senghor of Senegal, Julius Nyerere of Tanzania and Kenneth Kaunda of Zambia, "throughout the 1970s, the Bank strongly supported the development strategies of all the three through its lending" (Kapur *et al.*, 1997: 697).

21 Special Drawing Rights (SDRs) is the official currency of the IMF loan facility which allows a country to draw beyond its quota. In simple terms SDRs are overdrafts on a member's account.

22 Ethiopia had earlier (1947) applied to draw US$900,000 from the IMF, but was turned down.

23 This is the mechanism through which the IMF and the borrowing country make arrangements for the former to release tranches of a loan meant for BoP support at specified intervals. The release of a loan tranche is based on the continuous assessment of the borrowing country's performance on agreed policies. This was the most common form of lending by the IMF prior to the mid-1970s.

References

Arrighi, Giovani and Saul, John S. (1973). *Essays on the Political Economy of Africa*. New York: Monthly Review Press.

Ayres, Robert (1983). *Banking on the Poor: The World Bank and World Poverty*. Cambridge, MA: MIT Press.

Bates, Robert (1981). *Markets and States in Tropical Africa: The Political Basis of Agricultural Policies*. Berkeley: University of California Press.

Bishop, Annabel (2012). "Ratings Warning a Red Flag." *Mail and Guardian Business*, January 20–6.

Boas, Morten and McNeill, Desmond (2003). *Multilateral Institutions: A Critical Introduction*. London: Pluto Press.

Brown, B. Michael (1995). *Africa's Choices: After Thirty Years of the World Bank*. London: Pluto Press.

Calderisi, Robert (2006). *The Trouble with Africa: Why Foreign Aid Isn't Working*. New Haven/London: Yale University Press.

Davie, Kevin (2012). "How to Deal with a Downgrade." *Mail and Guardian Business*, January 20–6.

De Wilde, John (1967). *Experience with Agricultural Development in Tropical Africa: Synthesis* (Vols 1 and 2). Baltimore: Johns Hopkins Press.

Green, Reginald, M. (1993). "The IMF and the World Bank in Africa: How Much Learning?" in T.M. Gallaghy and J. Ravenhi (eds) *Hemmed In: Responses to Africa's Economic Decline*. New York: Columbia University Press. Chapter 2.

International Development Association (IDA/World Bank, 2010). "How IDA Resources are Allocated." Online, available at http://web.worldbank.org, accessed 18 October 2011.

International Monetary Fund (IMF) (2013). *Regional Economic Outlook May 2013: Sub-Saharan Africa – Building Momentum in a Multi-speed World*. Washington DC: IMF.

Kamarck, Andrew (1967). *The Economics of African Development*. New York: Praeger.

Kapur, Devesh, Lewis, John and Webb, Richard (1997) *The World Bank: Its First Half Century*, Vol. 1. Washington DC: The Brookings Institution.

Krugman, Paul (1996). *Development, Geography and Economic Theory*. Cambridge, MA: MIT Press.

Lancaster, Carol (1997). "The World Bank in Africa Since the 1980s: The Politics of Structural Adjustment Lending" in D. Kapur, J. Lewis and R. Webb (eds) *The World Bank: Its First Half Century*. Washington DC: The Brookings Institution: 161–94.

Lewis, W. Arthur (1954). "Economic Development with Unlimited Supplies of Labour." *Manchester School*, Vol. 20: 139–91.

Manson, E. and Asher, R. (1973). *The World Bank Since Bretton Woods*. Washington DC: The Brookings Institution.

McNamara, R. (1973). *Nairobi Speech: Address to the Board of Governors by Robert S. McNamara, President of the World Bank Group. Nairobi, Kenya. 24 September 1973*. Online, available at: http://www.juerg-buergi.ch/Archiv/EntwicklungspolitikA/EntwicklungspolitikA/assets/McNamara_Nairobi_speech.pdf, accessed 14 September 2012.

Mosley, Paul, Subasat, Turan and Weeks, John (1995a). "Assessing Adjustment in Africa." *World Development*, Vol. 23, No. 9: 1459–73.

Mosley, Paul, Harringan, Jane and Toye, John (1995b). *Aid and Power: The World Bank and Policy Based Lending*. Routledge: London.

Moss, Todd and Leo, Benjamin (2011). "IDA at 65: Heading Towards Retirement of a Fragile Lease on Life?" Centre for Global Development (CGD) Working Paper No. 246. Online, available at: www.cgdev.org, accessed 15 October 2011.

Moss, T., Standley, S. and Birdsall, N. (2004). "Double Standards, Debt Treatment and World Bank Country Classification: The Case of Nigeria". Centre for Global Development, Working Paper No. 45.

Moyo, Dumbisa (2009). *Dead Aid: Why Aid is not Working and How there is a Better Way for Africa*. New York: Farrar, Straus and Giroux.

Owusu, Francis (2003). "Pragmatism and the Gradual Shift from Dependency to Neoliberalism: The World Bank, African Leaders and Development Policy in Africa." *World Development*, Vol. 31, No. 10: 1655–72.

Peet, Richard (2003). *Unholy Trinity: The IMF, World Bank and WTO* (2nd edition). London/New York: Zed Books.

Polak, Jacques (1997). "The World Bank and the IMF: A Changing Relationship" in D. Kapur, J. Lewis and R. Webb (eds) *The World Bank: Its First Half Century*. Washington DC: The Brookings Institution: 473–521.

Ranis, Gustav and Fei, John (1961). "A Theory of Economic Development." *American Economic Review*, Vol. 51, No. 4: 533–65.

Stein, Howard (2004). "The World Bank and the IMF in Africa: Strategy and Routine in the Generation of a Failed Agenda." Centre for Afro-American and African Studies (CAAS), University of Michigan. Online, available at: http://www.macua.org/Howard_Stein.pdf, accessed 24 April 2009.

Stiglitz, Joseph (2000). "The Insider: What I Learned at the World Economic Crisis." *The New Republic*. Online, available at: http://www.tnr.com, accessed 17 October 2012.

United Nations Economic Commission for Africa (UNECA) (1989). *African Alternative Framework to Structural Adjustment Programmes for Socio-Economic Recovery and Transformation (AAF-SAP)*. UNEC. Online, available at: www.uneca.org, accessed 17 August 2009.

World Bank (1986). *Financing Adjustment With Growth in Sub-Saharan Africa 1986–90*. New York: IBRD/World Bank.

World Bank (1989). *Sub-Saharan Africa: From Crisis to Sustainable Growth*. Washington DC: World Bank.

World Bank (2001). "Poverty Reduction Strategy Source Book." Online, available at: http://www.worldbank.org/poverty/strategies/index.htm, accessed 21 January 2011.

World Bank (2007). *Challenges of African Growth: Opportunities, Constraints and Strategic Directions*. New York: IBRD/World Bank.

World Bank (2011). "Africa's Future and the World Bank's Support to it". The World Bank. Online, available at: http://www.worldbank.org/africastrategy, accessed 17 September 2011.

World Bank (2014). "Africa Pulse Rate: An Analysis of Issues Shaping Africa's Economic Future". April, Vol. 9. Online, available at: http://www.worldbank.org/content/dam/Worldbank/document/Africa/Report/Africas-Pulse-brochure_Vol9.pdf, accessed 13 June 2014.

3   The Bank and the IMF in Africa: the SAPs and beyond

Introduction

If the Bank's relationship with Africa, prior to the 1980s, can be referred to as cordial, this relationship can only be described as strained during the 1980s and 1990s. While many analysts focus on the Bank and the International Monetary Fund's (IMF's) dictating of economic and development policies to African governments (see Owusu, 2003; Lancaster, 1997), the Bank especially has had its own share of trials in its engagement with Africa. In the years following the second oil crisis of 1979 there was much at stake for the World Bank, not only in terms of the resources it committed to Africa, but also its integrity as an institution that could effectively analyse economic problems and provide guidance regarding measures necessary to address the challenges. As the African crisis got worse during the 1980s, the situation turned into a nightmare for the Bank, and one of long-term pain for most people in Africa. The doctor-patient analogy captures well the Africa-Bank/Fund relationship during the 1980s and 1990s. Even if the doctor is emotionally and psychologically detached from his or her patient, the mere fact that the patient's illness gets worse by the day can be painful for the patient, but equally frustrating for the physician whose ability to help seems limited.

In the case of the World Bank's work in Africa, the prolonged crisis has several possible interpretations. The first is that the crisis was poorly understood and therefore the wrong policies were prescribed; the second is that the policies were not properly implemented (the latter is the Bank's view). The third view is that not only were the wrong policies prescribed, programmes were improperly implemented due to the fact that they were inappropriate in the first place. Ironically, like the map-making process mentioned in Chapter 1, it was at the time when more information became available that the African economic crisis undoubtedly deepened, leading to a number of analysts (including those from within the Bank) referring to the 1980s as the "lost decade" for Africa (World Bank, 2007). Although the accuracy and reliability of the data on which the Bank based its policy recommendations were questionable (see Srinivasan, 1994), the Bank, among all the development agencies, was probably the only one capable of gathering up-to-date data at the continental level – such that one may be justified in expecting a better understanding of the challenges.

As noted in the previous chapter, while prior to the 1980s the Bank's engagement with Africa was largely limited to technical advice related to projects funded by the Bank, during the 1980s and beyond the policy-based lending adopted led it into the policy arena, focusing on three broad areas: incentive structures (markets and pricing of agricultural commodities), institutional reform (mainly public sector reforms) and policy reform (liberalisation of exchange rates, trade and interest rate regimes). In all these reforms the emphasis throughout this period was on shifting the "onus of price setting from government to markets by liberalising markets" (Kapur *et al.*, 1997: 734–5).

Structural Adjustment Programmes (SAPs) in Africa

A great deal of literature has been produced about Structural Adjustment Programmes (SAPs) in Africa, ranging from the nature of SAPs, their intended goals, the sequencing of these reforms, and, most of all, the impact of the reforms on the ground. The intention here is not to restate the debate, but to highlight the point that SAPs indirectly reflect the World Bank and IMF's understanding of, and response to, the economic growth and development challenges in Africa. Aside from the debate about whether these programmes were appropriate to address the African challenges, or whether they were successful or not, SAPs dominated the policy space in most African countries which borrowed from the Bank and from the Fund – to the point that the local state's role in policymaking was reduced to one of being an implementing agent. Indeed, if one were to look at the policy documents coming out of many African countries during the 1980s and 1990s, it would not be hard to see that SAPs were ubiquitous. Both the Bank and the Fund "barely blinked, delivering the same medicine to each ailing nation that showed up on [their] doorstep" (Stiglitz, 2000).

Policy-based lending

Though economy-wide, performance-related, conditions lingered in the project assistance lending years (see Chapter 2), the nature and scope of policy-based lending during the 1980s was unprecedented. Officially, policy-based lending was introduced in 1979 by the World Bank and the Fund when the executive board of the two institutions approved new lending policy proposals. The reasons for the shift from project- to policy-based lending relate to several factors, chief among them being pressure from some senior Bank staff who felt that the project lending approach did not provide sufficient incentive for the borrowing countries to keep their houses, and their national accounts, in order (see Kapur *et al.*, 1997). Paul Mosley *et al.* (1995b), for example, have observed that the shift to policy-based lending was not sparked by the second oil crisis, as it is often claimed, but rather by the changing economic and political environment, and, most importantly, by pressure from within the Bank as it reassessed the effectiveness of its lending programmes. In addition to this, it is also evident that the size of resources committed to developing countries, together with the fact that most countries – particularly in Africa – became heavily dependent on the Bank and Fund's resources, explain the more intrusive approach reflected in SAPs, as well as the greater attention by the Bank.

The two policy-based lending instruments, Structural Adjustment Lending (SAL) and Sectoral Adjustment Loans (SECAL), (which together constituted SAPs), were conceived as "quick-disbursement loans supporting a reform programme which addressed the structural causes of macroeconomic imbalances and poor economic performance" (World Bank, 1998: 2). Understood in this way, SAPs were both diagnostic as well as prescriptive. Of these two dimensions, it was the prescriptive component of SAPs which has been monumentally dominant via the conditionality attached to the loans aimed at supporting the reform programme. In general, the "conditions attached to the Bank's SALs and SECALs consist essentially of measures to remove what it [the Bank] sees as harmful state interventions in particular markets, in particular the markets for agricultural produce, energy, credit and foreign exchange" (Mosley *et al.*, 1995b: 69). In the case of Sub-Saharan Africa (SSA), these reform recommendations are clearly evident in some of the Bank's regional reports.

The rationale behind SAPs

The rationale behind the SAPs was that state interventions in markets led to the distortions of market operations, leading to inefficiency and poor allocation and use of resources – a condition that makes sustainable economic growth and development difficult to achieve. For instance, one of the World Bank's vice presidents during the 1980s – Ernest Stein – argued that most developing countries "postponed domestic policy reforms or introduced them slowly" and that this poor policy environment resulted in the "misallocation of resources and ... an incentive system biased against exporters ... inadequate price incentive for producers, and the mismanagement of agencies handling credit, marketing, and export promotions" (cited in Mosley *et al.*, 1995b: 98). Thus, the Bank was clear that in order to promote conditions suitable for sustained economic growth, policy reforms which reduced these distortions in the economy were indispensable. It was essentially for this reason that SAPs focused on the liberalisation of commodity, factor, capital, financial and foreign exchange markets. Other reforms such as the removal of government subsidies, the cutting of public spending, trimming public services, and the introduction of user fees, were all tailored towards creating an environment in which distortions of any kind would be reduced significantly – thus allowing the market to function optimally.

The implicit logic behind this was that a well-functioning market would be the engine for growth, and with growth the borrowing countries would be in a better position to repay their loans. There was certainly an element of self-interest on the part of the Bank, though poverty reduction and growth concerns were still cited as the main reason for providing loans. Therefore, apart from the goal of improving the policy environment and providing resources in low-income countries, SAPs had an in-built mechanism to protect the Bank's financial interests in borrowing countries. Policy-based lending within the Bank and the Fund was also seen as an instrument of preventing 'moral hazard' – rewarding countries for failing to adopt and implement the 'right' policies (see Moss *et al.*, 2004). In retrospect it has been widely acknowledged, even within the Bank, that such policies did not achieve the intended objective anywhere, especially in SSA. In one of the World Bank's Africa reports it is acknowledged that "after sixteen years of experience with adjustment lending, a consensus in the World Bank is that while adjustment lending promoted sound policies, it had not achieved high rates of economic growth nor reduced poverty" (World Bank, 1998: 2).

Policy objectives of SAPs

The main objective of SAPs, according to the World Bank, was to help member countries restructure and stabilise their economies so as to create conditions which would promote equitable economic growth and development (see World Bank, 1981). From 1982 the Bank adopted a two-sided strategy of stabilising (short-term programmes) and restructuring (medium-term programmes) in SSA economies to achieve this objective. Restructuring of an economy, on the one hand, is often used to refer to reforms which remove what the Bank considers as impediments to growth, including inefficient allocation of resources, poorly defined and protected property rights, bloated public services, and, in general, anything that obstructs the optimal functioning of markets. Stabilisation, on the other hand, often focuses on restoring fiscal balance (i.e., reducing budget deficits, usually achieved through cuts in government expenditure or increasing public taxation), removal of subsidies on all non-essential goods and services, reduction of the current account deficit through policies that promote export growth such as devaluation of the local currency (trade and foreign exchange liberalisation), and cutting down on the public wage bill. Overall, stabilisation addresses the demand-side issues in the economy, while adjustment is directed towards the supply-side (Mosley *et al.*, 1995a). In a sense, structural adjustment constitutes a long-term measure taken to promote economic growth, while stabilisation is envisioned as a short-term intervention aimed at creating a stable internal macroeconomic environment which can promote long-term growth. In this sense, the two are different sides of the same coin.

For the IMF and the Bank, stabilisation has often been understood as a prerequisite for structural adjustment. As noted in Chapter 2, while prior to the 1980s there was a division of labour – with the Bank funding the latter while the Fund funded the former set of programmes – prolonged crisis in SSA forced the two institutions to do both. For instance, the IMF's Structural Adjustment Facility (SAF) and Enhanced Structural Adjustment Facility (ESAF) "replicated to a large extent the Bank-IDA structure, with a similar list of countries eligible for near-zero interest rates – although the lending period of SAF and ESAF remains at the ten-year limit" (Polak, 1997: 481). Consequently, from the mid-1980s, the line dividing the Bank and the Fund's operations has almost disappeared. While this melting of boundaries has sometimes resulted in strained relations between the Bank and the Fund,[1] it has also resulted in the convergence of policy prescription and conditionality – giving rise to a situation whereby failure by a borrowing country to meet the Fund's conditions automatically excluded that country from accessing the Bank's resources, as well as other major creditors such as the Paris Club. The other important development from this scenario is that while in earlier work stabilisation was largely seen as creating conditions for adjustment, during the 1980s these programmes were implemented simultaneously (Mosley *et al.*, 1995a).

High stakes, high risks in Africa

It is also important to note at this point that by the end of the 1980s, Africa had become the most challenging region for the Bank. A close review of the Bank's activities in the continent suggests that there was a lot of learning, especially during the turbulent years of the 1980s and 1990s when the Bank literally treated Africa as a "research lab for economic reform experimentation" (Michaels, 1993: 100). Contrary to the widely held view by critics of the Bank and the Fund that the Bretton Woods institutions (BWIs) enjoyed administering 'shock therapy' to most African countries, the Bank's work in Africa proved to be more challenging, at times leading to nervousness and panic among the Bank's senior staff. This is clearly elaborated in one of the Bank's briefing notes just before the incoming president (Berber Conable) took office in 1986:

> We must recognise that the role and reputation of the Bank is at stake in Africa. To be frank, the Bank has stuck its 'neck out a mile' in Africa. We have said publicly on many occasions that we are giving Africa the highest priority among development problems in the world. We have been telling Africa how to reform, sometimes in great detail … If these programmes fail, for whatever reasons, our policies will be seen widely to have failed, the ideas will be a set-back for a long time in Africa and elsewhere.
>
> (cited in Kapur *et al.*, 1997: 730)

In a statement to the World Bank board of directors in November 1990, the then vice president for Africa, Edward Jaycox, expressed similar concerns, noting that the "World Bank's reputation is on the line in Africa … Half of the IDA for example is now allocated to Africa. If we do not succeed in Africa, therefore, it seems to me that the very rationale for IDA may well be undermined" (cited in Lancaster, 1997: 186).

As the African economic crisis deepened, doubts emerged within the Bank regarding its understanding of the situation and the appropriateness of the measures it had prescribed. This waning of confidence expressed itself in the Bank's solicitation of support from other institutions, especially the IMF. A memo from Ernest Stern (World Bank vice president for operations) to William Dale (IMF director) illustrates the Bank's waning of self-confidence: "The purpose of such meeting [between the IMF and the World Bank] would be to consider whether the tools, approaches, and concepts we are using are appropriate, whether there are other approaches we might explore" (cited in Kapur *et al.*, 1997: 748).

Thus, the relationship between Africa and the Bank, especially during the 1980s, has been one of a chronic patient and an extremely worried physician. Part of the physician's anxiety, as may be evident in the cited memos above, arose from doubts about whether the patient's condition was properly diagnosed. Thoughts of the possibility of an inaccurate diagnosis and an erroneous prescription seem to have emerged as early as the mid-1980s. As the African crisis worsened, so did the nerves of the physician. With time, even the patient started to protest against the prescribed cure, arguing that the concoction was misguided and would only worsen the condition. In a number of instances, as noted in Chapter 2, some patients abandoned the treatment for a while, though out of desperation they resumed it later.

Other than the Bank's reputation, there was also a challenge regarding its understanding of the African condition in general. From the 1980s the Bank's view that it was largely domestic factors (mainly overvalued currency, poor incentives in agriculture, and deficient administrative capacity) that accounted for poor economic performance in Africa was challenged, most prominently, by the Economic Commission for Africa (UNECA), which put the emphasis on external factors, beyond the continent's control; mainly, deteriorating terms of trade and the unequal international economic order.[2]

One of the challenges which the Bank recognised from the start was how to deal "with criticism and resistance by Africans" (Lancaster, 1997: 168). Although African leaders were aware of the economic challenges and had requested a thorough analysis of the economic crisis in Africa, they disagreed with the Bank's diagnosis and prescription – although they did not directly oppose the prescription. One example of this was the Lagos Plan of Action (LPA) which laid the blame for Africa's poor economic performance on external factors.

While a number of reasons have been advanced to explain resistance from African governance, disagreements about the causes of poor economic performance in Africa between the Bank and most African governments was one of the main factors (see Lancaster, 1997). Criticism of the Bank's policies intensified as the economic crisis deepened, and it became evident that the prescribed cure was doing little to ameliorate the situation. Criticism was not just about the policy content, but also about issues around the sequencing and timing of reforms, lack of concern for human impact of reforms, and also around the Bank's lack of sensitivity to the political cost of the reforms. African critics saw the Bank and the IMF's operation as a subtle way of recolonising Africa, leading to the continuation of the transfer of African resources and capital to developed countries.

> They [IMF and World Bank] work closely with the imperialist countries to systematically transfer huge amounts of economic surplus from Africa to the metropolitan countries, de-capitalise the poor countries, sustain technological backwardness and intensify their mass poverty. This is how unequal development and underdevelopment of Africa and the rest of the Third

World are nurtured in the post-colonial era. This re-colonialism is precisely the heart of the African crisis.

(Onimode, 1988: 21)

By the end of the 1980s growing criticism seems to have damaged the self-esteem and the initial enthusiasm and self-confidence of the Bank's staff, with a degree of humility and self-doubt creeping in during the 1990s (see Collier, 1993). However, in spite of this, the Bank did not scale down its activities in Africa, nor did it back down on its core strategy. If anything, it intensified its study and analysis of SSA, as evidenced by the number of reports produced during the 1980s and 1990s (see Table 3.1).

The Bank's approach to Africa in the 1980s

In discussing the Bank's work in Africa, there are two important points to keep in mind. First, "Africa is the only operational region for which, from the early 1980s onwards, the Bank regularly undertook region-wide analysis" (Kapur *et al.*, 1997: 684). In other regions, the Bank usually undertook country studies and issued country reports. The reason for taking the regional approach in SSA, as we shall see later, was the view that most economies in the region had similar economic structures and challenges. Second, starting from the 1980s, the pace, scope and scale of the Bank's activities in SSA increased more than in any other developing region. Apart from increases in the number of studies and reports conducted on Africa between 1980 and 1995 (see Table 3.1), the number of staff, the number of offices in the region, and meetings and resources committed to the region[3] increased significantly. By the mid-1980s, for instance, the Economic Development Institute allocated more than half its resources to Africa.

Part of the explanation for this surge in the Bank's activities in Africa is the fact that during the 1980s there "were strong signals from the Bank's hierarchy indicating that Africa was an institutional priority, service in and on Africa caught on rapidly within the institution", though it is noted that this momentum was actually short-lived (ibid.: 745). Many executive board members of the Bank pushed for stronger Bank commitment to Africa. For example, the Dutch executive director, Ferdinand van Dam, is reported to have argued that "We have recognised Africa as a priority area; we should make available the best staff to deal with Africa's problems" (cited in ibid.: 731).

The decision to prioritise Africa was provoked by the alarming review of the prevailing economic and social conditions and a worse than expected economic growth outlook, especially following the 1983 report. This, together with the fact that by the mid-1980s most African countries had become heavily dependent on the Bank and the Fund for balance of payments (BoP) support, made the Bank more deeply engaged in Africa than in any other underdeveloped region: "There is no region of the world where the World Bank is more visible and more influential than in Sub-Saharan Africa" (Lancaster, 1997: 161). This widely acknowledged influence of the Bank and the Fund in Africa's development policy, strategy and views makes it imperative to look at how the Bank conceived and interpreted the challenges of economic growth and development in Africa.

Of course the Bank and the Fund are massive institutions with staff who do not share the same position on such a controversial topic as development challenges in Africa. It must be noted here that individual members of staff within the Bank and the Fund do not always have a common view about the problems of Africa's development, or how to address these (Stern and Ferreira, 1997). However, the BWIs operate under an institutional vision and strategy which constitutes the ideological and theoretical basis for the Bank and the Fund's policy and programmes. As noted earlier, the Bank and the Fund are largely influenced by the dominant thinking of the major donor countries (stakeholders) such as the USA, Japan, France, Germany and Canada. Howard Stein (2004) in particular argues that the Bank has always followed US foreign policy and functioned as an extension of the US treasury and Federal Reserve (FED). Other analysts observe that while the Fund is less affected by US policies, it has also remained loyal to its biggest shareholders, and works in close collaboration with the US treasury (Stiglitz, 2000).

Furthermore, in both institutions the predominance of orthodox economic thinking orient them in a particular way, adopting a particular viewpoint in interpreting economic situations globally.

The World Bank's understanding of the challenges in Africa

In terms of building knowledge about African economies and development strategies, the Bank conducted or commissioned several studies, followed by reports discussing the African economic crisis and outlining the measures required to address the crisis. Table 3.1 provides a list of some of the major regional reports published by the Bank, the year they were published, and the focus of each one. Though there are several studies and reports produced by the Bank on Africa's development challenges, only the major ones are referred to in this chapter. Similarly, while the Bank commissioned and published several reports on individual countries, here focus is given to regional studies and reports. These reports provide a general overview of the Bank's position on various issues related to development in Africa.

The first regional study was commissioned in 1980, and led by Elliot Berg. The report, entitled *Accelerated Development in Sub-Saharan Africa: An Agenda for Action* (widely known simply as the *Berg Report*), was published in 1981. According to the Bank, the study was conducted in response to a request from the "African governors[4] of the World Bank" to examine the economic prospects of African countries in the context of a growing perception of a dim economic outlook. To many analysts, the *Berg Report* is the most influential one – with the Bank elaborating its view on the economic crisis in Africa and what was needed to fix the malaise; subsequent reports featured only minor adjustments to the *Berg Report* (Mosley *et al.*, 1995a).

Table 3.1. World Bank major reports/studies on Africa (1980–2011)

Name	Focus	Year	Source
Accelerated Development in SSA: An Agenda for Action (Berg Report)	Identify structural problems in African economies and recommend reforms	1981	Based on study led by Elliot Berg (hence, Berg Report)
SSA: Progress Report on Development Prospect and Programme (APRD)	Review of reform programmes in SSA since the Berg Report	1983	Prepared by Bank staff based on work conducted in SSA
Towards Sustainable Development in SSA: A Joint Programme of Action (TSD)	Emphasise donor assistance, investment and debt problems	1984	Prepared by Bank staff based on views of donors and officials in Africa
Financing Adjustment with Growth in SSA 1986–90 (FAG)	Financial needs of 29 SSA countries relying heavily on ODA/IDA resources	1986	Prepared by the Bank's Special Office for African Affairs
SSA, From Crisis to Sustainable Growth: A Long Term Perspective Study (LTPS)	Policies and programmes needed to attain sustainable growth	1989	Based on research conducted by the Bank staff
Africa Adjustment and Growth in the 1980s (AAG)	Assessment of the outcome of SAP in SSA	1989	Joint report by World Bank and UNDP
World Bank Adjustment Lending and Economic Performance in SSA in the 1980s (ALEP)	Contribution of SAP to SSA's economic outcome in the 1980s	1992	Staff working papers
Adjustment Lending in Africa: Reforms, Results and the Road Ahead (ALA)	Policy reforms and their impact on Africa's performance	1994	Based on study commissioned by the Bank's vice president
A Continent in Transition: SSA in the Mid-1990s (ACT)	Five-year review of conditions in SSA	1995	Prepared by Bank staff based on workshops in SSA and donors
Higher Impact Adjustment Lending (HIAL) in SSA: An Update	Examine the Bank's adjustment operations in SSA since 1995	1998	Prepared by the chief economist of the Africa region
Can Africa Claim the 21st Century? (CAC)	Africa's prospects for economic and social development in the twenty-first century	2000	Based on a joint study by AfDB, AERC, WB and GCA
Meeting Africa's Development Challenges (MADC)	Devise an Africa Action Plan (AAP), a result-oriented framework	2005	World Bank staff in collaboration with donor countries
Challenges of African Growth: Opportunities Constraints and Strategic Directions (CAG)	Identify opportunities, constraints and strategic choices in SSA	2007	Based on long-term studies conducted by Bank staff since 1998
Africa's future and the World Bank's Support to it (DS)	Outlines a two-pillar economic growth strategy for Africa	2011	Based on 31 meetings with African leaders, civil society, private sector and other parties

Source: compiled by author.

Note: the abbreviation of the report's name is given in brackets.

In addition to the reports listed in Table 3.1, the Bank has also annually produced the *World Development Report* (WDR, starting from 1978) and its statistical companion, the *World Development Indicators* (WDI), which comment on development trends and challenges in Africa, though not entirely dedicated to African issues.

It is important, however, to note that these reports are written by different people, often staff members at the World Bank, in collaboration with researchers, analysts, academics, consultants and politicians outside of the Bank and the Fund. Much of the empirical work on which the Bank and the Fund rely to formulate policies and programmes is conducted by staff from the two institutions and other affiliated organisations. Some of these studies on Africa, which form the empirical basis for policy, are discussed in Chapter 4.

Although these reports have the Bank's name on them, they all carry a disclaimer that the ideas and views contained in them do not necessarily reflect the Bank's views nor those of the board of directors. However, each publication is approved by a senior staff member at the Bank, sometimes by the director of programmes but often by senior staff from the Operation and Evaluation Department – which reviews and clears material for publication. For example, the *Berg Report* and its recommended policy programmes were discussed by the Bank's executive directors before being published (see World Bank, 1983). By means of a review conducted by the Bank on any major publication bearing its name, care is taken to ensure that these documents reflect the Bank's institutional vision and are in line with its core mission. Views opposed to the Bank's vision may be presented in the reports, but it is clearly stated that the Bank holds a different view on the matter.

As noted above, not all staff members at the Bank have the same position on complex issues such as economic growth and development; nonetheless through public documents such as the regional reports, a general view reflecting the institution's position on the issue is communicated, and this is why approval of a publication bearing the World Bank's name has to be granted by a senior staff member. While these reports may not reflect any particular individual's view, they do express the institution's position on a particular issue. Although as Nicolas Stern and Francisco Ferreira (1997: 589) have noted, the "Bank is not a bureaucratic institution in which uniformity of views or outlook may be found" – some form of 'common ground' is not only desirable but is necessitated by the institution's values, strategic objectives and ideological disposition. As Devesh Kapur *et al.* (1997) observe, the Bank is a "strongly hierarchical" institution with every decision revolving around its headquarters in Washington DC. Although many field offices have been opened in Africa since the beginning of the 1980s, "most of these operations [have] little power. Except when it travelled with the president, the organisation's centre of gravity never stayed outside of Washington D.C." (Kapur *et al.*, 1997: 1211). With specific reference to the IMF, it has been observed that no open debates are allowed, and staff who have a different opinion are often not consulted (Stiglitz, 2000).

Thus, some kind of allegiance to institutional values and disposition is tacitly required from Bank staff. For example, a World Bank staff member who argues for the position that the spread of the market mechanism is the cause of poor economic performance in Africa would not only find fewer sympathisers within the Bank, but would likely be sidelined to the point where his or her suitability might be seriously questioned. In institutions like the World Bank and the IMF, a certain way of thinking is to be expected given the strong influence that big countries like the USA exercise over its policy and operations. Thus, the rationale for treating these reports as the World Bank's official position on economic, social and political challenges in SSA is the very fact that these reports bear the Bank's name, and presumably are approved by some senior member of the Bank. While the views in the report in question may not necessarily reflect those of the executive directors, they at least reflect a broader institutional position and commitment, and most importantly inform the Bank's policy advice and design. As the *Report on Adjustment Lending II* (RAL-2, 1991) asserts, "Findings of this research and the research carried out elsewhere provide important underpinnings for the Bank's advice on the design of adjustment lending operations" (World Bank, 1991).

Consistency on core policy areas

One thing that is quite amazing when looking at the Bank's reports on Africa is that there is a certain degree of consistency over time regarding the core issues and the recommended strategies. For instance, low returns to investment in SSA, as one of the major factors which constrains investment and productivity growth especially in agriculture, is listed in all the major reports from the *Berg Report* to the 2011 strategic plan document. The LTPS, for example, argues that "low return on investments is the main reason for Africa's recent decline" (World Bank, 1989b: 3). Some 18 years later, we are told that "investment in Africa yields less than half the return, measured in growth terms, found in other developing countries" (World Bank, 2007: 145). Similarly, 30 years after the *Berg Report*, a World Bank report argues that "at 15 per cent of GDP, the private investment rate [in Africa] is about half of Asia", and that for Africa to grow at a higher and more sustainable rate it needs to attract more private resources into its economies (World Bank, 2011: 4).

On a number of core issues, the recommended solutions to Africa's economic problems since 1981 have largely remained the same: "reducing transaction costs for private enterprises, particularly indirect costs, supporting innovation to take advantage of new technological opportunities; and improving skills and institutional capacity to support productive growth and competitiveness" (World Bank, 2007: 145–6).

Other examples of consistency that one finds across the reports include the challenge of slow demographic transition (persistently high fertility rates), the impact of geography, poor domestic policies – including exchange rates – trade policies, and poor administrative capacity in public institutions, all resulting in inefficient allocation and use of resources. These appear almost consistently in all the reports and are given the same credence in 1981 as they are in 2011. In the *Strategic Plan for Africa*, it is observed that unemployment is due to the rapidly growing population compounded by "a poor investment climate". This poor investment climate is due largely to "(a) poor infrastructure, (b) poor business environment (policies and access to finance), and (c) insufficient technical skills" (World Bank, 2011: 10).

This consistency in diagnosis and policy recommendations has led some analysts to argue that in fact the key policies coming from the World Bank were laid out in the *Berg Report*; everything else coming after is a mere refinement (see Stein, 2004; Mosley *et al.*, 1995a). Maintaining the same policy recommendation in a changing environment is a serious indictment against the Bank unless the conditions in which African economies operate have not changed since the 1980s. If this consistency in policy is due to the fact that little has changed in Africa, then one is bound to ask: what have the Bank's programmes achieved over the years if everything has remained the same?

From country to regional report

As is evident from Table 3.1, the Bank's work on SSA regional economies gathered momentum during the 1980s. Previously, as noted in Chapter 2, the Bank took a country-based approach, relying on country mission reports and other documents. Although from the 1980s the Bank published regional reports on SSA, it continued to produce country reports as well; however, it could be argued that the emphasis in understanding economic challenges in Africa shifted from country to regional reports, an approach that has been referred to as the "regional strategic perspective" (World Bank, 2007: 145). What prompted this regional approach in understanding the development challenges faced by African countries is not very clear, other than the view that this was what the African governors at the World Bank wanted in their effort to entice the Bank to increase lending to African countries by means of a "special programme of action" (Lancaster, 1997). Whatever the reasons were for embarking on a regional approach for understanding economic challenges in Africa, the practical convenience of publishing one report instead of 48 different reports is implicit. Of course the authors of the *Berg Report* and subsequent reports on SSA were well aware that the continent of Africa is neither a single country nor a single economy.

Certainly, the countries that constituted SSA in the late 1970s and early 1980s were different from each other in many respects, including their economic resources, structures, opportunities and challenges. While this is clearly acknowledged in the *Berg Report*, the rationale for taking a regional approach to explaining the economic crisis in SSA was that most of the countries faced similar challenges, had similar economic production and output structures, and similar geographical constraints and policy challenges. The report argued that although there is heterogeneity in the region,

There is, nonetheless, considerable homogeneity within the region. African economies for the most part are small in economic terms, a result of low average income and small population. Of the 45 states in the region, 24 have fewer than five million people ... They are specialised economies, most of them agricultural, dependent on the export of two or three primary commodities. Even in mineral exporting countries, the bulk of the population – rarely less than 70 percent – works in agriculture, and subsistence oriented production still accounts for half or more of total agricultural output. Only 20 percent of the population is urban, and modern wage employment absorbs a very small proportion of the labour force – in most countries less than 10 percent. In addition to these similarities of economic structure, other characteristics are common: the scarcity of educated people, the dominance of land-extensive agricultural systems, and an extreme ethnic diversity and consequent political fragility. All are new states, recently emerging from colonial rule, except Liberia and Ethiopia. All are tropical, with the exception of Lesotho and Swaziland. In almost all, fertility is high and population is growing rapidly – more rapidly than in any other regions of the world. Finally, there is an extraordinary degree of similarity throughout the region in the nature of the policy problems that have arisen.

(World Bank, 1981: 2)

The commonality argument turns out to be a very important one which justifies the design of the same policy to fix the challenges in all the countries. Asserting "an extraordinary degree of similarity" makes it easier to justify the 'one-size-fits-all' approach. It has been suggested in the literature that since the early 1980s, "the entire edifice of internationally sponsored aid programmes such as ... the IMF and WB jointly sponsored Structural Adjustment Programmes, has been built on this classification of commonality" (Hoogvelt *et al.*, 1992: 92).

The strategy of establishing commonalities among all African countries has been challenged on the grounds that it lacks a legitimate "scientifically appropriate method" for validating them. In contrasting the Bank and the Fund's approach to the LPA in which African leaders also look at the continent as a single entity, Ankie Hoogvelt *et al.* (1992) argue that LPA affirmation of commonalities can be justified on the grounds that it is a result of a political process in which African leaders speak of a common strategy for development – which does not require any other grounds for asserting commonalities other than the political agreement to treat all the countries as a collective. According to this view the Bank and the Fund's approach does not emanate from a political consensus; rather the basis of commonality is alleged to be a scientific analysis of the economic characteristics of the countries in the sub-region, such as the percentage of the labour force in agriculture, the size of the region's economies, the structure of production and, indeed, economic policies. Because of the inadequacy of the scientific justification as a basis for asserting commonality in Africa, Hoogvelt *et al.* (1992) argue for the need to distinguish between what they call the "uniformity of treatment" adopted by the Bank and the Fund – which can be 'oppressive' in that highly

differentiated units are forced into one analytical unity – and the "unity of purpose" evident in LPA, which can be liberating in as far as it builds upon widely
accepted aspirations by the constituent member countries.

This distinction is important to keep in mind because the underlying dynamic
behind the two approaches has a bearing on how to interpret the commonality. In one case, the commonality is self-imposed and may not have any motive
other than to define a common aspiration and strategy, while in the other,
commonality is externally imposed which may be used as grounds for justifying
externally defined strategy and objectives. With hindsight, it is perhaps fair
to argue that the commonality perceived by the Bank and the Fund in SSA
formed the basis for prescribing the same reforms for all countries across the
region. The view that "the explanation for Africa's slow economic growth since
the 1960s … stems from the internal 'structural' problems" (World Bank, 1981:
16), somehow justified prescribing structural adjustment for the region since
all countries were seen to have common problems. Without establishing these
commonalities it would be irrational to prescribe the same policy reforms for
all of them. Thus, in as much as the approach of treating SSA countries as a
single unit of analysis may appear to be methodologically convenient, it serves
more subtle purposes.

Although it has been argued by some analysts that the claims of uniformity of
policy programmes designed by the World Bank and the IMF are "quite untrue"
(Mosley and Weeks, 1993: 1589), there is evidence that suggests certain policy programmes – especially for countries involved in adjustment lending programmes – have shared a commonality between them. For instance, the Bank's
internal Country Performance Rating for the period 1980–1998 shows that in
all 35 SSA countries involved in SALs since the 1980s, macroeconomic stability (mainly a competitive exchange rate and a stable BoP profile) and structural
reforms (mainly pricing of agricultural commodities) were prescribed (World
Bank, 1998). Mosley *et al.* (1995b) also argue that the design of programmes
implemented during the 1980s and onwards was based on the understanding
that every country that was experiencing BoP problems had messed with the
markets – in particular, the price incentive mechanism – and to fix this the
Bank and the Fund prescribed market reforms everywhere they went (see also
Stiglitz, 2000).

However, in questioning the grounds for affirming homogeneity in SSA, there
is also an inherent danger of overlooking commonalities in the region, a danger
which has led some analysts to argue that these countries are so different that they
each can be categorised in their own class. Such views often tend to disregard the
self-perceived commonalities among African leaders, or peoples in general, as
evidenced by the efforts of the Organisation of African Unity (OAU) and its
successor, the African Union (AU), which have pursued a self-defined strategy as
the central unifying factor for the continent. Emphasis of extreme heterogeneity
can be as dangerous as externally imposed homogeneity. While Hoogvelt *et al.*
(1992) challenge the grounds for asserting commonality in SSA, they also doubt
whether the region's 49 constituent countries can be treated "as one continent".

Using "statistical cluster analysis", as well as "discriminant analysis", they divide SSA countries in the continent into four clusters, which seemingly constitute four different continents!

Explaining the African growth experience

In terms of the World Bank's understanding of growth and development experiences in SSA, the reports in Table 3.1 and other documents on SSA provide a clue to the Bank's understanding of these challenges. A central feature of the Bank's understanding of Africa's growth and development experience – which runs through most of the reports – is the fact that they are largely a result of inappropriate domestic policies and low institutional capacity, which blocks the emergence of a favourable climate for economic growth and development. While the *Berg Report* does mention external factors as part of the explanation for the economic growth and development crisis in SSA, it puts emphasis on internal factors relating to domestic policies. This emphasis on internal factors in explaining the African crisis is particularly evident in the prescribed reforms aimed at addressing the challenges. A Bank report published two years after the *Berg Report* (*Sub-Saharan Africa: Progress Report on Development Prospect and Programmes* (APRD) (World Bank, 1983), summarises the Bank's view as follows:

> The poor economic performance of African countries was not attributed in the Bank's Africa Report [*Berg Report*] to any major extent to international trade and financial environment which they faced. For most countries, movements in the terms of trade had been favourable or neutral and market access, while important, had not been a critical problem.
>
> (World Bank, 1983: 2)

This position has been restated in subsequent reports. For example, the LTPS (1989) argues that even if most countries were affected by the sharp fall of commodity prices in the global market, poor economic performance since the late 1970s is largely explained by "declining levels of efficiency of investment, compounded by accelerating population growth – and not primarily external factors" (World Bank, 1989a: 3). In the Bank's view, weak public sector management, poor investment choices, price distortions (especially overvalued exchange rates, price controls, subsidies, and credit and foreign currency rationing), high wage costs *vis a vis* low productivity, bloated bureaucracy and arbitrary decision-making account for SSA's economic growth and development crisis. An earlier report published in 1984 (TSDA) also argues that the root causes of Africa's growth and development challenges are inappropriate domestic policies which have led to inefficient allocation and use of resources (see World Bank, 1984). In most reports, issues of governance, private sector investment, infrastructure, and management of public resources are seen to be responsible for SSA's economic growth and development crisis (World Bank, 2000: 12). While it is hard to deny that all these issues can have a negative impact on the performance of an economy, attributing the economic crisis in Africa to domestic factors tells an incomplete story.

At the beginning of the 1980s, external factors that were identified focused mainly on the donor's inability to meet their aid pledges, and the argument was that reform of internal policies could not succeed without adequate levels of aid from the international community (World Bank, 1984, 1986). A strong conviction that domestic policies are responsible for poor economic growth in Africa is reflected in the emphasis on reforming the internal economic, and, later, political, structures in Africa. External factors are rarely mentioned in the reports, and if addressed in programmes they are dealt with indirectly by fixing the internal environment.

A closer look at the different reports suggests that there seems to be a strong assumption that once you restructure domestic policies and institutions, any external 'effects' will be neutralised by a well-functioning internal environment. For instance, in most of the earlier reports by the Bank there seems to be an implicit understanding that once you get your exchange rate right, this is going to address issues of incentives, low export volumes, and eventually improve a country's BoP profile. Similarly, the underlying assumption in focusing on internal factors seems to be that if you provide the right incentive through a correct price structure and marketing mechanism, a country can solve the problems of low productivity, which in turn can create surplus resources for industrial development. Given this understanding, there has been no attention paid to addressing external factors such as terms of trade, unfair competition from developed countries, or agricultural subsidies in the USA or European Union (EU). There is no single report that recognises USA, Japanese or EU farm subsidies as a factor affecting Africa's economic performance. In the prescribed dosage for Africa's malaise, no attention is given to addressing the vexing problem of capital flight from Africa (see Ndikumana and Boyce, 2008). In all this, the dominant view seems to be clear: that you address the external constraints by fixing the internal weaknesses.

In a way, this is not surprising in a growth framework where the market solutions are seen as the 'first-best' solutions. In this framework, it is assumed that once the markets are sorted, everything falls in place. However, the main problem here is that markets are rarely sorted; and less so in Africa where a lot of them are either missing or very thin. Furthermore, even in cases where markets are functioning optimally, they do not operate in isolation; in a globalised world domestic markets are linked to and affected by global markets, such that focusing on fixing the domestic environment may be compared to treating cancer by massaging the tumour.

The challenge of failing to acknowledge and respond to external factors was noted in Robert McNamara's 1973 *Nairobi Speech*, in which he refers to the failure by rich countries to dismantle "discriminatory trade barriers against poor countries". However, this assertion did not translate into policy, and subsequently no programme was designed to address this problem. Focus has been on reforming the domestic economic environment and domestic policy to create favourable conditions for market operations, giving the impression that the external environment and forces do not matter much.

The market's supremacy

In the case of Africa, the adjustment programmes have been summarised as reforms and measures "aimed at giving prices, markets, and the private sector a greater role in promoting development in Africa. In particular, they reflect a desire to reduce administrative intervention in setting prices; to end monopolies on trade and marketing; and to reduce the government's role in allocating credit" – in order to create more scope for the private sector (World Bank, 1986: 15). In this understanding, the emphasis should be on markets in allocating resources, and in unlocking productive capacities through appropriate incentives. Of course it is not surprising in this framework that more attention is directed towards addressing internal problems, since the main problem is understood to lie with poor *domestic* conditions harming the operation of markets. There is probably nowhere where the primacy of markets has been more strongly affirmed than in the words of the former US chairman of the Federal Reserve, Alan Greenspan: "Markets are an expression of the deepest truths about human nature and … as a result, they will ultimately be correct" (cited in Wade, 2002: 201).

While the Bank and the Fund have consistently argued that the right way to address Africa's development challenges is through the promotion of markets, some analysts have challenged this, arguing that such an approach demonstrates a remarkable lack of understanding of local, historical and international conditions which have contributed to Africa's challenges (see Carlsson, 1983; Loxley, 1983; Stein, 2004). Critics of this view have pointed out that such an approach is only appropriate for middle-income countries (see Kapur *et al.*, 1997: 749). For this reason, it has been suggested that despite a long history of engagement with Africa, the Bank's understanding of its economic, political, social and cultural conditions has been deficient (see Lancaster, 1997: 174). This deficient understanding of the African context could be linked to the narrow focus on economic issues on the Bank's part, especially during the early days of SAPs. Focusing narrowly on economic factors has been acknowledged by the Bank as one of the mistakes made in its earlier programmes and policies:

> Too often, we have focused too much on the economics, without a sufficient understanding of the social, the political, the environmental, and the cultural aspects of society. We have not thought adequately about the overall structure that is required in a country to allow it to develop in an integrated fashion.
>
> (Wolfensohn, 1998: 12)

There are two key factors which explain the Bank's initial view that the African economic growth crisis was largely caused by internal factors. First, the Bank's analysis was overly economistic, reducing the problem of economic growth to economic factors only. But as later became apparent, economic growth is not just an economic matter which can be resolved by a correct pricing structure, or by simply promoting an environment in which the 'right incentives' are created. This position was later criticised by many, including the World Bank president – who argued that "development is not about adjustment ... Development is about putting all the component parts in place – together and in harmony", including political, social, environmental and cultural parts (Wolfensohn, 1998: 11). A more balanced understanding of economic growth and development should include more than just the 'economic'; it is more than just a matter of ensuring that the macroeconomic environment is stable (stabilisation), or just a matter of restructuring the public sector (privatisation or retrenchment). Undoubtedly, a stable macroeconomic environment is critical to sustained growth, but it is not the only condition that brings about economic growth and development. More importantly, the conditions that lead to a stable macroeconomic condition are broader than interest rates, exchange rates, a healthy BoP profile and low inflation rates. These factors are not determined independently of cultural, political, religious, social and historical and international factors. What this suggests is that creating macroeconomic stability requires understanding and consideration of the broader context in which the stability objective is being pursued.

The second reason that explains the narrow and short-term approach taken by the Bank in the initial SAPs has to do with the perception that the Bank was the only institution with the necessary technical and intellectual capacity, resources, and ability to analyse economic and development problems. In other words the Bank (and much less the IMF) has been less open to wider consultation and dialogue. While it may be true that there are few institutions which can match the technical capacity and expertise of the Bank and the Fund, there exist several other institutions that conduct research and analysis, and offer policy advice. Most importantly, development is not something you do *for* people; it is something you do *with* people; hence the need to listen broadly to people. To a large extent this perception, on the part of the Bank, has led to intellectual hegemony and arrogance among some of its staff. For those outside the Bank, this "perceived intellectual leadership made [the Bank] the most visible target" for criticism, especially if things did not go according to plan – as has been the case in Africa (Kapur *et al.*, 1997: 766). On matters of growth and development the Bank and the Fund have often presented themselves as 'intellectual and moral gurus' – dominating, liquidating, subjugating, and sidelining, not by armed force but by way of 'soft power' (Wade, 2002). As for the IMF, it has been suggested that its officials believe that "they are brighter, more educated and less politically motivated than the economists in the countries they visit" (Stiglitz, 2000).

Other than the intellectual hegemony, the drive towards short-term goals within the Bank has sometimes been blamed on the influence of the IMF, whose mandate falls within the short-term framework. Senior Bank officials complained of pressure from the IMF to focus on short-term goals such as increasing adjustment resources to avoid debt rescheduling in preference to long-term strategies such as increasing investment to sustain and improve production, and eventually income and levels of consumption (see Lancaster, 1997: 182). Later views within the Bank confirm that the narrow focus on short-term financial stabilisation in Africa was not going to be an effective way of addressing the crisis; a long-term as well as a broader approach was needed, as the former World Bank president later acknowledged:

> We must go beyond financial stabilization. We must address the issues of long-term equitable growth, on which prosperity and human progress depend. We must focus on the institutional and structural changes needed for recovery and sustained development. We must focus on the social issues.
>
> (Wolfensohn, 1998: 4)

An underestimated challenge

The most important lesson that emerges from analysis of the Bank's work in Africa is that there was little thought directed towards addressing the issue of how African economies, and society at large, would respond to SAPs. From the outset of the SAP regime, the Bank in particular assumed that the economic crisis in Africa would be fixed within a short period of time, between three and five years. The expectation was that after implementing the reforms for three years, recovery would begin around the mid-1980s, and countries faithful to the prescription would be restored to full sustained growth by the end of the decade. Indeed, the *Berg Report* acknowledges that its work in Africa was short-term in nature. Long-term strategies were understood to be the responsibility of the African leaders themselves. Though the Bank's Africa staff were aware of the tension between the short-term goals contained in the stabilisation strategies and debt management programmes, and the long-term objective of sustained growth and development, yet more attention was directed to BoP challenges which were short-term in nature (see Kapur *et al.*, 1997: 784–5, Brown and Cumming, 1984). In retrospect, it can be argued that at the beginning of the 1980s, the Bank underestimated the challenges of economic growth and development in SSA, and, consequently, the programmes it designed to address the challenges were unlikely to be effective.

Interestingly, after a decade of implementing SAPs in Africa, the Bank has acknowledged not only the complexity and enormity of the problem at hand, but also that its understanding of Africa's economic growth and development challenges was deficient: "we are only too conscious of our inadequate understanding of many issues covered" (World Bank, 1989b: 2). A similar view is echoed in the MADC report which acknowledges that the "Bank alone cannot deal with Africa's problems" and that "Sub-Saharan Africa presents the world with the most formidable development challenges" (see World Bank, 2005). Evidently, the earlier confidence and certitude apparent in the *Berg Report* waned as the reality of the African challenges became clearer. Given the complexity and scope of the problem, one would be expecting too much to think that a single institution could come up with a rounded diagnosis and a complete set of solutions to the complex question of achieving sustained economic growth in Africa. However, the Bank, at the beginning of the 1980s, portrayed itself as having the supreme knowledge and capacity to study, analyse and understand the crisis on behalf of African leaders and the African people.

Africans' response to the Bank's activities

From the time the *Berg Report* was published, many Africans, especially African government leaders, were not happy about the proposed reforms, but grudgingly signed up (mostly under pressure from the growing need for BoP support). This is one of the reasons why their implementation has been poor, with many African governments only committing themselves to the reforms as a means to access much needed foreign currency. They had no intention of implementing the reforms (Callaghy and Ravenhill, 1993). However, the World Bank blames poor implementation on lack of capacity rather than on lack of commitment[5] (World Bank, 1994). Looking at the experience of SAPs in Africa it is apparent that the debtor countries were "torn between a desire to maximise financial inflow and a desire to minimise the political costs imposed by implementing the associated conditionality" (Mosley *et al.*, 1995b: 73).

Apparently this tension was downplayed by assuming that the dire need for resources would be a strong enough stimulant for poor countries to comply with the stipulated reforms. As might be expected, however, the results were disappointing, with some countries – including Tanzania, Zambia, Cote d'Ivoire, the former Zaire, Cameroon and Zimbabwe – openly abandoning the Bank reform programmes at one point or another. During the 1990s it became clear that the Bank underestimated the political costs of SAPs. As noted earlier, some of the programmes, such as removal of subsidies and the introduction of user fees, wage cuts or freezes, and even devaluation of the local currency, were politically risky; only a naïve or a very courageous politician could wholeheartedly implement such reforms concurrently.

Further, while many African politicians and ordinary people were being asked to shoulder the burden of the reforms, the Bank's staff bore no similar costs, apart from senior level staff concerns about the reputation of the Bank in Africa. This unequal share of the burden of reform was a major source of criticism:

> The borrowers were being told to institute major changes, many of which were risky both personally for their leaders and for the economies ... Meanwhile, the advisers making those demands faced no personal risk, and the institutions they represented were subject to little accountability, at either institutional or personal level.
>
> (Kapur *et al.*, 1997: 767)

Many Africans, critical of the Bank's approach to Africa's growth and development challenges, pointed to the fact that its approach was mono-dimensional (focusing mainly on internal economic structural problems), and that the recommendations it made were not only contrary to the LPA, but insensitive to the "political, economic and social aspirations of Africa" (Kapur *et al.*, 1997: 718). The social and political costs that the Bank's reform policies championed were again, retrospectively, acknowledged by the Bank's president: "We have learned that when we ask governments to take the painful steps to put economies in order we can create enormous tension. It is people not government that feel the pain" (Wolfensohn, 1998: 5).

In an opinion poll conducted to gauge the reaction of African bureaucrats to the analysis and recommendations of the *Berg Report*, many noted that the often young and arrogant Bank officials tended to ignore local institutions and conditions, that they were inflexible in their views, and in some cases they tended to "bully African technocrats" (in Kapur *et al.*, 1997: 719). It is also reported that most African officials complained about the "tendency of the Bank staff to preach to them and at times to appear to be giving instructions to them" (Lancaster, 1997: 169).

Although the Bank was aware of such criticism from African officials – including the ministers of finance – they were often ignored and the Bank proceeded with reform implementation anyway. Criticism sparked by the *Berg Report* came from a wide range of observers, including foreign experts working in Africa – who complained about structural adjustment being so intrusive that it bordered on interfering with the national sovereignty of the borrowing countries. For many African critics of the Bank and the Fund, including many African heads of state, this was a form of neo-colonialism. Some of the complaints noted in the *Africa Perception Survey* include the arrogance and insensitivity of Bank staff, their inadequate knowledge of Africa, the sidelining of the resident mission teams, and the imposition of expatriate consultants on African governments when local analysts could do a better job (see Lancaster, 1997).

During the early days of SAPs there were reports of members of a World Bank delegation from Washington DC going straight to the minister of finance or Central Bank governor (and sometimes the head of state),[6] and after a few minutes staring at the figures on inflation, fiscal balance, interest rates and exchange rates, opening up their briefcases and pronouncing what the country and its officials were expected to do. Many African officials complained that they were not being given a chance to say what *they* thought was the best way forward.

This approach on the part of the Bank and the Fund, while it demonstrates a high level of confidence, carried the danger of being labelled arrogant, as most African clients of the Bank and the Fund have often reported. In the later periods, the Bank realised that this attitude was unproductive and later programmes started to emphasise participation and even ownership of policies by local state officials. For example, the ALA (1994) report emphasises government ownership of any reform process, arguing that, "government ownerships of an economic reform program is a prerequisite for its success" (World Bank, 1994: iv). Similar calls are made in the LTPS report which states that "It should be clear that the reform program is the government's – expressed in its own policy papers and internalised through local seminars and workshops" (World Bank, 1989b: 14).

However, although there have been calls for ownership of reform programmes by participating governments, the Bank often formulated them with little input from local people, especially during the early days of SAPs. Though the Bank often justified this by arguing that most African countries had low capacity to design complex reform policies and programmes, it is clear that this approach undermined the borrowers' responsibilites and commitment to such programmes. Even in the case of the Poverty Reduction Strategy Papers (PRSPs), which were supposed to be drawn up through a participatory process involving civil society and other stakeholders, there are reports of Bank officials taking over the process of drafting the papers and then holding a series of seminars to satisfy the participatory requirement (see Jubilee South, 2000).

The problem of narrow constituency and lack of political support for reforms

The other point which emerges from the review of the Bank's activities in Africa is the narrow focus on who was to be involved in the reform process itself. Little attention was given to issues of governance, institutional capacity, participation and political support for reform programmes (see Sandbrook, 1990, 1993). Where there is mention of building local capacities, it is capacities to absorb international aid that feature on the agenda. This inevitably led to taking a narrow scope and set of objectives. Since the problem was defined narrowly, to address the problem required focusing on a narrow constituency – influence the finance minister and his (rarely her) entourage, and policies will be implemented. This approach is confirmed by the former World Bank's Africa region vice president,

> we fell prey to another old habit of the Bank which is that we tended to think that if we influenced a small number of decision-makers rather than helping governments establish conditions for broad-based ownership, everything would be alright. The fact of the matter is that we have learnt the hard way that the finance ministers signing off a piece of paper does not mean that things will happen on the ground.
>
> (Madava, 1997: 4)

A later Bank report also acknowledged the narrow definition and focus of reforms during the earlier periods as a key weakness, and argues that economic growth-oriented reforms must go "beyond the focus on correcting policy failures – an approach dominant in the 1990s – to identifying growth opportunities and binding constraints to exploit these opportunities" (World Bank, 2007: 144).

Defining the challenge narrowly may have served the practical objective of narrowing the constituency which the Bank had to deal with – the so-called "Finance Ministry agenda" (Wade, 2002: 205). Reducing the challenge to the technical and professional level made it easier for the Bank to concentrate on a small section of the population to address the challenge – there was no need, for instance, to consult the farmer; all that was needed was to ask government bureaucrats to dismantle the marketing boards and things would improve as long as the price of cabbage or maize was set by the impersonal forces of the market and not some government minister or committee. This practical convenience, however, had a much higher cost, mainly in the form of widespread opposition to SAPs and lack of local political support from the masses, which in turn made the implementation of SAPs difficult and the realisation of the Bank's SAPs' objectives almost impossible. An attempt to correct this approach was made in later programmes, especially starting from the LTPS – which realised that to address the African crisis it was essential to go "beyond the issues of public finance, monetary policy, prices and markets to address fundamental questions relating to human capacities, institutions, governance, the environment, population growth and distribution, and technology" (World Bank, 1989b: 1).

Lessons learned

Although from this point on there seemed to be an appreciation of the fact that policy reform could only work when there were institutions capable of carrying them out, the Bank largely ignored the importance of local political support. Even with the growing criticism during the 1990s, as it became evident that SAPs had not improved the situation in Africa, the Bank's approach continued to focus on winning the support of African bureaucrats and other technocrats. Part of the difficulty in galvanising the support of local people in Africa lies in the widespread perception among ordinary Africans that SAPs (indeed anything emanating from the World Bank and the IMF) were not in their interest, a perception largely shaped by the initial experience with them.

Admittedly, political support is difficult to generate when implementing programmes such as removal of subsidies or introduction of user fees, which appear to be against the people's interest. Indeed, the Bank was aware, from the beginning, that the reforms in Africa would be "technically difficult and politically thorny" (World Bank, 1981: 133), and that these reforms would be difficult and "delicate" (World Bank, 1981: 7), but still the Bank opted to go ahead with reforms without clearing the ground for building broad-based support. As a result the programmes were not only opposed by vigilant activists, but even by the government officials who were expected to implement them.

The Bank's technocratic approach towards economic growth and development challenges has been attributed to the fact that the Bank is dominated by economists of a particular ideological persuasion. For instance, one analyst has observed that, "you do not get to be a Bank research economist without having demonstrated your commitment to the presumptions of neo-liberalism and to the analytical techniques of Anglo-American economics" (Wade, 2002: 219).

During the 1980s the Bank responded to this criticism by employing people with different educational and professional backgrounds (see Hart, 2006).

However, a review of the Bank's profile shows that during the earlier days (during Eugene Black and George Wood's days) the Bank's personnel was largely multidisciplinary – consisting of technical, legal and public administration experts. The dominance of economists in the Bank was a later development (see Kapur *et al.*, 1997: 1181). Nevertheless, the crucial question is not whether one is an economist or not – though it might be argued that one's training influences how one sees the world, and interprets and responds to its challenges. The crucial point regards the realisation that one's knowledge is not definitive – one can learn from others. Interaction between the Bank's staff and its African clients, however, has certainly not exhibited this virtue, regardless of whether the staff in question were economists, anthropologists, public administrators, agronomists, sociologists or geographers.

The role of agriculture in Africa's development

As noted in Chapter 2, the Bank's understanding of the African challenge since the 1960s has centred around the role of agriculture, though with changing emphasis along the way. During the 1960s and 1970s agriculture was seen as the core of Africa's development potential, for the reason that most of the people in the continent worked (and still work) in agriculture and related activities. Prior to the *Berg Report*, the de Wilde report (1967), Andrew Kamarck's book (1967), McNamara's *Nairobi Speech* (1973), and Robert Bates' (1981) study all highlighted the importance of agriculture to Africa's development. Picking up on this, the *Berg Report* locates agriculture at the heart of Africa's economic growth and development, stating that, "agricultural output is the single-most important determinant of overall economic growth and its sluggish record of recent years is the principal factor underlying the poor economic performance of the countries in this region" (World Bank, 1981: 45).

Because of the importance attached to agriculture, a significant number of the reform programmes prescribed during the 1980s focused on making it more efficient, particularly by improving incentives and productivity through market reforms. In a significant way other issues such as population control, exchange rates, pricing and marketing reforms, trade liberalisation and public sector reforms were all linked to the central issue of making agriculture more productive and efficient. The *Africa Progress Report* (World Bank, 1983), which followed the *Berg Report* (World Bank, 1981), reiterated the centrality of dealing with institutional and policy issues that were blocking the growth of the agricultural sector in Africa. Later reports, too, maintain the central role of agriculture in the region's economic growth and development. For example, the LTPS argues that "in contrast to the past, the future strategy sees agriculture as the primary foundation for growth" (World Bank, 1989b: 8).

Somehow, this fits in well with the mainstream development paradigm which sees the increase of productivity in the subsistence sector as key to generating surplus financial and human capital to drive industrialisation. W. Arthur Lewis (1954) sets out the main scaffolds for this model, which is developed by later

Table 3.2. Agricultural productivity (1990–1992 and 2005–2007, in 2000 US$ per worker)

	1990–1992	*2005–2007*	*Change 1990–2007 (%)*
Angola	176	222	26
Burundi	117	70	−40
Cameroon	409	703	72
Chad	209	246	18
Côte d'Ivoire	652	875	34
DRC	209	162	−22
Ghana	352	367	04
Kenya	379	367	−03
Madagascar	210	182	−13
Malawi	86	126	47
Mozambique	117	173	48
Niger	242	..	..
Uganda	175	191	0.09
Sudan	526	844	0.60
Tanzania	261	324	0.24
Zambia	189	232	23
SSA	305	318	4

Source: author, based on data from the *World Development Indicators* (2010).

analysts. The rationale was that since agriculture in low-income countries such as those of SSA accounted for more than 70 per cent of the labour force and almost half of Gross Domestic Product (GDP) in most countries, even during the 1980s (see World Bank, 1981), increasing productivity and efficiency in this sector would not only result in increased income, but would also generate more resources that could be channelled towards industrialisation. Based on this reasoning it has been asserted in mainstream development economic theory that "it is agriculture which finances industrialisation" (Lewis, 1954: 21). Thus, for some analysts, the simple fact that there has been no significant improvement in productivity in the subsistence agriculture sector in Africa, explains why development has been elusive. As Table 3.2 shows, productivity in agriculture, on average, barely changed between the early 1990s and 2007, and there has been little improvement in the last five years.

The performance of different countries, of course, varied, with Madagascar, Kenya, Burundi and the Democratic Republic of the Congo (DRC) recording a decline in productivity while other countries such as Malawi, Mozambique, Sudan and Cameroon recording a productivity growth of close to 50 per cent during the reference period.

Low productivity in agriculture, in general, and the subsistence sector in particular, has persisted despite the Bank's efforts and initiatives. While this situation raises questions about the efficacy of the Bank's initiatives, it also suggests that the challenges are probably more complex than simply addressing incentive structures through price reforms.

Table 3.3. Labour productivity, agricultural population and vulnerable employment for SSA

	Labour productivity growth/ worker (%)[a]		% of total population in agriculture[b]	% of labour force in agriculture[c]	% employed at rates below US$1.25/day[d]
	1990–1992	2003–2005	2010	2010	2004–2008
Angola	−5.0	12.0	69.2	69.0	59.9
Burundi	..	..	89.2	89.0	87.2
Cameroon	−6.7	1.1	40.9	48.0	39.9
Chad	..	..	65.6	66.0	72.1
DRC	−12.9	4.2	57.2	57.0	69.6
Côte d'Ivoire	−3.6	−0.3	37.9	38.0	26.3
Ghana	2.8	3.0	53.8	54.0	37.6
Kenya	−3.9	2.1	70.6	71.0	22.9
Madagascar	−5.9	1.5	70.1	70.0	76.7
Malawi	−1.9	1.9	72.9	79.0	79.8
Mozambique	−3.0	6.2	75.9	81.0	81.2
Niger	−5.7	0.2	82.9	83.0	76.6
Uganda	−1.1	3.3	73.4	75.0	55.7
Sudan	−1.3	−0.2	51.5	52.0	..
Tanzania	−2.4	4.8	73.2	76.0	90.0
Zambia	−2.5	3.2	63.2	63.0	76.6
SSA	−5.3	3.7	..	..	..

Source: author, based on data from *World Development Indicators*, *Human Development Report*, and FAOSTAT.

Note: figures for 1990–1992, 2003–2005 and 2004–2008 are averages for the period.

[a] = data from *World Development Indicators*, 2010 (WDI, 2010); [b] and [c] = data from FAOSTAT, available at: http://faostat.fao.org/site/348/default.aspx); [d] = data from *Human Development Report*, 2010 (HDR, 2010).

Given the large percentage of the population working in agriculture in most of SSA, it is perhaps justifiable to stress the important role agriculture can (and should) play in economic growth and development, and as such, raising productivity is central to any realistic growth strategy in these countries. Accordingly, the Bank's emphasis on agriculture in explaining SSA's growth and development challenges may be justified by the mere fact that this is the single sector in which the largest section of the population earns its living. In countries such as Tanzania, Malawi, Mozambique, Uganda, Niger and Burundi, more than three-quarters of the labour force worked in agriculture in 2010 (Table 3.3). While productivity per worker figures generally show some signs of recovery in the period 2003–2005 – when compared to earlier periods (see Table 3.2) – productivity levels still appear very low in most countries when compared to high performers such as Venezuela, which has an annual productivity growth rate of about 15 per cent over the same period. Low productivity per worker is also reflected in the high proportion of workers reported to be earning below US$1.25 per day (the working poor), most of them involved in subsistence agriculture.

Agriculture's fall from grace

Although agriculture in earlier reports occupied a central place in understanding SSA's economic and growth challenges, there seems to have been a shift of emphasis in later reports starting from the mid-1990s. It is not clear what justifies this shift, but it is evident that agriculture's role in explaining the SSA's growth experiences seems to have been declining. For example, the World Bank's strategy document for Africa's development does not even mention agriculture as one of its priority areas; it is economic infrastructure and competitiveness which are seen as the pillars for the future of Africa's economic growth and development (see World Bank, 2011). Similarly, the Bank's action plan for Africa's development which talks about identifying drivers of growth in Africa, although mentioning increasing productivity in agriculture as one of the objectives, focuses mainly on improving the investment climate for the private sector (see World Bank, 2005).[7]

Though agriculture seems to be disappearing from the policy radar within the Bank, the share of the labour force and the population in general in agriculture is still exceptionally high in many countries, as Table 3.3 suggests. It is not clear if the Bank assumes that structural transformation (diversification of the production structure) has occurred in SSA economies such that the role of agriculture in economic growth is no longer that critical. In the Bank's reports from the mid-1990s onwards, agriculture is largely seen as an instrument for alleviating rural poverty (World Bank, 1995) and not necessarily as a "foundation for growth", as was the case in the earlier reports. For example, the CAC report, when listing the factors which explain SSA's "slow growth", mentions factors such as geography, population, ethnic fragmentation, lack of democracy, social conflict, aid dependence and poor economic management, with no mention of agriculture. Similarly, the CAG report when drawing lessons from the experience of the past five decades, does not mention agriculture as a growth strategy; instead the crucial factors mentioned concentrate on policy and governance, geography (mainly in the climatic dimension) and high population growth rates (World Bank, 2007: 145–6).

While the conventional neoclassical view of economic growth and development is that as the economic development progresses, agriculture's contribution to GDP declines – as well as its importance as a source of growth and employment (Ndulu and O'Connell, 2008) – there is little evidence to suggest that such a transformation has already taken place in most African countries. As Table 3.3 shows, most of these countries still have more than half of the labour force in agriculture and more than 30 per cent of GDP comes from agriculture. If agricultural production declines as a result of flood, drought or other natural causes, we not only see a decline in GDP growth rates in most of these countries but also a negative effect on their BoP situations, exchange rates and even their inflation since more foreign reserve resources are used to import food to cover the shortfall. So the seemingly dwindling role of agriculture in explaining Africa's growth and development challenges could be a case of a premature pronouncement of economic 'take-off' and transformation in Africa. As argued in Chapter 7, if the 'take-off' has indeed occurred, it has only carried with it a third of the population, leaving behind the other two-thirds on the runway, watching.

Agriculture and policy reforms

Analysts within the Bank, especially at the beginning of SAPs, strongly believed that "an improvement in agricultural incentive is unlikely to occur without a marked improvement in efficiency with which agricultural outputs and inputs are marketed and without a greater willingness by governments to use exchange rate policy more actively" (World Bank, 1983: 2). Accordingly, the Bank argued that reforms in trade and exchange rate policies provided the right incentives to farmers by removing the excessive tax on agricultural production that resulted from overvalued local currencies. These reforms were seen as central to increasing productivity and efficiency in agriculture. In the literature on SSA's development challenges, high input costs and low producer prices were widely believed to be responsible for strangling growth in the agriculture sector.

Thus, while the focus on devaluation may have been narrowly defined and targeted, addressing an overvalued currency had implications on the agriculture sector through medium-term changes in producer and input prices. An overvalued local currency effectively shifted the internal terms of trade in favour of the urban population, who obtained foodstuff at prices subsidised by the agricultural producer. Often, in cases where prices for agricultural produce were raised either by devaluation of local currency or by increasing the market price for such products, the shifting terms of trade in favour of the rural sector were subsequently reversed by either the urban workers demanding higher incomes, or by the rising input costs.

Other reforms

At the beginning of the structural reform programme in Africa, as noted above, the focus was on short-term reforms, with an understanding that the long-term challenges could be addressed by fixing short-term problems like BoP and fiscal imbalances in the economy. Within the short-term reforms, areas such as public finance (mainly fiscal deficit reduction), public enterprise reform (privatisation), trade, financial and capital market reforms (liberalisation), and public wage bill reduction (as part of the move to reduce fiscal deficit), were seen as crucial. Adjustment lending, as well as technical support, was, from the early 1980s, strictly tied to the implementation of these reforms. Although wide-ranging conditionalities regarding exchange rates through to public sector reform and population policy were attached to every loan, the focus during the earlier period was on macroeconomic reforms which were linked to reforms in agriculture – as noted above.

Within the macroeconomic reforms, exchange rate policies, interest rates and fiscal balance were seen as critical areas. However, exchange rate policies and maintaining a fiscal balance were the most controversial areas, and they came with a high political cost for most African governments. The Bank was well aware of this: "exchange rate is perhaps the most controversial issue" (World Bank, 1989b: 5). The justification for focusing on exchange rates within the Bank was that "Overvalued exchange rates encourage imports and discriminate against local producers. A competitive exchange rate is essential to boost domestic production and employment" (ibid.). With regard to SSA's economic growth challenges the Bank was convinced that since the early 1980s "exchange rate policy is at the heart of the failure to provide adequate incentive for agricultural production and for exports in much of Africa" (World Bank, 1983: 7). In a way this was in line with the thinking that 'getting the price right' was the magic bullet that would resolve all other problems (Ravenhill, 1993), including the political malaise. This is clearly summed in the view that,

> Experience worldwide convincingly demonstrates that the countries with highest growth rates have kept their exchange rates competitive, avoided excessive protection of manufacturing industry and under-pricing their agricultural products, kept real interest rates positive and real wages in line with productivity, priced utilities to recover costs, and avoided high and accelerating inflation by following disciplined fiscal and monetary policies. Structural adjustment programmes have reflected these themes ... They are critical to Africa's recovery.
>
> (World Bank, 1989b: 5)

Even though in later years there has been an acknowledgement that most SSA countries have improved their macroeconomic environment, and that most of the countries' macroeconomic policies are converging towards the global average in areas such as inflation, interest rates, real exchange rates and trade policies (see IMF, 2013), sticking points such as low productivity, low returns on investment in agriculture and low export growth – which are basically incentive-based dynamics – still remain major constraints for SSA (World Bank, 2007). The focus on exchange rates and fiscal balance within the SAPs could be explained by the Bank's commitment to the market as an institution that promotes efficiency in resource use and allocation. Whether these reforms achieved their intended objectives is a contested matter.

The scope and outcome of SAPs in Africa

Although the adjustment lending programmes started off very slowly with only six SSA countries (Kenya, Cote d'Ivoire, Malawi, Mauritius, Senegal and Togo) reported to have designed and started implementing these reforms by 1983 (World Bank, 1983: 21), by the end of 1987 a total of 18 countries had initiated SAPs and another 14 had borrowed from the Bank on condition that they would initiate structural reforms (World Bank, 1989b: 20). By the end of the decade 34 SSA countries were on SAPs. In 90 per cent of cases, reduction of fiscal deficit was prescribed, and in half the countries (except the in the CFA (*Communauté*

Financière Africaine) zone, which had exchange rates linked to the French Franc) exchange rate policy conditionality was attached to all loans. Countries participating in adjustment lending programmes, either in the form of SALs or SECALs, were expected to implement these programmes before disbursement of loans could be made. The justification for tying concessional loans to a set of conditionalities was that performance-based lending would provide an incentive for governments to implement the policies – a safeguard against the 'moral hazard'. Conditionality around fiscal deficit or exchange rate policies covered numerous reforms (though economistic in nature) from privatisation to contract management and adoption of specified accounting and auditing systems. Often, when talking about conditionality, there is an impression that few performance variables were included, but in reality one finds a long list of reform prescriptions. However, since the focus was on macroeconomic policy reforms, most of these revolved around markets for products, inputs and currencies.

Debates on the outcome of the Bank's operation in SSA have been widespread, and extend into the present. Generally, the performance of SAPs has not been impressive in SSA compared to other regions. The Bank itself has been aware of this below-par performance in SSA since the mid-1990s:

> No African country has achieved a sound macroeconomic policy stance – which in broad terms means inflation under 10 percent, a very low budget deficit, and a competitive exchange rate. In a third of the countries, macro-economic policies actually deteriorated over the decade. Furthermore, countries are still taxing their farmers heavily, through marketing boards and/or overvalued exchange rates. Most countries have further to go in eliminating nontariff barriers and adopting a moderate, tariff-based level of protection. Social spending, while not showing an overall decline during the adjustment period, is misallocated within the health and education sector. And the politically difficult reform of the public enterprise and financial sectors lags well behind.
>
> (World Bank, 1994: 1–2)

However, the Bank has always argued that the reason why these policies have performed badly is because they have not been consistently implemented (World Bank, 1994; 1989b). Poor compliance with agreed conditionality, as well as weakness in the design and sequencing of programmes, have been noted to be responsible for the poor record of the Bank's operations in SSA (World Bank, 1998; Dollar and Svensson, 2000). Over the three years since the 2009 financial crisis, the Bank in particular has been arguing that the sustained growth recorded in Africa since 2000 is the result of the SAP policies implemented during the 1990s which are now beginning to bear fruit (World Bank, 2011; 2013).

One of the major problems in assessing the impact of programmes such as SAPs is that they are not a single policy – various elements of the reforms are interlinked to everything else from interest rates, export promotions, terms of trade, public borrowing, productivity growth, wages, labour laws, skills, inflation and public perception. For instance, the first adjustment loan given to Senegal in 1980 attached fiscal deficit reduction, increased saving, devaluation of the local currency, privatisation of parastatals (especially the marketing boards), and removal of subsidies and import duties to its terms. In this instance, the impact of each of these policies is difficult to disentangle, although there has been widespread consensus that the outcomes were a disaster (see Brown, 1995).

Because of this dominant view, SAPs in Africa have been criticised from different angles. Critics have argued that SAPs were "simply incapable of either assessing the nature of Africa's problems or putting in place policies that will put African countries on a trajectory of sustainable development" (Stein, 2004: 153). Nonetheless, some critics have accused the Bank of shying away from its duty to provide guidance on development policy and decisions. With particular reference to the LTPS report, Paul Collier argues that the Bank gives a low profile to macroeconomic policy as a way of avoiding friction, particularly with the United Nations Economic Commission for Africa (UNECA) (Collier, 1991).

From short-term to long-term interventions

As noted earlier, there was strong belief that at the beginning of the reforms focusing on key short-term constraints would eventually address the identified long-term challenges such as population growth, human capital shortfalls, infrastructure deficits, low agricultural research and low institutional capacity. But as the Bank gained more experience of working in SSA, this view changed with the realisation that SSA's challenges could not be fixed by focusing on stabilisation programmes. A summary of the evolving approach of the Bank's strategy in SSA is provided in a review report on adjustment lending, which points out that

> Adjustment lending has increasingly focused on long-run structural and institutional reforms, both across and within sectors. In the area of economic management, adjustment lending support has shifted from a short-term focus on stabilization and getting relative prices right to longer-term structural reforms to restore the basis for sustained growth. During the 1980s, adjustment lending mainly addressed fundamental distortions resulting from decades of import-substituting industrialization policies. During the 1990s, it increasingly supported reforms in public sector management, in the financial and private sectors, and in the social sectors. This change is reflected in a decline in the share of adjustment loan conditions in the areas of industry, energy, and agriculture policy from 22 percent in FY80-88 to 5 percent in FY98-00. Meanwhile, the share of public sector management conditions rose from 15 percent to 24 percent, and the share covering the financial and private sector from 28 percent to 41 percent.
>
> (World Bank, 2001: xiii–xiv)

Part of the reason for this change in approach, as the report acknowledges, is external criticism of the Bank's programmes. To a large extent the shift in the

LTPS from a narrow and short-term focus to a broader and long-term strategy was a response to criticisms from UNECA and other institutions – even within the UN system – about the nature and pace of SAPs (see Kapur *et al.*, 1997; Owusu, 2003). UNECA in particular (which has been described by many as the most vicious critic of the Bank and SAP in SSA (see Sandbrook, 1990; Ravenhill, 1993, Mosley and Weeks, 1993), argued that the recommended policies undermined SSA's ability to recover from economic crisis, and that if the policies continued there was little prospect that the region could ever recover (see UNECA, 1989).

Criticisms from the UNECA were provoked by a joint World Bank/UNDP report which claimed that the reforms prescribed by the Bank during the 1980s resulted in improved economic performance in the region. The report argued that improved performance was recorded in countries that implemented SAPs more consistently, and weak performance recorded in countries which did not do so (World Bank/UNDP, 1989: 27).

This is not the place for assessing the merit of the arguments on both sides; the full content of the debate can be accessed in the paper by Paul Mosley and John Weeks (1993). It suffices here to note that the UNECA's criticism of SAPs in SSA may have influenced the Bank's shift in dealing with the challenges of economic growth and development in SSA. In a report that followed the World Bank/UNDP report, there is seemingly an acknowledgement that the Bank did not fully understand the complexity of SSA's economic and growth challenges (World Bank, 1989b: 2). There is a shift in tone in the report, which is different from earlier ones that were written without much conviction and self-confidence.

However, although there was a humble admission of inadequate understanding of SSA's complex situation at the end of the 1980s, the core policy prescription and approach remained the same during the 1990s and 2000s apart from the addition that governance issues should also be part of the adjustment programmes. The core policy issues of pricing and market reform, less state intervention in the economy, and emphasis on fiscal austerity, have remained unchanged even today.

The Bank and the Fund in post-structural adjustment Africa

By the mid-1990s it was becoming apparent that the Bank and the Fund's economic restructuring programmes had registered little success in bringing about the anticipated economic turn around, transformation and poverty reduction. Reports from within the Bank indicated that 27 countries in SSA experienced negative growth in terms of their annual average Gross National Product (GNP) per capita for the period 1988–1994, with countries such as Cameroon (–9 per cent), Zaire (–7 per cent), Cote d'Ivoire (–4.5 per cent) and Ethiopia (–3 per cent) experiencing large annual declines (see World Bank, 1995: 6). Other indicators – such as the proportion of primary commodities in total exports, investment-to-GDP ratios, domestic savings, manufacturing, aid inflows, and especially, external debt – showed no signs of improvement. At the end of 1993 the overall debt burden for SSA was estimated at 254 per cent of the region's export earnings, and 28 countries had rescheduled their debts, some of them 13 times since 1980 (ibid.: 12).

A much more negative picture emerged regarding poverty. An assessment of poverty levels in SSA in 1994 revealed that up to 50 per cent of the population was living below the poverty line of US$1 per day (see World Bank, 1994). Although the Bank and the Fund blamed this poor result on the failure by most African governments to implement the prescribed programmes consistently, criticism of the Bank's policies in Africa in particular, intensified, with reproaches coming from international and local non-governmental organisations (NGOs), broader civil society, as well as the various agencies of the United Nations – especially the United Nations Children's Fund (UNICEF), which argued that the obsession with economic variables resulted in neglect of the social and human dimensions of the Bank and Fund's work. These criticisms forced the Bank and the Fund to critically review their approach to the economic crisis in Africa, and it became apparent that it was not just an economic one; the crisis also had social, political as well as human dimensions. In an effort to incorporate these dimensions into its reform programmes, issues of poverty started to receive serious attention again,[8] especially within the World Bank – resulting in a number of initiatives meant to give their programmes a 'human face'. Important examples of this are the two initiatives introduced in the second half of the 1990s – the Highly Indebted Poor Countries (HIPC) Initiative, jointly introduced by the Bank and the Fund in 1996, and the Poverty Reduction Strategy Papers (PRSPs) for the World Bank, and Poverty Reduction and Growth Facility (PRGF) for the Fund, introduced in 1999.

From SAPs to HIPC/PRSPs-PRGF

There has been a lot of debate about whether the initiatives introduced in the second half of the 1990s constituted a complete policy turnaround or whether they were just a repackaging of 'old wine' into 'new skins'. Those critical of these initiatives have argued that they were just a new way of carrying on old programmes under new acronyms. Jubilee South (an international coalition of NGOs involved in the Debt Cancellation Campaign), for instance, argued that those initiatives appearing to be concerned with poverty were the "newest justification for the aging prescriptions geared to increasing the overall opening of the 'host countries' to external economic actors and free market rules" (Jubilee South, 2000: 2). Other analysts critical of the BWIs have observed that while the new initiatives presented opportunities for linking issues of poverty, accountability, participation and the redistribution of the benefits of growth,

> PRSPs continue to impose a narrow neo-liberal economism that seems unacceptably hard and sharp in the face of growing evidence that the much hoped for general and robust relation between its precepts and growth, equity and poverty reduction may simply not be there.
>
> (Craig and Porter, 2003: 58)

However, others see the mid-1990s' initiatives as a "retreat from classical free market" fundamentalism, occasioned mainly by the crisis of confidence and uncertainty within the World Bank and the IMF (see Pender, 2001: 398).

A close look at the earlier programmes (SAPs, mainly the SALs and SECALs) of the World Bank – and the ESAF of the IMF – suggests that there has been no paradigm shift, although a number of accommodating tactics have been introduced. As illustrated below, although issues of poverty, vulnerability, participation and social policy have been taken on board, PRSPs and PRGF still carry stringent conditionality which the recipient country has to fulfil in order to be eligible for debt relief.

The HIPC initiative

Due to the disappointing outcome of SALs and SECALs, and ESAF programmes, the World Bank and the IMF jointly launched the HIPC initiative in 1996 with the aim of reducing the external debt burden of HIPC. This initiative was introduced amidst the growing debt burden experienced by many countries in the developing world, particularly in SSA. Not surprisingly, like the International Development Association (IDA) loans, the HIPC initiative, from its inception in 1996, has been dominated by African countries, with 18 out of 22 countries eligible for debt relief in 2000 being located in SSA (see IMF, 2002). This situation has not changed, as shown in Table 3.4.

Initially, HIPC was conceived as a means, by both multilateral and bilateral lenders, to facilitate the debt-ridden poor countries' 'robust exit' from the debt crisis situation (Oxfam International, 1999: 5). According to the IMF, the main purpose of the HIPC Initiative is to deal with the debt problem of heavily indebted countries so as to reduce the debt burden to sustainable or manageable levels (IMF, 2002: 45). In 1999, the Bank and the Fund made adjustments to the original programmes and came up with what has been called the enhanced HIPC-2 – but linked to the PRSPs. Although in practice there has been no noticeable difference between HIPC-1 and HIPC-2, the IMF argues that HIPC-2 was an improvement on the earlier form in that it embarked on providing "broader, deeper and faster relief" (IMF, 2002: 45). In 2005 the HIPC-2 initiative was supplemented by the adoption of the Multilateral Debt Relief Initiative (MDRI) following the Gleneagles meeting of the G8, with the promise of 100 per cent debt relief for poor countries by multilateral lenders.

The critical components of HIPC include the eligibility criteria, the determination of sustainable debt, and the degree of relief granted to HIPC countries. On the eligibility criteria, the HIPC framework as applied by the Fund and the Bank uses a two-threshold qualifying point system which consists of the Net Present Value (NPV) of debt-to-export ratio and the NPV of debt-to-government revenue ratio. Under HIPC-2 a country can qualify for debt relief if its NPV of debt-to-export ratio is more than 150 per cent, and if its NPV debt-to-government revenue ratio is more than 250 per cent. This means that countries with NPV debt-to-export ratios of less than 151 per cent are excluded, just as countries with

Table 3.4. HIPC countries in SSA (2011)

Country	Decision point	Completion point	Current status
Benin	2000	2002	2nd Generation PRSP (2008)
Burkina Faso	1999	2000	2nd Generation PRSP (2004)
Burundi	2003	2009	PRSP progress Report (2009)
Cameroon	2000	2003	2nd Generation PRSP (2010)
Cape Verde	2002	2004	2nd Generation PRSP (2008)
Central African Rep.	2000	2006	Joint Staff Assessment (2007)
Chad	2000	Not yet	2nd Generation PRSP (2010)
Comoros	2005	Not yet	Joint Staff Assessment (2006)
DRC	2002	2006	2nd Generation PRSP (2007)
Congo Republic	2004	Not yet	Joint Staff Assessment (2004)
Cote d'Ivoire	2002	Not yet	PRSP Progress Report
Ethiopia	2000	2002	Joint Staff Advisory Note
Gambia	2000	2002	2nd Generation PRSP (2007)
Ghana	2000	2003	PRSP Progress Reports
Guinea	2000	Not yet	PRSP Progress Reports
Guinea-Bissau	2000	Not yet	PRSP Progress Report
Kenya	2000	2004	2nd Generation PRSP (2010)
Lesotho	2000	2005	2nd Generation PRSP (2006)
Liberia	2007	2008	PRSP Progress Report
Madagascar	2000	2003	2nd Generation PRSP (2007)
Malawi	2000	2002	2nd Generation PRSP (2006)
Mali	2000	2002	2nd Generation PRSP (2008)
Mauritania	2000	2002	3rd Generation PRSP (2011)
Mozambique	2000	2001	3rd Generation PRSP (2004)
Niger	2000	2002	2nd Generation PRSP (2008)
Nigeria	2005	2005	PRSP Progress Report
Rwanda	2000	2002	2nd Generation PRSP (2008)
Sao Tome and Prin.	2000	2005	PRSP Progress Report
Senegal	2000	2002	3rd Generation PRSP (2007)
Sierra Leone	2001	2005	PRSP Progress Report
Tanzania	1999	2000	3rd Generation PRSP (2010)
Togo	2008	Not yet	Joint Staff Advisory Note
Uganda	1999	2000	3rd Generation PRSP (2004)
Zambia	2000	2006	2nd Generation PRSP (2007)

Source: based on data from the World Bank website at: www.worldbank.org, Country Papers, and JSANs/JSAs-Sub-Saharan Africa.

Note: Out of the 39 eligible countries for HIPC in 2010, 33 are in SSA – the other six being Nicaragua, Bolivia, Haiti, Honduras, Guyana and Afghanistan. Of the 33 SSA countries, 26 have reached completion point, while seven are still operating under the interim PRSP. Eritrea, Somalia and Sudan have not yet reached decision point (see IMF, 2009).

NPV debt-to-government revenue ratios of less than 249 per cent are excluded on the grounds that they have achieved sustainable debt levels (IMF, 2002: 4). According to the IMF, a sustainable level of debt is reached when a country is "able to continue servicing its debt without an unrealistically large future correction to the balance of income and expenditure"; in other words without requiring debt rescheduling, further borrowing, or further debt accumulation (ibid.).

With specific reference to HIPC, and although many critics have argued for total debt cancellation, it has been widely acknowledged that the initiative is a better and more efficient mechanism than the concessional lending facilities (CAFOD *et al.*, 2002: 2; Gunter, 2003: 101). Since 1999 the key mechanism through which HIPC and, later on, MDRI, have been implemented, is the PRSP-PRGF processes.

Linking PRSPs/PRGF to HIPC

PRSPs-PRGF are linked to HIPC in the sense that to be considered eligible for debt relief under HIPC, a country has to go through the process of designing a PRSP. As may be evident, these initiatives have both an element of *carrot* and *stick*, with the PRSP containing a set of tasks which an aspirant country had to implement before being eligible for debt relief. While the main objective of HIPC is to reduce the debt burden of poor countries, the envisioned objectives of PRSPs are many, including coordination of donor funding, directing the attention of recipient governments to focus on poverty reduction, promoting the participation of citizens in issues of development which affect their lives, and promoting ownership of reform programmes by participating countries (see World Bank, 2001). However, while these objectives are clearly stated, the PRSPs' aim is to "describe a country's macroeconomic, structural and social policies and programmes over a three year or longer horizon, to promote broad based growth and reduce poverty" (cited in Craig and Porter, 2003: 53).

Compared to the earlier programmes of SAPs (which focused narrowly on macroeconomic stability through fiscal and monetary discipline), the new initiatives, without relaxing the commitment to maintaining macroeconomic stability, have taken on board a wider spectrum of issues. The broader view taken by PRSP compared to SAPs is reflected in the new policy components which were not present in SAPs. These include the recommendation that the new programmes be 'country driven', result-oriented, comprehensive, long-term in approach, and based on partnership. These components reflect the four principles contained in the Comprehensive Development Framework introduced by the World Bank in 1999 (see Wolfensohn, 1999).

The focus on poverty in the PRSP-HIPC approach also stands out in contrast with the SAPs, which relegated poverty to being a secondary concern to be addressed *after* achieving sufficient economic growth. Focus on poverty reduction was highlighted in the *World Development Report 2000/2001*, in which the Bank outlined the main approaches as creating opportunities for the poor, facilitating their empowerment, securing their livelihoods, and enhancing their access to basic social services – realising that while market reforms can deliver growth, they can also be a source of dislocation (World Bank, 2001: 32–3). While such differences between SAPs and PRSPs are evident on paper, critics have argued that they are all merely a reframing of the same strategies, though with appendages on poverty alleviation, plurality, decentralisation and participation (Craig and Porter, 2003). The process of becoming eligible for debt relief and HIPC status is quite revealing in this regard.

The HIPC process

For a country to be eligible for debt relief under the HIPC Initiative, it has first of all to express an interest in participating in the initiative, and be a poor country with unsustainable debt levels.[9] On the part of the Bank and the Fund there are four main conditions which must be met before a country is considered for debt relief: a country should (i) be eligible for IDA loans, (ii) satisfy the unsustainable debt burden requirement, (iii) have a track record of implementing sound reform policies suggested by the Bank and the Fund, and (iv) prepare a PRSP. Once these conditions are met and the lenders are satisfied, the country is said to have reached what is known as the *decision point*. Countries which have reached the decision point are eligible for interim debt relief on debt service payments that are due. For full debt relief support, a country needs to "establish a further track-record of good performance under programmes supported by loans from the IMF and the World Bank; implement satisfactorily key reforms agreed at the decision point; and adopt and implement its PRSP for at least one year" (IMF, 2011: 3).

The requirement to implement reforms supported by the Bank and the Fund is one set of conditions which has continued from the SAPs, with little adjustment. For example, while under SALs the key performance conditions included a reduction in current account deficit, the cutting of subsidies, achieving fiscal balance, a competitive exchange rate, low inflation and liberalisation of markets (see World Bank, 1991), similar conditions are set as performance requirements for being eligible for debt relief under HIPC. Thus the PRSP-HIPC approach still carries macroeconomic conditionality, which remains the core performance requirement, even if it is combined with other requirements such as demonstrating that the PRSP process was participatory and that the resources to be freed through debt relief will be spent on programmes which are going to benefit the poor. Countries which fail to meet these requirements, especially the macroeconomic one, often fail to reach the *completion point*, and thus are unable to receive full debt relief.

Table 3.4 shows SSA countries participating in the PRSP-HIPC Initiative, the year when the country presented an interim PRSP, the year when the full PRSP was completed, and the current status. It is interesting to note that for some countries it took a long time to move from the *decision point* to the *completion point*. The longer period taken to reach completion point is often due to failure to meet the stipulated conditionality, especially macroeconomic performance indicators. Since a PRSP is a poverty reduction strategy for a specified period of time, there are some countries which are implementing the third generation PRSPs, while others have not yet reached the *completion point*. By the end of 2011 there were 26 African countries which had attained completion point status out of the total of 32 countries globally; four African countries were at the interim stage (between decision and completion points) and three were at the pre-decision stage (i.e., had not reached decision point, and were not yet participating in the HIPC Initiative, see IMF, 2011).

The process of a country graduating to full HIPC status is complex and involves at least three stages: decision point, interim period and the completion point (see Gunter, 2003: 99; CAFOD *et al.*, 2002: 7). In cases where a country fails to meet the stipulated performance conditions, the completion point is then taken to be a '*floating one*', which can be reached only after meeting the conditionality stipulated at the decision point. In the case of Zambia, for instance, the interim PRSP indicated that completion point would be reached at the end of 2003, but when the interim PRSP was presented at the end of 2003 it was not accepted until 2005. This was entirely because some of the conditions agreed upon (particularly, inflation, budget deficit levels, and various aspects of public sector reform, including finalising the privatisation of the mines) were not met. In the meantime, the country was asked to reduce inflation by half, reduce public spending and complete the privatisation of the outstanding state-owned enterprises. To achieve completion point the government had to, among other things, impose a wage freeze for the whole year (2004) for public service employees.

The principles of PRSPs

There are three key features of the PRSP initiative:

(i) **Ownership:** Again, based on the experience with SAPs, the Bank and other development agencies slowly realised that for structural reforms to succeed there must be a "broad country ownership" of the whole process (World Bank, 2004: 14). Emphasis on ownership reflects the recognition that individual governments should elaborate their strategies on how poverty should be tackled. Indeed, "successful adjustment must 'faithfully reflect' domestic goals and priorities" (Brown, 2000: 123). While ownership should be promoted, this can also be a way of shifting the responsibility for failing programmes to the participating government. With programme ownership offloaded to individual countries, the World Bank and the IMF can dodge the blame for failure of the programmes.

(ii) **Participation:** One of the requirements for a final PRSP is that the process should involve all stakeholders, including the poor themselves. For a PRSP to be approved, it must demonstrate that the government extensively consulted all stakeholders, including NGOs, civil society groups, church groups, as well as local government leaders (World Bank, 2004: 30). Although participation has been highly recommended, it has been observed that it must be genuine participation where stakeholders have the chance to give inputs at every stage of the process – from formulation through monitoring and evaluation. And for participation to be meaningful, "those involved need to feel they 'own' the process to a significant extent" (IDS, 2000: Issue 13)

(iii) **Good governance and accountability:** As has been noted earlier, the purpose of a PRSP was to ensure that resources released from "debt relief provided under the HIPC initiative, and concessional loans from the international financial institutions, are directed towards poverty reduction. Given this intention, then making sure that the resources freed under HIPC serve the intended purpose becomes one of the essential component of PRSP" (IDS, 2000). It is for this reason that issues of good governance, which include accountability of state institutions, become an indispensable component of the entire programme. Highlighting this point, Jubilee South (2000: 4) notes that accountability does not merely involve giving charts and electronically generated tables to donors or funders, it essentially requires that governments be accountable to "their people and domestic constituencies rather than to external funders so that the poor become active participants not just passive recipients".

PRSP/PRGF *outcome*

While most of these initiatives have currently lost the momentum that they had at the beginning of the 2000s, a number of observations can be made about what such programmes have meant in terms of addressing economic development and poverty challenges in Africa. Compared to SAPs, PRSPs represent some degree of adjustment. As observed earlier, SAPs were premised on a very narrow understanding of economic growth and development challenges. This changed somewhat under the HIPC-PRSP Initiative. A close review of these new programmes suggests that the scope has been widened; a lot more has been taken on board. For example, the emphasis on good governance, institutional capacity and social issues such as poverty and inequality, and social capital (Mosley *et al.*, 2004: 275), reflects a wider scope than the earlier programmes.

However, the reported shift in approach, while a commendable one, is actually not far from the old goalpost. First of all, although openness, ownership, participation and consultation have been applauded as steps in the right direction, the underlying factors remain to be addressed. Of particular importance is the process of drawing up PRSPs. While the Bank and the Fund give the impression that PRSPs are drawn up on a 'blank sheet' entirely by individual governments, in practice this is not the case: "PRSP designs in most countries [do] not start with a blank sheet of paper. Some [of the] most important decisions [are] pre-empted by prior government–IFI [international financial institutions] agreements; for example, on PRGF conditionality and HIPC triggers" (Booth, 2003: 148). Similar views have been expressed by Jubilee South (2000: 3), that "in most countries, the policy environment was and is … dominated by the World Bank, IMF, regional development banks and the UNDP who physically write the policy paper [PRSP]".

Further, a continued emphasis on conditionality as a basis for lending and accessing aid (World Bank, 2004: 32) simply undermines the level of participation and involvement of stakeholders. As David Craig and Dough Porter (2003) have noted, it seems as though the Bank and the Fund have employed catchwords such as 'participation', 'consultation' and 'partnership' as a way of responding to critics. A sincere commitment to participation would entail a clean slate for all stakeholders. But as can be seen from the various World Bank reviews, preset hurdles based on narrow macroeconomic stability concerns have to be complied with before even preliminary negotiations can begin, making it difficult for genuine participation to occur (Booth, 2003: 149). What this does, in effect, is to shift attention from the real issues – that is, poverty reduction through growth – to merely satisfying the conditionality. In some instances, governments, under pressure to meet these conditions, simply sign the documents as the only means of accessing much-needed relief resources, without much commitment to poverty reduction.

Moreover, a critical look at the current approach by the Bank and the Fund suggests that while the approach has changed, no changes to the core economic assumptions have been made. Even in the new approach, stabilisation, liberalisation and privatisation still remain as the core orientation of the reforms. Final PRSPs are not allowed to 'step outside' these core policies, and a number of elements are not included in PRSPs "because they do not fit within the obligatory neo-liberal parameters" (Jubilee South, 2000: 2). Consequently, the foundations on which SAPs were built have emerged unscathed as the cornerstone for the new approach. Similarly, a continuous insistence on debt relief being tied to PRSPs has led some critics to argue that PRSPs are simply SAPs dressed in new clothes (Craig and Porter, 2003: 55).

Africa's future and the Bank's role

Even though currently the Bank argues that reforms implemented during the 1990s were responsible for the sustained growth experienced in SSA since 1998, there is little evidence to show that most SSA countries have actually addressed concerns recognised during the 1980s. A good example is the concern that most African countries are still heavily dependent on primary commodity exports (Rowden, 2013). The challenge of diversifying the economy to provide a strong base for sustained growth remains unresolved, even in the current growth episode. The larger share of export earnings for most SSA countries still comes from agriculture (see Chapter 7). In countries – including Benin, Burundi, Burkina Faso, Ethiopia, Ghana, Malawi, Sierra Leone, Tanzania and Uganda – three-quarters of export earnings come from agriculture commodities. For countries such as Cameroon, Mozambique, Niger, Nigeria, Sudan and Zambia, their export earnings still come mainly from either oil or metals and ores. For instance, oil accounts for 87 per cent of Nigeria's exports and 91.3 per cent of Sudan's; coffee and tea account for 85 per cent of Burundi's exports; uranium and oil account for over 93 per cent of Niger's exports; and copper accounts for 71.8 per cent of Zambia's exports. Economies with such a production structure remain very vulnerable to commodity price volatility.

From this perspective it is clear that the current sustained growth experienced in SSA will remain very fragile as long as the economic structures are not transformed, and there is little evidence suggesting that the windfall revenue from high commodity prices are being used to restructure the production base of these economies. Furthermore, the weakness of economies in SSA are revealed by the fact that value-added growth is only occurring in manufacturing and services, which are relatively small sectors (see Chapter 7).

Looking back at the Bank's activities in Africa, and its views on African economic growth and development challenges, it is apparent that there has been a learning curve not just for the Bank but also for African governments and people. As Kapur *et al.* observe,

> The Bank – through countless analyses, papers, and reports, meetings, seminars, and discussions with African officials and intellectuals, bilateral donors, multilateral agencies, and academics outside Africa – had shaped views on African development, but these interactions, in turn, also shaped and changed the Bank's views.
>
> (Kapur *et al.*, 1997: 798–9)

While relations between Africa and the Bank have often been seen as a one-sided affair by many critics, it is apparent that the Bank's engagement with Africa has been a process of great turbulence for both the lender and the borrower. As for the future role of the Bank and the Fund in Africa, this will depend on how African economies perform from now on. If the current growth momentum grinds to a halt we will see the Bank becoming more influential; if the growth episodes continue the Bank's role will diminish even further.

This chapter and the previous one have discussed views based on market-oriented explanations of Africa's economic and development experience. The next chapter looks at the empirical evidence provided to support these market-oriented explanations.

Notes

1 For a full account of developing tension between the two Bretton Woods institutions (BWIs), see Polak (1997: 481ff).
2 For a detailed analysis of the differences in policy direction between the Lagos Plan of Action (LPA) and *Berg Report*, see Browne and Cummings (1984).
3 It is noted that by the mid-1980s, the Bank committed one-third of its staff resources to the region though the ratio of financial resources committed to SSA was only one-sixth. However, the administrative budget for Africa was larger than any other regional development bank (see Kapur *et al.*, 1997: 731).
4 In some literature these are sometimes mistakenly referred to us "African leaders"; these are the finance ministers or Central Bank governors of African countries who are ex-officio members of the Bank's executive board of directors. They are not African heads of state.
5 Some analysts have termed the Bank's lending to countries demonstrating little evidence of reform as "throwing money at Africa" (see Kapur *et al.*, 1997: 756). Others have actually praised the astuteness of the African politician in being able to trick the international community into believing that the money would buy reforms in Africa when in actual fact the only intention of using the donated resources is to perpetuate conditions of underdevelopment (see Chabal and Daloz, 1999; Chabal, 2002; Bayart, 1993). However, it appears the Bank had little choice but to continue lending to African governments even in situations like the former Zaire where there was absolutely no evidence of commitment or capacity to implement reforms. Cold War politics, in the case of Zaire, is cited as an explanation for the Bank's action.

6 In one incident, one of the Bank's senior officials for Africa reportedly requested a meeting with the former Tanzanian president, Julius Nyerere. During the meeting the World Bank official bluntly declared that he "had come for his check". This angered Nyerere so much that he instructed his aides to pay the Bank regardless of the impact on the country's financial position (see Lancaster, 1997: 169). A similar story involving junior World Bank staff and President Kamuzu Banda of Malawi is reported by Kapur *et al.* (1997).

7 Plans to increase agricultural productivity in the AAP, "includes measures to: (a) increase physical investment in agriculture, especially for irrigation, water resources management, rural roads and other infrastructure, and research and extension; (b) increase public service delivery in rural areas, and (c) achieve higher productivity through the use of more fertilizers and improved agricultural practices" (see World Bank, 2005: ix).

8 It is often noted that poverty concerns featured more strongly in the Bank's work during the McNamara presidency as a result of his focus on agriculture, basic needs and integrated rural development. But this focus on poverty fell away in the post-McNamara years, from 1981 up to the early 1990s – when concerns about poverty started to feature more strongly in the Bank's policies (see Ayres, 1983; Mosley *et al.*, 1995b; Kapur *et al.*, 1997; Craig and Porter, 2003; Stein, 2004). At the beginning of the 1990s the World Bank came up with a motto: "A World Free from Poverty", which is inscribed on one of its main buildings in New York City.

9 There are some poor countries eligible for HIPC who refused to participate. According to the IMF update on HIPC/PRGF, the Nepal and Kyrgyz authorities decided not to participate in the initiative, although is it claimed that these countries' income levels are above the IMF/MDRI threshold (see IMF, 2009).

References

Ayres, Robert (1983). *Banking on the Poor: The World Bank and World Poverty*. Cambridge, MA: MIT Press.

Bates, Robert (1981). *Markets and States in Tropical Africa: The Political Basis of Agricultural Policies*. Berkeley: University of California Press.

Bayart, Francois (1993). *The State in Africa: The Politics of the Belly*. London: Longman.

Booth, David (2003). "Introduction and Overview." *Development Policy Review*. Vol. 21, No. 2: 131–59.

Brown, B. Michael (1995). *Africa's Choices: After Thirty Years of the World Bank*. London: Pluto Press.

Brown, William (2000). "Restructuring North-South Relations: ACP-EU Development Cooperation in a Liberal International Order." *Review of African Political Economy*, Vol. 27, No. 85: 367–83.

Browne, S. Robert and Cummings, J. Robert (1984). *The Lagos Plan of Action Versus the Berg Report*. Lawrenceville: Brunswick.

CAFOD, Oxfam and UNICEF (2002). "A Joint Submission to the World Bank and IMF Review of HIPC and Debt Sustainability." Online, available at: http://eurodad.org/uploadedfiles/whats_new/reports/eurodad_debtsustainability_hipcreview.pd, accessed 31 July 2004.

Callaghy, Thomas and Ravenhill, John (1993). "How Hemmed In? Lessons and Prospects of Africa's Response to Decline" in T. Callaghy and J. Ravenhill (eds) *Hemmed In? Responses to Africa's Economic Decline*. New York: Columbia University Press. Chapter 13.

Carlsson, Jerker (1983). "Introduction" in J. Carlsson (ed.) *Africa in Recession*. Uppsala: Scandinavian Institute of African Studies: iii–xi.

Chabal, Patrick (2002). "The Quest for Good Governance in Africa. Is NEPAD the Answer?" *International Affairs*, Vol. 78, No. 3: 447–65.

Chabal, Patrick and Daloz, Jean-Pascal (1999). *Africa Works: Disorder as Political Instrument*. London: James Currey.

Collier, P. (1991). "African External Economic Relations 1960–90." *African Affairs*, Vol. 90, No. 360: 339–56.

Collier, Paul (1993). "Africa and the Study of Economics" in R. Bates, V.Y. Mudimbe and J. O'Barr (eds) *Africa and the Disciplines: The Contribution of Research in Africa to the Social Sciences and Humanities*. Chicago/London: University of Chicago Press: 58–82.

Craig, David and Porter, Dough (2003). "Poverty Reduction Strategy Papers: A New Convergence." *World Development*, Vol. 31, No. 1: 53–69.

De Wilde, John (1967). *Experience with Agricultural Development in Tropical Africa: Synthesis* (Vols 1 and 2). Baltimore: Johns Hopkins Press.

Dollar, David and Svensson, Jacob (2000). *What Explains the Success or Failure of Structural Adjustment Programs?* Policy Research Working Paper No. 1938. Washington DC: The World Bank.

Gunter, B. (2003). "Achieving Long Term Debt Sustainability in Heavily Indebted Poor Countries (HIPC)" in A. Buira (ed.) *Challenges to the World Bank and IMF – Developing Country Perspectives*. London: Anthem Press. Chapter 4: 91–117.

Hart, Gillian (2006). "Post-apartheid Developments in Historical and Comparative Perspective" in V. Padayach (ed.) *The Development Decade? Economic and Social Change in South Africa 1994–2004*. Pretoria: HSRC Press: 13–32.

Hoogvelt, Ankie, Phillips, David and Taylor, Phil (1992). "The World Bank and Africa: A Case of Mistaken Identity." *Review of African Political Economy*, No. 54: 92–96.

Institute for Development Studies (IDS) (2000). "Poverty Reduction Strategies: A Part of the Poor?" *Policy Briefing*, Issue 13. IDS.

International Monetary Fund (IMF) (2002). "Assessing Sustainability." Online, available at: http://www.imf.org/external/np/hipc/2002/lteds/041502.pdf, accessed 11 October 2004.

International Monetary Fund (IMF) (2009). "Heavily Indebted Poor Countries (HIPC) Initiative and Multilateral Debt Relief Initiative (MDRI) – Status of Implementation." Online, available at: www.imf.org, accessed 13 January 2012.

International Monetary Fund (IMF) (2011). "Debt Relief Under the Heavily Indebted Poor Countries (HIPC) Initiative (Fact sheet), 15 December 2011. Online, available at: http://www.imf.org, accessed 30 January 2012.

International Monetary Fund (IMF) (2013). *Regional Economic Outlook October 2013: Sub-Saharan Africa – Keeping Pace*. Washington DC: IMF.

Jubilee South (2000). "The World Bank and the PRSP: Flawed Thinking and Failing Experiences." Memo. Online, available at: http://www.aidtransparency.org/at/images/ docs/resarch_results/les_dsrp_et_la_societe_civile_africaine/the_world_bank_and_ the_prsp_flowed.pdf, accessed 12 July 2004.

Kamarck, Andre (1967). *The Economics of African Development*. New York: Praeger.

Kapur, Devesh, Lewis, John and Webb, Richard (1997) *The World Bank: Its First Half Century*, Vol. 1. Washington DC: The Brookings Institution.

Lancaster, Carol (1997). "The World Bank in Africa Since the 1980s: The Politics of Structural Adjustment Lending" in D. Kapur, J. Lewis and R. Webb (eds) *The World Bank: Its First Half Century*. Washington DC: The Brookings Institution. Chapter 5: 161–94.

Lewis, W. Arthur (1954). "Economic Development with Unlimited Supplies of Labour." *Manchester School*, Vol. 20: 139–91.

Loxley, John (1983). "The Berg Report and the Model of Accumulation in Sub-Saharan Africa." *Review of African Political Economy*, Nos 27/28: 197–204.

McNamara, R. (1973). *Nairobi Speech: Address to the Board of Governors by Robert S. McNamara, President of the World Bank Group. Nairobi, Kenya. 24 September 1973.* Online, available at: http://www.juerg-buergi.ch/Archiv/EntwicklungspolitikA/EntwicklungspolitikA/assets/McNamara_Nairobi_speech.pdf, accessed 14 September 2012.

Madava, Callisto (1997). "Evolving Relationship between Africa and the World Bank: What Have We Learned Together?" James Coleman – An Appreciation. Los Angeles, 8 October 1997. Online, available at: http://worldbank.org, accessed 24 October 2011.

Michaels, Marguerite (1993). "Retreat from Africa." *Foreign Affairs*, Vol. 72, No. 1: 93–108.

Mosley, Paul and Weeks, John (1993). "Has Recovery Begun? 'Africa's Adjustment in the 1980s' Revisited." *World Development*, Vol. 21, No. 10: 1583–606.

Mosley, P., Hudson, J. and Verschool, A. (2004). "Poverty Reduction and the New Conditionality." *Economic Journal*, Vol. 14: 217–43.

Mosley, Paul, Subasat, Turan and Weeks, John (1995a). "Assessing Adjustment in Africa." *World Development*, Vol. 23, No. 9: 1459–73.

Mosley, Paul, Harringan, Jane and Toye, John (1995b) *Aid and Power: The World Bank and Policy Based Lending.* Routledge: London.

Moss, T., Standley, S. and Birdsall, N. (2004). "Double Standards, Debt Treatment and World Bank Country Classification: The Case of Nigeria." Centre for Global Development, Working Paper No. 45.

Ndikumana, L. and Boyce, J. (2008). "New Estimates of Capital Flight from Sub-Saharan African Countries: Linkages with External Borrowing and Policy Options." *Political Economy Research Institute (PERI) Working Paper Series*, No. 166.

Ndulu, Benno and O'Connell, Stephen (2008). "Policy Plus: African Growth Performance" in B. Ndulu, S. O'Connell, R. Bates, P. Collier and C. Soludo (eds) *The Political Economy of Economic Growth in Africa: 1960–2000.* Cambridge: Cambridge University Press: 3–75.

Onimode, Bade (1988). *A Political Economy of the African Crisis.* London: Zed Books.

Owusu, Francis (2003). "Pragmatism and the Gradual Shift from Dependency to Neoliberalism: The World Bank, African Leaders and Development Policy in Africa." *World Development*, Vol. 31, No. 10: 1655–72

Oxfam International (2000). *Make Debt Relief Work: Proposals for the G7.* London: Oxfam International. Online, available at: http://www.caa.org.au/oxfam/advocacy/index.html, accessed 19 August 2004.

Pender, John (2001). "From 'Structural Adjustment' to 'Comprehensive Development Framework': Conditionality Transformed." *Third World Quarterly*, Vol. 22, No. 3: 397–411.

Polak, Jacques (1997). "The World Bank and the IMF: A Changing Relationship" in D. Kapur, J. Lewis and R. Webb (eds) *The World Bank: Its First Half Century.* Washington DC: The Brookings Institution: 473–521.

Ravenhill, J. (1993) "A Second Decade of Adjustment: Greater Complexity, Greater Uncertainty" in T. Callaghy and J. Ravenhill (eds) *Hemmed In? Responses to Africa's Economic Decline.* New York: Columbia University Press. Chapter 1.

Rowden, Rick (2013). "The Myth of Africa's Rise." Online, available at: http://www.twincities.com/ci_22327262/rick-rowden-myth-africas-rise, accessed 17 November 2013.

Sandbrook, Richard (1990). "Taming the African Leviathan." *World Policy Journal*, Vol. 7, No. 4: 673–701.

Sandbrook, Richard (1993). *The Politics of Africa's Economic Recovery*. Cambridge: Cambridge University Press.

Srinivasan, T.N. (1994). "Data Base for Development Analysis." *Journal of Development Economics*, Vol. 44: 3–27.

Stein, Howard (2004). "The World Bank and the IMF in Africa: Strategy and Routine in the Generation of a Failed Agenda." Centre for Afro-American and African Studies (CAAS), University of Michigan. Online, available at: http://www.macua.org/Howard_Stein.pdf, accessed 29 April 2009.

Stern, Nicolas and Ferreira, Francisco (1997). "The World Bank as Intellectual Actor" in D. Kapur, J. Lewis and R. Webb (eds) *The World Bank: Its First Half Century*. Washington DC: The Brookings Institution. Chapter 12: 523–609.

Stiglitz, Joseph (2000). "The Insider: What I Learned at the World Economic Crisis." *The New Republic*. Online, available at: http://www.tnr.com, accessed 17 October 2012.

United Nations Development Programme (UNDP) (2010). *Human Development Report 2010: The Real Wealth of Nations*. New York: UNDP.

United Nations Economic Commission for Africa (UNECA) (1989). *African Alternative Framework to Structural Adjustment Programmes for Socio-Economic Recovery and Transformation*. Addis Ababa: UNECA.

Wade, Robert (2002). "US Hegemony and the World Bank: The Fight Over People and Ideas." *Review of International Political Economy*, Vol. 9, No. 2: 201–29.

Wolfensohn, James (1998). "The Other Crisis." Address to the IMF and World Bank Group Board of Directors. Online, available at: www.worldbank.org/NEWS/Resources/jdwsp100698-en.pdf, accessed 14 March 2012.

Wolfensohn, James (1999). "A Proposal for a Comprehensive Development Framework." Online, available at: http://www.imf.org/external/np/prsp/pdf/cdfprsp.pdf, accessed 11 April 2012.

World Bank (1981). *Accelerated Development in Sub-Saharan Africa: An Agenda for Action* [The Berg Report]. New York: IBRD/World Bank.

World Bank (1983). *Sub-Saharan Africa: Progress Report on Development Prospects and Programmes*. New York: IBRD/World Bank.

World Bank (1986). *Financing Adjustment with Growth in Sub-Saharan Africa 1986–90*. New York: IBRD/World Bank.

World Bank (1984). *Towards Sustained Development in Sub-Saharan Africa*. New York: IBRD/World Bank.

World Bank (1989a). IBRD Articles of Agreement (as amended, effective 16 February 1989). Online, available at: http://siteresources.worldbank.org/EXTABOUTUS/Resources/ibrd-articlesofagreement.pdf, accessed 12 August 2011.

World Bank (1989b). *Sub-Saharan Africa: From Crisis to Sustainable Growth*. Washington DC: World Bank.

World Bank (1991). *Report on Adjustment Lending II: Lessons for Eastern Europe*. Working Paper No. 693: 1–46.

World Bank (1994). *Adjustment in Africa: Reforms, Results and the Road Ahead*. New York: IBRD/World Bank.

World Bank (1995). *A Continent in Transition: Sub-Saharan Africa in the mid-1990s*. New York: IBRD/World Bank.

World Bank (1998). "Higher Impact Adjustment Lending (HIAL) in Sub-Saharan Africa: An Update." Online, available at: www.worldbank.org, accessed 18 October 2011.

World Bank (2000). *Can Africa Claim the 21st Century?* [The Gelb Report]. New York: IBRD/World Bank.

World Bank (2001). "Poverty Reduction Strategy Source Book." Online, available at: http://www.worldbank.org/poverty/strategies/index.htm, accessed 21 January 2011.

World Bank (2004). "From Adjustment Lending to Development Policy Lending: Update of World Bank Policy." World Bank Operations Policy and Country Services. Online, available at: www.Worldbank.org.

World Bank (2005). *Meeting the Challenge of Africa's Development: A World Bank Group Action Plan.* New York: IBRD/World Bank.

World Bank (2007). *Challenges of African Growth: Opportunities, Constraints and Strategic Directions.* New York: IBRD/World Bank.

World Bank (2010). *World Development Indicators 2010.* New York: IBRD/World Bank.

World Bank (2011). "Africa's Future and the World Bank's Support to it." The World Bank. Online, available at: http://www.worldbank.org/africastrategy, accessed 17 September 2011.

World Bank (2013). *Africa Pulse Rate: An Analysis of Issues Shaping Africa's Economic Future. October 2013.* Vol. 8. Online, available at: http://www.worldbank.org/content/dam/Worldbank/document/Africa/Report/Africas-Pulse-brochure_Vol8.pdf, accessed 13 February 2014.

World Bank/UNDP (1989). *Africa's Adjustment and Growth in the 1980s.* New York: World Bank/UNDP.

4 Africa's economic growth experience in empirical growth studies

Africa's economic growth performance has attracted a lot of attention from researchers and analysts across the disciplines. In an attempt to understand Africa's economic growth experience, many studies have been conducted and have offered different explanations for the observed growth patterns. Since the 1980s, when the impact of Africa's 'growth failure' became visible and incontrovertible, the challenge that has occupied most researchers and analysts has been how to explain this phenomenon. As has been observed, "Explaining Africa's slow growth in the second half of the 20th century remains a major challenge to economists and other analysts" (World Bank, 2000: 23). This challenge has actually become more pronounced in the current period when most African countries have recorded sustained economic growth, with serious questions being asked about whether this growth is another 'false start' in what has come to be known as the Africa Rising narrative (ARN). Despite a wealth of empirical studies on Africa's growth experience, it is evident that explaining it has proved to be as elusive as achieving sustained growth.

From a review of existing studies, it is apparent that although many have identified myriad variables which are alleged to account for the observed growth experience, actually explaining it has remained elusive, with little guidance from theory and empirical evidence. For example, at the heart of mainstream growth theories is the assertion that all the different paths that economies traverse "converge to a long-run equilibrium" (see Atkinson, 1969: 137), suggesting that, over time, the income gap between rich and poor countries shrinks as poor countries 'catch up' with rich ones. Since the mid-1950s this has not been the experience of Africa (Ndulu and O'Connell, 2008). Instead, African economies have actually been diverging. This observation has been confirmed even by the proponents of the convergence thesis, who observe that while on "average the developing world is now converging on the rich world, Africa is the only region to have been characterized by long-term divergence" (Collier, 2006: 188). If it is true that there is a growing gap between the income of rich (industrial) countries and poor countries in Africa, this constitutes 'anomalous data' in the paradigm, and the failure to adequately account for such data could be one indication of the inadequacy of the paradigm (see Kuhn, 1970).

Interrogating the paradigm

The call for a different paradigm and approach to understanding growth in developing countries is not new. During the 1940s and 1950s, as discussed in Chapter 5, the emergence of the 'sub-discipline' of development economics was predicated on the argument that "neoclassical economics did not apply terribly well to underdeveloped countries" (Sen, 1983: 746). Pioneers of development economics argued that developing countries had specific economic characteristics which could not be explained by the conventional neoclassical theories, adding that traditional economic analysis was not able to capture fundamental economic dynamics in non-industrial countries (see Hirschman, 1958, 1981). This assertion led to the rejection of what Albert Hirschman has referred to as "monoeconomics", and the call for a recasting of the neoclassical framework in order to understand conditions in developing countries. While this recasting within development economics did not amount to a paradigm shift, it has been observed that the mild rebellion against orthodox economic theory should not come as a surprise, because neoclassical economics has never applied too well anywhere (see Ruttan, 1998).[1] In the African context, arguments about whether the neoclassical framework is able to provide insights on Africa's development experience have been raised, and some analysts have argued that it is unable to explain the continent's growth experience and constraints (see Onimode, 1988, Nabudere, 1997; 2006, Murunga, 2005).

In trying to understand Africa's growth and development experience, there are two important reasons for looking at empirical studies on growth. The first is that these studies provide the empirical basis for the policies adopted by most international development agencies and financial institutions, especially the World Bank and the International Monetary Fund (IMF). Most of the policies and approaches discussed in Chapter 2 and Chapter 3 are supported by the findings of these empirical growth studies, often taking the findings of growth regression analysis literature as the basis for policy directives (Wade, 2002: 211). The second is that apart from providing empirical support for mainstream development policy, the explanations provided by these studies strongly influence and shape the dominant thinking on economic growth and development policy globally (see Jerven, 2009). As one would expect, not all empirical growth studies come to the same conclusion regarding the factors responsible for Africa's economic growth and development performance. Factors which are seen to significantly affect Africa's growth in one study, do not seem to do so in other studies. A number of factors may be common across the studies, but there are as many factors responsible for Africa's growth as there are empirical growth studies themselves. Thus, while each of the studies offers some empirically grounded explanations for Africa's economic performance, there is no agreement on what factors account for this experience and which ones are most significant.

Explaining elusive growth in Africa

Within the development research community there has been wide agreement that economic growth and development in Africa have been elusive. A joint

World Bank/UNECA (United Nations Economic Commission for Africa) report entitled *Can Africa Claim the 21st Century?* summarises the challenge of economic growth and development in Africa as follows:

> many development problems have become largely confined to Africa. They include lagging primary school enrolments, high child mortality, and endemic diseases – including malaria and HIV/AIDS – that impose costs on Africa at least twice those in any other developing region … Making matters worse, Africa's place in the global economy has been eroded, with declining export shares in traditional primary products, little diversification into new lines of business, and massive capital flight and loss of skills to other regions … the region's average income per capita averaged just $315 in 1997 when converted at market exchange rates … When expressed in terms of purchasing power parity (PPP) – which takes into account the higher costs and prices in Africa – real income averaged one-third less than in South Asia, making Africa the poorest region in the world. The region's total income is not much more than Belgium's, and is divided among 48 countries with median GDP of just over $2 billion – about the output of a town of 60,000 in a rich country.
>
> (World Bank, 2000: 1, 7)

Current sustained economic growth recorded since 2000 has not changed much of this portrait, especially regarding social development dimensions including education, healthcare and poverty.

In a study investigating the trend in Africa's Gross Domestic Product (GDP) per capita growth over a 45 year period, E.V. Artadi and Xavier Sala-i-Martin (2003) describe the African growth experience as the "worst economic tragedy of the XXth century". Similarly, William Easterly and Ross Levine (1995) refer to Africa's growth experience since the 1960s as a "tragedy: potential unfulfilled, with disastrous consequences". In a report entitled, *Economic Growth in the 1990s: Learning from a Decade of Reforms* (2005), the World Bank acknowledges that while in the 1960s it was believed that most African countries were "richer" than their Asian counterparts, and that the growth prospects for Africa were more positive, Africa's growth experience in the last 40 years has been below expectations.

> Over the last four decades, in the 28 countries[2] that have complete gross domestic product (GDP) series data for this period, the median growth rate has gradually but persistently declined and 11 countries now have income levels lower than at the time of their independence. Ranked by their growth performance since 1960, 15 of the world's 20 slowest performers and only two of the 20 best performers are in Africa.
>
> (World Bank, 2005: 274; see also Table 1.1)

While there has been wide agreement that economic performance in Africa has been relatively weak, there has been little agreement on the reasons for this. Similarly, whereas the extent and impact of Africa's weak economic performance has been loudly proclaimed, understanding and explaining this experience has proved to be quite difficult. Efforts to explain this growth experience have produced myriad empirical studies with numerous (often contradictory) explanations for the observed growth pattern. Difficulties in understanding Africa's growth experience have sometimes been expressed in pessimistic terms, with some analysts being smugly contemptuous of the continent – feeding into the 'Africa bashing' attitudes. While one can understand their frustration with this bewildering growth scenario, adopting a disdainful attitude towards Africa's growth experience is like blaming the data for not fitting into the theory. There seems to be a fundamental question here of whether the problem is with the data or the paradigm used to explain what we are observing in the data.

From the available evidence on economic growth in the continent, it is apparent that economic performance since the mid-1970s has fallen way below the levels anticipated by the dominant growth models (World Bank, 2005, Easterly and Levine, 1997, Collier and Gunning, 1999a; Ndulu and O'Connell, 2008). And the big question is, why? It is in trying to answer this question that numerous empirical growth studies on Africa emerged, initiated by Robert Baro's (1991) seminal work on cross-country growth regressions.

Currently, most explanations and the empirical evidence come mainly from neoclassical growth models and their mutations.[3] However, despite a wealth of empirical growth studies on Africa, it is apparent that explaining the observed growth pattern in the continent has proved to be as elusive as growth itself (see McPherson and Rakovski, 2001; Block, 2001), and the debate on the empirical evidence and theoretical approaches has intensified (see Jutta and Dirk, 2008). A critical review of these studies suggests that while tremendous effort has been made with regard to *identifying* factors that are believed to strongly influence Africa's growth experience, there has been little headway in explaining how these factors account for the observed growth dynamic. An even more unsatisfactory result is evident with regard to understanding why these factors are more fateful in Africa than elsewhere.

On the question of tools used to explain the African growth experience, it is important to bear in mind that most of the influential growth theories and models since the 1950s (particularly, Robert M. Solow, 1956 and Trevor Swan, 1956 [the Solow-Swan Model]) – which are still taught and used today – were devised to understand mid-twentieth century US economic growth dynamics (see Lucas, 1988). The big question is whether these theories and models are appropriate for understanding growth under conditions that are substantively different. Arguably, growth theories and the subsequent growth models "like much else in macroeconomics, [were] a product of the depression of the 1930s" and the war that followed it (see Solow, 1988: 308), and as such their application in other contexts is questionable (Ruttan, 1998: 2). For instance, some of the assumptions made in these models – such as perfect competition, market clearance, factor mobility and full employment – are not easily obtainable under conditions prevailing in most developing countries (see Ranis, 2003).

Further, cross-country growth regression analysis using time series data, which most empirical growth studies rely on, has many limitations (see Levine and

Renelt, 1992; Sala-i-Martin, 1997; Ndulu and O'Connell, 2008), making it even more difficult to yield any clear insight into complex issues such as growth in developing countries. The limitations are not just with the nature of the data on which the analysis relies (Srinivasan, 1994), but also the interpretation of the outcome of regression models. What, exactly, we can learn from the regression coefficients is 'the' big question. In most cases "the variables that are said to explain why Africa is different need some explanations themselves" (Lawrence, 2010: 32). For critics, "a little number-crunching rarely provides adequate insight into [the] development strategy of an entire nation" (Stiglitz, 2000), and many have questioned the usefulness of the aggregate figures on growth and other indicators (Freund, 2010).

In the African context this problem is worsened by the apparent lack of, or poor nature of, the data (Jerven, 2013, Deverajan, 2013), especially when proxies are created to make up for unavailable information. The resulting picture can only be fuzzy at best. Because of this, it becomes more difficult to provide clear understanding of the crucial issues on how to improve growth performance and development outcomes in the continent. Claims and counter-claims among the empirical growth analysts about what accounts for Africa's slow growth leave many observers wondering whether the actual problems have been grasped. Some analysts have tried to escape the need for understanding Africa by arguing that the actual problem is the way Africa *is*; the way 'Africa works'.

Empirical growth studies on Sub-Saharan Africa

Following Baro's (1991) seminal work on growth regression analysis using cross-country time series data, there has been an outburst of empirical studies conducted by individuals as well as team researchers. These studies have identified a wide range of explanatory variables which are believed to account for growth in developing regions, including Africa. With specific reference to the African empirical growth story, the variables offered include the standard right-hand growth regression variables such as geography, population dynamics, institutions and policy (Sachs and Warner, 1997); ethnic fractionalisation (Easterly and Levine, 1997); political assassination, aid dependence, lack of social capital, lack of financial depth, and corruption (Collier and Gunning, 1999a, Baro, 1996); precarious rainfall, lack of civil and political rights and inflation (Ghura and Hadjimichael, 1996); dictatorship (Chou and Khan, 2004); state legitimacy (Englebert, 2000a); and anti-growth policy syndromes (Fosu, 2009).

Due to the large number of empirical growth studies on Africa, the major studies discussed here are divided into four main categories. First there are those studies which refer to Africa's growth experience as a '*tragedy*'; second is a group of studies which focus on identifying sources of poor growth in Africa; third is a group of studies that seek to understand whether Africa's *growth dynamics are essentially different* from other regions; and finally a number of studies that focus on explaining Africa's growth experience in terms of *structural constraints*.

Africa's growth tragedy studies

The first Easterly-Levine study (1995)

Among the influential empirical growth studies on Africa are the two studies conducted by Easterly and Levine: "Africa's Growth Tragedy: A Retrospective 1960–89" (Easterly and Levine, 1995) and "Africa's Growth Tragedy: Policies and Ethnic Division" (Easterly and Levine, 1997). The first study uses the standard 'right-hand' growth regression variables[4] including initial GDP per capita, schooling, political stability, trade indicators, exchange rate and financial sector development. In addition to these, the study also includes variables on infrastructure, ethnic diversity, and the 'neighbourhood effect'. Using a ten-year annual average of per capita GDP growth rates between 1960 and 1987, Easterly and Levine (1995) find that policy variables – particularly overvalued local currencies (measured by the size of the black market premium as a proxy), the depth of the financial sector, infrastructure, ethnic diversity, geography and the neighbourhood effect – strongly affect growth in Africa. Interestingly, political instability (estimated by using assassinations and *coup d'etat* as proxies), trade indicators (openness) and inflation are found not to be significant and have no effect on the outcome of the core regression (see Easterly and Levine, 1995: 7).

The neighbourhood effect in this study occupies a central place in explaining the economic growth experienced in African countries. Using the weighted average GDP growth rates of neighbouring countries, Easterly and Levine observe that "each country's neighbours' growth rate has a surprisingly large and statistically significant effect on each country's own growth: one percentage point more growth by the neighbour in a given decade translates into higher own growth of .55 percentage point" (Easterly and Levine, 1995: 15).

If growth is that 'contagious', it can be expected that negative growth in a neighbouring country can have a drag effect on the growth of an adjacent country. This has been noted in the study, though the emphasis is on the fact that the 'contagion' often generates positive effects rather than negative ones, and the reason is that governments often do not copy bad policies or practices, and when they do, they may use them in ways that produce good effects (Easterly and Levine, 1995: 17). Again, if the neighbourhood factor had such strong positive effects, the sustained growth that we have seen in a few African countries would have pulled the neighbouring countries' growth rates to levels where Africa would have avoided the "worst tragedy of the twentieth century" (Artadi and Sala-i-Martin, 2003).

Certainly, if the neighbourhood effect was a true growth vector, being in a 'growing neighbourhood' would imply sustained growth even for a country that fails to create conditions for growth. But even a cursory inspection of growth trends in Africa shows that what we have are isolated cases of sustained growth in the sea of erratic growth that characterises the 1960–2007 period (see Table 1.2). Examples of sustained growth islands are Botswana, South Africa, Equatorial Guinea, Seychelles, Tunisia, Cape Verde, and Egypt, with low average coefficients of variation in Gross National Product (GNP) growth rates between 1960 and 2010, surrounded by Zimbabwe, Zambia, Angola and Namibia with high to extremely high volatility in growth (see Table 1.2). Even in the case of South Africa and Botswana, where one can make a claim of the neighbourhood effect, Botswana's economy experienced rapid growth when the South African economy was actually declining during the 1970s and 1980s and right up to the beginning of majority rule in 1994. Thus, one is at a loss regarding the direction in which the neighbourhood effect operates.

The other interesting variable that features prominently in the first Levine-Easterly study is ethnic diversity, or fractionalisation[5]. This variable accounts for a large percentage of the growth variance between Africa and other regions. According to Easterly and Levine (1995), results from the regression show that "ethnic diversity independently accounts for about 35% of Africa's growth differential with the rest of the world", and this figure rises to 45 per cent if the impact of ethnic diversity on policies is taken into account. The main reason why ethnic diversity explains much of the variance is that

> ethnically fragmented societies are prone to competitive rent-seeking by the different ethnic groups and have difficulty agreeing on public goods like infrastructure, education, and good policies. Furthermore, ethnic diversity may favour policies destructive to long-run growth like financial repression and overvalued exchange rates if such policies create rents for the group in power at the expense of the other groups.
>
> (Easterly and Levine, 1995: 12–13)

Another interesting finding of the first Easterly-Levine study is that when the Africa dummy[6] variable is entered alongside the 'neighbourhood' variable in the model, the former becomes insignificant (Easterly and Levine, 1995: 15). Results from the core regression show that when entered in the absence of the neighbourhood variable, the Africa dummy accounts for a large part of the difference in growth rates, accounting for 1.5 of the 2.3 percentage points in growth variance. The explanation given for this is that since the dummy represents what we cannot explain by standard growth regression variables, the neighbourhood effect introduced in the regression takes away the significance of the Africa dummy. A conclusion drawn from this result is that 'spill-over effects' from neighbours operate in many ways to account for a sizeable proportion of observed growth differentials. If the neighbourhood effect was so crucial, it is still not clear why countries in the same neighbourhood – such as Uganda, Kenya, Tanzania and Rwanda on the one hand, and the Democratic Republic of the Congo (DRC) on the other – grow in opposite directions.

The second Easterly-Levine study (1997)

The second Easterly and Levine study is a continuation of the investigation started in the first, but focusing on whether ethnic diversity impacts on the

Table 4.1. Ethnolinguistic fractionalisation indices for selected countries

15 most fractionalised	No. of ethnic groups	15 least fractionalised	No. of ethnic groups
Tanzania	93	Haiti	1
Uganda	90	Japan	1
Zaire (DRC)	90	Portugal	1
Cameroon	89	Hong Kong	2
India	89	Yemen	2
South Africa	88	Germany	3
Nigeria	87	Burundi	4
Cote d'Ivoire	86	Dominican Rep.	4
Central African Rep.	83	Egypt	4
Kenya	83	Ireland	4
Liberia	83	Italy	4
Zambia	82	Norway	4
Angola	78	Iceland	5
Mali	78	Jamaica	5
Sierra Leone	77	Jordan	5

Source: author, based on data from Easterly and Levine (1997: 1220).

quality of public institutions, public choices made, and eventually on growth. The study finds that ethnic diversity has direct as well as indirect effects on long-run growth. This study concludes that high ethnic diversity is strongly linked to a high black market premium, low schooling, poor infrastructure development and poor public service delivery. According to this study, "ethnically diverse societies not only by definition have distinct groups, but are also empirically less likely to have the kind of political institutions that create effective checks and balances, i.e., democratic institutions and rule of law" (Easterly and Levine, 1997: 1215). The explanation for this is that

> ethnic diversity influences economic performance, and most of this effect works indirectly through public policies, political stability, and other economic factors. We illustrate the economic importance of ethnic diversity by demonstrating that it helps account for Africa's growth tragedy.
>
> (Easterly and Levine, 1997: 1205)

The broader theoretical argument for this view is that a more fragmented society lacks the cohesion that is required to establish effective democratic institutions and instead promotes the emergence of several power bases or strong interest groups to which local politicians respond – instead of responding to the electorate as a whole. Table 4.1 shows a list of the 15 most ethnically fragmented and the 15 least ethnically divided countries based on the 'Soviet Measure' of ethnic fractionalisation.

Using countries such as those shown in Table 4.1, Easterly and Levine make a case for the effect of ethnic division on Africa's growth, arguing that 14 out of the 15 most ethnically fragmented countries in the world are in Africa, while eight out of the countries classified by the World Bank as high-income countries are among the least ethnically diverse countries, and none of the 15 most ethnically divided countries is among the high-income group (Easterly and Levine, 1997: 1219). Examples from Kenya and Ghana are used as typical cases of ethnically diverse countries, while Botswana represents a typical case of ethnic homogeneity. From this it is inferred that the episodic growth seen in Kenya and Ghana and the sustained economic growth recorded in Botswana over the past 40 years is evidence of the impact of ethnic diversity (Easterly and Levine, 1997: 1218). This assertion is based on results from a growth regression which produces a regression coefficient with a negative sign (−0.023), suggesting that ethnic diversity is negatively associated with growth. According to the authors, this magnitude of coefficient

> indicates that going from complete homogeneity to complete heterogeneity is associated with a fall in growth of 2.3 percentage points. A one-standard-deviation increase in ETHNIC [this is the variable representing ethnic diversity] is associated with a decrease in per capita growth of about 30 percent of a standard deviation in growth across countries.
>
> (Easterly and Levine, 1997: 1223–4)

There are, however, many serious concerns which can be raised with the evidence presented. Here I focus on the problems with the measure of ethnicity. Though the second Easterly-Levine study has made reference to four different measures of ethnicity, it has relied on the Soviet Measure and Soviet data.[7] Not only does the Soviet Measure have its own shortcomings (Easterly and Levine, 1997: 1221), there are serious controversies about the significant impact of ethnic diversity on growth. For instance, Jeffrey Sachs and Andrew Warner find ethnic fractionalisation to be statistically insignificant when entered into the model with other variables such as policy, location in the tropics, and demographic dynamics, though the coefficient has the predicted negative sign (Sachs and Warner, 1997: 345). Similarly, Block (2000) finds that the impact of ethnographic fragmentation on the quality of institutions and policies is insignificant. In another study looking at the relationship between state legitimacy and economic growth, the regression results show that ethnic fragmentation has little influence on economic growth in most African countries; a more legitimate state is said to score up to two percentage points higher than a less legitimate one – via the governance effect – regardless of its ethnic composition (see Englebert, 2000a). With these contradictory results from regression analysis, the evidence of the impact of ethnic diversity on growth can only be described as fragile, so far.

Further, the ethnolinguistic fractionalisation thesis assumes that policy decisions are made in an open and democratic manner where ethnic groups can exert considerable sway. But that is a bold assumption to make if one takes into account the fact that policy decisions, even in the most democratic nations, are not directly open to public vote. Even if one was to adopt the 'collective choice model' of the public choice theory (Buchanan and Tullock, 1962), it is not clear that the 'calculus of consent' will operate along ethnic lines. Even if policy processes were open to collective choice dynamics, it is mostly true that activities that lead to rent-seeking rarely operate on ethnic lines; they are often a result of the promptings of the 'economic man' in each of the individuals forming particular interest groups or specific class interests. Thus, the likelihood of selecting socially sub-optimal policies may not necessarily be a function of ethnicity, but more an effect of the special interest groups – which need not be ethnically constituted. If, for the sake of the argument, one attributes the brute 'rational egoistic' instinct to all politicians in Africa, it is more probable that the expected policy choices are likely to be influenced by the median voter, regardless of his or her ethnicity, unless one assumes that the median voter (the swing voter) in Africa is synonymous with ethnicity.

The Artadi and Sala-i-Martin study

The other research that refers to Africa's growth experience as a 'tragedy' is the Artadi and Sala-i-Martin (2003) study. This study, however, did not carry out growth regression analysis; instead, it relies on findings from other empirical studies. Key variables identified to explain Africa's growth tragedy include investment (especially foreign direct investments, FDI), human capital (education, health and life expectancy), geographic variables, and institutions. According to this study, one of the key constraints to Africa's growth is lack of investment – which is the result of the high risk and low return nature of investments in the continent. This makes capital expensive, hence there is low capital investment, and this in turn affects economic growth. Factors identified to have worsened Africa's investment climate include political instability, price volatility, failure of governments to respect private property and general macroeconomic instability (Artadi and Sala-i-Martin, 2003: 10).

While this study has profiled Africa's growth experience, it provides no explanation as to why price volatility or political instability, for instance, have become so crucial in accounting for Africa being the "worst economic tragedy of the XXth Century". Surely, price volatility is not only confined to Africa. Lack of investment as a result of low returns on investment in Africa appears in many explanations, including the World Bank's reports – but it is not clear whether low returns on investment are in turn a function of low investment itself. The circularity of the argument here makes it difficult to identify other possible underlying causes of low investment, such as poor infrastructure and the high costs of services including transport, communications and energy. This problem has been spotted by Benno Ndulu and Stephen O'Connell (2008) as the general problem of endogeneity associated with growth regression analysis.

Sources of growth studies

The Sachs-Warner study

Among the most influential studies in this category is Sachs and Warner's (1997) work, "Sources of Slow Growth in African Economies". The other studies considered in this paper are Amor Tahari *et al.*'s (2004) "Sources of Growth in Sub-Saharan Africa" and O'Connell and Ndulu's (2000) "Africa's Growth Experience: A Focus on Sources of Growth". Like other empirical growth studies, Sachs and Warner use cross-country growth regression to identify the variables which they believe account for the variance in growth between and within regions. This study argues that Africa's growth dynamics can be explained by the standard right-hand variables. As such there is no need for "a special Africa theory" to explain growth dynamics in Africa (Sachs and Warner, 1997: 336). Although they admit that there are unique features in Africa such as prolonged colonialism, ethnic diversity and geographical features, they argue that these don't affect Africa's economic growth differently from other parts of the world. In Sachs and Warner's view, what explains the larger part of Africa's poor growth performance is a cluster of variables which can be summarised into two categories: poor policy and institutional quality.

Notably, the Sachs and Warner study makes a number of innovations including the construction of an institutional quality index,[8] an openness index,[9] and the ranking of variables in order of the size of their impact on growth. This study also added the natural resource abundance variable to the regression and finds it to be negatively correlated with growth. Abundance of natural resources, especially minerals and oils, is reported to affect growth negatively via the 'Duct Disease' and 'resource curse'. Although Sachs and Warner (1997) note that this association is questionable, the natural resources variable has an estimated coefficient of −3.26 in the regression, and on the basis of this it has been estimated that an increase in the share of natural resources in exports from 0.1 to 0.2 per cent reduces growth by 0.33 percentage points (Sachs and Warner, 1997: 348). Other studies have confirmed this negative association between growth and natural resource abundance (see Sachs and Warner, 2001; te Velde, 2006).

Interestingly, Sachs and Warner do not find the Africa dummy or the neighbourhood effect variable significant (1997: 350). In terms of ranking variables in order of the magnitude of impact on growth, 'openness' has the biggest impact – accounting for 0.9 of a percentage point – followed by life expectancy at 0.7, institutional quality and central government saving, both at 0.6, natural resources abundance at 0.5, growth in the economically active population and tropical climate, both at 0.4, and land-lockedness at 0.3 (Sachs and Warner, 1997: 350). Although other variables are said to affect growth in one way or another, openness and the quality of institutions have received remarkable attention in this study.

This finding confirms the mainstream economic theory that integration into the global economy is an engine for growth through dynamics such as the diffusion of technology, increased efficiency in resource allocation, factor mobility – especially physical and financial capital – and best practices, all of which increase total factor productivity. It is therefore not surprising that Sachs and Warner (1997: 346) reach the conclusion that "for the average country in the sample, a switch from a closed regime to a completely open regime is estimated to raise the annual growth rate by 2.21 percentage points". The influence of these findings on the policies prescribed by the World Bank and the IMF in Africa is obvious.

From a large number of variables examined, Sachs and Warner found ten variables that significantly influence growth in Africa, and it is estimated that these account for 90 per cent of the cross-country growth variance observed between 1965 and 1990 (Sachs and Warner, 1997: 349). The overall conclusion in this study is that much of Africa's poor economic performance originates from the policy variable (mainly openness, government savings) and institutional quality. Consequently, it is argued that if issues related to these factors were 'appropriately' addressed, we could have seen Africa's GDP per capita growing steadily at an average rate of 4.3 per cent during the period under observation (Sachs and Warner, 1997: 358).

The Tahari study

This study examined sources of growth in Africa, focusing on the role of policy. The study relies on growth accounting techniques to identify the source(s) of poor economic performance in Africa between 1960 and 2002. A key source of growth identified in this study is total factor productivity (TFP). Tahari *et al.* (2004) find that growth in Africa has been affected by factor accumulation, reflected by lack of growth in factor productivity and averaging zero over the observation period. The evidence presented shows that from 1960 to 2002, close to half of the countries in Sub-Saharan Africa (SSA) experienced a decline in TFP, with only five countries (Botswana, Equatorial Guinea, Mauritius, Swaziland and Uganda) experiencing growth in TFP of over 1 per cent. The study asserts that the improved growth rates observed in the region between 1990 and 2002 coincides with the growth in TFP, especially in countries that consistently implemented IMF and World Bank prescribed reforms. From this assertion, it is argued that the "increased TFP growth during 1997–2002 in countries whose programmes were on track reflected the efficiency gains from the implementation of macroeconomic and structural reforms" (Tahari *et al.*, 2004: 8).

The obvious question that this assertion begs is, if TFP is so critical to growth, what causes an increase in TFP? Tahari *et al.* (2004) suggest four ways that can lead to the growth in TFP; namely, good quality institutions, human capital development, a favourable macroeconomic policy environment, and diversification in the economy. A critical issue that has not been explained is, why do these factors hinder growth in Africa such that we end up with a growth tragedy? In a way, the explanation provided runs the danger of becoming a circular argument. If poor institutions and policy affect TFP growth in Africa, why is this so endemic in Africa? A typical response to such a question is that poor growth is associated with poor development of public institutions and policy, which have a negative impact on growth (Easterly and Levine, 2002). But since the failure to address policy constraints is itself seen as a consequence of poor economic growth and development conditions, the explanation does not go beyond stating that good policies are important for growth – which is obvious.

The O'Connell-Ndulu study

This study tries to explain Africa's growth experience by focusing on the indirect impact of bad policies. The study uses an augmented Solow model, similar to Anke Hoeffler's (2000) and Sachs and Warner's (1997) models. Using a three-step approach (starting with a baseline regression, followed by estimation of partial correlations with the policy variable, and finally the full specification of the model with both baseline and policy variables), the study identifies policies which affect factor accumulation as the major source of Africa's poor growth. Results from the core regression show that low factor productivity growth accounts for half of the variance observed in the growth rates between African and non-African cases. According to O'Connell and Ndulu (2000: 19), the other half of the variance can be accounted for by low physical and human capital accumulation. Policy variables in this study, though robust in the growth literature on SSA, are only found to operate indirectly by limiting capital accumulation and productivity growth. A conclusion reached is that "Africa's slow growth is explained by relatively slow accumulation of capital, low productivity growth, and pressures from high population growth rates" (O'Connell and Ndulu, 2000: 19).

Here again we see explanations similar to the Bank and the Fund's account of the causes of economic growth and development challenges in Africa, with an emphasis on internal factors as the main causes. There is also a danger of running into a circular argument here which arises from the general problem of endogeneity typical of most regression analyses (see Ndulu *et al.*, 2008).

Does Africa grow differently?

The Africa dummy

A number of empirical studies have tried to investigate the question of whether Africa's growth dynamics differ from those in other parts of the world. Empirical investigation of this question has largely been framed in terms of the Africa or regional dummy (Hoeffler, 2000: 30, O'Connell and Ndulu, 2000: 13), and the argument has been that if the Africa dummy variable is consistently significant, then this can be taken as evidence of Africa's growth dynamics being substantively different from the rest of the world. In other words, the Africa dummy represents the unexplained variance in growth rates between Africa and the rest of the world (Ndulu and O'Connell, 2008). Many empirical studies (especially the third generation empirical growth studies) find that the Africa dummy is not consistently significant, and therefore conclude that growth dynamics in Africa are not substantively different from those found in other parts of the world (Sachs and Warner, 1997, Rodrick, 1998, Easterly and Levine, 1997, Bloom and Sachs, 1999; Hoeffler, 2000, O'Connell and Ndulu, 2000). Notably, Hoeffler (2000) addresses the question of whether Africa grows differently from the rest of the world, and the results from an augmented Solow model show that the Africa dummy is insignificant when the "unobserved country specifics" – mainly investment and population growth – are controlled for.

But there are some studies which have maintained that the growth dynamics in Africa, because of differences in underlying conditions, operate in a significantly different manner. Block (2001), Collier and Gunning (1999a; 1999b,), Baro (1991, 1996), and McPherson and Rakovski (2001) are some of the studies which support this conclusion. A common observation regarding the Africa dummy is that, like most other variables in the empirical growth regression literature, the outcome of whether a variable is significant or not depends much on what other variables are simultaneously entered in the model. Results from most empirical growth studies show that the Africa dummy variable is significant when regressed alongside some variables, while insignificant alongside others. A typical example of this is the Easterly and Levine (1997) study referred to above. In the core regression, the coefficient on the Africa dummy is negative and significant, but when the neighbourhood variable is added to the model, while the negative sign remains on the coefficient the Africa dummy becomes insignificant. Thus, the Africa dummy in the empirical growth studies yields very little explanatory insight into the economic growth and development challenges in Africa.

The Block study (2001)

On the basis of results from an 'augmented reduced form' regression model, Steven Block (2001) concludes that the assumptions made by empirical studies which assert non-difference in growth dynamics between Africa and the rest of the world are not valid for two reasons. First, equality between African and non-African cases is dubious, given the difference in the coefficient slopes obtained in the regression parameters. Second, the assumptions fail to take into account the relevant channels of growth transmission through which the variables operate. Aware of these problems, Block explores whether the same variables, such as population growth, can have a different marginal impact on Africa when compared with the rest of the world, and "whether the determinants of the variables are the same in Africa as elsewhere" (2001: 444). On the basis of the results from the augmented model, Block contends that by

> limiting the analysis to a single 'reduced form' equation, and by forcing growth rates in Africa and elsewhere to have the same sensitivity to given influences, previous studies have assumed away potentially important differences in the mechanisms of growth in Africa. Several of these differences can have important implications for policies designed to promote economic

growth, and may help to explain the mixed results to date from policy reform efforts.

(Block, 2001: 445)

He further argues that the equalisation of Africa with the rest of the world has actually contributed to a dangerous policy approach of 'one-size-fits-all' adopted by the international financial institutions (IFIs). When estimating the impact of fixed effects, Block (2001) finds that population and education dynamics affect growth differently in Africa when compared to non-African countries. For example, while one year of education is found to be significant in reducing population growth in non-African samples, it is insignificant in the African sample. According to Block, this suggests that there are "indirect growth penalties" on certain variables in Africa which do not exist elsewhere. He further argues (2001: 462) that there are "important ways in which Africa does grow differently, usually failing to reap the indirect benefits of several positive influences and paying a harsher penalty for several negative influences on growth".

The McPherson and Rakovski study

Using different regression techniques to control for autocorrelation among the variables in the model, Malcolm McPherson and Tzvatena Rakovski (2001) reach a similar conclusion, arguing that the use of single regression equations fails to capture the unique growth experience in Africa, and the underlying conditions for it. They point out that the ratio of formal to informal economy, at different growth stages, has given rise to errors that are not captured by single equation regression models. McPherson and Rakovski (2001) further contend that extended periods of slow growth have a unique reinforcement factor that makes Africa's growth dynamics different from other regions.

The Collier and Gunning study

However, Paul Collier and James Gunning (1999b), while identifying a number of factors – including soil quality, low population density, tropical climate, colonial effects, the average size of African economies and inappropriate agricultural policies which are unique to Africa – all of which predispose Africa to slow growth, conclude that the poor policy environment explains the divergent growth path observed in Africa.

> Coastal Africa is not intrinsically markedly worse-endowed in any geographical sense than much of coastal Asia or Brazil … By contrast, it is easy to point to policies which until recently have been dysfunctional. Even as of 1998, Africa had the worst policy environment in the world.
>
> (Collier and Gunning, 1999b)

These often contradictory outcomes from empirical growth studies make it difficult to ascertain the usefulness of empirical growth studies in explaining the African growth experience. A useful explanation would clarify, for instance, whether African economies respond differently to openness, or fiscal deficit, or population growth, or schooling – and if so, why.

Structural constraint studies

The Ghura-Hadjimichael study

Other than the World Bank reports discussed in Chapter 3, there have been a number of empirical studies which explain Africa's growth experience in terms of structural rigidities. Among these studies are the Ghura-Hadjimichael (1996) study, and the Calamitsis-Basu-Ghura (1999) study. Daneshwar Ghura and Michael Hadjimichael focus on the impact of structural and institutional reform on growth. The basic argument advanced is that structural distortion – such as the price controls, subsidies, state monopolies, trade restrictions, overvalued exchange rates and large budget deficit ratios present in many African economies – create constraints which hamper growth in the long-run via inefficient allocation and use of resources. Examining variables such as population growth, the ratio of private and public investment to GDP, human capital development, inflation levels and trends, the levels of government deficit, real exchange rates, terms of trade, growth of export volume and a dummy on the implementation of structural reforms, including variables on political rights and inadequacy of rainfall, the study finds that countries that have higher growth rates are those which have been consistent in implementing structural and institutional reforms. Results from ordinary least square (OLS) regressions support the view that consistent implementation of reforms have resulted in higher investment ratios to GDP, low population growth, high primary and secondary enrolments, lower budget deficits and increased export volumes. The study also finds that

> an increase in the private investment ratio of one standard deviation is estimated to raise growth by 1 percentage point, and an increase in the government investment ratio of one standard deviation is estimated to raise growth by about 0.5 percentage point.[10]
>
> (Ghura and Hadjimichael, 1996: 622)

The obvious conclusion drawn from this is that private sector investment provides more growth momentum than public investments, and that the former should be promoted.

The Calamitsis-Basu-Ghura study

The Calamitsis-Busa-Ghura (1999) study is, in fact, an adaptation of the Ghura-Hadjimichael (1996) study. It employs the same regression model and examines the same variables, except that it replaces the 'inadequate rainfall' variable with a dummy on the occurrence of war, and discards the CFA dummies. Consequently, most of the findings are the same, mainly that policy variables (budget deficit to GDP ratio, effective exchange rate, trade regimes, private investment and institutional reforms) are all significant, together with a few standard growth variables such as population, terms of trade and human capital accumulation. From these results, it is argued, that "countries that implemented IMF-supported programs on a sustained basis were able to achieve faster growth than other countries" (Calamitsis *et al.*, 1999: 11). Both studies come to the conclusion that the empirical evidence supports the view that implementation of IMF-driven structural reform programmes has a positive and significant correlation with growth in the continent.

Without going much into the technical details of these studies, it is apparent that the two overlooked the fact that the implementation of structural reforms has been itself a function of institutional capacity and initial conditions. Most importantly, the impact of structural reforms is highly contested, and has not been measured accurately (see Easterly, 2005). Even the World Bank and the IMF have not been clear about what such reforms have achieved and whether the failure or success of reforms can be attributed to the content of the programmes or the implementation process. Further, there are countries within the SSA region which have consistently implemented reforms and yet have experienced episodic growth (see UNECA, 1989). Examples include Zambia, Ghana, Benin, Malawi and Madagascar, which are reported to be the "sustained reformers", yet they are the worst performers in terms of per capita growth between 1980 and 2001, with average growth rates ranging from 0.1 per cent for Ghana to –1.3 per cent for Madagascar (World Bank, 2007: 275, 278). Conversely, there are countries in the region (Botswana, Mauritius and Equatorial Guinea) which are not "reformers" in the conventional sense and yet they have recorded the highest growth rates (World Bank, 2007: 275). Therefore, claims that the sustained growth experienced in Africa since 2000 is a product of the IMF-World Bank reforms implemented during the 1990s (World Bank, 2011) are not supported by the evidence. Many of the fastest growing economies in Africa since 2000 – Nigeria, Ethiopia, Mozambique, Angola, Chad and Sierra Leone – have not consistently implemented IMF/World Bank reforms.

One important discrepancy to note about the structural constraint studies is that, in general, while there have been significant improvements in structural and institutional variables in many countries on the continent[11] (World Bank, 2007), there is no convincing evidence correlating growth with implementation of reforms, especially in Africa. Such a correlation is often spurious and intractable. As Paul Krugman has pointed out, while policy variables such as the black market premium, openness and the size of the public sector have all improved in many developing countries, "the real economic performance of countries that had recently adopted Washington consensus policies ... was distinctly disappointing" (cited in Easterly, 2001: 3). Thus, the result from implementation of structural reforms on growth can only be described as mixed. The World Bank assessment of the outcome of these reforms arrived at a similar conclusion, not-ing that structural reforms have yielded disappointing results. To echo Easterly, although "extremely bad policy can probably destroy any chance of growth, it does not follow that good macroeconomic or trade policy alone can create the conditions for high steady state growth" (Easterly, 2005: 3).

What have we learned from empirical growth studies on Africa?

At this point it is important to note that there are several other empirical studies conducted on Africa; the ones discussed above are only some of the influential studies. Similarly, there are several other attempts at explaining Africa's growth experience other than the empirical studies. But, from the growth studies dis-cussed above, a number of general observations can be made.

First, it is clear that these studies have identified a substantial number of vari-ables which are said to be crucial in understanding growth, particularly in Africa. While some of the variables overlap across studies, the number of variables identi-fied seems to be growing with time. For instance, while Levine and David Renelt (1992) reported over 50 variables which different studies found to be correlated with growth, Sala-i-Martin (1997) gathered about 60, and in 2000 Michael Bleaney and Akira Nishiyama reported 86. Given this large number of variables it is increasingly difficult to identify the *crucial* from the *opportunistic* regressors.

What is even more confusing is the fact that different studies identify differ-ent variables to be influential in accounting for the observed growth pattern in Africa, leading to an unresolved controversy over which variables really matter. For example, in the studies discussed above, while the Sachs and Warner (1997) and Easterly and Levine (1995) studies found the Africa dummy variable to be statistically insignificant, Baro (1991), Collier and Gunning (1999a; 1999b), Block (2001), and Sala-i-Martin *et al.* (2004) found it to have a significant influ-ence on growth. After a review of some of these studies, it has been suggested that the statistical significance of the Africa dummy reported by other empirical studies is due to the omission of critical variables entered into the regression model (Burger and du Plessis, 2006: 10). There are many other disputed vari-ables. For instance, while the neighbourhood variable is found to have a "sur-prisingly large and statistically significant effect" by Easterly and Levine (1995: 15), Sachs and Warner (1997) find it to be insignificant in explaining Africa's slow growth.

In three different studies (Sachs and Warner, 1997, Baro, 1996 and Easterly and Levine, 1997), out of the total 26 regressors used in them, only one (log of initial per capita GDP) is found to be significant in all three. Similarly, in a well-known study to test the robustness of the variables often used in empirical growth studies, Levine and Renelt (1992) and Levine and Sara Zervos (1993) find that there are 'very few' *consistently* robust variables. Most of them are sig-nificant when entered into a model along with certain variables, but become insignificant when entered with other variables. One of the implications of these inconsistencies is that the problems of endogeneity and attribution are perennial in most empirical growth studies, despite the incorporation of various techniques to control for these effects. As Ndulu and O'Connell (2008: 29) contend, the "typical growth regression is … likely to be subject to some degree of endogeneity bias, whether from true simultaneity – investment determines growth, but growth also determines investment – or from the omission of key determinants that are correlated with the included variables".

Commenting on the status of empirical evidence in growth studies, Solow notes that evidence

> seem[s] altogether too vulnerable to bias from omitted variables, to reverse causation, and above all to the recurrent suspicion that the experience of very different national economies are not to be explained as if they represent different 'points' on some well-defined surface.
>
> (Solow, 1994: 51)

A review of the various empirical studies suggests that the empirical evidence provided is not only weak in most of the studies (Levine and Zervos, 1993), but that it is also contradictory (Burger and du Plesssis, 2006). This has generally weakened the explanatory power of these studies.

Second, what seems evident from the above discussion is that it is easy to identify variables that are seemingly associated with growth. However, using these variables to explain how they contribute to poor economic performance has remained a difficult and controversial task. In the current situation where we have a proliferation of variables from growth regressions models (Solow, 1994, Fine, 2003), even appealing to theory does not seem to help resolve the diverging empirical evidence (see Sala-i-Martin, 1997). Clearly, it is one thing to identify variables associated with growth, but it is quite another to explain how the identified variable(s) operate or contribute to the observed phenomenon, and, most importantly, to explain why they are more entrenched in particular regions. Further, there seems to be a big question on the gap between statistical and economic significance; what is *statistically* significant may not necessarily have a significant bearing on economic growth dynamics. Making this distinction is even critical when theory itself gives little guidance in deciding which variable(s) are robust and economically important (see Levin and Zervos, 1993; Sala-i-Martin, 1997). Moreover, drawing an inference from coefficient statistics to explain growth dynamics requires greater caution. A more fundamental and philosophical question is, what exactly do the regression coefficients tell us?

Third, most of the empirical studies discussed above provide proximate explanations of the growth experience observed in Africa, which tends to lead to a circular argument. If, for instance, one claims that lack of TFP growth accounts for slow growth in most African countries, the question that follows is why has there been a lack of TFP growth in Africa? The standard reply is to point to institutions and policies (see Sachs and Warner, 1997; Ghura and Hadjimichael, 1996) as being the cause of poor factor productivity performance. However, this does not explain the underlying reasons as to why TFP has affected growth in the way it does; what this does is demonstrate that TFP is important for growth. Little insight is generated on why poor TFP growth affects general growth in Africa in the way that it does. While the Robert Hall and Charles Jones (1998) study scored some significant success in explaining the impact of TFP on growth across countries, the differential impact of TFP remains to be explained. It is not clear why TFP affects growth in Africa differently from other regions. As in other studies, what needs to be explained is offered as the explanation (see Lawrence, 2010). Here one is inclined to agree with Vernon W. Ruttan (1998) that explanations beyond identifying 'sources of growth' are probably beyond the capability of the models on which the empirical studies rely.

Fourth, all the studies discussed above assume that the neoclassical, or new growth models, provide the appropriate framework for explaining economic growth everywhere. No question is raised regarding whether this is an appropriate framework for understanding growth in conditions that are different. Given that the neoclassical models were formulated to understand growth experienced in the mid-twentieth century USA (see Lucas, 1988; Ruttan, 1998), why should we assume that these same models are capable of explaining economic growth dynamics in circumstances that are substantively different? In a more general debate, Gustav Ranis (2003), Ruttan (1998) and Lant Pritchett (1997) have raised questions about the suitability of neoclassical and new growth theories in explaining growth dynamics in developing countries. Ranis (2003) in particular is sceptical of using models which are based on assumptions that rarely occur in developing (and even in many developed) countries.

Although in some instances the researcher can see that these theories and models do not explain the data adequately, there is little questioning of the underlying assumptions. When faced with model dilemmas, many researchers resort to 'augmenting models', and the use of 'instrumental variables' – trying by every means to make the data fit the model (Romer, 1994). Under these circumstances it becomes difficult to have a clear picture of what is going on. Thus, while the models have certainly identified sources of growth,

> answers to more fundamental questions, such as why some countries save and invest more than others, why some countries invest a larger share of GNP on education or on R&D ... remain beyond the reach of the models employed by both neoclassical and new growth economists.
>
> (Ruttan, 1998: 12)

One of the major obstacles in developing a clearer understanding of the growth experience in the many regions outside the industrialised economies can be attributed to the failure to go beyond core neoclassical assumptions. As a result, discussions on theory and policy of economic growth have remained insensitive to the difference in underlying conditions (Pritchett, 1997: 15). In a way, the growth theories that are meant to help understand the economic dynamics are themselves becoming *obstacles* to a clear grasp of them.

Growth models and economic growth

Full discussion of growth theories and models is beyond the scope of this chapter. The purpose of this brief overview is to provide the context to the current debate. A growth theory provides a set of simple assumptions that help to explain what happens to an economy under a specified set of conditions, and a growth model is an econometric instrument used to mathematically represent these assumptions and the relations they imply. In this sense, a growth theory is not a forecasting tool that gives precise information or determines the exact course of events in the economy (Harold, 1939). Such a model will be mathematically intractable and less useful, practically (Fine, 2003). Fundamentally, a growth theory should be a useful tool for distinguishing the "*crucial*" from the "*obvious*" in the growth process (Lucas, 1988: 13).

Up to the present, several growth models have been proposed, but the most dominant can be classified into three categories: the classical (static), neoclassical (old or exogenous) and the endogenous (new) growth models. Although the endogenous (new) growth models seem to have elicited great excitement and interest since the late 1980s and throughout the 1990s, most of the empirical studies continue to employ the neoclassical growth models (Baro, 1996). This, however, might not be surprising given that it is the neoclassical models, especially Solow's model, which are taught in schools and are found in most text books on macroeconomics and development economics.

One of the fundamental principles of the exogenous (old) growth theory is that growth rates across countries have the tendency to converge to the Steady-state Balanced Growth (SSBG) or long-run equilibrium, in spite of the differences in the initial condition – such as per capita income, technology taste and saving rates among countries. A key assertion in this principle is that countries with low initial income per capita (poor countries) are expected to grow faster than countries with higher per capita income (rich countries), resulting in the convergence (narrowing/catching up) of per capita income over the long-run if they are not closed economies. To capture the several disclaimers that should accompany this assertion, many analysts refer to this narrowing of the per capita income gap as '*conditional* convergence'. According to the conditional convergence hypothesis, African countries should have experienced higher than average growth rates because of their low initial income per capita (Hoeffler, 2000: 31).[12] Since poor countries like Mali, Gambia, Ethiopia, Liberia and Zambia are anticipated to grow faster, it is believed that, in the long-run, per capita income of the poorer countries can be expected to 'catch up', and therefore close the per capita income gap with industrialised countries like Australia, Canada, Japan, Germany, the UK and the USA.

However, when it comes to the empirical evidence, whether one is referring to 'sigma' (λ)[13] or 'beta' (β)[14] convergence, the African context is not borne out by the available evidence. As Figure 4.1 shows, there is no sign of convergence between the per capita income of SSA and the high-income countries of the Organisation for Economic Cooperation and Development (OECD) club.

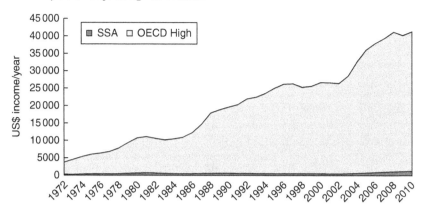

Figure 4.1. Gross National Income (GNI) per capita of SSA and high-income countries

Source: author, based on data from the World Bank's World Databank (http://databank.worldbank. org/ddp/home.do).

Note: 1972 is the earliest year for which comparable per capita income data for OECD and SSA countries are available.

While there may have been convergence among OECD countries, the notion of convergence evaporates when other poor countries from the developing world are included. In terms of the current empirical evidence of income per capita, "All of us know that much of the convergence since 1870 disappears when the net is widened to include Eastern Europe ... and if it were widened still further to include the Third World convergence would totally evaporate" (Williamson, 1995: 2). Therefore, when talking about convergence one has to answer several critical questions: convergence among whom? Convergence over what period? Convergence of what (Williamson, 1995: 2)?

These unresolved discrepancies between theory and reality in the exogenous growth theory motivated the emergence of the new or endogenous growth theories and models (see Romer, 1994). One of the key discrepancies in endogenous growth theory is the apparent inability to account for what seems to be divergence of income across countries (Romer, 1994, Pritchett, 1997, Ruttan, 1998). A number of studies have indicated that existing data support the convergence hypothesis only when high and middle-income countries are considered[15] (Baumol, 1986, Baro and Sala-i-Martin, 1992, Romer, 1994, Pritchett, 1997, Easterly, 2001). Baro's (1991) study shows that there is no evidence in the data to support the convergence hypothesis across countries. He argues that the "hypothesis that poor countries tend to grow faster than rich countries seems to be inconsistent with the cross-country evidence" (Baro, 1991: 408). Pritchett's study (1997: 10) also shows that convergence is obtained only when the per capita incomes of developed countries are compared; when poor countries are included in the sample, there is "substantial divergence between the top and bottom" countries.

Countries in the SSA region show a clear example of divergence in per capita income by any measure. Available data do not show any evidence of catching up, as Figure 4.1 shows. Since the mid-1970s the gap between the per capita income of OECD countries[16] and SSA has been growing. If convergence was in fact taking place, we should have seen the income per capita gap between these two groups of countries closing. Even if one includes the period from 2000 to 2010, a time period when per capita income in Africa has been growing at an average of 2.5 per cent (see Chapter 7), there is no sign of catching up. Whether one considers real wages, labour productivity or per capita income, there is no evidence that any of these indicators for Africa are closing the gap with those in developed countries.

Although it appears as if there is some catching up taking place during the 2000s, the gap has in fact been growing since the 1970s. Even if the purchasing power parity (PPP) dollar is used instead of the official exchange rate dollar, the gap between these two sets of countries is indisputable. This discrepancy between theory and evidence has resulted in what some authors have referred to as the enduring "convergence controversy"[17] (Romer, 1994).

In more recent growth models (the endogenous or new growth models), some of the assumptions of the neoclassical growth models have been revised. Paul Romer (1986), Robert Lucas (1988) and Sergio Rebelo (1991) in particular have revised the old growth model by dropping the diminishing returns assumption, and adopting the constant returns to scale, especially capital (Solow, 1988; 1994). By dropping the diminishing returns to capital assumption, the models have been able to do away with the unconditional convergence principle, demonstrating that per capita growth rates in the long-run "need not converge; growth may be persistently slower in less developed countries and may even fail to take place" (Romer, 1986: 1003). Lucas proposes a similar model under which a country with low human capital accumulation may continue with low per capita growth rate, "permanently below an initially better endowed economy" (Lucas, 1988: 25).

While this may help account for the existence of divergence (Rebelo, 1991), the growth dynamics in many parts of the developing world remain poorly understood (Ruttan, 1998). If there is low human capital accumulation in Africa, for instance, why are we not seeing the technological catch-up or spillover effects that the theory predicts? If Africa has low human capital accumulation, human capital theory predicts that physical capital would have higher marginal returns and we should therefore see growth in capital inflows into Africa. But what we have seen is just the opposite: human capital is moving from where it is scarce to regions where it is more abundant (Lucas, 1988). The same goes with capital; there is more capital flight from Africa than any other region of the world (see Chapter 7).

More broadly, the challenge of growth models revolves around the use of cross-country growth regression. With the assemblage of an international database by Robert Summers and Alan Heston[18] (1991), cross-country *growth* studies have become a common feature in the *empirical* growth literature. This proliferation of empirical research, however, cannot only be attributed to the availability of comparable data, but also to the growing controversy within the growth the-oretical framework (Bleaney and Nishiyama, 2000, Fine, 2003). As alluded to earlier, evidence from the empirical studies points to an enduring controversy regarding which variable(s) explain much of the variance across countries. Part of the controversy arises from the reliance on regression results which have many limitations, as noted above. Levine and Zervos (1993), Levine and Renelt (1992) and Sala-i-Martin (1997) have extensively discussed some of the weaknesses of growth regressions.

Crisis in the paradigm?

So far, it is apparent that empirical growth studies have probably made little pro-gress in coherently explaining Africa's growth experience apart from identifying more than 80 variables which are alleged to be responsible for the observed growth pattern. Multiplicity of variables and lack of consistency in the empirical support may be a sign of the failure to account for the observed growth experience by the theories themselves. Existence of unaccounted for 'data' within a given theory can be taken as a sign of cracks in a paradigm (see Kuhn, 1970). In the case of Africa's growth experience, the controversy and proliferation of variables may be a signal of the failure of existing growth paradigms to accommodate the Africa growth data. As Thomas S. Kuhn has argued, the proliferation of explanations and models is itself an indication of the inability of the paradigm to sufficiently accommodate all the data – a situation that is equivalent to a paradigm crisis. Using examples from natural sciences, mainly physics and chemistry, Kuhn observes that the "pro-liferation of versions of a theory is a very usual symptom of crisis", an indication of the decreasing utility of the existing paradigm (1970: 71).

Since the African growth experience amounts to an anomaly in the orthodox growth paradigm, it presents a great opportunity to stimulate debate about alter-native paradigms that can better account for the existing data. But as in natural science, the revision or even abandoning of long-serving paradigms is often not occasioned by the mere existence of unaccounted for data (Kuhn, 1970: 67–8). When a paradigm is challenged, the response is often to explain away the unfit-ting data, and the discussion on growth can be reduced to testing and rejecting deviant (unorthodox) views and evidence (Romer, 1994). In an effort to safe-guard the paradigm, the problem is shifted from the observed inconsistency in the data to the quality of data and the poor tools we have – we are limited by the data and the lack of an effective methodology, is a common story. As Romer (1994: 11) has noted with regard to growth theories, it is as though "data are the only scarce resources in economic analysis".

Typical of a research community, growth researchers have been focusing on modifying elements of the paradigm by augmenting Solow's model with all sorts of instrumental variables and proxies to control for this and that. It is as though nature (observations) has violated the paradigm's expectations (Kuhn, 1970). Even if the African growth anomaly has attracted the attention of eminent men and women in the profession (Hoeffler, 2000: 30), the focus has been on providing explanations to eliminate the anomalies rather than question theory itself or reassess the efficacy of the paradigm. There are many analysts and researchers who strongly believe that, in the long-run, Africa will eventually catch up. But as the famous Keynesian adage runs, "in the long run, there will be no long run, we will all be dead!"

In view of the fact that current growth theories and models have not adequately accounted for Africa's growth experience, it is probably appropriate to begin to critically examine the framework and the tools used. In the Kuhnian sense, a crisis in the paradigm signals two things. The first is that the puzzle-solving qualities of the paradigm have diminished; there is failure to account for all the evidence (Kuhn, 1970). The second is that a crisis often directs the research efforts towards finding ways to account for the deviant data, which may lead to a search for a new paradigm. The search for a new paradigm which can adequately account for the observed phenomenon may lead to the refinement of the paradigm, or the abandoning of the old one, in favour of the paradigm that offers adequate explanation of the existing data. The critical question is: what would such a paradigm entail? As indicated earlier, the main task of this chapter is not to propose a growth theory or model, but rather to highlight the fact that current models have not adequately explained the African growth experience. As the research community critically assesses the existing growth paradigm(s), there are a few things to reflect on.

First, a shift in the way we think about growth is probably inevitable if new insights into growth dynamics are to be generated (Stiglitz, 1998; Pritchett, 1997; Ruttan, 1998). Failure to think or experiment outside of the current paradigm may prolong the tendency to force data to fit models.

Second, a serious attempt at understanding Africa's growth dynamics will have to pay attention to the unique features of the structures of the continent's economies. These include the pronounced dualism (rural-urban, traditional-modern, agricultural-industrial (Bourguinon and Morrison, 1997), informal-formal (Ranis, 2003), large percentage share of agriculture in employment, national income and labour force, and the negative feedback from persistent negative perception of the continent.

Third, the identification of key variables to explain the African growth experience needs to be shifted from a narrow focus on economic variables to more broad and participatory approaches, with information about poor growth broadly generated (see Nabudere, 2006). As experience shows, the made-in-Washington approach has left a lot of things unexplained. To construct a more credible view of understanding what is happening, a participatory approach to the definition of growth and development is likely to be more useful (Stiglitz, 1998).

Last, due to the complexity of the matter, it may be necessary to shift attention from a differential equation approach to an approach that balances the micro with the macro information. It is not enough to just construct an empirical model that regresses openness on per capita growth or quality of institution, etc. Moreover, a variable may be robust in a model but that may not be enough to explain the economic significance of the variable.

This chapter has looked at explanations for Africa's economic growth and development experiences from the empirical growth studies perspective. The next chapter looks at explanations that focus on the state, and state institutions.

Notes

1 Some analysts have suggested that though the 'new' or 'endogenous' growth models – such as Romer's (1986), Lucas's (1988) and Rebelo's (1991) – sought to upgrade the neoclassical Sollow-Swan models, they did not go far beyond the neoclassical assumptions (Ruttan, 1998; Solow, 1994).

2 For a summary of real GDP per capita growth for all 53 African countries over the 1960–2012 period, see Chapter 1.

3 The 'new' or endogenous growth theories were notably pioneered by Romer (1986), Lucas (1988) and Rebelo (1991).

4 There is no agreed list of growth regressors, but there are certain variables that appear frequently in the many growth regression models. Some of the most common include educational attainment of the population, initial per capita income, policies (mainly the exchange rate regime, openness, public savings, and depth of the financial sector), geography (access to the sea, diseases and soil quality), political stability, and demography (life expectancy and population growth rate). However the data used for most of these are proxies.

5 This has been defined as the "probability that two randomly selected individuals in a country will belong to different ethnolinguistic groups" (Easterly and Levine, 1995: 13).

6 The Africa dummy variable refers to some characteristics unique to Africa which are not captured in the conventional growth model. If the Africa dummy variable is significant, it means that there are unique features in Africa which account for the difference in growth rates when compared to other regions (see Ndulu *et al.*, 2008).

7 Easterly and Levine use a measure and data constructed by a Soviet-based team of researchers working at the Miklukho-Maklai Ethnographical Institute, which compiled a database called *Atlas of the Peoples of the World* [Atlas Narodov Mira]. The other three measures were compiled by Taylor and Hudson (1972), Roberts (1962) and Muller (1964).

8 The institutional quality index consists of five sub-indexes, namely: (i) the rule of law, i.e., citizens' willingness to accept established institutions and laws, (ii) a bureaucratic quality index measuring the autonomy of civil servants from politicians, (iii) corruption in government, referring to the prevalence of illegal payment/transactions, bribery, nepotism, cronyism, patrimonialism, (iv) the risk of expropriation, which measures the probability of an "outright confiscation", and (v) repudiation of contract, referring to the possibility of changes in contracts due to government activity. See Sachs and Warner (1997: 341).

9 The openness index was actually developed in Sachs and Warner's (1995) work: "Economic Reform and the Process of Global Integration". This index also has five sub-indices which are used to determine the level of openness in an economy. An economy is said to be open if it meets all five indices: a tariff rate averaging less than 40 per cent, a parallel market premium rate of less than 20 per cent, average quota and licensing on exports of not more than 40 per cent, an absence of high (extreme) taxes, quotas, and state monopolies on exports, and the fact that a country is not regarded as a socialist country based on the Kornai Standard.

10 This figure is raised to two percentage points in the regression that takes into account the effects of simultaneity.

11 This report describes the SSA policy environment as approaching the "global mean" and no longer a valid variable for explaining Africa's growth challenges.

12 Hoeffler estimates that the initial per capita income for SSA was only 37 per cent of the average per capita income, though it is not clear what period this refers to.

13 This refers to the narrowing of the gap in living standards between rich and poor countries which can occur as a result of poor countries catching up, or as a result of declining living standards in rich countries.

14 This refers to a situation where poor countries' GNP per capita grows faster than richer ones – which may not necessarily lead to the narrowing of the living standard gap between rich and poor countries.

15 In both the Baumol (1986) and Baro and Sala-i-Martin (1992) studies, it is clear that convergence is only apparent when low-income countries are excluded from the sample. Furthermore, even among industrialised countries, convergence seems to be visible only in the post-World War Two period. Prior to this there is no evidence of convergence (see Romer, 1994; Pritchett, 1997).

16 There are currently 34 OECD member countries, with Chile, Slovenia, Israel and Estonia becoming members in 2010. But OECD high-income countries exclude Chile, Hungary, Mexico, Poland, Slovakia, Slovenia and Turkey, whose per capita incomes fall under the middle-income band (below US$12,000 in 2009).

17 Romer (1994) notes that it was this discrepancy between what the evidence and what the theory predicts that motivated him and Lucas (1988) to "drop the two central assumptions of the neoclassical models", namely that, (i) technology is exogenous, and, (ii) technological opportunities are the same across countries (see Romer, 1994: 4).

18 The Penn World Tables present a set of national accounts data denominated in a common currency and prices covering a large number of countries. The data set is upgraded and published in version from PWT1 to the most recent PWT 6.2. Presenting of data in standardised form makes it possible for cross-country analysis to be conducted, unlike data from the National Accounting system which only allow within country comparisons.

References

Artadi, E.V. and Sala-i-Martin, Xavier (2003). "The Economic Tragedy of the XXth Century: Growth in Africa." National Bureau of Economic Research (NBER) Working Paper No. 9865, Cambridge, MA: MIT Press.

Atkinson, B.A (1969). "The Timescale of Economic Models: How Long is the Long Run?" *The Review of Economic Studies*, Vol. 36, No. 2: 137–52.

Baro, Robert (1991). "Economic Growth in a Cross Section of Countries." *The Quarterly Journal of Economics*, Vol. 106, No. 2: 407–43.

Baro, Robert (1996). "Determinants of Growth: A Cross-Country Empirical Study." National Bureau of Economic Research (NBER) Working Paper No. 5698. Cambridge, MA: MIT Press.

Baro, Robert and Sala-i-Martin, Xavier (1992). "Convergence." *Journal of Political Economy*, Vol. 100, No. 2: 157–73.

Baumol, William (1986). "Productivity Growth, Convergence and Welfare: What Long-run Data Show." *American Economic Review*, Vol. 76, No. 5: 1072–85.

Bleaney, Michael and Nishiyama, Akira (2000). "Explaining Growth: A Contest Between Models." Centre for Research in Economic Development and International Trade, CREDIT Research Paper No. 00/11. University of Nottingham.

Block, S. (2001). "Does Africa Grow Differently?" *Journal of Development Economics*, Vol. 65: 443–67.

Bloom, David and Sachs, Jeffrey (1999). "Geography, Demography, and Economic Growth in Africa." Brookings Papers on Economic Activity, No. 2: 207–73.

Bourguinon, Francois and Morrison, Christian (1997). "Inequality and Development: The Role of Dualism." *Journal of Development Economics*, Vol. 57: 230–57.

Buchanan, J. and Tullock, G. (1962). *The Calculus of Consent: Logical Foundations of Constitutional Democracy.* Indianapolis: Michigan University Press.

Burger, Ronelle and du Plessis, Stan (2006). "Examining the Robustness of Competing Explanations of Slow Growth in African Countries." CREDIT Research Paper No. 06/02. Centre for Research in Economic Development and International Trade (CREDIT), University of Nottingham.

Calamitsis, Evangelos, Basu, Anupam and Ghura, Dhaneshwar (1999). "Adjustment and Growth in Sub-Saharan Africa." IMF Working Paper WP/99/51.

Chou, Yuan and Khan, Hayat (2004). "Explaining Africa's Growth Tragedy: A Theoretical Model of Dictatorship and Kleptocracy." Department of Economics Research Paper No. 922, University of Melbourne. ISSN 081 2642.

Collier, Paul (2006). "African Growth: Why a Big Push?" *Journal of African Economies*, Vol. 00, Supplement 2: 188–211.

Collier, Paul and Gunning, James (1999a). "Explaining African Economic Performance." *Journal of Economic Literature*, 37: 64–111.

Collier, Paul and Gunning, James (1999b). "Why Has Africa Grown Slowly?" *Journal of Economic Perspectives*, Vol. 13: 3–22.

Deverajan, S. (2013). "Africa's Statistical Tragedy." *Review of Income and Wealth*, Vol. DOI: 10.1111/roiw.12013, 2013.

Easterly, William (2001). "Developing Countries' Stagnation In Spite of Policy Reforms 1980–98." Online, available at: http://siteresources.worldbank.org/INTRES/Resources/469232-1107449512766/The_Lost_Decades.pdf, accessed 28 May 2008.

Easterly, William (2005). "National Policies and Economic Growth: A Reprisal" in Philippe, A. and Steven, D. (eds) *Handbook of Economic Growth*, Vol. 1A. Amsterdam: Elsevier. Chapter 15.

Easterly, William and Levine, Ross (1995). "Africa's Growth Tragedy: A Retrospective, 1960–89." Policy Research Working Paper No. 1503, World Bank.

Easterly, William and Levine, Ross (1997). "Africa's Growth Tragedy: Policies and Ethnic Divisions." *The Quarterly Journal of Economics*, Vol. 112, No. 4: 1203–10.

Easterly, William and Levine, Ross (2002). "Tropics, Germs and Crops: How Endowments Influence Economic Development." Centre for Global Development, Working Paper No. 15.

Englebert, Pierre. (2000a). *State Legitimacy and Development in Africa.* Boulder: Lynn.

Englebert, Pierre (2000b). "Pre-colonial Institutions, Post-colonial States and Economic Development in Tropical Africa." *Political Research Quarterly*, Vol. 53, No. 1: 7–36.

Fine, Ben (2003). "New Growth Theory" in Ha-Joong Chang (ed.) *Rethinking Development Economics.* London/New York: Anthem Press: 201–17.

Fosu, K. August (2009). "Understanding the African Growth Record: The Importance of Policy Syndrome and Governance." United Nations University/World Institute for Development Economics Research (UNU/WIDER) Discussion Paper No. 2009/02.

Freund, Bill (2010). "The Social Context of African Economic Growth 1960–2008" in V. Padayachee (ed.) *The Political Economy of Africa.* London/NewYork: Routledge: 39–59.

Ghura, D. and Hadjimichael, M. (1996). "Growth in Sub-Saharan Africa." *International Monetary Fund*, Vol. 43, No. 3: 605–34.

Hall, Robert and Jones, Charles (1998). "Why Do Some Countries Produce So Much More Output per Worker Than Others?" *Journal of Economic Literature*, Vol. 22: 1–50.

Harold, F. Roy (1939). "An Essay in Dynamic Theory." *The Economic Journal*, Vol. 49, No. 193: 14–33.

Hirschman, Albert (1958). *The Strategy of Economic Development*. New Haven: Yale University Press.

Hirschman, Albert (1981). *Essays in Trespassing: Economics to Politics and Beyond*. Cambridge: Cambridge University Press.

Hoeffler, A.E. (2000). "The Augmented Solow Model and the Africa Growth Debates." *Centre for International Development (CID) Working Paper No.36*, Harvard University.

Jerven, Morten (2009). "The Quest for the African Dummy: Explaining African Post-colonial Economic Performance Revisited." *Journal of International Development*, DOI: 10.1002/jid.1603.

Jerven, Morten (2013). "Comparability of GDP Estimates in Sub-Saharan Africa: The Effect of Revision in Sources and Methods Since Structural Adjustment." *Review of Income and Wealth*, Vol. DOI: 10.1111/roiw.12006, 201.

Jutta, Bolt and Dirk, Bezerner (2008). "Understanding Long-Run African Growth: Colonial Institutions or Colonial Education? Evidence from a New Data Set." Munich Personal RePEc Archieve (MPRA) Paper No. 7029. Online, available at: www.mpra. ub.uni-muenchen.ed/7029/pdf, accessed 12 May 2010.

Kuhn, Thomas S. (1970). *The Structure of Scientific Revolutions* (2nd edition). Chicago: Chicago University Press.

Lawrence, Peter (2010). "The African Tragedy: International and National Roots" in V. Padayachee (ed.) *The Political Economy of Africa*. London/New York: Routledge: 19–38.

Levine, Ross and Renelt, David (1992). "A Sensitivity of Cross-Country Growth Regressions." *The American Economic Review*, Vol. 82, No. 4: 942–63.

Levine, Ross and Zervos, Sara (1993). "What Have We Learnt About Policy and Growth from Cross-Country Regression?" *The American Economic Review*, Vol. 83, No. 2: 426–30.

Lucas, Robert (1988). "On the Mechanics of Economic Development." *Journal of Monetary Economics*, Vol. 22: 3–42.

McPherson, Malcolm and Rakovski, Tzvatena (2001). "Understanding the Growth Process in Sub-Saharan Africa: Some Empirical Estimates." *African Economic Policy Discussion Paper No. 54*. Belfer Centre for Science and International Affairs, Harvard University.

Muller, Siegfried (1964). *The World's Living Languages: Basic Facts of Their Structure, Kinship, Location, and Number of Speakers*. New York, NY: Ungar.

Murunga, Godwin (2005). "A Note on the Knowledge Question in Africa's Development." *CODESRIA Bulletin*, Nos. 3–4: 8–10.

Nabudere, Dani (1997). "Beyond Modernisation and Development, or Why the Poor Reject Development." *Human Geography*, Vol. 79, No. 4: 205–15.

Nabudere, Dani (2006). "Development Theories, Knowledge Production and Emanicipatory Practice" in V. Padayach (ed.) *The Development Decade? Economic and Social Change in South Africa 1994–2004*. Pretoria: HSRC Press: 33–52.

Ndulu, Benno and O'Connell, Stephen (2008). "Policy Plus: African Growth Performance" in B. Ndulu, S. O'Connell, R. Bates, P. Collier and C. Soludo (eds) *The Political Economy of Economic Growth in Africa: 1960–2000*. Cambridge: Cambridge University Press: 3–75.

Ndulu, B., O'Connell, S.A., Azam, J.-P., Bates, R.H., Fosu, A.K., Gunning, J.W. and Njinkeu, D. (2008). "Introduction" in *The Political Economy of Economic Growth in Africa 1960– 2000* (Vols 1 and 2, Country Case Studies). Cambridge: Cambridge University Press.

O'Connell, S.A and Ndulu, Benno (2000). "Africa's Growth Experience: A Focus on Sources of Growth." Prepared for the AERC Explaining the African Economic Growth Project, April 16: 1–54. World Bank. Online, available at: http://www.swarthmore.edu/ SocSci/soconne1/documents/revision2.pd, accessed 11 June 2008.

Onimode, Bade (1988). *A Political Economy of the African Crisis*. London: Zed Books.

Pritchett, Lant (1997). "Divergence Big Time." *The Journal of Economic Perspectives*, Vol. 11, No. 3: 3–17.

Ranis, Gustav (2003). "Is Dualism Worth Revisiting?" Economic Growth Centre, Discussion Paper No. 870. University of Yale. Online, available at: http://www.econ. yale.edu/~egcentre/research.htm, accessed 19 July 2008.

Rebelo, Sergio (1991). "Long-Run Policy Analysis and Long-Run Growth." *Journal of Political Economy*, Vol. 99, No. 3: 500–21.

Roberts, Janet (1962). "Sociocultural Change and Communication Problems" in Frank A. Rice (ed.) *Study of the Role of Second Languages in Asia, Africa, and Latin America.* Washington DC: Center for Applied Linguistics of the Modern Language Association of America: 105–23.

Rodrik, Dani (1998). "Where Did All the Growth Go? External Shocks, Social Conflict and Growth Collapses." Online, available at: http://www.ksg.harvard.edu/rodrik, accessed 13 July 2008.

Romer, Paul (1986). "Increasing Returns and Long-Run Growth." *Journal of Political Economy*, Vol. 94, No. 5: 1002–37.

Romer, Paul (1994). "The Origins of Endogenous Growth." *The Journal of Economic Perspectives*, Vol. 8, No. 1: 3–22.

Ruttan, W. Vernon (1998). "The New Growth Theory and Development Economics: A Survey." *Journal of Development Studies*, Vol. 35, No. 2: 1–26.

Sachs, Jeffrey and Warner, Andrew (1995). " Economic Reform and the Process of Global Integration." Brookings Papers on Economic Activity. Online, available at: http:// citeseerx.ist.psu.edu/viewdoc/download;jsessionid=4CB4540A80E3F80A79718627499 69F60?doi=10.1.1.296.6542&rep=rep1&type=pdf, accessed 17 June 2006.

Sachs, Jeffrey and Warner, Andrew (1997). "Sources of Slow Growth in African Economies." *Journal of African Economies*, Vol. 6, No. 3: 335–76.

Sachs, Jeffrey and Warner, Andrew (2001). "The Curse of Natural Resources." *European Economic Review*, Vol. 45, Nos 4–6: 827–38.

Sala-i-Martin, Xavier (1996). "Regional Cohesion: Evidence and Theories of Regional Growth and Convergence." *European Economic Review*, XL: 1325–52.

Sala-i-Martin, Xavier (1997). "I Just Ran Two-Million Regressions." *American Economic Review (Papers and Proceedings)*, Vol. 87: 178–83.

Sala-i-Martin, Xavier, Doppelhofer, G. and Miller, G.I. (2004). "Determinants of Long-Term Growth: A Bayesian Averaging of Classical Estimates (BACE) Approach." *American Economic Review*. Vol. 94, No. 4: 813–35.

Sen, Amartya (1983). "Development: Which Way Now?" *The Economic Journal*, Vol. 93, No. 372: 745–62.

Solow, Robert M. (1956). "A Contribution to the Theory of Economic Growth." *Quarterly Journal of Economics*, Vol. 70, No. 1: 65–94.

Solow, Robert M. (1988). "Growth Theory and After." *The American Economic Review*, Vol. 78, No. 3: 307–17.

Solow, Robert M. (1994). "Perspectives on Growth Theory." *American Economic Review*, Vol. 8, No. 1: 45–54.

Srinivasan, T.N. (1994). "Data Base for Development Analysis." *Journal of Development Economics*, Vol. 44: 3–27.

Stiglitz, Joseph (1998). "Towards a New Paradigm for Development Strategies, Policies, and Processes". A paper presented as a Prebisch Lecture at the UNCTAD, Geneva, 19 October 1998.

Stiglitz, Joseph (2000). "The Insider: What I Learned at the World Economic Crisis." *The New Republic*. Online, available at: http://www.tnr.com, accessed 17 October 2012.

Summers, Robert and Heston, Alan (1991). "The Penn World Table (Mark 5): An Expanded Set of International Comparisons, 1950–1988." *Quarterly Journal of Economics*, Vol. 106, No. 2: 327–68.

Swan, Trevor (1956). "Economic Growth and Capital Accumulation". *Economic Record*, Vol. 32, No. 2: 334–61.

Tahari, Amor, Ghura, Dhaneshwar, Akitoby, Bernardin and Brou Aka, Emmanuel (2004). "Sources of Growth in Sub-Saharan Africa." IMF Working Paper WP/04/176.

Taylor, Charles Lewis, and Hudson, Michael C. (1972). *World Handbook of Political and Social Indicators* (2nd edition). New Haven: Yale University Press.

te Velde, Dirk Willem (2006). "Foreign Direct Investment and Development: An Historical Perspective." Background paper for World Economic and Social Survey for 2006. ODI (Commissioned by the UNCTAD).

United Nations Economic Commission for Africa (UNECA) (1989). "African Alternative Framework to Structural Adjustment Programmes for Socio-Economic Recovery and Transformation (AAF-SAP)." UNECA. Online, available at: www.uneca.org, accessed 17 August 2009.

Wade, Robert (2002). "US Hegemony and the World Bank: The Fight Over People and Ideas." *Review of International Political Economy*, Vol. 9, No. 2: 201–29.

Williamson, Jeffrey (1995). "Globalisation, Convergence and History." National Bureau of Economic Research (NBER) Working Paper No. 5259.

World Bank (2000). *Can Africa Claim the 21st Century?* [The Gelb Report]. New York: IBRD/World Bank.

World Bank (2005). *Economic Growth in the 1990s: Learning from a Decade of Reform*. New York: IBRD/World Bank.

World Bank (2007). *Challenges of African Growth: Opportunities, Constraints and Strategic Directions*. New York: IBRD/World Bank.

World Bank (2011). "Africa's Future and the World Bank's Support to it." The World Bank. Online, available at: http://www.worldbank.org/africastrategy, accessed 17 September 2011.

5   The state and development in Africa

Introduction

The role of the state in economic growth and development in Africa has been a widely debated topic. From the 1950s through to the mid-1970s, development economists were very clear that to achieve sustainable economic growth and development, the state not only had to play an important role, but had to be a 'prime mover'. Various concepts such as the "Big Push" (Rosenstein-Rodan, 1943, and later, Nurkse, 1953), the "Two-sector model" (Lewis, 1954), "Take-off" (Rostow, 1959), "Backward and Forward Linkages" and "Unbalanced Growth" (Hirschman, 1958), as well as Harvey Leibenstein's "Critical Minimum Effort", all bore an underlying assumption that the state should be the driver, planner, coordinator and deliverer of growth and development. Most pioneers of development economics had a strong conviction that development and industrialisation in less developed countries (LDCs) needed deliberate, coordinated, guided and intensive effort from the state (see Hirschman, 1981). During the post-World War Two period right up to the mid-1970s, the view that the markets were "inadequate for the 'great development project' on account of several failures necessitating the use of planning to address coordination failures" was dominant (Ndulu, 2008: 320). While in the three decades following the end of World War Two the state's role in economic growth and development was taken for granted, serious debates about what role it should play in the economy emerged during the 1980s.

To discuss how the state and the associated institutions are deployed in explaining Africa's economic growth and development experience, this chapter focuses on two different schools of thought. One set of ideas originates from development economics and the other from what is known as state-centric theories. While the two schools come from different traditions of thought, with development economics diverging from mainstream economics (see Lewis, 1984), and the state-centric school originating from political sociology, they both see the state (not the market) as central in understanding the processes of economic growth and development. Nevertheless, the two schools highlight different aspects of the state as an economic and development actor. Whereas the development economics school largely focuses on the developmental aspects of the state as an agent of industrialisation – mobilising capital (human and physical), planning, coordinating and directing public and private investments in the economy (the *developmental state*),[1] the state-centric school emphasises the nature and quality of state institutions, state formation, formalisation of state institutions, and focuses more on issues of state capacity and functions – the political processes behind the formalisation of state institutions and internal state structures (*the bureaucratic state*).[2]

Of course between these different emphases there is an area of intersection: the 'developmental state', though it is not the same as the 'bureaucratic state' (see Johnson, 1999: 53), reflects most of the essential features of the bureaucratic state. Peter Evans and James Rauch (1999), for instance, see the developmental state as largely coinciding with the Weberian bureaucratic state. In fact, it has been argued that it is only an effective bureaucratic state that can be a developmental state. Such a state is seen as critical even to the optimal functioning of markets: "an effective state … [is] an essential prerequisite of the formation of market relations" (Evans, 1995: 29; see also North, 1992).

State and development: the second best option

To distinguish development economics from mainstream economics (both Keynesian and neoclassical), W. Arthur Lewis (one of the founding fathers of this sub-discipline) defines development economics as a branch of economics which "deals with the structure and behaviour of economies where output per head is less than 1980 US$2,000" (Lewis, 1984: 1). The main reason for defining development economics this way, according to Lewis, is that countries with per capita income below US$ 2,000, in 1980 prices, have features which are different from advanced economies such that understanding the former calls for a different set of tools and concepts – hence development economics. For instance, in the early days of development economics, it was argued that "certain special features of the economic structure of the underdeveloped countries make an important portion of orthodox analysis inapplicable and misleading" (Hirschman, 1981: 5). Thus, development economics was built on the understanding that the "conventional body of economic thought and policy advice are not applicable to the poorer countries". The new sub-discipline[3] was given the task of developing appropriate tools which could not only "slay the dragon of backwardness virtually by itself" (ibid.), but also enhance the understanding of the unique conditions in these countries. It was mainly for this reason that development economists during the 1950s insisted on "separating development economics from the rest of economics" (Sen, 1988: 11). Thus, the basic question on which development economics was to be justified was whether developing "countries differ in structure or [and] in behaviour from the richer countries, in ways that require different concepts or tools to understand their functioning" (Lewis, 1984: 2). For many early development economists, the answer was a resounding 'yes', and this gave rise to a flourishing sub-discipline which has survived until today, albeit with a different mission, scope and focus.

The role of the state in development: the pioneers' view

One of the central proposals of the pioneers of development economics was that mainstream economics was politically naïve in prescribing a minimal role for the state in economic growth and development. A strong affinity for 'macro-strategies' among the early development theorists convinced them to believe in the idea that the state should initiate, plan, direct and drive the process of economic transformation in LDCs (see Lewis, 1984), and "development economics [should] provide the rationale and instruments for its implementation" (Ndulu, 2008: 319). This elevated role for the state in development economics is sometimes attributed to the influence of the dominant economic paradigm of the time (Keynesianism), which advocated for strong state intervention in the context of The Great Depression: "the claim of development economics to stand as a separate body of economic analysis and policy derived intellectual legitimacy and nurture from the prior success and parallel features of the Keynesian Revolution" (Hirschman, 1981: 7). The Keynesian idea of "two economics" – one which applies to the "*special economics*" of full employment (obtained under conditions of economies operating at full capacity with optimal competitive markets), and the "*general economics*" which apply to conditions of widespread unemployment and underemployment, market failures and imperfect competition (most prevalent in underdeveloped countries) – had a strong influence on the earlier development economists who were convinced that the latter situation required a special set of ideas for understanding the economic dynamics and accordingly devised a required strategy for addressing these conditions.[4]

However, it must be noted here that the reason for development economists' faith in the state was not that they did not have faith in the markets; their explicit confidence in the state was some sort of 'second best' option, precisely because they believed that markets were underdeveloped in all LDCs and therefore could not function optimally. Arthur Lewis explains this more concisely: "One reason why government is closer to the developing economy is that the market works less efficiently there than in the developed economy. So the government is constantly asked to rectify market error or market inequity" (Lewis, 1984: 4). Thus,

> To say ... [that the state should correct market failure] is not to imply that government action in the market always gives a better answer than the uncontrolled market, whether in allocation or distribution. [In LDCs] it is often the case that the imperfect solution of the market could be better than that of the government.
>
> (Lewis, 1984: 4)

This idea of the state intervening in the economy to correct market failure is sometimes referred to as the 'Pigouvian paradigm', named after the twentieth century English economist, Arthur Cecil Pigou. In this view, the first generation of development economists' confidence was not because states were seen to be better than markets; it was based on the belief that a "developing country did not have a reliable market price system, that the supply of entrepreneurship was limited, and that large structural changes – not merely marginal adjustment, were needed", which justified an activist state approach (Meier, 2001: 14–15).

The role of planning

Economic development debates in the post-World War Two era were dominated by development theorists who proposed ways of transforming underdeveloped societies by means of national planning and coordination of investments.[5] A common idea among these thinkers was that underdeveloped countries had either poorly developed or missing markets, resulting in rampant market failures, such that the state was vital in mobilising and coordinating resources for development. Paul Rosenstein-Rodan, one of the pioneers of the sub-discipline of development economics, argued, for example, that the development of underdeveloped areas would be too slow (or impossible) without the state mobilising capital for investment, and planning how these investment resources were to be deployed sectorally and geographically. Though he was mainly concerned with Eastern and South-Eastern Europe, the argument in favour of "large-scale planned industrialisation" (the *Big Push*) was seen to be appropriate for the development of any "depressed area" (Rosenstein-Rodan, 1943: 205). According to this view, private sector-led development was seen as inappropriate in underdeveloped countries, for various reasons including the small size of private firms, the inappropriateness of private sector investment in labour training, the lack of coordination of private sector investments, high political risks for large-scale private investments, lack of technology and, most especially, the large overhead capital investments required. After considering all these factors, the conclusion was that

> If the industrialisation of internationally depressed areas were to rely entirely on the normal incentive of private entrepreneurs, the process would not only be very much slower, the rate of investment smaller and (consequently) the national income lower, but the whole economic structure of the region would be different. Investment would be distributed in different proportions between different industries, the final equilibrium would be below the optimum which a large E.E.I.T would achieve.
>
> (Rosenstein-Rodan, 1943: 207)

It is interesting to note that the term *industrialisation* is used almost synonymously with economic development, reflecting the dominant view at the time (maybe even now) that industrialisation was the hallmark of economic development. Though Rosenstein-Rodan is thinking in terms of the supranational investment agency the East and South-Eastern Investment Trust (EEIT) – whose role would be to mobilise investment resources, plan and coordinate investments – the equivalent at the national level would be the state: in particular the national planning department or agency. Similarly, Arthur Lewis[6] (1954), although emphasising the important role of a capitalist class in the transformation of both the agricultural and industrial sectors in the early stages, accords an important role to the state – especially in the initial stages of the transformation process when capital accumulation through the extraction of 'surplus value' from the subsistence sector can only be achieved through state intervention.

The influence of state-led development strategies in Africa

Many of these ideas found themselves in Africa largely through the visiting missions and expatriate advisors during the colonial and post-colonial periods. These economic advisors understood Africa's state of underdevelopment to be a direct consequence of a lack of capital in the broad sense – both human and fixed/physical capital – for industrialisation. This understanding of the African condition inevitably put the state at the centre of the development enterprise, with the idea being concretised in the national development plans which most African countries formulated throughout the 1960s. For the newly independent African countries yearning to 'catch up' with the developed world (but also because of the strong socialist preferences among many African states during the 1960s), the idea of the state being at the helm of the development enterprise was very attractive (see Biney, 2008). Throughout the 1960s many governments in Africa cooperated with some of the development experts in designing the famous five- or ten-year development plans. For instance, Arthur Lewis himself was seconded to the newly independent state of Ghana to assist with designing strategies for economic growth and development during the later 1950s and the early 1960s. Specific development strategies such as import substitution industrialisation (ISI), which many African countries adopted from the early days of independence, were formulated in a context in which the state played a central role (Meier, 2001).

For many independent African countries during the 1960s, it was often taken for granted that the responsibility to grow the economy and improve the living conditions of the African people fell squarely on the new independent state. Some analysts have even argued that improving the living conditions of the African people, largely neglected during colonial rule, was one of the *raisons d'être*[7] of the nationalist movement and the liberation struggles across the continent (Mkandawire, 2003, Green, 1965). Strong nationalist sentiments gelled well with the idea of the state being at the helm of the economic and development project, with the state controlling and directing the resources into strategic sectors which could fulfil the nationalist goal of reducing dependence on the former colonial masters: the quest for economic independence. The other reason why the idea of state-led development was very attractive to the newly independent African states was that capitalism was largely associated with the policies of the colonial masters; many nationalist leaders were suspicious that the free market approach was a form of maintaining control over Africa (see Nkrumah, 1963; Mohan, 1966).

The state-led approach to development also gained intellectual and political support in most African countries during the 1960s because it offered what appeared to be a quicker way of industrialisation and *catching up* with the rest of the world (Ake, 1981). Apart from being suspicious of market-led development, many African leaders believed that market-led industrialisation would be very slow – having the state active in the economy offered a shortcut to the challenge of industrialisation. In hindsight we now know that the post-colonial developmental state in Africa failed to emerge in most African countries (for various reasons), although modest successes in some countries were scored in the earlier periods of the post-colonial era (see UNECA, 2011; Bates, 1981).

State-led development debates

Debates about the role of the state in the economy have gone through three major phases. From the 1940s up to the mid-1970s, state intervention in the economy was widely accepted. This was a period which was dominated by what some analysts have referred to as "big D-development" (see Hart, 2001, 2006). From the early 1980s until the mid-1990s, state interventions in the form of state planning and state ownership of large enterprises were seen as harmful to the economy and society (Harvey, 2005). During this period the popular policy recommendation, especially in poor countries, centred on rolling back the state from the commanding heights. However, a third phase, from the mid-1990s – in which there has been a resurgence of interest in state-led strategies, particularly in developing countries – has led to the emergence of the 'second generation' development plans in Africa (see p. 153). Bueno Ndulu (2008: 317) also observes three phases in the evolution of the paradigms of development from the 1950s to the present day, arguing that "the development paradigms have been shaped … by the dominant ideologies of the time" which in turn have influenced attitudes towards the role of markets, the state, and the private sector in the economy.

Generally, while state intervention was being favoured from the 1940s until the 1970s – supported by the Pigouvian theory – the sort of rampant state failure which became evident during the 1970s led to strong anti-state sentiments in the 1980s and onwards. Before the 1980s, regardless of whether a state was leviathan, predatory, kleptocratic or prebendal, state intervention was widely acknowledged as the *only* effective way of doing development (see Meier, 2001). However, by the mid-1980s the pendulum had swung in an entirely opposite direction, sweeping away states in favour of markets as the most efficient mobiliser, coordinator and allocator of resources in the economy. Emerging views about the role of the state countered the earlier belief that it was generically better placed to promote economic growth and development in developing countries. Various studies began to highlight the view that the earlier idea that the state should intervene in the economy to correct market failures had often led to 'state-failure' – which some analysts claimed was much worse than 'market-failure' (Collier and Gunning, 1999). Thus, the neo-market failure thesis argued that, "We need to recognize both the limits and strengths of markets, as well as the strengths and limits of government interventions aimed at correcting market failure" (Stiglitz, 1989: 202).

Unfortunately, in the African case, notions of state failure produced strong anti-state sentiments among international development agencies such that the mood shifted from the state playing a central role in the economy to what has been referred to as "anti-state neoliberalism" (Mkandawire, 2001: 294). Strong arguments against state-led development strategies rested on the view that state intervention in the economy produced much worse results than the malfunctioning markets. Anne Kruger's (1974) study on rent-seeking and efficiency, though not focused on Africa, has been influential in this respect. In diagnosing the causes of the crisis in Sub-Saharan Africa (SSA) during the 1980s, state intervention became the Achilles heel, and the resulting reform proposals focused on strict application of a special form of neoclassical fundamentalism which restricted the state to a watchdog role in the economy (Singh, 1992). As noted in Chapter 3, the overriding "aim of structural adjustment in Africa (and elsewhere) [was] to remove the impediments caused by state interference in the operation of … markets" (Stein, 1994: 1834). In the rush to "avoid what was seen as the dangers of state intervention", the question of what kind of state structures were most likely to promote economic growth was easily lost (Evans and Rauch, 1999: 749). The expectation was that through programmes such as public sector reform, privatisation of state-owned enterprises, public service streamlining, and dismantling of the infamous marketing boards, the "African Leviathan" could be "tamed and redirected" (Sandbrook, 1990).

The orthodox paradox

However, this purging of the African Leviathan seems to have gone too far, to the extent that it rendered most states in Africa incapable of even carrying out such basic functions as implementing the Structural Adjustment Programme (SAP). This situation, which has often been referred to as the 'orthodoxy paradox' (see Callaghy and Ravenhill, 1993), exposed the contradictions inherent in the reforms proposed by the World Bank and the International Monetary Fund (IMF): while implementation of these programmes required a strong and effective state, the actual effect of SAPs was to weaken and reduce the capacity and effectiveness of most African states, to the point of paralysis (Mkandawire, 2001: 306).

Nevertheless, aware of these contradictions, some analysts began to take serious interest in the importance of understanding the relationship between the way the state is constituted, how it functions, and economic growth and development. While the Bank was promoting reliance on markets to bring about economic growth and development in Africa, a number of analysts highlighted the importance of the state, and a whole range of institutions, not just in creating an environment in which markets can function optimally, but also in coordinating and mobilising investment capital. In retrospect, the strong anti-state views adopted during the 1980s generated a backlash which led to growing emphasis among some analysts that economic growth is in fact stifled under conditions where the state is weak and ineffective. Evidence from the Asian Tigers, though disputed (see Stiglitz, 1989), generally supported the view that effective state interventions provided the 'steroids' that stimulated the growth of such 'tigers' (see Smith, 2001; Wade, 1990). Empirical studies conducted during the 1980s and 1990s began to suggest that the main issue was not about state intervention *per se*, but more about the nature of the state and the quality of state institutions.

> The issue is not one of state intervention in the economy. All states intervene in their economies for various reasons ... The United States is a good example of a state in which the regulatory orientation predominates, whereas Japan is a good example of a state in which the developmental orientation predominates.
>
> (Johnson, 1982: 17, 19)

As a result of these views, especially from the mid-1990s, a revival of interest in state-led development strategies gained ground. Accompanying this revival was the resurgence of development economics – which was declared dead in the early 1980s – most notably by one of the pioneers of development economics, Albert Hirschman (see Hirschman, 1981). In his eulogy for development economics, Hirschman laments: "as an observer and long-time participant I cannot help feeling that the old liveliness is no longer there, that new ideas are ever harder to come by and that the field is not adequately reproducing itself" (Hirschman, 1981: 1). The reason for this loss of faith in development economics was that since the sub-discipline's main objective was to address issues of poverty and underdevelopment in LDCs, the persistence of these conditions in developing countries amounted to the failure of the sub-discipline. From a development economics, perspective, the economic growth and development challenges in Africa can be explained largely in terms of the inability of states in Africa to mobilise resources (through whatever means) and coordinate investments at the national level.

Bringing the state back

Attention to the role of the state in economic growth and development was also highlighted by the proponents of the New Institutional Economics (NIE), who argued that institutions other than markets had an impact on economic performance. For example, Douglas North (1997), one of the main proponents of NIE,[8] maintained that economic performance is greatly influenced by the set of local institutions to which economic actors respond. He further contended that the neoclassical narrow focus on markets underestimated the role of other non-market institutions in promoting their efficient functioning. According to North, "A set of political and economic institutions that provides low-cost transacting and credible commitment makes possible the efficient [functioning of] the factor and product markets underlying economic growth" (North, 1997: 2).

   In addition, during the 1990s a number of cross-country studies, particularly Paulo Mauro's (1995), Stephen Knack and Phillip Keefer's (1995) and Evans and Rauch's (1999) – which reported a strong correlation between growth and the quality of public institutions – provided empirical support for the rebound of the state as a key player in economic growth and development. By the mid-1990s, a number of case studies had been conducted in different countries which suggested that the way the state was structured had a bearing on economic growth and development. Concepts such as a 'fully institutionalised state', 'political penetration' (Coleman, 1985), 'embedded autonomy' and 'internal coherence' (Evans, 1995) and 'developmental state' (Johnson, 1982) were used to describe organisational and institutional arrangements within the state as essential to promoting economic growth and development.

Some authors point to the poor performance of the market-oriented strategies in Africa as the main reason for the resurgence of the state-led development strategies, starting from the mid-1990s. For instance, Devesh Kapur and Richard Webb (2000) have argued that the repeated failure of the Bank's market-centred strategies to revive economic growth and development in Africa led to the call to "roll back" the state. From this angle, the resurgence of state-led development is a counter-revolution to the strong anti-state momentum generated during the 1980s. Other factors cited for the revival of interest in state-led development include the fact that globalisation had changed what has been referred to as the "international political culture" in which civil society has become more vigilant in demanding capable and effective public institutions (Kapur and Webb, 2000: 2).

However, it is important to note here that although this revival of interest in the state coincides with the popular discourse of good governance, these ideas are different in that the good governance approach still views the state as playing a minimal role of enforcing contracts and maintaining the rule of law (the minimalist approach), while the idea of a developmental state goes beyond the state playing a facilitatory role.[9] Proponents of the developmental state see the state and its accompanying institutions playing critical roles including "altering incentives in the markets, reducing risks, offering entrepreneurial vision, and managing conflicts"[10] (Johnson, 1999: 48).

A similar view is expressed by the United Nations Economic Commission for Africa (UNECA) when it argues that the developmental state's role is to "promote capital accumulation, utilise reserves of surplus labour, undertake policies of deliberate industrialisation, relax the foreign exchange constraints through import substitution, and coordinat[e] the allocation of resources through programming and planning" (UNECA, 2011: 116). While one can question whether any such state exists in Africa – i.e., one that performs all these functions effectively – it has been argued that such a state is indispensable for delivery of the sort of industrial, social and economic transformation needed in Africa. As noted above, even during the anti-state era researchers and policymakers from developing countries saw the state as an important player in economic development, and not just limited to creating a 'market-friendly' environment. Former Mexican minister of finance Pedro Aspe, and Mexican under-secretary for international affairs Angel Gurria, in a keynote speech at the World Bank's Annual Conference on Development Economics in 1992, courageously[11] stated that,

> during the early phases of development, when an economy is no more than
> a collection of fragmented markets ..., the *direct participation of the state* in

some areas of the economy [is] not only desirable but an indispensable pre-condition for the growth process.

> (Aspe and Gurria, 1992: 9, emphasis added)

Although the anti-state counter-revolution at the beginning of the 1980s argued that "government intervention in the economy is by definition distortionary and counterproductive" (Todaro, 2000: 96), by the end of the 1980s some analysts were challenging this view, arguing that even in advanced industrial economies state intervention was not only inevitable but part of the normal operation of these economies (see Dutt, 1992; Johnson, 1999). This argument went beyond the market failure thesis, pointing out that

> it would be wrong to conclude ... that government is not only the solution ..., but actually the problem itself. Such critics suggest that, were it not for the interference of government, natural economic forces would have led to a burst of economic energy, lifting billions ... out of poverty.
>
> (Stiglitz, 1992: 61)

Recognition of market as well as state failures has led to the realisation that simply 'getting the prices right' is not enough, just as 'bringing back the state' may not be a sufficient enough condition for generating the necessary momentum for sustained growth and development (see Singh, 1992).

States, markets and development in Africa

In the African context, what this debate has highlighted is the fact that both markets and states require not only adjustment but serious reform to achieve sustained growth and development. In this vein, it is not just the state but the quality of the state *institutions* which is crucial, just as it is not just markets which are critical, but the environment in which those markets operate. The either/or approach has proved to be severely defective in responding to the challenges in SSA, and has in fact led to detrimental effects. The *Economic Report on Africa 2011*, for example, argues that

> Advocating a stronger role for the state in development should neither be seen in terms of the old and tired debate of state versus market nor should it be understood that the private sector should not remain the engine of economic growth. This is because the issue is not whether the state – like the market or the private sector for that matter – should play a role in economic transformation and development but rather how to construct developmental states in Africa.
>
> (UNECA, 2011: 91)

Experience from the past half century (since the mid-1960s) of development efforts in Africa and other developing regions suggests that the predominant assumption during the 1950s and 1960s that the state would act in a benevo-lent, selfless and neutral way, is far from the reality; so too is the view that the market is the magic bullet for economic growth and development. Both state- and market-led strategies have their own limitations. This realisation has been widely acknowledged, even by the World Bank, which is now arguing that it is promoting a development model which allows "mixes of government and market interventions" (World Bank, 2011: 7). Awareness of both market and state fail-ures has, in recent times, led to the rediscovery of the importance of coordinating investment and resource allocation in the economy, those very core ideas which the 1950s analysts highlighted (Meier, 2001).

The grand planning era

As noted earlier, the idea of state-led development was widely adopted by many African countries at independence. Indeed, most of the newly independent states adopted the five- or ten-year development plans in which the state was expected to mobilise, coordinate and direct investment resources and kick-start industri-alisation. Five- or ten-year development plans were common in self-proclaimed socialist states such as Ghana, Tanzania, Ethiopia, Togo, Mozambique, Angola, Guinea and Senegal as well as other countries which did not officially embrace socialist ideologies such as Cote d'Ivoire, Kenya, Malawi, Cameroon, Nigeria, Zambia, Swaziland and Gabon. For this reason the 1960s and 1970s in Africa can rightly be referred to as the grand planning era. These national development plans provided an overarching framework which guided economic and social development efforts in various sectors such as education, agriculture, rural and urban service provision, transport and communications, industrial development, administration, and defence and security. In these plans, most governments out-lined the basic structure of their economies and defined the national economic and social development goals and priorities.[12] Although the colonial govern-ments also formulated and implemented development plans, it was only after independence that a broader strategy for social and economic transformation was designed and implemented (see Green, 1965). Prior to independence, the devel-opment plans focused on the narrow interests of the colonial government and a few indigenous urban dwellers, such that development efforts were only directed to 'enclave projects' (see Rivkin, 1963; Mackay, 2008).

Generally, these national development plans were a symbol of independence in as far as they enabled African governments to determine their country's des-tiny by deciding how available resources were to be used.

> African states … see national social and economic planning as a logical historical development from the national independence effort, now to be channelled into the rapid improvement of standards of life and of economic capacity. The national plan is both a symbol of that effort and a means of bringing it about.
>
> (Green, 1965: 249)

However, apart from these plans being vaguely formulated and lacking national and economy-wide linkages, some critics have observed that they were often not followed, the resources planned for were beyond what most countries could mobilise, and that the plans did not often reflect the priorities according to the situation on the ground (see Kapur *et al.*, 1997). One of the major problems was that they were taken as development blueprints, which had to be followed rigidly at any cost. Reflecting on the Nigerian experience, Adebayo Adjedeji argued that

> it would be a great mistake to regard a plan as a blueprint for action. Rather … a plan … [is] a document assessing a country's problems, stating broad conclusions about the scale and direction of development efforts and indicating some of the main projects, programmes, and policies to be executed.
>
> (cited in Green, 1965: 250)

In most independent African countries development planning was also justified on the grounds that during the earlier period of independence, there was high expectation and confidence that the state would bring about an improvement in the lives of the majority of the people. Thus, planning and direct participation in the economy was the mechanism through which most Africans governments hoped to transform their economies and societies.

> There were very high expectations about the role the state would play … in all development efforts. Whether in agriculture, industrialisation, education or other sectors, the burden of formulating and implementing the policies … was laid squarely with government. The state was to pull the whole society in an all-out development drive.
>
> (Doornbos, 1990: 182)

Second generation development plans: Vision 2020 and Vision 2030

Though the grand planning era was interrupted during the 1980s, we have seen, since the beginning of the mid-1990s, a growing interest in development planning across Africa. Many African states are now developing long-term development plans such as the Vision 2020 developed in Ghana (1996) and Nigeria (2009), the Vision 2030 developed in Zambia (2006), Kenya (2008), South Africa (2011) and Namibia (2004), and the Vision 2063 developed by the African Union (AU). Although these are not the same as the development plans of the 1960s, they do reflect the importance of strategic thinking and goal-setting. Further, while the role of the state in these visions is not the same as the state's role during the grand planning era, and although these (new plans/visions) have been criticised as part of the African governments' rhetoric, in most countries there has been a realisation that without a vision in which the aspirations of the people are expressed, a nation is as good as lost.

Different from the earlier planning and strategies, the emphasis in the second generation development plans is on the view that the vision should not be that of government officials only, but should reflect the general aspirations of the people. This is particularly evident in the Namibian vision which states

> Unless it is a shared vision, it may not be socially and politically accept-able. Therefore, as a tool for social dialogue and part of good governance, the Vision process in Namibia involved ... the major social groups, at the national and regional levels in various aspects of the formulation process.
>
> (Republic of Namibia, 2004: 20)

Although most of these visions may be nothing more than the usual shopping list of the great things that the nation plans to do, there does seem to be a realisa-tion that development is not something that is achieved by a few development specialists who formulate 'grand development models' based on what some critics have referred to as the "high development theories" (Krugman, 1996). To the contrary, there is a growing awareness that both economic growth and devel-opment come about as a result of what we do as a people, as a nation, and as a continent; and that development should embrace collective aspirations, goals, efforts, energies and commitments.

In many countries this revived interest in national planning may still be a reflection of the dreams and ambitions of those in charge of state policy and plan-ning. Whether this will mean anything positive for the people on the ground is yet to be seen; what we can see in these documents are 'finishing lines' towards which countries are expected to strive. One of the advantages of having a national vision is that if a country does not even have an idea of what it wants to be, it is difficult to direct any effort at anything. As Chalmer Johnson (1999) argues, the essence of state-led development is goal-setting such that the legitimacy of the state becomes dependent on the achievement of these set goals. Hopefully, within these new visions, there will also emerge ideas that will reshape and redefine the state and its role in the economic growth and development of Africa.

State and development: a state-centric view

Economic growth performance in Africa, in analytical debates, especially during the 1980s and 1990s, has had a strong state dimension, and for some analysts this is where the key to explaining Africa's growth and development experience lies. A number of analysts have sought to explain the widely and loudly proclaimed failure of development in many African countries by analysing the nature of states in Africa and how they function (see Sandbrook, 1993). According to this view, the nature of the state and state institutions in Africa is a central explana-tory variable, and should be given more attention in an attempt at understand Africa's growth and development challenges. However, explaining the economic growth and development crisis in Africa via the state has been a tricky business, not just in terms of the analytical content in the debates, but also in terms of finding a methodology that succeeds in generating useful insights. Mahmood Mamdani (1996) attributes the analytical and methodological crunch to what he calls the dominance of the "unilinear social science" (modernisation, dependency, structuralism or Marxist theories), all of which use a binary framework – modern-traditional, capitalist-precapitalist, centre-periphery. Largely because of this approach to the state and development in Africa, it has been fashionable for many analysts to cast doubts even on the existence of *states* in Africa (see Hill, 2005).[13]

Analysts who try to explain economic growth and development challenges in SSA by locating the problem within the structure and functions of the state in Africa try to compare the performance or role of African states with either states in developed or emerging countries – Western Europe and East Asia in particular. In the literature on states and development in Africa, it is common to come across statements such as, "While the state has been a crucial element in the success of Japan and the Newly Industrialising Countries (NICs), it is part of the problem of economic stagnation in much of Sub-Saharan Africa" (Sandbrook, 1986: 319). Reasons why states in Africa have been a problem instead of a solution, as far as economic growth and development is concerned, are surprisingly divergent across a wide range of analysts, with some attributing the defects in African states to the underdevelopment of capitalism (Hyden, 1986; Cox and Negi, 2010; Leys, 1996), while others point to poor institutionalisation of the state, resulting in entrenched neo-patrimonialism (Chabal and Daloz, 1999).

However, there seems to be some consensus among these analysts that the main cause of poor economic growth and lack of development in Africa is the state and its accompanying fragile or semi-institutionalised institutions. While in the previous chapters economic stagnation in Africa is explained in terms of the distortions of prices due to state intervention in the economy, proponents of the state-centric approach focus on the nature of the state and its institutions. Although most state-centric analysts are aware of the diversity of states in Africa, they argue that most of the states in Africa exhibit similar features which largely account for the weak economic growth experienced over the past four decades. For instance, when discussing corruption, there are few African countries in which this is not recognised as a major problem.

Part of the problem with this seemingly sophisticated approach arises from the over-extension of the comparative or analogy methodology as an instrument for understanding the African development crisis. Understandably, human knowledge develops through association and analogy; building on what one already knows. However, stringent projection of what one already knows may actually prove to be counter-productive in understanding and interpreting new experiences. For example, while it is perfectly sensible to try and understand the state in Africa through the Western or Eastern models, such models can be cruel masters which can suppress and ignore anything *alien* to them. As Mamdani (1996: 13) points out, a researcher operating within the analogy methodology searches for the right analogy to fit Africa, he proceeds by dismissing, one after another, those that do not fit. In the process, he establishes his main conclusion: Africa is *not* like Europe, where the peasantry was 'captured' through wage labour, nor ... Asia or Latin America, where it was captured through tenancy arrangements.

What this approach succeeds in doing is to show that Africa is different from Europe, but it does not go beyond that to explain that which is different from what the analyst knows. This may probably be due to the assumption that whatever is different from what the analyst knows is unimportant, and, worse still, does not have its own existence. Herein lay the strength and the weakness of the analogy approach. Strength because by analysing different situations through the same framework one is able to easily identify the differences which can lead to growth of knowledge by association or analogy. If, for instance, patrimonialism is something foreign to states in the West, using the Western Model of state when analysing African states will illuminate and isolate patrimonialism as a unique feature which can either attract the analyst's attention or may be simply dismissed. It is at this point that the weakness may or may not arise, depending on how the analyst deals with the novel experience. Serious weakness may arise in the analogy approach if there is no effort made to look at the unfamiliar features with an open mind; if the unfamiliar is quickly classified as bizarre, wired, unconventional, residual, deviant, uncivilised, or simply brushed aside as something irrational, primitive, traditional, underdeveloped, pre-capitalist, sacrilegious or pathological, then the analogy approach can be quite inhibitive. The strength of the analogy approach may sometimes lead to identifying what some analysts are now acknowledging as the 'knowledge gap' in our understanding and thinking about economic growth and development in Africa (Booth, 2011, Kelsall, 2008). In a sense, this knowledge gap in understanding African states may lead to rampant vilification of African states from both neo-Marxists and neo-liberals, as Mkandawire (2001) has argued.

Neo-patrimonialism and the state in Africa

For analysts who use the concept of neo-patrimonialism to explain the African crisis in general, the starting point is that poor state formation and the resulting weak state institutions in many African countries has made it impossible for the state to play an effective role in promoting economic growth and development. According to proponents of this view, lack of formalisation of the state has meant that it is not autonomous, and this makes it susceptible to capture by a few political elites who use its machinery for self-enrichment and for staying in power. Hence, while there is recognition that the state plays (and should play) a central role in economic growth and development, it is contended that the nature of states in Africa makes it difficult for the state to play a constructive role in the process of economic growth and development.

A common view among analysts operating within this framework is that the "Failure of the state to be emancipated from society has profoundly limited the scope of 'good governance' in Sub-Saharan Africa". It is further argued that, "such [a] poorly institutionalised state has not had the means seriously to spur sustainable economic growth on the continent" (Chabal and Daloz, 1999: 14). This failure to institutionalise the state, it has been argued, results in most of the functions which should be performed by the formal state institutions being carried out by *informal*, underground institutions (Chabal, 2002). This is because "governments in Africa have never achieved the level of institutionalisation" required for a formal functioning of the states; "they have remained unemancipated from society" (Chabal and Daloz, 1999: 28). A similar point is made by Jean-Francois Bayart (1993: 37), who argues that the "incompleteness and ambivalence" of African states makes it easy for the political elite to use the state as an instrument of control and domination. For some analysts the main reason explaining the informal nature of African states is "precisely because they lack Weberian-style bureaucracies and strong institutions through which to impose their agenda" (see Menocal, 2004).

Institutionalisation of the state is a key concept in this approach and it is developed further to link it to the notion of *disorder* as a functional condition which serves very specific ends. From this it is argued that what seems to be *disorder* is actually a well-ordered realm, characterised by the "rush for spoils in which all actors – rich and poor – participate in the world of networks. 'I chop you chop' was the promise of a Nigerian party" (Bayart, 1993: 235). Other analysts argue that because of the *personal* nature of African states, "the political requirement of regime and personal survival take precedence over and can contradict the economic policies and practices needed to promote sustained economic expansion" (Sandbrook, 1986: 321).

Relying on this understanding of the state, most analysts operating within the state-centric framework have concentrated on the impact of *patrimony* and its progeny, *neo-patrimonialism*, to explain economic growth and development challenges in Africa. In this regard, the main argument advanced is that neo-patrimonialism and rampant rent-seeking in most (if not all) African states, prevents the state from using resources for investment; instead resources are used to sponsor lavish consumption of patrons and their clients in the networks.

> Within a neo-patrimonial system the much trumpeted 'public' sector is in reality appropriated by private interests. The consequence is double: on the one hand, public service remains personalised …; on the other, access to the public institutions of the state is seen as the main means of personal enrichment.
>
> (Sandbrook, 1986: 9)

In a similar vein, Naomi Chazen and Donald Rothchild (1993) also argue that the *incomplete* institutionalisation of the state has meant that a small section of the political elite – one made up of powerful networks – controls and monopolises state resources to the detriment of economic growth and development.

Here the key argument is that when such a state intervenes in the economy, it only promotes rent-seeking, corruption and looting of public resources to the benefit of a tiny section of the elite:

> involvement of the state in the economy has allowed individual politicians and bureaucrats to manipulate markets as means of generating profits through non-competitive mechanisms and to use them not only to enrich themselves but also to build ... political support. This pervasive dynamic has led to the antithesis of development.
>
> (Menocal, 2004: 766)

The two publics thesis

Related to the notion of incomplete state institutionalisation is the idea that post-colonial African states are characterised by the existence of 'two publics': the *primordial* (kin relationships) and *civil* (state-citizen relationship) publics. Robert Bates *et al.* (1993) refer to this feature as the "dual political authority". Using this concept it is argued that most individuals in Africa operate in both publics. However, while an individual operates in both, he or she is *moral* in the former and *amoral* in the latter. In the primordial public, on the one hand, the "individual sees his duties as *moral* obligations to benefit and sustain a primordial public of which he is a member". On the other hand, while "the individual seeks to gain from the civic public, there is no *moral* urge for him to give back to the civic public in return for his benefits" (Ekeh, 1975: 106–7, emphasis in original). This amoral nature of an individual in the civic public, it is argued, is responsible for the perception that the "civic public can never be impoverished" (Ekeh, 1975: 108).

The consequence of citizens operating in the two publics is that it becomes easy for the political elite to use the civic public's resources to support their networks in the primordial public, from where they receive, in return, non-material benefits including psychological security. As a result, public resources and privileges can be used to advance personal or narrow interests in ways that harm economic growth and development. While this feature of African societies benefits a few individuals in a particular network, some analysts have warned that the benefit for the few comes at a huge cost in terms of the missed development opportunities for the majority.

A general observation made in this regard is that while academics have described and analysed the nature, costs and operation of neo-patrimonial rule, the impact that such systems impose on society at large, and development prospects in particular, are often ignored (Hyden, 2000: 20). Resources channelled to political loyalties, which could have gone into development projects, often come from public sources such as taxation and royalties on agricultural producers, exporters of natural resources, importers, foreign aid, loans and foreign investments; operations of state-owned corporations; and from appointments to the public sector. In such a system, officials are under "constant pressure to capture new resources to maintain the loyalty of subalterns" (Sandbrook, 2005: 1123).

Ironically, despite being aware of the social cost of patrimonial rule, some analysts have suggested that reforming this system may have a negative impact on societies in Africa, especially in cases where the restructuring of *informal* institutions results in state failure which is worse than even a "poorly functioning neo-patrimonial system" (Sandbrook, 2005: 1122). It has further been argued that in the context of entrenched neo-patrimonial rule, the political competition introduced by the democratic multi-party system in Africa since the beginning of the 1990s has resulted in a fierce contest for scarce resources between rival elite groups, resulting in conflict and civil wars in many countries (Chabal, 2002). While political competition that comes with multi-party politics has been heralded by some as the starting point for rescuing the state from rent-seeking behaviour and clientelism, there are also suggestions that this has actually resulted in the intensification of the fight to capture the state (Bayart, 1993). According to this view, the current relatively high price of commodities on the global level should lead to more contestation for the state in the bid to control the channels for extracting rents. This, in turn, should lead to an increase in civil conflict, coups, state failures and collapse. However, this might not be happening currently because, as some analysts have suggested, the level of contestation around the state is the function of the degree of state legitimacy, such that the "weaker the legitimacy of the state … the more likely it is that political contestation will turn into challenges to the state itself" (Englebert, 2000a: 14).

Broadly, the connection between neo-patrimonialism and the economic growth and development challenges in Africa is the idea that in a situation where state or public resources are used to oil the joints of the 'looting' networks, the basic elements required for the normal functioning of a 'modern' state and economy – such as an autonomous bureaucracy (in the Weberian sense), accountability, impartiality, an impersonal formalised set of rules, certainty, discipline, professionalism and transparency – are disregarded. Instead fraud, corruption, arbitrariness, discretional rule according to the wishes of the patron leader, manipulation, rent-seeking, tax evasion, informal exchange, the shrinking of the formal realm of the state, and the pillaging of state resources become the order of the day.

Because of its informal and clandestine nature, so the argument goes, neo-patrimonial rule recruits people to public office not on merit but on other factors such as ethnicity, loyalty to the patron, kinship ties and other non-meritocratic principles. Consequently, since the civil service is filled with incompetent party cadres and network clients, not only does the quality of services suffer, but effective state intervention on behalf of the broader public interests, including creating conditions conducive to economic growth and development, is rendered futile. Under these circumstances, "production suffers as rulers invest the scarce resources to realise these non-economic objectives. They divert resources from public investments in high quality roads, schools, and health facilities in order to favour cronies and their cronies' clienteles" (Sandbrook, 2005: 1123). It is further argued that in such circumstances the elites are more likely to resort to neo-patrimonialism than developmental policies, ... [and] the more neo-patrimonial the nature of the ruling system, the weaker the effectiveness of government institutions, the poorer the quality of governance, and the worse the choice of economic policies.

(Englebert, 2000a: 14)

The roots of patrimony

Since the concepts of patrimony and neo-patrimonialism occupy a central place in the state-centric perspective, it is important to briefly elaborate on these ideas. The concept of patrimony is not a new invention peculiar to the African situation. The term was popularised by Max Weber to describe the type of relationship which existed between the members of the feudal estate and the feudal lord prior to the development of capitalism in Europe. The defining features of this feudal relationship included the arbitrary exercise of power on the part of the estate-owner, and the demand for unflinching allegiance or loyalty from tenants or subjects. In Weber's formulation, this arbitrariness in the exercise of power, predominant in feudal societies, is clearly distinguished from capitalist (industrial) societies in which relations are not based on any form of allegiance, but are regulated by formal contracts which recognise individual rights (Weber, [1911] 1968).

Thus, the most important feature of the patrimonial system is that one person (the patron or patroness, feudal lord, etc.) controls (owns) and distributes the privileges or resources in the feudal estate or manor. The patron(ess) personalises the power in the community such that whatever he or she decrees has to be carried out. Therefore the patron(ess) becomes a law unto him/herself in as far as the ruler's wishes are not limited by prescribed or prior agreed rules.

In the African case, some scholars have suggested that the widespread patrimonial tendencies seen in post-colonial African leaders have their roots in the pre-colonial political institutions – such as chieftaincy or kingship – under which it was believed that traditional leaders exercised power arbitrarily, in the same way as the feudal lord in fourteenth century Western Europe (see Medard, 1982, Clapham, 1985). Analysts who espouse this view have triumphantly referred to patrimonialism in Africa as a form of "retraditionalizing" the continent (Chabal, 2002: 452). Some have gone further and attributed neo-patrimonialism in Africa to what they describe as "excessive economic regulation which was widespread during the 1970s and 1980s – the socialist and Marxist 'control regimes'"(Collier, 2006: 192).

However, relating neo-patrimonialism to pre-colonial African societies creates several analytical hurdles. For example, what constitutes pre-colonial society is hard to properly reconstruct after encounters with other cultures (see Mamdani, 1996). But even if one manages to reconstruct how power was exercised in these societies prior to the encounter with the West or near-East, some analysts have contended that the exercise of power in pre-colonial African societies was not arbitrary (Davidson, 1992). "Restraint on pre-colonial authority flowed from two separate, though related tendencies: one from peers, the other from people" (Mamdani, 1996: 43). Lungisile Ntsebeza (2006) makes a similar point, arguing that the tyrannical feature of traditional leaders in African societies was a form of corruption introduced by the colonial system of appointing loyalists as chiefs or kings. Mamdani's (1996) central argument on this issue is that the checks and balances within pre-colonial societies in Africa were compromised by the colonial administration's introduction of what he calls "decentralised despotism". Careful analysis of the administrative structures and exercise of power in traditional African societies, even today, supports the view that power is not personalised upon the king or chief; the leaders in society follow collectively approved norms and guidelines. Even the chief or king is subject to these norms. While there are some traditional leaders who have abused their roles and positions in society for personal enrichment, they cannot justify their actions on the basis of customary norms and practice. To the contrary, a traditional leader is expected to be the custodian of these cultural norms and principles.

Is neo-patrimonialism peculiar to Africa?

While it has been acknowledged by many analysts that distributing resources and privileges on a party, ethnic or kinship basis is not unique to African states and societies (Hyden, 2000: 22; Collier, 2006), there is wide agreement among proponents of this view that the African form of neo-patrimonialism is different from that which one finds anywhere else in the world. One example that is used as evidence for the uniqueness of the African brand of neo-patrimonialism is the widespread nature of this scourge. Patrick Chabal and Jean-Pascal Daloz (1999), for instance, argue that even if corruption, bribery, nepotism, discrete political and economic exchanges, and clientelism exist everywhere, it is the widespread nature of this problem in Africa which makes it unique. As the quote from Bayart on p. 157 suggests, there is an impression created that everyone ('rich and poor') is participating in some form of network or discrete exchange; that everyone operates with the "I chop, you chop" maxim. Although some authors acknowledge that such practices are also found in developed democracies with *formalised* states, including those in Western Europe and North America, a distinction is made between the pervasive form of neo-patrimonialism found in Africa (referred to as the '*vertical* corruption'), and the *horizontal* corruption found in Western countries, which, they argue, is limited to top-level officials. Critics often argue that whereas corruption in the West and other developed countries is restricted to the top level (horizontal), involving the top managers in the corporate world, in Africa corruption "concerns the whole population and operates essentially according to a vertical relation of inequality. Everyone, everywhere tries to benefit. Examples abound: in airports, each official (passport, health, customs, baggage, etc.) wants his/her cut" (Chabal and Daloz, 1999: 102).

Some proponents of neo-patrimonialism contend that in Africa, "Contrary to the popular image of the innocent masses, corruption and predatoriness are not found exclusively amongst the powerful. Rather they are modes of social and political behaviour shared by a plurality of actors on more or less a greater scale" (Bayart, 1993: 238). The conclusion drawn is that these widespread informal activities make economic growth and development impossible. According to this view, the situation turns into a vicious circle which reproduces economic stagnation as long as it is easy for the patron to control and sustain his or her networks. Bayart, for instance argues that lack of development – manifested in scarcity of resources and widespread poverty – makes it easier for the patrons to regulate political power and maintain loyalty among clients. "Nothing is done without his order. No operation is undertaken unless he has ordained it. The President of Guinea has become the *Papa Bondieu* giving out thousands of francs CFA here, sheets of metal, a sack of cement, a motorbike or a bag of sugar there" (Bayart, 1993: 233). The outcome is a self-reinforcing situation whereby the scarcer in a society the resources are, the more widespread are the informal exchanges, and the more the state is captured for private gain.

'Big Men', the state and Africa's development

While Weber used the term patrimony in the context of pre-capitalist societies, modern analysts have added the prefix 'neo' to adapt the term to the current context in which power is not exercised over a small manor, feudal estate or village, but over the entire state machinery. However, the modern use of the term neo-patrimonialism also conveys the meaning of arbitrary, personified, informal, totalitarian use of state power and other resources by a political leader or people in his/her network. Chabal (2002), who has been a faithful observer and analyst of neo-patrimonial rulers and states in Africa, has defined a neo-patrimonial state as one where despite the existence of *formal* state structures, exercise of power takes place in the *informal*, wily structures where state power is not only personalised but is discretionarily exercised. By extension, a neo-patrimonial leader is one who presides over a neo-patrimonial state, and, in the literature, he is often referred to as the 'Big Man' or 'Number One'; his/her real names are rarely mentioned in informal dealings. Typical 'Big Men' in Africa are often portrayed as follows:

> He is the centrifugal force around which all else revolves … His physical self is omnipresent … [his] picture is plastered on public walls, billboards and even in private homes. His portrait also adorns stamps, coins, paper money, and even the T-shirts and buttons often distributed by the party 'faithful'.
>
> (Sandbrook, 1986: 323–4)

If pressed for examples, proponents of the neo-patrimonial thesis would string out a list of African political leaders who perfectly match this portrait. Though some, however, have argued that this portrait matches Africa's 'political entrepreneurs' of the 1980s and 1990s and noted that the era of the 'Big Man' has passed, and that "Africa no longer needs strong men – it needs strong institutions"[14] (Joseph, 2011: 324), the neo-patrimonial literature still populates the African states with myriad Big Men who often backslide into despotism and authoritarianism (Mattes and Bratton, 2007). Descriptions of what Bayart (2000) refers to as the "native princes" (or the 'political entrepreneur') is often so poetically depicted that the resulting caricature becomes hard to trust for someone who has never met such a human being; he (there has been no *she* yet) is often over-coloured, beyond any human resemblance, and without conscience or sense of shame.

The hollowing of the state

In the context of the state in Africa, neo-patrimonialism has often been used to mean the capture of the state machinery by the 'Big Men' or the 'native princes', and the network which they[15] operate to advance personal interests. The rule of law, transparency, impersonal rule, accountability and rationality in state operations (including resource allocation and investment decisions) only receive lip-service. The result is obvious: *disorder*, uncertainty, cronyism, clientelism, systemic corruption and lack of accountability. All these features contribute to the 'hollowing' of the state, to the extent that the state's formal structures are bypassed, and the state bureaucracy only responds to the promptings of clients in the network. Thus, in patrimonial states, instead of being accountable to the people, the bureaucracy is accountable to the patron leader and his/her network. Consequently

> government is not held to account by its supporters for the delivery of public goods, but rather for its ability to divert resources from other groups. Short-term considerations of inter-group transfers crowd out the consideration of a longer-term vision.
>
> (Collier, 2006: 194)

For most of the authors who have written on this topic, this form of political and social organisation is predominantly found in SSA (see Collier, 2007), though a couple of countries in other developing regions are often mentioned. In recent years the World Bank has also added to this prognosis, arguing that while problems of poor governance are found in other developing regions, the "challenge in Africa is particularly acute for three reasons": (i) too many 'fragile states', (ii) political instability in many countries, and (iii) the resource curse (World Bank, 2011: 20). Though not on the same wavelength as the World Bank, proponents of neo-patrimonialism offer similar reasons why this patrimony is more prevalent in SSA compared to other regions. The widely cited factors include the view that African leaders inherited the patrimonial rule from pre-colonial traditional authorities, as mentioned above (see Mattes and Bratton, 2007); that Africa lacks a true bureaucracy because of a lack of the sort of industrialisation which was the precursor of a modern bureaucratic state in the West (Sandbrook, 1986); that the special nature of colonial rule in Africa created conditions for patronage politics (Bayart, 1993); that extreme ethnic diversity provided a fertile ground for special interests to capture the state (Suberu, 2000); that the material conditions of most SSA countries create a favourable climate in which informal exercise of power becomes ubiquitous (Sandbrook, 2005, Chazen and Rothchild, 1993). Some analysts have argued that the absence of a strong and well-defined indigenous class makes state formation difficult (Leys, 1976), and that the absence of strong civil society has resulted in states that are susceptible to elite capture (Chabal and Daloz, 1999).

A bureaucratic-developmental state in Africa: lessons from Asia

Analysts who focus on the nature of the state in SSA as the main explanatory variable for SSA's economic and development experience often point to countries in South East Asia, where it is believed that the development of a strong, autonomous and effective state contributed to rapid economic growth, accompanied by massive improvements in the living conditions of the people.

> South Korea is the obvious point of comparison ... In the years immediately after the Second World War, Korea was governed by ... the personalised, corrupt administration of Syngman Rhee. In its rent-seeking and pursuit of patronage politics, and subordination of economic rationality to short-term political gain, the Rhee regime was similar to many of the governments that have hastened Africa's economic decline ... While the Korean state under Rhee may have been similar to many contemporary African states; that which evolved after the military coup of 1961 was very different. The military leadership that seized power justified its moves as necessary for ending corruption and for achieving real economic development ... Pivotal to this was the centralisation of political power, the gaining of autonomy from societal pressure groups, and institutionalisation of centralised decision-making by technocrats who enjoyed substantial autonomy from societal pressures.
>
> (Callaghy and Ravenhill, 1993: 35–6)

In this comparison, the argument has been that most African states had similar economic and political institutions to states in South East Asia, such as South Korea during the 1960s. But the latter succeeded in implementing political transformation which paved the way for rapid economic growth and development. Key in this transformation was the role of the state, which itself was transformed from being a predatory, patrimonial, rentier state into an autonomous bureaucratic state, free from the influence of the politicians' narrow interests.

Critics of African states observe that the successful transition in Korea, guided by authoritarian governments, pre-empts any argument that puts the blame for economic challenges in Africa on the spread of military rule or authoritarian one-party states. To the contrary, there have been suggestions that authoritarian regimes are more ideal for countries at the early stages of economic development. For example, Gunnar Myrdal (1970) argued for "strong states" (in contrast to "soft states"), as indispensable for economic growth and development in underdeveloped countries. A similar view is expressed in Johnson's view that the Japanese state's role in economic growth amounted to some form of state absolutism (and Johnson's emphasis on the state's autonomy has been criticised as defending authoritarianism and fascism). In Johnson's view, the Japanese state, through the Ministry of International Trade and Industry (MITI), exercised absolute control over the running of the economy, including the introduction of protectionist measures, quotas and the rationing of foreign currency (see Johnson, 1982: 38).

The main reason for preferring 'strong states' in developing countries is that 'soft states', because of their lack of 'social discipline' are prone to arbitrariness, deficient legislation, failure to observe and enforce laws, and collusion with powerful personalities – giving rise to corruption which, in turn, weakens state capacity, resulting in what Myrdal (1970) calls "circular causation". On the other hand, 'strong states' are seen to be able to institute social discipline, making it possible to implement development plans. Myrdal (1970), however, argues that 'softness' or 'strongness' of the state is not related to any particular *form* of government (authoritarian or democratic); it relates to the condition of the state.

On the basis of this, there have been numerous suggestions in the literature urging Africa to learn from the East Asian model of development (see Morrissey, 2001; Smith, 2001). Today, debates about the developmental state (not necessarily authoritarian states) emphasise the creation of an autonomous state capable of pursuing broader national developmental goals without being pressured by political elites or interest groups. However, some have argued that replication of the Asian style of development is almost impossible in Africa today for various reasons, including the 'softness' of African states, a lack of ideology to guide development, the dependent nature of African governments, lack of technical capacity within the state, and the difference in global environment in which the protectionist approach adopted by most Asian countries is no longer tenable (see Mkandwire, 2001).

While calls for the developmental state in Africa, similar to the Asian models, have resurfaced (see UNECA, 2011), with some analysts emphasising that such a state should not only be 'developmental' but also 'democratic' – giving rise to the idea that Africa needs a 'democratic developmental state' (see Edigheji, 2005) – there is no reason to believe that what worked in East Asia will perform the same miracle in Africa. Critics have argued that the replication approach is not likely to work; what is critical is the transformation of African states in ways which can overcome the patrimonial burden that most of them struggle with. For this reason proponents of the state-centric approach, though mostly agreeing that economic policy reforms are important for ensuring sustained economic growth and development, emphasise that reforming state institutions is key to addressing Africa's economic growth and development crisis. Hence, some have chastised structural adjustment for failing to dismantle patrimonial states in SSA (Chabal and Daloz, 1999, Chabal, 2002), while others have argued that adjustment programmes – by emphasising the operation of the markets, the privatisation of state-owned enterprises, and public service reforms – have contributed to freeing state institutions from capture by the political elite (Chazen and Rothchild, 1993).

State bureaucracy and development

Discussions around the role of the state in economic growth and development often deploy notions of the modern bureaucratic state as the appropriate concept that captures the state–development connection. As noted earlier, whether one is using the concept of a developmental or modern bureaucratic state, there is wide agreement that the way state apparatus is configured has an impact on economic growth and development outcomes in a country. While Georg F.W. Hegel has been credited with being the intellectual father of the concept of the modern state (see Nettl, 1968: 573), it can be argued that views on the formation and functions of modern state institutions are varied and debates on the concept and application is far from settled. However, some of the common ideas about the modern state are widely traced to Weber's concept of modern bureaucracy.

A central concept in the Weberian view of the state is this idea of *rationality*, or the *impersonal nature* of the state; the idea that the state should not be identified with any person who holds or exercises power within it. Weber develops his idea of modern bureaucracy by linking it to his theory of *social action* and the *origins of authority* and *power*. In Weber's theory of *social action*, human actions are derived from three main motives: emotion (affective action), custom (traditional action) and rationality (rational action based on legal, formalised rules). Consequently, the three types of social action generate the corresponding types of legitimacy and authority in associative (public) life; affective action results in legitimacy and authority based on an individual's emotional attraction to a charismatic figure who can be a religious leader, politician, activist, or even an anarchist. The social and political structure in this instance revolves around the perceived charismatic qualities of the leader, and the exercise of power resulting from this is what Weber refers to as 'charismatic authority' (Weber, [1911] 1968).

The other source of legitimacy and power is custom, based on 'traditional practice'. In the Weberian concept of authority and power, customary practice gives rise to a form of legitimacy built on the belief that something is right because *that is the way it has always been done*. A classic example of legitimacy based on customary authority is the belief that members of a royal family should always rule because that has been the custom, with the legitimacy generated by people's submission to the traditional authority conferred by customary norms. In this way the traditional leaders, nobles and kings command authority, obedience and submission not on the basis of their charismatic qualities, but purely on the basis of their inherited status, although some may actually have strong charismatic and leadership qualities.

The third source of legitimacy in the Weberian framework is rationality. Different from charismatic and traditional authority, rational authority is based on collectively agreed upon principles which guide public interactions and the exercise of power. Rational authority arises from the rational actions of individuals guided by formally elaborated rules and principles. Consequently, legitimacy and exercise of power are based on formally agreed *impersonal* rules which define the limits of power and authority of those in positions of leadership, such that the exercise of power is based on fixed jurisdiction, prescribed rules and an autonomous agent – the 'bureaucratic *agency*'. It is important to note that Weber calls these three types of authority and organisational structures "ideal types".

According to Weber, the charismatic and traditional forms of authority characterise pre-industrial, pre-capitalist societies, while a bureaucratic state based on rational authority is emblematic of modern industrial capitalist society: "Bureaucracy, thus understood, is fully developed in political and ecclesiastical communities only in the modern state, and in the private economy only in the most advanced institutions of capitalism" (Weber, [1911] 1968: 956). Although Weber had his own worries about the dangers of rational authority, he clearly identified this form of legitimacy as being superior to the other two. An effective state bureaucracy or civil service, in Weber's view, is seen as an indispensable structure of industrial capitalist societies which is expected to perform administration on a large scale.

Central to this conception of the state is the idea of depersonalisation, or the separation of the *public* from the *private* realm and interest.

> In principle, the modern organisation of the civil service separates the *bureau* from the *private domicile* of the official and, in general segregates official activity from the spheres of private life. Public monies and equipment are divorced from the private property of the official.
>
> (Weber, [1911] 1968: 957, emphasis added)

In this way, it is apparent that the state (and its institutions) takes up a 'life of its own', and this is perhaps the most important feature that distinguishes the Weberian notions of the state from other notions of it (see Nettl, 1968). In the Weberian view, it becomes difficult to imagine how the state can sustain the complex structures of regulating, coordinating and administering the multitude of intricate tasks without an efficient and competent bureaucracy. Weber defines bureaucracy in an industrial capitalist state as a hierarchical organisation designed rationally to coordinate the work of many individuals in the pursuit of large-scale administrative tasks and organisational goals (Weber, [1911] 1968).

However, identifying the appearance of state bureaucracy with industrial capitalism raises the question of whether different state formations are to be expected in non-industrial countries. Thus, one can argue that since industrial capitalism has not fully developed in many African countries, it should not be surprising to find African states displaying traits different from the Weberian state. In other words, Weber's close association of a depersonalised state with industrial capitalism can justify the argument that the absence of this feature in most African states is a clear manifestation that industrial capitalism has not taken root in the continent. In fact a number of authors such as Goran Hyden, Colin Leys, Kevin Cox and Rohit Negi have argued that the poor state formation in Africa and the subsequent weak economic growth performance should be explained by the incomplete development of capitalism in the continent. "Our diagnosis is rooted in the general absence of the necessary precondition for capitalist development", argue Cox and Negi (2011: 72). According to this view, African states are weak and underdeveloped precisely because capitalist development failed to take root in the continent. Here the crucial debate centres on the soundness of the major premise of the argument: is state bureaucracy a feature of industrial capitalism only?

In the Weberian conception of a modern state, although all the features of a well-functioning bureaucracy are interlinked and important, appointment to public office on the basis of merit (an individual's competence, skill and ability to perform his or her duties) and no other criterion are key. In other words, civil servants should not be recruited because they know someone or because they belong to a particular party or race or ethnic group, but because they meet the required competencies. In Weber's view, it is only when civil servants are recruited on merit that they will be able to implement the rules in an impersonal way, and more effectively because they are the best people for the job. Otherwise, civic officials may fail to discharge their duties in an impersonal, professional manner because they have to respond to those people who influenced their appointment. According to Weber, "bureaucratic administration means fundamentally the exercise of control on the basis of knowledge. This is the feature of it which makes it rational" (Weber, [1911] 1968).

Professionally competent and autonomous civic officials are also seen to be instrumental in effectively mobilising resources (public and private) and coordinating the way these resources are used. When civil servants with these features occupy public office, it is argued that state power cannot be easily hijacked for the personal and arbitrary interests of any single individual or group of individuals. This feature of state bureaucracy is sometimes referred to as "embedded autonomy" (Evans, 1995), i.e., the bureaucracy enjoys a level of freedom and legitimacy (see Johnson, 1982). When a state develops such qualities, it is argued that the state is freed from society or that the state is fully institutionalised, meaning that the functions of it are separated from the private interest of groups and individuals – including the head of state. In this sense, the modern Weberian state is conceived as "a complete break from the notion that the holders of political power possess any legitimate claim on the assets or resources which they administer. The public and private spheres become functionally distinct" (Chabal and Daloz, 1999: 5).

Of course in reality it is hard to find any state bureaucracy which exhibits all the features of the Weberian ideal state. Even in the industrial capitalist states which Weber was writing about, party deployment to public office is a common practice such that the winning party always has the prerogative of appointing its own cadres to key positions, including top civil service offices. These in turn may influence the recruitment of officials to intermediate and lower level public offices, for various reasons. Thus, the real modern state is highly unlikely to be immune from the politics of patronage, clientelism and cadreism, and all the abuses this may entail, even in industrial capitalist countries. Further, the key notion of the separation of public office from private activities, while a conceptually appealing idea, is not always easy to practise even in advanced capitalist countries. Often, either states or individual office bearers are too pervasive to the point that the "lines between public and private, political and personal, formal and informal, official and non-official, government and market, legal and customary … are blurred". As was the case with most countries in East Asia, "states are organisationally pervasive, without clear-cut boundaries" (Johnson, 1999: 60).

Weber himself was aware of the limitations of his framework of the modern bureaucratic state. Apart from his fears about creating "specialists without spirit", trapped by conforming to the rigidities of formalised, impersonal interactions, he was also aware that such concentration of power can be prone to abuse by those who have control over the state bureaucracy. However, what is widely accepted is the view that the development of an efficient state machinery anchored around an efficient, competent and skilful, professional, highly trained, and most importantly, autonomous civil service, can provide the momentum required to achieve sustained economic growth.

State bureaucracies in Africa

In the case of African states, analysts who attribute Africa's poor economic performance to neo-patrimonial rule argue that since state institutions are not fully institutionalised or liberated from society, state resources are not only vulnerable to being used to serve the interests of the 'Big Men' and their networks, the elite have no interest in promoting broad-based, orderly, development – and as such they cannot be developmental. Proponents of this view have argued that this institutionalisation of what may appear to be irrationality or disorder in many African states is deliberate because it serves rational ends for those who operate in the patrimonial networks. It has been argued, for instance, that in a patrimonial state, there is no incentive for those operating in the network to *liberate* the state and fully institutionalise the bureaucracy, since a partially emancipated state may not advance the interests of the networks: "[T]he very weakness and inefficiency of the state has been profitable to the African political elite. The development of political machines and the consolidation of clientelistic networks within the formal political apparatus has been immensely advantageous" (Chabal and Daloz, 1999: 14). Chabal and Daloz (1999) and Bayart (1993) in particular argue that the patrimonial state is not in the business of development. Development in its broader definition would undercut the spaces in which the patron operates. Thus, the 'politics of the belly' is not just about the desperate move to survive biologically, but also about the politics through which the 'political entrepreneurs' or 'native princes' amass and redistribute wealth in exchange for honour and loyalty (Bayart, 2000). "In other words, the social struggles which make up the quest for hegemony and the production of the state bear the hallmark of the rush for spoils in which all actors – rich and poor – participate in the world of networks" (Bayart, 1993: 235). In this framework it is noted that a patrimonial state will not have the incentive to provide public services to build the human capital needed to staff a technocratic and efficient civil service which can clamp down on rent-seeking and corruption.

The empirical challenge of neo-patrimonialism

Although claims about rampant neo-patrimonialism in Africa have been made, there is an empirical challenge to this analysis. In the first instance, most of the accounts rely on anecdotal evidence (Hungwe, 2000), and public opinion polls (Mattes and Bratton, 2007). In this way, the neo-patrimonial approach is similar to the map-making exercise of the sixteenth and seventeenth centuries, which generated many myths about Africa and the people who live there. While it is equally suspicious to dismiss the existence of patronage in Africa, one struggles to find any serious attempt to provide the empirical support for the existence of the same. It seems that the discourse is "rarely based on analysis of actual experiences, but merely on first principles, ideological convictions or faith" (Mkandawire, 2001: 290). For a long time scholarship on African states has struggled to relate theory to reality – to move from theory to the empirical – primarily because the reality is often dismissed as aberrant or deviant, and whatever is left, every effort is made to ensure that it fits into the already structured units of analysis (see Hill, 2005). As some analysts have pointed out, "the understanding of power and culture suggest an essential need to interpret the local and the proximate, because of the way they are constituted and experienced" (Dorman, 2009: 13).

The failure to connect with local realities in the dominant approach adopted when studying states in Africa has led to the disconnection between the theoretical and the empirical such that most works in this area "tell us surprisingly little about the state in Africa" (Nugent, 2010: 35). In this regard it is not only the conceptual disconnections; there are also questions about the suitability of the various tools that are used to investigate state performance in Africa, especially now, when myriad governance indices – such as the Governance Indicators of the United Nations Development Programme (UNDP), the Freedom House Index, the Ease of Doing Business Index, the MO Ibrahim Index, the Polity IV Classification Scale, the Afrobarometer, the Corruption Perception Index, the Economist Intelligence Unit Democracy Index, the World Bank's Country Policy Institutional Assessment (CPIA) – have proliferated. With specific reference to the Ease of Doing Business Index, compiled by the World Bank, it has been observed that using this index to explain variance in growth across countries has "yielded ambiguous results". It has also "suffer[ed] from the same econometric woes as all other cross-country growth regressions" (Page, 2012: 15). It has been further observed that such indices have focused on rewarding "the quantity of ranking changes but does not assess whether the changes constitute important or meaningful reforms", and as such they are seen to have "diverted attention and resources from serious and public action needed to address investment climate constraints to faster growth" (Page, 2012: 15).

In recent analyses of the challenge of development and growth in Africa, some analysts are highlighting this empirical challenge, pointing out that there is an empirical gap inherent in the dominant assessments of African states, including the role of the state in economic growth and development analysis. Research initiated by the Africa Power and Politics Programme (APP) in 2003 has now gained momentum in identifying what it calls the "knowledge deficit" and the "lack of understanding and a shared inability to conceive alternative scenarios and pathways" in Africa (Booth, 2011: 1). Failure to critically understand African realities is seen as an inevitable outcome promoted by the international development agencies which since the early 1960s have seen aid as a perfect substitute for understanding African societies. It is thus argued that

> no one really knows how to build the type of governance that Africa needs. The forms of governance that might work better for development … are not known. We know what is wrong, but we do not know for sure what would work better.
>
> (Booth, 2011: 2)

In a sense, the acknowledgement of a knowledge gap as far as Africa's development challenge is concerned is an honest acceptance of the fact that our understanding has been hazy, and therefore further effort is needed to improve this.

Unfortunately, most of the analysts who have used the concept of neo-patrimonialism in Africa have not provided systematic analysis of this scourge in Africa. For example, although Chabal and Daloz claim that their main task is to help make sense of what seems senseless (making sense of the so-called "mysteries of Africa's barbarism") – by making "empirical observation of present-day realities and not from preconceived notions of what ought or ought not to be analysed" (Chabal and Daloz, 1999: 17) – there is no evidence of any systematic gathering of data which informs their analysis. When discussing corruption, loyalty to the patron, and recruitment of personnel into public service, the evidence given is this:

> The head of the national radio station of a major West African country confided recently that he was constantly under pressure to hire relatives of the members of the political elite. He explained that to resist such pressure would inevitably mean he would lose his job
>
> (Chabal and Daloz, 1999: 6–7)

Evidence of nepotism and corruption cited include the claim that "Benin's N. Soglo" is known to be corrupt and that "Zambia's Chiluba" is reported to have fired the director of the national TV station for opposing the allocation of air-time to a religious group to which Chiluba belonged (Chabal and Daloz, 1999: 6–7).

Just as one cannot deny the occurrence of such activities in the continent, unless there is sufficient credible evidence to support their existence it is equally questionable to affirm their occurrence on the basis of anecdotal evidence. However, this is a general problem associated with informal state structures and networks which operate clandestinely. Given the nature of these operations, it is difficult to empirically investigate neo-patrimonialism and all that it implies.

No one records the informal transactions which take place outside of formal state institutions. In fact, it is difficult even to obtain data on formal state transactions such as the amount of public resources allocated and disbursed to various sectors. Thus, while one can make observations of incidences that point to the existence of patrimonialism and clientelism, the principle of parsimony calls for a cautious generalisation in cases where the evidence is far from convincing.

For this reason, case studies investigating the nature and quality of the state and how state institutions operate can provide meaningful insights into the connection between state bureaucracy (quality of governance) and economic growth. Earlier cases that have looked at these issues include the seminal case study of the Japanese MITI by Johnson (1982), Alice Amsden's (1989) study of South Korea, and Robert Wade's (1990) study of Taiwan – all of which have provided some helpful insights into the functioning of state bureaucracy. Unfortunately, very few (if any) similar case studies in Africa look into state structure, capacity and operations and how these can impact on economic growth. The very fact that the way African states function has been cited as a major contributing factor in their erratic economic performance should be a strong motivation for conducting serious investigation into how states are constituted, the nature of state bureaucracy, how these states operate, and what influences the *way* they operate.

Crude indices and proxies of state institutions – such as the Ease of Doing Business Index and the World Wide Governance Indicators (WWGI), as well as the Country Policy and Institutional Assessment (CPIA) published by the World Bank's International Finance Corporation (IFC), and other similar measures of the effectiveness of state institutions – shed little light on the organisational structure and constraints that these institutions face. In focusing on narrowly defined indicators such as the number of days it takes for someone to set up a business, the time it takes for someone to obtain a work or business permit, the time it takes to obtain an export or import permit, clear customs, and so on, the indices only provide an operational assessment of state institutions; they say very little about the nature and organisation of these institutions. Because of such a narrowly defined scope, these measures and the studies[16] that use them have failed to provide useful insights into the nature of state bureaucracy in Africa, and how such measures can be strengthened. Broadly aggregated indices, such as those covering corruption, rule of law, regulation quality, governance effectiveness, political stability and accountability, reveal little about the nitty-gritty of the way states operate and how this impacts on the lives of their citizens. Some analysts have questioned the suitability of such indices:

> For example, the various indicators used for surveying political issues ... are rarely suitable for Africa. Also there is no clarity on what is being measured: process or outcome? Beyond these issues of conceptual relevance are other technical problems of the surveys of political issues.
>
> (Adetula, 2011: 21)

Notably, most of these indices are tailored to the needs and interests of investors, on whose behalf some of the data sets are compiled. Little effort, if any, is made to understand how these weaknesses in state institutions arise, the nature of the weaknesses, and how they can be addressed. The primary interest is in classifying countries on a binary scale of those which provide an 'investor friendly environment' and those that do not. A country's position on the scale can be determined by how well a country treats the business class (especially foreign investors) regardless of what happens to the rest of the population. In this regard the Mo Ibrahim Index of African Governance (Mo Ibrahim Foundation, 2011) – which includes an index based on citizens' assessments of their own governments – may be a more useful tool for understanding issues around state capacity and constraints on the one hand, and challenges on the ground on the other.[17]

Thus, the challenge of understanding the role of states in Africa's economic growth and development today lies in finding appropriate concepts and tools for evaluating states, as well as suitable tools for systematically gathering information in ways that allow African states and state formation to be examined in their concrete contexts.

This chapter has discussed the role of states in understanding the economic growth and development challenges in Africa, focusing on views from development economics and political sociology. The next chapter looks at the various political-economic views on explaining Africa's economic and growth challenges.

Notes

1 Amartya Sen, for instance, identifies, (i) industrialisation, (ii) rapid capital accumulation, (iii) mobilisation of underemployed resources (particularly manpower), and (iv) planning, as the "major strategic themes pursued" by development economics since the 1940s (Sen, 1983: 746). The central focus of development economics can also be formulated in terms of the question "how can we account for differences in the levels of income and the rates of growth between the developed and less developed economies?" (Stiglitz, 1989: 197; see also Lewis, 1984: 5).
2 For instance Bayart (1993) and Chabal and Daloz (1999) emphasise that poor institutionalisation of the state and the failure to "emancipate the state from society" in Africa has impacted negatively on economic growth.
3 There are controversies about whether development economics was actually a subdiscipline or simply a set of themes and beliefs still deeply rooted in neoclassical economics (see Hirschman, 2001; Sen, 1983).
4 The notion of 'two economics' is reminiscent of Albert Einstein's *general* theory of relativity and *special* theory of relativity.
5 It should be noted here that the central planning referred to is not the same as the planned or command economies of the former USSR or Cuba. These ideas were rooted within the classical economic and Keynesian paradigms. See Arthur Lewis's (1954) model, for instance.
6 Arthur Lewis was invited to Ghana by Nkrumah and served as the economic advisor to both the colonial and post-colonial government (Ranis, 2004).
7 Other major reasons for the liberation struggle included the land question (especially in settler colonies), the fight for justice, and the restoration of the humanity of Africans who were either de-or sub-humanised by colonialism (see Rodney, 1972).

8 The award of a Nobel Peace Prize in economics to Ronald Coase and Douglas North in 1991 brought the ideas of NIE into the mainstream academic and research community.

9 While issues of good governance raised by the World Bank and the IMF during the 1990s may seem to be congruent with some of the ideas of a developmental state, the former focuses more on the functional aspects of the state such as accountability, transparency, and human rights; while the latter emphasises the structural features of the state such as the formalisation or depersonalisation of the state (an effective, autonomous, impersonal state bureaucracy).

10 Similar views are expressed in Chang's (1994) *The Political Economy of Industrial Policy*.

11 Courageously, because encouraging direct state participation in the economy at a World Bank gathering in the 1990s was tantamount to blasphemy.

12 See the First National Development Plans for Ghana (1963/64–1969/70), Tanzania (1964–1969), Nigeria (1962–1968), Kenya (1964–1970) and Zambia (1966–1970).

13 For instance, in an edited book on the role of the state in development, Callaghy and Ravenhill (1993: 540) cast doubt on the notion of states in Africa, and argue that most countries in SSA lack "stateness and cosmopolitanism" which are central to engendering autonomy within the state. Chabal and Daloz (1999) also come close to arguing that because the state has not been institutionalised (liberated from society), the state in Africa is "vacuous" or even non-existent.

14 These are apparently the words of Barack Obama to African leaders during his 2009 visit to Ghana.

15 So far there have been only 'he's; therefore it may be justified here to use what may sound like sexist language.

16 Most studies have relied on the data gathered by the International Country Risk Guide (ICRG), the Business and Environmental Risk Intelligence (BERI), and Business International (BI). Cross-country data sets such as the Penn World Tables have also been used by a number of analysts to investigate the impact of state institutions on growth. But very little has been learned from these (see Evans and Rauch, 1999).

17 Different African states are ranked based on their score on a number of indicators. There is an overall ranking as well as the ranking based on indicators such as safety and rule of law, sustainable economic opportunity, human development, and participation and human rights (see Mo Ibrahim Foundation, 2011).

References

Adetula, Victor (2011). "Measuring Democracy and 'Good Governance' in Africa: A Critique of Assumptions and Methods" in K. Kondlo and C. Ejiogu (eds) *Governance in the 21st Century*. Pretoria: Human and Social Sciences Research Council: 10–25.

Ake, Claude (1981). *A Political Economy of Africa*. Lagos: Longman Nigeria.

Amsden, Alice (1989). *Asia's Next Giant: South Korea and Late Industrialization*. New York: Oxford University Press.

Aspe, Pedro and Gurria, Angel (1992). "The State and Economic Development: A Mexican Perspective" in L. Summers and S. Shah (eds) *Proceedings of the World Bank Annual Conference on Development Economics*. Washington DC: World Bank: 9–14.

Bates, Robert (1981). *Markets and States in Tropical Africa: The Political Basis of Agricultural Policies*. Berkeley: University of California Press.

Bates, Robert, Mudimbe, V.Y. and O'Barr, Jean (1993). "Introduction" in R. Bates, V.Y. Mudimbe and J. O'Barr (eds) *Africa and the Disciplines: The Contribution of Research in Africa to the Social Sciences and Humanities*. Chicago/London: University of Chicago Press. Chapter 1.

Bayart, Jean-Francois (1993). *The State in Africa: The Politics of the Belly*. London: Longman.

Bayart, Jean-Francois (2000). "Africa in the World: A History of Extraversion." *African Affairs*, Vol. 99: 217–67.

Biney, Ama (2008). "The Legacy of Kwame Nkrumah in Retrospect." *Journal of Pan African Studies*, Vol. 2, No. 3: 129–59.

Booth, David (2011). "Introduction: Working with the Grain? The Africa Power and Politics Programme." *Institute of Development Studies (IDS) Bulletin*, Vol. 42, No. 2: 1–10.

Callaghy, Thomas and Ravenhill, John (1993). "How Hemmed In? Lessons and Prospects of Africa's Response to Decline" in T. Callaghy and J. Ravenhill (eds) *Hemmed In? Responses to Africa's Economic Decline*. New York: Columbia University Press. Chapter 13.

Chabal, Patrick (2002). "The Quest for Good Governance in Africa. Is NEPAD the Answer?" *International Affairs*, Vol. 78, No. 3: 447–65.

Chabal, Patrick and Daloz, Jean-Pascal (1999). *Africa Works: Disorder as Political Instrument*. London: James Currey.

Chang, Ha-Joon (1994). *The Political Economy of Industrial Policy*. New York: St. Martin's Press.

Chazen, Naomi and Rothchild, Donald (1993). "The Political Repercussions of Economic Malaise" in T. Callaghy and J. Ravenhill (eds) *Hemmed In? Responses to Africa's Economic Decline*. New York: Columbia University Press. Chapter 5.

Clapham, Christopher (1985). *Third World Politics: An Introduction*. Madison: University of Wisconsin Press.

Coleman, James (1985). "The Concept of Political Penetration" in M. Twaddle (ed.) *Decolonisation in British Africa: A New Historiographical Debate*. Copenhagen: University of Copenhagen.

Collier, Paul (2006). "African Growth: Why a Big Push?" *Journal of African Economies*, Vol. 00, AERC Supplement 2: 188–211.

Collier, Paul (2007). *The Bottom Billion: Why the Poorest Countries are Failing and What Can Be Done About it*. New York: Oxford University Press.

Collier, Paul and James W. Gunning. (1999). "Why Has Africa Grown Slowly?" *Journal of Economic Perspectives*, Vol. 13: 3–22.

Cox, Kevin and Negi, Rohit (2010). "The State and the Question of Development in Sub-Saharan Africa." *Review of African Political Economy*, Vol. 37, No. 123: 71–85.

Davidson, Basil (1992). *The Black Man's Burden: Africa and the Curse of the Nation States*. New York: Times Books.

Doornbos, Martin. 1990. "The African State in Academic Debate: Retrospect and Prospect." *Journal of Modern African Studies*, Vol. 28, No. 2: 179–98.

Dorman, Sarah. 2009. "Patrick Chabal: An Appreciation." *Critical African Studies*, Issue 2: 10–18.

Dutt, Amitava K. (1992). "Two Issues in the State of Development Economics" in Dutt, Amitava K. and Jameson, Kenneth P. (eds) *New Directions in Development Economics*. Aldershot: Edward Elgar: 1–34.

Edigheji, Oman (2005). "A Democratic Developmental State in Africa? A Concept Paper." Centre for Policy Studies, Research Paper No. 105. Online, available at: www.cps.org.az, accessed 27 April 2009.

Ekeh, Peter (1975). "Colonialism and the Two Publics in Africa: A Theoretical Statement." *Comparative Studies in Society and History*, Vol. 17, No. 1: 91–112.

Englebert, Pierre (2000a). *State Legitimacy and Development in Africa*. Boulder: Lynne.

Englebert, Pierre (2000b). "Pre-colonial Institutions, Post-colonial States and Economic Development in Tropical Africa." *Political Research Quarterly*, Vol. 53, No. 1: 7–36.

Evans, Peter (1995). *Embedded Autonomy: States and Industrial Transformation*. Princeton, NJ: Princeton University Press.

Evans, Peter and Rauch, James (1999). "Bureaucracy and Growth: A Cross-national Analysis of the Effects of the Weberian State Structures on Economic Growth." *American Sociological Review*, Vol. 64, No. 5: 748–65.

Green, Reginald (1965). "Four African Development Plans: Ghana, Kenya, Nigeria and Tanzania." *Journal of Modern African Studies*, Vol. 3, No. 2: 249–79.

Hart, Gillian (2001). "Development Critiques in the 1990s: Culs de Sac and Promising Paths." *Progress in Human Geography*, Vol. 25, No. 4: 649–58.

Hart, Gillian (2006). "Post-apartheid Developments in Historical and Comparative Perspective" in V. Padayach (ed.) *The Development Decade? Economic and Social Change in South Africa 1994–2004*. Pretoria: HSRC Press: 13–32.

Harvey, David (2005). *A Brief History of Neoliberalism*. Oxford: Oxford University Press.

Hill, Jonathan (2005). "Beyond the Other? A Postcolonial Critique of the Failed State Thesis." *African Identities*, Vol. 3, No. 2: 139–54.

Hirschman, Albert (1958). *The Strategy of Economic Development*. New Haven: Yale University Press.

Hirschman, Albert (1981). *Essays in Trespassing: Economics to Politics and Beyond*. Cambridge: Cambridge University Press.

Hirschman, Albert (2001). "A Dissenter's Confession: 'The Strategy of Economic Development' Revisited" in G. M. Meier and J. Stiglitz (eds) *Frontiers of Development Economics: The Future in Perspective*. New York: Oxford University Press: 87–114.

Hungwe, Kedmon (2000). "Africa Works: Disorder as Political Instrument (Review Essay)." *Zambezia*, Vol. 27, No. 2: 269–81.

Hyden, Goran (1986). "The Anomaly of the African Peasantry." *Development and Change*, Vol. 17, No. 3: 677–705.

Hyden, Goran (2000). "The Governance Challenge in Africa" in G. Hyden, D. Olowu and O. Okoth Ogendo (eds) *African Perspectives on Governance*. Trenton: Africa World Press: 5–32.

Johnson, Chalmer (1982). *MITI and the Japanese Miracle: The Growth of Industrial Policy 1925–1975*. Stanford: Stanford University Press.

Johnson, Chalmer (1999). "The Developmental State: Odyssey of a Concept" in M. Woo-Cumings (ed.) *The Developmental State*. Cornell, CA: Cornell University Press: 32–60.

Joseph, Richard (2011). "Democracy and the Reconfiguration of Power in Africa." *Current History*, November: 324–30.

Kapur, Devesh and Webb, Richard (2000). "Governance-related Conditionalities of the International Finance Institutions." Research Papers for the Intergovernmental Group of Twenty-Four on International Monetary Affairs, G-24 Discussion Paper Series. Geneva: UNCAD.

Kapur, Devesh, Lewis, John and Webb, Richard (1997). *The World Bank: Its First Half Century*, Washington DC: The Brookings Institution.

Kelsall, Tim (2008). "Going with the Grain in African Development?" *Development Policy Review*, Vol. 26, No. 6: 627–55.

Knack, Stephen and Keefer, Phillip (1995). "Institutions and Economic Performance: Cross-Country Tests Using Alternative Institutional Measures." *Economics and Politics*, Vol. 7, No. 3: 2007–27.

Kruger, Anne (1974). "The Political Economy of the Rent-seeking Society." *The American Economic Review*, Vol. 64, No. 3: 291–303.

Krugman, Paul (1996). *Development, Geography and Economic Theory*. Cambridge, MA: MIT Press.

Lewis W. Arthur (1954). "Economic Development with Unlimited Supplies of Labour." *Manchester School*, Vol. 20: 139–91.

Lewis, W. Arthur (1984). "The State of Development Theory." *The American Economic Review*, Vol. 74, No. 1: 1–10.

Leys, Colin (1976). "The 'Overdeveloped' Post-Colonial State: A Re-Evaluation." *Review of African Political Economy*, No. 5: 39–48.

Leys, Colin (1996). *The Rise and Fall of Development Theory*. London: James Currey.

Mackay, Peter (2008). *We Have Tomorrow: Stirrings in Africa 1959–1967*. Norwich: Michael Russell.

Mamdani, Mahmood (1996). *Citizen and Subject: Contemporary Africa and the Legacy of Late Colonialism*. Princeton, NJ: Princeton University Press.

Mattes, Robert and Bratton, Michael (2007). "Learning about Democracy in Africa: Awareness, Performance and Experience." *American Journal of Political Science*, Vol. 51, No. 2: 199–217.

Mauro, Paolo (1995). "Corruption and Growth." *Quarterly Journal of Economics*, Vol. 110: 681–712.

Medard, Jean-Francois (1982). "The Underdevelopment of State in Tropical Africa: Political Clientelism or Neo-Patrimonialism?" in C. Clapham (ed.) *Private Patronage and Public Power: Political Clientelism in the Modern State*. London: Frances.

Meier, Gerald (2001). "The Old Generation of Development Economists and the New" in G.M. Meier and J. Stiglitz (eds) *Frontiers of Development Economics: The Future in Perspective*. New York: Oxford University Press: 13–49.

Menocal, Alina R. (2004). "And If There Was No State: Critical Reflections on Bates, Polanyi and Evans on the Role of the State in Promoting Development." *Third World Quarterly*, Vol. 75, No. 4: 756–77.

Mkandawire, Thandika (2001). "Thinking about the Developmental States in Africa." *Cambridge Journal of Economics*, Vol. 25, No. 3: 289–313.

Mkandawire, Thandika (2003). "African Intellectuals and Nationalism." A Paper Presented at the Conference on the 30th Anniversary of CODESRIA, Dakar, Senegal.

Mo Ibrahim Foundation (2011). "2011 Ibrahim Index of African Governance." Online, available at: http://www.moibrahimfoundation.org/en/section/the-ibrahim-index, accessed 28 October 2011.

Mohan, Jitendra (1966). "Varieties of African Socialism" in R. Milliband and J. Sauville (eds) *The Socialist Register, 1966*. London: Merlin Press: 220–66.

Morrissey, Oliver (2001). "Lessons for Africa from East Asian Economic Policy" in P. Lawrence and C. Thirtle (eds) *Africa and Asia in Comparative Economics*. London: Palgrave: 34–48.

Myrdal, Gunnar (1970). *The Challenges of World Poverty: A World Anti-Poverty Programme in Outline*. Harmondsworth: Penguin.

Ndulu, J.B. (2008). "The Evolution of Global Development Paradigms and their Influence in African Economic Growth" in B.J. Ndulu, S.A. O'Connell, R. Bates, P. Collier, C. Soludo (eds) *The Political Economy of Economic Growth in Africa 1960–2000*. Cambridge: Cambridge University Press: 315–47.

Nettl, J. (1968). "The State as a Conceptual Variable." *World Politics*, Vol. 20, No. 4: 559–92.

Nkrumah, Kwame (1963). *Africa Must Unite*. London: Panaf.

North, Douglas (1990). *Institutions, Institutional Change and Economic Performance.* Cambridge: Cambridge University Press.

North, Douglas (1992). "The New Institutional Economics and Third World Development" in J. Harris, J. Hunter and C. Lewis (eds) *The New Institutional Economics and Third World Development.* London: Routledge: 17–26.

North, Douglas (1997). "The Contribution of the New Institutional Economics to an Understanding of the Transitional Problem." World Institute for Development Economics Research (WIDER), Annual Lecture 1, Helsinki.

Ntsebeza, Lungisile (2006). *Democracy Compromised: Chiefs and the Politics of Land in South Africa.* Cape Town: HSRC.

Nugent, Paul (2010). "States and Social Contracts in Africa." *New Left Review*, Vol. 63, May–June: 35–68.

Nurkse, Ragnar (1953). *Problems of Capital Formation in Underdeveloped Countries.* Oxford: Oxford University Press.

Page, John (2012). "Aid, Structural Change and the Private Sector in Africa." *United Nations University (UNU) World Institute for Development Economic Research (WIDER) Working Paper No. 2012/21.* UNU-WIDER.

Ranis, Gustav (2004). "Arthur Lewis's Contribution to Development Thinking and Policy." *Economic Growth Centre, Discussion Paper No. 891.* Yale University.

Republic of Namibia (2004). *Vision 2030: Prosperity, Harmony, Peace and Political Stability.* Windhoek: National Planning Commission Secretariat.

Rivkin, Arnold (1963). *The African Presence in World Affairs: National Development and its Role in Foreign Policy.* London: Macmillan.

Rodney, Walter (1972). *How Europe Underdeveloped Africa.* Washington DC: Howard University Press.

Rosenstein-Rodan, Paul (1943). "Problems of Industrialisation of Eastern and South-Eastern Europe." *Economic Journal*, Vol. 53, Nos 210–211: 202–11.

Rostow, Walter W. (1959). "The Stages of Economic Growth." *The Economic History Review (New Series)*, Vol. 12, No. 1: 1–16.

Sandbrook, Richard (1986). "The State and Economic Stagnation in Tropical Africa." *World Development*, Vol. 14, No. 3: 319–32.

Sandbrook, Richard (1990). "Taming the African Leviathan." *World Policy Journal*, Vol. 7, No. 4: 673–701.

Sandbrook, Richard (1993). *The Politics of Africa's Economic Recovery.* Cambridge: Cambridge University Press.

Sandbrook, Richard (2005). "Africa's Great Transformation?" *Journal of Development Studies*, Vol. 41, No. 6: 1118–25.

Sen, Amartya (1983). "Development: Which Way Now?" *The Economic Journal*, Vol. 93, No. 372: 745–62.

Sen, Amartya (1988). "The Concept of Development" in H. Chenery, T. Srinivasan and P. Streeten (eds) *Handbook of Development Economics Volume 1.* Hague: Elsevier: 9–26.

Singh, Ajit (1992). "The Actual Crisis of Economic Development in the 1980s: An Alternative Policy Perspective for the Future" in Amitava K. Dutt and Kenneth P. Jameson (eds) *New Directions in Development Economics.* Aldershot: Edward Elgar: 81–116.

Smith, Peter (2001). "Should Africa Try to Learn from Asia? Lessons for and from Uganda" in P. Lawrence and C. Thirtle (eds) *Africa and Asia in Comparative Economics.* London: Palgrave: 49–64.

Stein, Howard (1994). "Theories of Institutions and Economic Reform in Africa." *World Development*, Vol. 22, No. 12: 1833–49.

Stiglitz, Joseph (1989). "Markets, Market Failures, and Development." *The American Economic Review*, Vol. 79, No. 2: 197–203.

Stiglitz, Joseph (1992). "Alternative Tactics and Strategies for Economic Development" in Amitava K. Dutt and Kenneth P. Jameson (eds) *New Directions in Development Economics*. Aldershot: Edward Elgar: 57–80.

Suberu, Rotimi (2000). "Governance and the Ethnic Factor" in G. Hyden, D. Olowu and O. Okoth Ogendo (eds) *African Perspectives on Governance*. Trenton: Africa World Press.

Todaro, Michael P. (2000). *Economic Development* (7th edition). New York: Addison-Wesley.

United Nations Economic Commission for Africa (UNECA) (2011). *Economic Report on Africa 2011: Governing Development in Africa*. Addis Ababa: UNECA.

Wade, Robert (1990). *Governing the Markets: Economic Theory and the Role of Government in Taiwan's Industrialisation*. Princeton, NJ: Princeton University Press.

Weber, Max [1911] (1968). *Economy and Society* (edited by G. Roth and C. Wittich). New York: Bedminster.

World Bank (2011). "Africa's Future and the World Bank's Support to it." The World Bank. Online, available at: http://www.worldbank.org/africastrategy, accessed 17 September 2011.

6 The political economy of Africa's economic growth and development experience

Introduction

In trying to understand and explain the economic growth and development experience in Africa, while the market-oriented approach (MOA) emphasises markets as the key to its understanding, and state-oriented approaches (SOA) take the state as pivotal to understanding Africa's growth experience, the political economy approach (PEA) takes a global focus, homing in on structures and relations between countries within the global economic system. Whereas MOA and SOA focus mainly on the internal conditions in which markets and states operate, PEA looks at power relations and the accompanying geopolitical structures emanating from the interaction of states and markets at a global level. In this sense, PEA's starting point is that there is a global system (predominantly economic in nature, much less political or social), which shapes the relations and actions between states, as well as the relations between markets and states. Therefore, PEA locates the state-market-development dynamics in the global arena, and the internal factors within a particular state are seen as largely outcomes of the global system. PEA does not regard the local states or markets as inconsequential for economic growth and development, but they are considered within the larger context of the international networks of economic and political relations.

It is important to note at this point that political economy (PE) encompasses a wide range of traditions from the classical political economists such as Adam Smith, David Ricardo, James Mill and Karl Marx, the rational political economy traditions (the Public Choice school) of James Buchanan and Gordon Tullock, the New Institutional Economics (NIE) school[1] popularised by Ronald Coase, Oliver Williamson and Douglas North, the New Political Economy (NPE) school of Torsten Persson and Guido Tabellini,[2] through to the structuralist theories of Raul Prebisch, Hans Singer, and to a lesser extent Gunnar Myrdal. The common factor in all PE traditions, however, is the idea that political issues (state, constitutions, public policy, public institutions, the behaviour of political actors) are intricately linked with economic issues (markets, resource allocations, production, investment, fiscal and monetary policy), in such a way that to understand how economics works requires a sound understanding of *real politick*. Although in different PE traditions there has been a tendency to emphasise one over the other of these aspects, there is wide agreement that the two (the economic and political spheres) influence each other and should be considered integrally.

While there is wide agreement about who the pioneers of a particular PE school of thought are, there is less agreement among the various schools on a number of concepts and their theoretical as well as practical implications. For example, as we shall see later in this chapter, there are significant differences in viewpoint – even among scholars who classify themselves as orthodox Marxists – about whether capitalism can exist without wage labour.[3] Instead of repeating or reclassifying the different PE schools of thought, this chapter focuses on analysing the influence PE scholars have had on the understanding of Africa's economic growth and development experience. The discussion in this chapter focuses on the Marxist and neo-Marxist, and structuralist and neo-structuralist, traditions of PE – sometimes referred to as radical political economy (RPE). The reason for focusing on these two PE schools of thought is that the other traditions – such as NIE, OIE, NPE, rational political economy and the public choice schools – largely draw from and rely on core concepts of the mainstream economic theory and assumptions, which have been discussed already in Chapters 2, 3 and 4.

The political economy of underdevelopment

As noted above, apart from being diverse, there have been sometimes acrimonious debates among political economists, even those from the same tradition. The diversity of views makes it difficult to present each and every shade of PE, or to elaborate on the various elements of each school. However, if there is any common feature to these diverse views it is the emphasis that the external factors related to underdevelopment are linked to, and in a fundamental way shape, the internal factors. Seeing the two (the external and internal dynamics) as parts of a unified system has resulted in most RPE scholars emphasising the systemic and structural origins of global economic growth and development challenges in Africa. In this regard RPE differs from both MOA and SOA, which tend to give lower weight to the role of the global (external) forces in explaining Africa's growth experience. Although MOA and SOA analysts, as we have seen in Chapters 2–5, acknowledge that external factors such as terms of trade play a part in explaining Africa's growth and development experience, such factors are often seen as tangential. For example, inappropriate domestic policies and poor administrative capacity are what the Bank and the Fund focus on in explaining Africa's growth experience. Though these factors may be linked to external forces, they are largely seen as outcomes of internal factors. Similarly, neo-patrimonialism, which is emphasised by most analysts within SOA – though it may be linked to external factors via colonialism and neo-colonialism – is largely seen as a product of the local socio-political dynamics. Consequently, the operations of a patron and his networks are internal phenomena, following an internal political, social and economic rationality. However, RPE takes an integral approach and looks at these activities as manifestations of a system in which external and internal factors interact, reinforced through existing structures and relations.

Arguably, the emphasis on the structural nature of the challenges of under-development globally is one of the key distinguishing features of RPE from other traditions of PE, with most RPE analysts arguing that economic growth and development challenges cannot be adequately understood by focusing on internal factors only. For instance, Immanuel Wallerstein (1974b) in his World System Theory, contends that the weakness of states in peripheral areas *vis à vis* strong states in the core is not accidental; it is an internal logic of the system which enables the latter to maintain its dominance over the former. According to this view, if states in the periphery and the core were equal in power and influence, no state would dominate other states, and the phenomenon of uneven development would not arise. If all states have equal power, they would all be in a pos-ition to effectively counteract any attempt to undermine each other's interests. But since the "strength of the state-machinery in the core states is a function of the weakness of other state-machinery" (Wallerstein, 1974a: 403), the structure of unevenness in political, economic and social terms is entrenched at the global level. This view is stated more clearly in the argument that

> One cannot reasonably explain the strength of various state-machineries at specific moments of the history of the modern world-system primarily in terms of a genetic-cultural line argumentation, but rather in terms of the structural role a country plays in the world-economy at that moment.
>
> (Wallerstein, 1974a: 403)

Other analysts, including Andre Gunder Frank, Fernando Henrique Cardoso, Singer, Prebisch and David Harvey, etc., also stress the importance of imbal-anced relations created and maintained systemically through global economic structures. For instance, it is argued that

> contemporary underdevelopment is in large part the historical product of the past and continuing economic and other relations between the satellite underdeveloped and ... metropolitan countries. Furthermore, these relations are an essential part of the structure and development of the capitalist system on a world scale as a whole.
>
> (Frank, 1970: 5)

This view has been employed by some analysts to explain African economic growth and development trajectory. For example, Walter Rodney (1972) argues that structures that perpetuated the underdevelopment of Africa dur-ing colonial rule were not limited just to trade (paying low prices for Africa's raw materials) or paying low wages to African workers, but formed an integral part of the system anchored around the division of labour, political, cultural, religious and psychological domination. According to this view inequality (or broadly uneven development) of state capacity, power, income, technology, productivity, etc., are part of the structural dynamism of a system which keeps reproducing unevenness.

Thus, the alleged lack of capacity, lack of formal institutionalisation of the state, low factor productivity, and low investment in Africa – according to this view – are not consequences of any peculiar characteristic of African leaders or peoples; they are inevitable outcomes of the way the global economic system is set up and functions. For some analysts this is the only valid explanation for the observed growth pattern in Africa:

> Africa south of the Sahara exists in a capitalist world, which marks and con-strains the lives of its inhabitants at every turn ... This is the fundamental truth from which any honest analysis must begin. This is what explains why sub-Saharan Africa's ... economies have responded worse than others.
>
> (Saul and Leys, 1999: 5)

Within this approach, Africa's economic growth and development challenges are seen as outcomes of the global economic system, which reproduces condi-tions of underdevelopment. Thus, according to this view, even if Africa were to be filled with 'Machiavellian princes' (as opposed to the 'native princes' or the 'Big Men'), these would have little effect as long as they operated in the prevailing global economic set-up. In fact, the emergence of such states and princes in Africa is undermined by the global system itself. While some analysts dismiss this as a tired tactic, typical of African leaders and their sympathisers playing the "old guilty" card to "conceal their own failures" (see Ayittey, 2004; Mills, 2011), this view has attracted the attention of many analysts within and outside Africa.

The core-periphery structure

Crucial to understanding the importance of structural conditions within the global economic system is the division of the world into core and periphery (Prebisch, 1950), developed and underdeveloped (Singer, 1950), metropole and satellite (Frank, 1970), and centre and periphery (Amin, 1974a). A com-mon view among proponents of this model is that it is the adverse interaction between the centre and periphery – through the economic structure of capital-ism, and supported by multilateral imperialism (see Shivji, 1990) – that largely explains the underdevelopment of Africa and other regions. As one would expect, the application of such views relating to Africa has been contested, with some authors arguing that such ideas are foreign and unable to provide insight into Africa's growth and development experiences. Referring particularly to the dependence theory, Anthony Hopkins (1975) argues that the "Frankian thesis", does not fit the African reality.

Interestingly, while dependence theory is rejected on the grounds that it is "incompatible to Marxist analysis", Samir Amin's analysis is endorsed as an argument "in harmony with central Marxist tradition because it is based on the assumption that it is the rate of capital accumulation which ultimately determines the distribution of wage profits" (Hopkins, 1975: 20). Other analysts have dismissed both views as neo-Marxist and neo-structuralist – misguided and inappropriate to the understanding of the African crisis (Bayart, 1993, Chabal and Daloz, 1999). Notably, while these views have arguably had noticeable influence among many African scholars and political leaders, especially during the 1960s and 1970s (see Mafeje, 1994), they are rarely deployed in explaining economic growth and development patterns in Africa today (Freund, 2010).

Underdevelopment as unequal relations

Analysts who use the RPE framework try to explain poor economic growth and underdevelopment in low-income countries by means of unequal relations between developed and underdeveloped countries. According to this view, the interaction between the developed and underdeveloped countries has not just been unequal, it perpetuates and reproduces the unevenness in the relations. Proponents of this view argue that prolonged periods of unequal interactions between industrialised and non-industrialised countries create structures which condition the relationship into that of subordination and domination, not only in the economic sphere but also in other spheres of interaction including cultural, political, technological and religious (see Amin, 1974a). Any effort by the periphery to industrialise, for instance, is frustrated by the same mechanism of domination and subordination generated by these unequal interactions.

Some authors argue that part of this structural trap has been created through the theory of modernisation, which takes the unevenness between countries as part of the development process – arguing that underdeveloped countries are expected go through the same stages that industrialised countries went through (Frank, 1970). Thus RPE challenges the modernisation paradigm which sees the developed countries as a future version of what the underdeveloped countries will become. Some analysts have contended that 'catching-up' is not possible as long as the imbalance in the relationship is maintained, particularly because the "now-developed countries have never been underdeveloped, though they may have been undeveloped" (Frank, 1970: 5).

Although there have been controversies among scholars[4] on which of these views account for the observed growth patterns in Africa most accurately, some became very popular among African policymakers during the 1960s and 1970s (see Mafeje, 1994).

The Commercial Revolution as a precursor of underdevelopment

Within PE, several views have emerged on how this subordination of underdeveloped regions by the industrial countries started and was sustained. For analysts, uneven development on the global scale is produced and sustained over the years through mercantilism, imperialism, colonialism, neo-colonialism, and conspiracy among African political elites. One dominant mechanism through which unevenness has been perpetuated is trade. Interaction in the form of exchange of goods between societies (trade) has a long history and a rich theoretical background – from the pre-mercantilist period, when exchange of scarce, luxury goods such as gold, spices, perfumes, and metal coins between noble families dominated the exchange, to the present complex and diverse trade relations.

In the case of Africa, in the pre-mercantilist era, exchange was limited to a few light ('rich trade') goods which could be easily transported (since the transportation system was not sufficiently developed to handle heavy, bulky merchandise) (see Wallerstein, 1974b). Although there were no clearly defined nations at this time, the nature of the trade had elements of modern-day international trade, to the extent that goods were transferred from one territory/region/monarchy to another. International trade, as its name suggests, is often linked to the phenomenon of the centralisation of power in Europe following what is often referred to as the Commercial Revolution and the emergence of the nation states.[5] The growth of commerce effectively led to the centralisation of power in the form of sovereign territorial powers (see Polanyi, 1944). Seen within the context of the Westphalia Peace Treaty of 1648, territorial sovereignty became the rationale on which the mercantilist system was consolidated and spread throughout Western Europe (see Hobsbawm, 1996). In fact, there exists a close relationship between the growth and spread of trade and the emergence of nation states, with mercantilism as a dominant form of economic and political organisation. The resulting sovereign territories exercised their influence and power through trade, in such a way that the more merchandise a country controlled the more power a territory exercised over others. Thus, mercantilism did not only result in the extroversion of commercial power, it also occasioned an internal reorganisation, requiring the centralisation of territorial powers to support the growth of commerce, and with it, international influence. In this sense mercantilism was a response to both the external and internal political, economic and administrative challenges of the time.

Politically, the centralised sovereign state was a new creation called for by the Commercial Revolution that had shifted the centre of gravity of the Western world from the Mediterranean to the Atlantic seaboard, and thus compelled larger agrarian countries to organise for commerce and trade.

Mercantilism and the nation states

The creation of sovereign territories and powers became the rational response to the Commercial Revolution, with mercantilist statecraft involving the marshalling of resources of the whole territory for the purpose of controlling trade relations. Unification of the territories fragmented by feudal and municipal particularism was the necessary by-product of such an endeavour. Economically, the instrument of unification was capital, i.e., private resources available in the form of money hoards suitable for the development of commerce. Following the centralisation of power, the administrative technique underlying the policy of the central government was supplied by the extension of the traditional municipal system to the larger territory of the state (see Polanyi, 1944: 65).

This centralisation of territorial power, achieved by safeguarding commercial interests and resources from external intrusion by discouraging the importation of goods and encouraging exportation, led to the excessive protectionism of the seventeenth and eighteenth centuries – protectionism which pro-free trade advocates, including Adam Smith, protested against. Protectionism was seen as irrational behaviour aimed at advancing the private interests of manufacturers and merchants at the expense of the larger society.

> Our woollen manufacturers have been more successful than any other class of workmen, in persuading the legislature that the prosperity of the nation depended upon the success and extension of their particular business. They have not only obtained a monopoly against the consumers, by an absolute prohibition of importing woollen cloths from any foreign country; but they have likewise obtained another monopoly against the sheep farmers and growers of wool, by a similar prohibition of the exportation of live sheep and wool. The severity of many of the laws which have been enacted for the security of the revenue is very justly complained of, as imposing heavy penalties upon actions which, antecedent to the statutes that declared them to be crimes, had always been understood to be innocent. But the cruellest of our revenue laws, I will venture to affirm, are mild and gentle, in comparison to some of those which the clamour of our merchants and manufacturers has extorted from the legislature, for the support of their own absurd and oppressive monopolies.
>
> (Smith, [1776] 2005: 527)

In this sense, mercantilists constituted a form of special interest group conspiring against the public, and particularly against the poor. The special interest character of mercantilism is articulated by Adam Smith when he observes that commerce is "the industry which is carried on for the benefit of the rich and the powerful, ... That which is carried on for the benefit of the poor and the indigent is too often either neglected or oppressed" (Smith, [1776] 2005: 524).

It is interesting here to note that even during these early stages of the nation state, state institutions (the legislature) were used by a small section of society (the traders in this case) to advance narrow interests. Arguably, it is not necessarily trade which works against the poor sections of society (who are often the majority), rather it is the conditions and the structures under which trade is conducted which results in one group (a few powerful merchants) reaping all the benefits while piling the burden on the rest of society. When discussing imperialism and colonialism, John Hobson (1902) makes a similar point, arguing that while the cost of imperialism was borne by the general public, only industrial and finance capital owners benefited from the expanded market for finished products, and the securing of new and cheap supplies of raw materials (see also Cesaire, [1955] 2000).

The importance of international trade, since its earliest forms, is that it plays a crucial role in generating the unequal relations between developed and underdeveloped countries, even today. Here again the emphasis is on structures and the resulting relations surrounding the exchange. Even at this early stage of international trade, some elements of domination of one sovereign territory over others are discernible, to the extent that one country manages to use protectionism effectively to disadvantage others. Some analysts have even argued that it was this effective use of protectionism which contributed to the emergence of the Industrial Revolution in England and not in France or Wales (or Scotland for that matter), with the centralised power of the state playing a crucial role in safeguarding the interests of English merchants and manufacturers (Hobson, 1902). The logical explanation offered is that as a country accumulates wealth, it also accumulates power (political, military, informational, technological) which it uses to influence the way it interacts with other countries. According to this view, this configuration of power shapes the relations which exist between nations and explains the unevenness in the level of development among countries of the world. Testing this theory is beyond the scope of this book; suffice to note that power relations and the resulting structures are seen – within RPE – as central to explaining uneven development globally (see Harvey, 2000).

International trade and the division of labour

Although protectionism, which characterised the mercantilist period, was widespread in Europe, trade between the sovereign territories continued and increased over time. The increase in trade from the eighteenth century can be partly attributed to the impact of the Industrial Revolution, which saw massive increases in productive forces that in turn led partly to the growth of an urban population whose diverse needs could only be satisfied by importing food and other consumer goods. To a large extent, growth in trade between nations can be seen as a product of the division of labour and the resulting specialisation of production. International division of labour, which entails specialisation of production in goods or services that a country has either a relative or absolute comparative advantage in, arises out of natural factors such as climate, type of soil, geological formation, natural resource endowment, etc. Specialisation can also occur because of the difference in the level of technology, capital accumulation, labour and skills (human resources), and the stage of development.

However, within the RPE traditions it has been argued that the division of labour among the nations of the world constitutes a strategic set of decisions which results in certain regions being consigned to the performance of certain functions that are perpetually rewarded less than others. For example, Wallerstein contends that one of the key features of the capitalist economic system is the "extensive division of labour", with the task unevenly distributed between the periphery and the centre. Although he acknowledges that part of this division of labour can be accounted for by geographical and ecological differences, he maintains that, "for the most part, it is a function of the social organisation of work, one which magnifies and legitimizes the ability of some groups within the system to exploit the labour of others, that is, to receive a large share of surplus" (Wallerstein, 1974a: 29–30).

Division of labour is central within this view, such that the emergence of capitalism is squarely pinned on the occurrence of this specialisation of production, an event that is estimated to have taken place around 1450 CE. This assertion follows on from the view that it is impossible for the world system to survive if the different political units that constitute it are equal in power and influence. Thus, the international division of labour is the mechanism through which unequal relations among the constituting units of the world system are produced and reproduced. According to this view, since the capitalist system has always been global, the actual division of labour is a global phenomenon. Consequently, the world under capitalism is divided into the centres (which form the core of the world system, and in this case North-Western Europe), the periphery (the subordinated areas of the world, in this case Africa,[6] Latin America, Asia and the Middle–East), and also the semi-periphery (that is, countries conceived as the buffer between the centre and the periphery, in this case Eastern and Southern Europe – Spain, Portugal, Greece, Ireland and southern Italy).[7] This division of the world into regions based on what they each should produce is said to have been consolidated by 1640 into a well-functioning system (Wallerstein, 1974a: 29–30).

Scholars operating within the orthodox Marxist tradition have challenged this view, arguing that it presents a misconception of capitalism since it seems to assert the existence of capitalism on the basis of exchange relations, and not on modes of production. They accuse the Wallersteinian view of confusing "modes of production" with "participation in exchange relation" (see Laclau, 1971; Sweezy, 1950). In this debate there is a distinction made between agricultural and industrial capitalism, with some authors arguing that what emerged around the mid-seventeeth century was agricultural capitalism, while industrial capitalism appeared only towards the end of the eighteenth century. Even if one accepts this argument, a review of the debate reveals that the point when capitalism started is a controversial one – as we shall see later in this chapter; not because of disagreement about the date when capitalism emerged, but most importantly the analytical implications.

Africa in the capitalist world system

The concept of division of labour as a fundamental feature of the capitalist global economy is elaborated by Amin, who argues that it was during the mercantilist period (1600–1800) that the world was decisively partitioned into periphery and centre, with "Black Africa" becoming the "periphery of the periphery", reduced to supplying slaves to the American plantations (Amin, 1972: 110). Like Wallerstein, Amin also sees this period as having a decisive role in the future relations between the centre and the periphery, relations reinforced by successive stages of colonialism, imperialism and multilateral imperialism in post-colonial

Africa. For Amin, the fragmentation and brutality of this period "lie at the root of the most serious handicaps of contemporary Africa" (Amin, 1972: 110).

Unlike Amin, Wallerstein does not see Africa as part of the global system during the mercantilist system; during this period Africa is classified as "external" to the world system until the second half of the eighteenth century.

> From 1450 to 1750, West Africa[8] was in the external arena of the European World Economy and not part of the periphery; that up to 1750 the bulk of the trade could be considered as 'rich trades;'[9] and thus up to that point the two systems were separated.
>
> (Wallerstein, 1980: 29)

There are three reasons given for this. First, prior to 1750 Africa's trade with Europe was mainly in slaves, which is referred to as "rich trades". Second, the interaction between Africa and Europe did not involve the "significant transfer of surplus" since the capitalist mode of production had not yet been established on the continent. Third, interactions between the centre and the periphery in the world system resulted in the weakening of the political institutions of the latter, which was not the case for Africa prior to 1750. On this point it is argued that the slave trade in fact resulted in the strengthening of "state-structures in West Africa, and it strengthened the role of the indigenous commercial bourgeoisie" (Wallerstein, 1980: 27–8).

While the categorisation of Africa as external to the European world economy prior to 1750 has been explained, it is not clear what this category adds to the understanding of the core concepts of division of labour and unequal relations. This has resulted in some critics raising the concern that it is not clear if the defining feature of the system is extraction of surplus through the capitalist mode of production, bulky trade and weakening of the local political institutions, or merely the existence of unequal exchange that explains perpetual domination of the periphery by the core. A closer reading of this and other texts suggests that the division of labour and unequal exchange are at the heart of understanding the system. But then the application of this framework to Africa leaves a number of questions unresolved, especially if the claim that Africa was external to the European world system is taken seriously. One of the implications of this view is that Africa's unequal relations with Europe only surfaced during the second half of the eighteenth century. But as Amin (1974a) has noted, many analysts would agree that unequal relations with Africa started well before the eighteenth century.

What is clear in Wallerstein's view of the world system, however, is that a capitalist world economy is based on a division of labour between the core, semi-periphery and periphery in such a way that there is unequal exchange not only between the regions, but that there is also dependence of all the periphery and semi-periphery on the core, both economically and politically. This structural dependence of the periphery on the core ensures the continuation of unequal relations. While the features of this unequal relationship are not clearly spelt out by Wallerstein, Amin tries to elaborate on what this entails. For Amin, the unequal relationship between the centre and the periphery manifests itself in the different rewards for labour between the two – the same quantity of labour at the centre is rewarded much more than labour at the periphery. Differential wages represent unequal exchange, resulting in an increasingly higher surplus value being extracted from the periphery when compared to the centre (see Amin, 1974b). With this leakage of surplus value, in addition to the "visible transfer of the profits of foreign capital", peripheral regions remain scarce of capital such that they are always dependent on the centre for investment (Amin, 1974b: 13). According to this view, this leads to perpetuation of dependence for the periphery because any foreign capital from the centre reproduces the same mechanism of extracting a higher surplus and expropriating more capital from the periphery in the form of profits. One conclusion reached from all this is that, in these circumstances, participation in the world economy implies underdevelopment for the periphery: "Any development policy that accepts the framework of integration into this market, must fail: for it can only be a matter of pious wishes for needful external aid" (Amin, 1990: 32). A similar assertion is expressed by Frank (1970), who argues that the more a satellite region or country is tied to a metropole, the more underdeveloped it becomes. According to this view, Africa's underdevelopment can be largely explained in terms of the operation of such a system – the subordination of Africa to unequal exchange at the economic, political, cultural and religious level.

While the exchange takes various forms, it is the exchange through trade that explains the inequality that perpetuates and deepens underdevelopment in peripheral regions such as Africa. Recently this argument has been used against those who argue that Africa is poor because it is marginalised (not integrated into the global system, i.e., left out by the process of globalisation). Opponents of the integrationist thesis argue that "it is precisely the way in which Africa is integrated into the world economy, rather than its absence from or refusal to take part in it, that has contributed to the continent's predicament" (Bush, 2004).

Structuralist arguments

Views that rely on trade or international exchange to explain the phenomenon of underdevelopment can also be found in the works of analysts who are often referred to as structuralists[10] (mainly Prebisch, Singer, but also Myrdal to a lesser extent). In the literature they are classified as structuralists mainly because they pay more attention to explaining why there has been a lack of *structural* transformation in less developed countries (LDCs). Though not all three authors emphasise the same factors to explain the condition of underdevelopment, they all see structural transformation of the economies in underdeveloped countries – particularly the poor growth of the local manufacturing sector, together with agriculture – as the underlying factor. In this sense the structuralists' view is closer to the views of the pioneers of development economics – such as W. Arthur Lewis, Paul Rosenstein-Rodan, Albert Hirschman and Ranar Nurkse – who all understood

the problem of underdevelopment as largely that of 'delayed' or arrested industrialisation (see Chapter 5). The other area of commonality between the early
structuralists and development economists is the view that industrialisation
required deliberate state intervention, as explained in Chapter 5.[11]

While ideas developed by the structuralists have some commonality with those
developed by the pioneers of development economics, they differed fundamentally in the former's insistence that the distribution of the gains of international
trade between the centre and the periphery always results in the latter being
disadvantaged. Hirschman, for instance, confirms that one of the two central
themes of development economics is the assertion of what he calls the "mutual
benefit claim"; the claim that "economic relations between these two groups of
countries [developed and underdeveloped] could be shaped in such a way as to
yield gains for both" (Hirschman, 1981: 3).[12] This is essentially the pro-trade
argument which asserts a win-win outcome from exchange of goods under conditions of specialisation and division of labour.

For the structuralists, the central argument is that the unequal distribution of
the gains from trade between the centre and the periphery results in the exploitation of the latter by the former such that development is impossible in the latter unless the distribution of benefits from trade is radically altered. One key
feature of this structural inequality is that trade between industrial and underdeveloped countries is structured in such a way that developed countries export
manufactured goods while underdeveloped countries focus on exporting primary
commodities. This trading system results in unequal distribution of investment,
income and the general benefit from trade between the two sets of countries. The
explanation provided for the unequal share in the benefits of trade is that

> differences between industrial countries exporting manufactures and export-
> ers of primary commodities … set up a tendency for primary commodity
> prices to decline relative to those of manufactured goods, and for asymmet-
> rical changes in demand and volume. The effect would be for the benefits to
> be increasingly unequally distributed between the two groups of countries.
>
> (Singer, 1984: 281)

This analysis was supported empirically by a study[13] of the relative price of
exports and imports between industrial and underdeveloped countries between
1870 and 1939, a study which showed that the price of primary commodities
declined relative to the price of manufactured goods, over time.[14] What explains
the inequality in the share of the benefits from trade is the unfavourable terms of
trade against the primary commodity exporting countries (all of which happen
to be underdeveloped). Focusing on Latin America, Prebisch makes a similar
argument highlighting not just the unfavourable terms of trade, but also how this
comes about.

> Technological progress started at the centres and its fruits remained basic-
> ally there. For better or worse, they did not spread to the periphery through

a general fall in prices in relation to increases in productivity. Historically, the role of the periphery had been mainly restricted to the supply of primary products. This explains why the growth of income stimulated demand and continuous technological innovations at the centres ... gave great impetus to industrialisation. The periphery was left behind not because of malicious design but because of the dynamics of the system. This accentuated the tendency of the periphery to imitate the centres – to grow in their image and likeness. We tried to adopt their technologies and life styles, to follow their ideas and ideologies, to reproduce their institutions.

(Prebisch, 1984: 184)

In Prebisch's view, imitating the centre's technology, lifestyle and ideas did not work; it created a condition of perpetual dependency, where peripheral regions relied on the centre not just for investment, but also for ideas, productive forces and skills.

Taking a broader view, Myrdal uses the theory of "circular and cumulative causation" to explain how initial inequality in capital accumulation, skills, investment, income, and, to a large extent, trade relations, tends to operate in a vicious circle that deepens inequality. In one of his main works, *Economic Theory and Under-developed Regions*, he elaborates using concrete examples of how inequality between regions or nations in the initial stage intensifies and widens, arguing that the forces of the market – if left to operate on their own – "tend to increase, rather than decrease, the inequality between regions" (Myrdal, 1957: 26). According to this view, international trade – in as far as the developing regions begin from a disadvantaged position regarding levels of accumulated capital, technology, structure of income and demand, and investment patterns – cannot be an engine for development as claimed by the classical political economists; it can only work to intensify the inequality between industrial and underdeveloped countries. As noted earlier, this is an inversion of the classical trade theory which argues for a win-win outcome, although the gains from trade need not be equally shared among those involved. For a detailed theoretical discussion of the classical and neoclassical views on international trade and comparative advantage, see Arghiri Emmanuel's *Unequal Exchange* (1972).

It is, however, important to note here that while the theories of free trade and comparative advantage have attracted wide support within the broader economic scholarship, the idea of free trade enjoyed an astonishingly short career. The practice of free trade has been an exception rather than a rule, even in England – which has been a champion of free trade for centuries. Despite the post-mercantilist political economists' (from François Quesnay to Alfred Marshall) success in demonstrating the errors of protectionism and other barriers to free trade, it has been observed that, in practice, all governments have always (except for a short interlude between 1846 and the beginning of World War One) taken protectionism as the norm. "Year after year, decade after decade, the governments of every country in the world have practiced without interruption a policy of protection. This has gone on for centuries. The only break was the brief parenthesis of free trade that began for England in 1846 and ended completely in 1932" (Emmanuel, 1972: xiii).[15] According to Emmanuel, this discrepancy between theory and practice is a clear sign that "there are two worlds, the rational world of political economy and the crazy world of economic policy" (Emmanuel, 1972: xiv).

It is interesting to note here the point that while structuralist theorists have argued that trade between developed and underdeveloped countries essentially leads to underdevelopment of the latter, they do not dispute the main claim of classical trade theory that in fact trade between parties (whether within nations, regions or between nations) produces a win-win situation. One of the main observations made by the structuralists is that it is the *way* in which trade has been organised between countries that makes it difficult for the periphery countries to use trade as the means to promote economic growth and development. Singer (1984), in particular, argues that the win-win doctrine is not in itself a problem, it is the nature of relations between the trading partners which makes it unattainable.

However, several arguments have been advanced against the classical trade theory. For instance, critics argue that this doctrine assumes away the influence of conditions under which this exchange takes place. In this regard Singer and Prebisch raise important questions about the structures and conditions under which international trade is conducted. Further, the free trade doctrine has been accused of ignoring the real world of inequality of power, technology, capital, skills and other differences between the parties to a trade relationship that often influence how the benefits are shared. Nevertheless, the obsession with international inequality resulting from trade obscures the similar situation that arises at national level. It is for this reason that some analysts have argued that the international scenario is mirrored at the national level where certain classes benefit more from exchange relations than others (Amin, 1974b). Thus, analysis of unequal relations in trade needs to account for micro-level dynamics.

Terms of trade: the conveyor belt

In the structuralists' framework, terms of trade are central to explaining underdevelopment in the peripheral region of Africa. Unfavourable terms of trade against underdeveloped countries, according to this view, arise from the structure of international trade in which underdeveloped countries export mainly primary commodities while the centres export manufactured goods. If one accepts that the price of primary commodities has a tendency to decline over time relative to the price of manufactured goods, as Singer and Prebisch assert, the implication is that over time, countries in underdeveloped regions will have to increase their production of primary goods just to sustain current levels of consumption and investment. For example, if the Democratic Republic of the Congo (DRC) sell two tons of copper to buy one German tractor in 2010 (assuming that the price of copper on the world market is falling, say, by 20 per cent per year on average, while the price of tractors remains the same), by 2015 the DRC would need to sell four tons of copper to buy the same German tractor. This implies that the terms of trade between the DRC and Germany would have declined by 100 per cent for the DRC if we exclude the effect of inflation on prices and exchange rates, while Germany's terms of trade relative to the DRC would have improved by 100 per cent.

In this simple example, the value lost by the DRC due to the decline in the price of copper relative to the price of tractors equals the value gained by Germany due to the improvement in terms of trade for tractors. Though the nominal value of the German tractor remains the same, in price terms between 2010 and 2015 its real value, in relative terms (relative to DRC copper), doubles over the same period. Here even if trade between the DRC and Germany may still be a win-win situation in 2015 as long as the DRC may not be able to produce a tractor at a cost lower than the value of four tons of copper, the terms of trade are unfavourable against DRC.

The crucial question is, why does the price of primary commodities such as copper tend to fall, while the price of manufactured goods like the German-made tractor remain the same – or even increase? For the structuralists the answer to this question is that primary goods have "serious limitations" in the sense that the possibility of increasing commodity exports are "restricted by the relatively slow growth of demand in the centres because of the generally low demand elasticity for primary products and their protectionist policies" (Prebisch, 1984: 178). According to this view the situation is compounded by the fact that markets in underdeveloped countries are too small to compensate for the relative fall in demand for primary goods at the centres. Interestingly, protectionist policies are justified by their proponents on the basis of the slow growth in demand for primary goods. What this entails is that the expansion of primary commodity production at a rate faster than the growth in demand would lead to both a fall in prices and, subsequently, employment and income and the growth in productive forces in the periphery.

The cumulative effect of this "lack of an automatic multiplication in demand, coupled with the low price elasticity of demand for both raw material and food, results in large price falls, not only cyclically but also structurally" (Singer, 1950: 480). Conversely in the centres, because of advanced technology used in production, productivity increases and so do wages – which leads to an increase in demand – not for primary products but for manufactured products – as the standard of living changes. Singer (1950) notes in particular that while the demand for primary products at the centre grows slowly during boom times when the underdeveloped countries can export more, demand for secondary products increases rapidly in both the centre and the periphery – resulting in a secular rise in demand for manufactured products over time. Because of this it has been argued that

> The industrialised countries have had the best of both worlds, both as consumers of primary commodities and as producers of manufactured articles, whereas the underdeveloped countries had the worst of both worlds, as consumers of manufactures and producers of raw materials.
>
> (Singer, 1950: 479)

Foreign investment in underdeveloped countries

Although their main writings appeared in the 1950s, Singer and Prebisch have maintained the same position in later years, arguing that prices of primary commodities have continued to decline[16] (See Prebisch, 1984; Singer, 1984). In his 1984 paper, Singer, referring to his 1950s work, asserts that "the views then expressed have been well vindicated" (1984: 275). Both Singer and Prebisch have consistently argued against foreign investment directed towards the production of primary products in underdeveloped countries for export, pointing out that such investment only seeks to further entrench the unequal structure that makes development in underdeveloped countries impossible – which has occurred through the siphoning of profits, as well as the supply of cheap primary products, to those centres where investment capital originates. A similar view was expressed during the 1960s by Oskar Lange, who observed that,

> Investment of capital in underdeveloped countries from highly developed countries acquired a specific character. It went chiefly into the exploitation of natural resources to be utilised as raw material by the industries of the developed countries ... the profits which were made by foreign capital ... were exported back ... where capital came from.
>
> (cited in Arrighi and Saul, 1973: 106)

Such capital leakage makes it difficult for underdeveloped countries to mobilise the resources needed to embark on industrialisation. Ironically, it is the underdeveloped countries which have been urged to do everything they can to attract foreign investment as a way to develop. One of the World Bank's main explanations for weak economic performance and the failure to structurally transform economies in Africa and other low-income countries is the failure to attract foreign investment (see Chapter 3). Even in its 2011 strategy for Africa's development, the Bank argues that Africa's main constraint to economic growth and development is the low level of capital resulting from low foreign investment (see World Bank, 2011).

For the structuralists the argument advanced is that for the majority of people in underdeveloped countries, incomes, savings and capital formation are very low, making it difficult for them to industrialise. A lack of capital to embark upon industrialisation forces the underdeveloped countries to concentrate on extraction of primary products, reinforcing the dynamics which lead to low capital accumulation. This condition of low capital accumulation locks the underdeveloped countries in a perpetual relation of dependence. What sustains this structure of dependency are the various forms of leakage of resources, including tax avoidance practices such as transfer pricing, misinvoicing, profit-taking and illegal offshore investments and bank accounts – widely referred to as 'capital flight' (see p. 211). The conclusion drawn is that

> in the world economy, there are forces at work that make for uneven distribution of the gains from trade and economic progress generally, so that the

lion's share goes to the lions, while the poor are themselves swallowed up in the process.

(Singer, 1984: 286)

Unequal exchange and underdevelopment

The importance attributed to trade as the main mechanism through which the exploitation of underdeveloped countries occurs is also highlighted by analysts other than the structuralists. Emmanuel's *Unequal Exchange: A Study of the Imperialism of Trade* (1972) is one such example. This is a study primarily concerned with the theory of 'comparative costs'. According to Emmanuel, as soon as one introduces even partial factor mobility into the trade model, the win-win advantage of international free trade disappears, resulting in a situation where one country gains at the expense of another. The reason given for this is that

> Under the theory of comparative costs, values continue to coincide with costs, but as the factors are no longer competitive[17] as between countries, costs no longer coincide with the quantities of factors expended in production, … since no equalisation process takes place, the rewarding of the factors is no longer the same.

(Emmanuel, 1972: xi)

Borrowing from Marx's labour theory of value, Emmanuel argues that the exchange of goods through trade between nations results in an unequal rewarding of factors, particularly labour, such that workers in the developed capitalist countries receive higher rewards for equivalent work in underdeveloped countries. To elaborate upon this argument, Emmanuel makes a distinction between "unequal exchange in the broad sense" and "unequal exchange in the narrow sense". The former is understood to arise from the difference in the factor endowment between different regions within one country, a condition which he refers to as the "difference in organic composition". Unequal exchange in the 'strict sense' is a situation that arises at the international level where the difference in factor endowments leads to the difference not only in wages, but also, over time, profits, technology and labour productivity. Thus, in the latter case, there is difference in both organic composition and wages; the former condition exhibits difference in organic composition only, since the intra-country wage differentials are seen to be somewhat equalised by state action.

Emmanuel is not concerned with unequal exchange within a country; he focuses on the second type of unequal exchange involving two different countries, one developed, the other underdeveloped. And the main argument is that if two countries with different factor endowments engage in trade, unequal exchange is bound to occur and the inequality between the two will enlarge over time. The key distinction made between the two types of unequal exchange is that one occurring *within* a country does not involve a transfer of surplus value, whereas one *between* countries results in the net transfer of surplus value from one country to another. Emmanuel makes the fundamental point that if countries with differences in labour productivity engage in trade, the country with the lower labour productivity ends up exchanging large quantities of its labour contained in the exported goods as compared to a trade partner with higher labour productivity. Thus the inequality is not so much between the products exchanged, but the labour value contained in the products that are exchanged between the two economies.

Unequal exchange and the labour theory of value

In trying to elaborate his theory of unequal exchange Emmanuel employs Marx's labour theory of value, which sees value of the commodity to be constituted by the amount of labour power expended in the production of the use-value of a commodity or service. Marx defines use-value as "something capable of satisfying a want of some sort" (Marx, [1867] 1995). However, he made a subtle distinction between the conception of value under social conditions of production and capitalist production. Under the former, labour time which is used up in producing a product is not a commodity, but corresponds to the value of the materials used up to enable the labourer to produce it. This is referred to as the "socially necessary labour time". Under social conditions of production the labourer uses up only the labour power or value of labour which is necessary to keep him or her (and his or her family) alive and reproduce himself or herself; no surplus value is generated in the process. Under capitalist production, however, the labourer sells his or her labour power as a commodity, whose price is the wage that the worker gets. However, in the production process, the worker's labour power is transformed into a value that is greater than the value reflected in his or her wages. The difference between the value that labour power creates and the wage paid is what constitutes surplus value.

The essential point is that under both capitalist and social conditions of production, the value of the product is determined by the labour power used in producing it. This is where the view that the cost of production (which includes labour, inputs, and machinery costs plus profit) coincides with or determines the value of a commodity differs fundamentally from the Marxian notion of value. And the key difference is that the costs (especially of labour, and also of the previous labour embedded in the inputs and machinery) can be lower than the value of the total labour used up in the production of a commodity or service. Marx explains this at great length in Chapter 7 of *Capital, Volume 1*, pointing out that

> We know that the value of each commodity is determined by the quantity of labour expended on and materialised in it, by the working-time necessary, under given social conditions, for its production. This rule also holds good in the case of the product that accrued to our capitalist.

However, under capitalist production

> [the] capitalist has two objects in view: in the first place, he wants to produce a use-value that has a value in exchange, that is to say, an article destined to

be sold, a commodity; and secondly, he desires to produce a commodity whose value shall be greater than the sum of the values of the commodities used in its production, that is, of the means of production and the labour-power, that he purchased with his good money in the open market. His aim is to produce not only a use-value, but a commodity also; … but at the same time surplus-value.

Using this concept of surplus value and the difference in wages between industrial and underdeveloped countries, Emmanuel argues that the difference in wages between workers in an industrial and a poor country amounts to an "unequal exchange". By means of this exchange, the surplus value of a low wage country is effectively transferred to an industrialised country.

Emmanuel focuses on unequal exchange at the international and not the domestic level, for the simple reason that "inside a given country redistributive mechanisms wipe out the inequality of exchange that is due to differences in organic composition of capital between different branches or regions" (Emmanuel, 1972: 163). Unequal exchange which arises, for instance, from the unfavourable terms of trade between the urban and the rural sectors, or between the manufacturing and agricultural sectors in the same country, is eliminated by the deliberate action of the state through various redistributive measures. In contrast, the exported goods produced by paying low wages to workers in underdeveloped countries means that a net surplus value is transferred from the exporting country to the importing country. In this way the surplus value which should be the property of the exporting country is "irrevocably lost" to the importing country.

The difference in productivity of labour which may account for wage differentials between the low wage exporting and high wage importing country is explained by the idea of the difference in organic composition – which simply means the difference in factor endowments (particularly capital and technical progress or skills). Following on from this, is the argument that these differences at the national level do not actually matter much because the resulting surplus stays within national boundaries and so therefore a country does not lose out. This applies to multinational companies which operate in low wage countries producing goods for export to industrialised nations.

Here the view that wages increase in proportion to the increase in the productivity of labour is dismissed by the argument that wages change slowly compared to changes in productivity (in either direction, downward or upwards – wages tend to be sticky). According to this view, the ultimate result from the sticky nature of wages *vis-à-vis* the rapid shifts in productivity is increased profits, which signify an increase in the extraction of surplus value.

> Increased productivity does not directly increase [the] basket of goods; it reduces the time to produce them. The immediate effect, however, of increased productivity is an increase in surplus value not an increase in wages. Only when the quantitative changes in productivity have accumulated sufficiently … does the value of labour power change.
>
> (Emmanuel, 1972: 110)

Emmanuel further argues that the resulting exploitation of poor countries through trade with rich ones only leads to the widening of inequality, such that the development of the advanced nations inevitably leads to the underdevelopment of Third World countries. According to Emmanuel's view, if there was no such exploitation then wage labour, capitalist relations, profit accumulation and economic progress would not be possible, but the "mere fact that one of these things exist is sufficient proof" that unequal exchange is a reality (Emmanuel, 1972: 107).

While Emmanuel's analysis is focused at the international level, just like Prebisch and Singer, his view is different from them in that the analysis is not based on the type of commodity exported, but is applied to any exchange relations between nations with different wage levels, regardless of whether one is exporting primary commodities or manufactured goods or services. However, one could argue that the difference in productivity and wages between countries virtually translates into the fact that countries with low wages tend to produce and export primary commodities, while countries with higher wages tend to produce manufactured products. In a broad sense this is largely related to the factor endowment argument, which asserts that countries with low capital, and relatively lower capital-labour ratios, will have lower wages; while economies with higher capital-labour ratios tend to have labour as the scarce resource, which is relatively more expensive.

However, Emmanuel's analysis concentrates on the mere fact that trade between nations with different wage levels eventually leads to the irrevocable transfer of surplus value from a low wage to a higher wage country. This argument also challenges the comparative advantage doctrine which posits a win-win outcome from trade. In challenging this view it is argued that the international division of labour on which the free trade theory is based does not only lead to unequal exchange, it also results in a "suboptimal" system to the extent that the comparative advantages of individual countries are impossible to realise (Emmanuel, 1972: 164). This is mainly attributed to the fact that factors (capital and labour) within comparative advantage theory are assumed to be immobile between countries – thereby rendering the notion of comparative advantage ineffective – since there is no factor competition between nations that can account for factor price equalisation over time.

In this framework, while there is evidence for asserting partial immobility of labour (for example immigration laws, immigration costs, etc.), there is little evidence to support the view that capital is immobile across countries, especially in the current context when there has been a deeper integration of financial and capital markets across the globe. Even during the 1960s and 1970s, when many developing countries were hostile to foreign capital investment, capital was mobile (see te Velde, 2006) – though mainly between the industrialised countries and a few emerging markets.

Taking a broader approach to the issue of convergence of wages, factor prices and productivity over time, Jeffrey Williamson (1995) argues, using the Heckscher-Ohlin theory of factor proportions, that in fact trade in a globalised world can be a substitute for factor mobility such that even if one assumes total factor immobility, as long as there is trade between countries then factor prices (the differences which reflect inefficient allocation of resources in the global economy), wage differentials, and income, tend to converge to the long-term equilibrium, and both parties engaged in trade do in fact gain, though not equally. While the evidence for this claim again is restricted to industrialised countries, even here this can only be possible if there is an assumption of free trade. But free trade, even in the era of liberal trade policies (the golden age of capitalism 1870–1914), has remained the exception not the rule, as noted earlier. Although one could argue that capital mobility in LDCs is constrained, there is significant capital flow to middle-income countries in Latin America (mainly Brazil, Mexico, Argentina and Colombia) and East Asia (China, Indonesia and South Korea). It is, rather, what this capital does in these countries which should be the main concern.

Emmanuel's view that unequal exchange at the national level can be addressed by the redistributive mechanisms of the state, through regulation, is highly debatable. Literature on this topic has pointed out that operations of capitalist relations at the national level mirror the global picture such that the redistribution that he suggests may not actually lead to any reversal of intranational inequality. Thus, the distinction made between unequal exchange in the 'broad' and 'strict' senses seems to be an analytically necessary one.

Unequal exchange and modes of production

While Emmanuel's work constitutes a significant contribution to a critical analysis of the international trade doctrine (see Bettelheim, 1972), his views have been contested by both Marxist and non-Marxist commentators. An interesting and extended critique of Emmanuel's analysis has been provided by Charles Bettelheim, who has argued that Emmanuel has confused exploitative exchange relations with the core Marxist concept of modes and relations of production. By emphasising the exploitation arising from exchange, it is argued, the analysis has diverted attention from the root problem – which lies in the relations of production and not the exchange relations. "One of the serious weaknesses of the terms 'commercial exploitation' and 'unequal exchange' is that they obscure the fact that what is described by them is necessarily rooted in the production relations" (Bettelheim, 1972: 276). Other analysts argue that by focusing on exchange relations, this analysis ignores the root of the problem of underdevelopment – which lies in the extraction of surplus value, via wage labour. Extraction of surplus value through low wages and other extra-economic means has been emphasised by most of the analysts operating within the broader Marxist tradition, who argue that the crux of the matter is not exchange relations, but relations of production.

A similar debate arose between Frank and Ernesto Laclau (1971) concerning the claim by Frank (1967) that Latin America had been a capitalist region since the sixteenth century, with the latter arguing that this thinking is actually alien to Marxist theory.[18] Controversies which have long dominated this debate relate to whether there can be surplus value extracted under conditions where wage labour does not exist; whether the exchange relations under non-capitalist modes of production amount to the extraction of surplus value. Not surprisingly, some analysts, including Wallerstein and Amin, have answered this question positively, arguing that capitalism is not just about modes of production wrapped around wage labour. In Amin's view

> a society cannot be reduced to a mode of production. The concept of mode of production is abstract. It does not imply any particular order in the chain of historical events ... from the first differentiated society to the capitalist form of society.
>
> (Amin, 1972: 107)

Hamza Alavi, on the contrary, highlights the importance of modes of production and the resulting social relations of production in the Marxist conception of capitalism: "Modes of production and social relations of production structured by them, rather than relations of exchange, define capitalism in a Marxist conception. The trade links do not by themselves unify societal entities into a structurally single economic system" (Alavi, 1982: 173). Similarly, with particular reference to underdevelopment and dependence theories, Colin Leys (1977) identified the main weakness of these theories to be their failure to clarify the issues around the "articulation of modes of production" – which is central to Marxist analysis. Other analysts have argued that "a form of organisation of production in which the direct producers sell their labour power since alternative means of survival are increasingly constrained" is what constitutes capitalism (Sender and Smith, 1986: 35).

The main contention by those who are often referred to as neo-Marxists is that extraction of surplus is not just unique to capitalist modes of production, but to any interaction where exchange results in one party getting more than it has given to the other. From this it has been argued by theorists such as Wallerstein, Amin and Frank, that modes of production are not sequential such that capitalist modes appear *after* pre-capitalist modes – the two, in fact, often co-exist.[19] Proponents of this view argue that the main problem is the notion that "free labour is the defining characteristic of a capitalist mode of production" (Wallerstein, 1974b: 393). Rejecting the view that capitalism only appears where there are developed capitalist modes of production (free wage labour or capitalist relations of production), Amin argues that Emmanuel's analysis – which emphasises exploitation even in exchange situations, whether under capitalist relations of production or not – has revealed the true nature of the mechanism through which surplus value is transferred from the periphery to the centre (Amin, 1974: 23).

However, other analysts have contended that there cannot be capitalism without wage labour, a condition that is only possible under circumstances of 'free' labour engaging in a paid wage structure as a means of survival. Otherwise the resulting relations of production are not capitalist. Karl Polanyi (1944), for instance, argues that there can be no capitalism without free labour. Using England as an example, he argues that capitalism only became a reality after the abolition of the Poor Laws in 1832, which forced people to engage in wage labour as a necessary means of survival. "Not until 1834 was a competitive labour market established in England; hence, industrial capitalism as a social system cannot be said to have existed before that date" (Polany, 1944: 83). Similarly, John Sender and Sheila Smith (1986) also see the emergence of a "free market for labour" as the defining feature of capitalism. This debate has not been resolved even today, although the free labour thesis dominates.

Influence on Africa

The theories discussed above have, in different ways, influenced thinking about economic growth and development in Africa since the early 1960s. There is no doubt that some of the ideas discussed above have influenced African scholars, politicians and policymakers, in many countries, but it is important to note that there are some scholars within and outside Africa who doubt the relevance of these views when it comes to explaining the growth challenges there. For example, it is argued that the dependency theory "originated in the observation of Latin American economic patterns. Its application to Africa has given rise to an increase in dogma and hypocrisy rather than to a careful study of political dynamics" (Bayart, 1993: 5). A similar view is expressed by Hopkins (1975), who argues that the dependency theory has little conceptual relevance in Africa, though he acknowledges that orthodox Marxism offers Africa helpful insights.

The introduction of these theories and ideas into Africa by 'non-Africans'[20] is attributed to the idea that research in Africa is not sufficiently developed to challenge them. Other critics have argued that concepts borrowed from Marxist and neo-Marxist paradigms have in fact been misleading; it is difficult to identify corresponding ideas such as "social class" in Africa, thus rendering such concepts less helpful in understanding the continent (see Chabal and Daloz, 1999: 5). For some critics, both orthodox bourgeois *and* Marxist theories fail to offer appropriate tools for understanding the African crisis because their point of departure was developed in capitalist countries where conditions were very different (see Onimode, 1988).

A similar view is expressed by Mahmood Mamdani (1996) who argues that the bipolar paradigm which orthodox Marxism, structuralism and dependency theories employ in understanding Africa can actually do a disservice to the understanding of Africa's challenges. The crucial point, in Mamdani's view, is that while "the lead term [modern, capitalist or developed] had analytical content, the residual term [traditional, pre-capitalist, underdeveloped] lacked both an original history and an authentic future" (Mamdani, 1996: 9). In this binary framework, Africa's future, for instance, tends to be explained in terms of becoming modern, passing through the capitalist phases of development as conceptualised in the lead countries. This debate ties into the discourse on African intellectuals, and it is closely linked to the question of the 'relevancy' of African scholarship, discussed in Chapter 8.

Despite the above concerns, many African scholars and politicians have actually found these theories appealing (in particular ideas related to dependency and structuralism, especially during the 1960s and 1970s), and have used them to devise strategies for Africa's development (see Ki-Zerbo, 1994). A review of the economic strategies implemented in Africa during the 1960s and 1970s suggests that the structuralist, Marxist, dependency and modernisation theories had significant influence in many African countries. Some authors have attributed their appeal to the nationalist imperative of seeking a quick solution to underdevelopment. Arguably, the application of such theories did not essentially involve a total transplantation of foreign ideas into Africa; in many cases, there were attempts to adapt them to African conditions. One of the prominent though controversial examples is the notion of African socialism, which was initially seen to have adapted socialist ideas to African realities by emphasising the idea of social solidarity as fundamentally reflecting the African worldview and value system. A good example of this in early post-colonial Africa is the assertion by some African leaders that,

> from scientific socialism we have rejected atheism and violence, which are fundamentally contrary to our genius ... We have developed co-operation, not collectivist, but communal. For co-operation, in family, village, tribe, has always been held in honour in Africa, not its collectivist form.
>
> (cited in Mohan, 1966: 226)

In addition to the politicians, African scholars use the above ideas to explain Africa's underdevelopment as a specific consequence of structural relations with the industrial or developed countries. For example, Rodney (1972) argues that the interaction between Africa and Europe – not just during slavery but throughout the colonial and neo-colonial period (through multinational corporations) – constitutes the root cause of Africa's underdevelopment. In all these relations, so the argument goes, Africa is disadvantaged due to its structural weakness when compared to the other partners in the relationship. Exploitation of labour through various means, exploitation of natural resources, expatriation of surplus value from Africa, at various stages means the development of Europe is the converse of the underdevelopment of Africa, related in a dialectical manner (Rodney, 1972). Amin makes a similar point, arguing that through interaction between "Europe and Africa since the mercantilist period (1600 AD), Africa has been cumulatively weakened to the point which makes economic growth and development impossible as long as the structures which perpetuate Africa's subordinate position in the relation continues" (Amin, 1972: 107). Seen in the larger framework of PE, this assertion seems to justify the idea that exploitation was not only peculiar to the establishment of capitalist modes of production in the continent, but also to unequal relations and exchange between Africa and the West in particular. For this reason, some analysts have argued that the only way forward for Africa is to delink from the world system. The reason for proposing the delinking strategy is that as long as Africa remains part of the world capitalist system it will continue to be subordinated to the external capitalist rationality of uneven development whereby the leakage of surplus value from Africa will continue to strengthen the advanced capitalist nations on the one hand, but further weaken African nations on the other. In this view, explanations such as those by the World Bank and others who argue for further integration of Africa into the global economy are only a superficial analysis of the African reality (see Amin, 1990; Bush, 2004). The reason offered for rejecting integration into the global capitalist system is that such a system produces opposite effects for Africa and the advanced capitalist countries:

> Capitalist expansion has directly inverse effects in the centres and in the peripheries of the system: It integrates the societies in the former, but in the latter it disintegrates the society, fragments it, alienates it, and eventually destroys the nation or destroys its potential.
>
> (Amin, 1990: 57)

In this view, the various problems identified by the World Bank and the International Monetary Fund (IMF) as the major causes of Africa's economic growth and development challenges – such as poor incentives to agriculture, overvalued exchange rates, low investment, low skills, high population growth rates, poor state institutions and inappropriate domestic policies – should all be seen as outcomes of a capitalist system which generates conditions unfavourable for the development of Africa.

Import substitution industrialisation strategy in Africa

As noted earlier, the influence of the different PE views discussed above has not been limited to academic analysts and researchers; these ideas filtered into policies at various times, especially during the 1960s and 1970s. One of the ideas which influenced a number of policymakers in Africa is the import substitution industrialisation (ISI) strategy that has its roots in the ideas of the early structuralists, mainly Prebisch and Singer. As discussed above, the Prebisch-Singer model asserts that reliance on the export of primary commodities and import of manufactured products from industrialised countries by the underdeveloped countries undermines the latter's prospect for economic growth and development via the unfavourable terms of trade against suppliers of primary commodities. To lessen the negative impact of this structural constraint, both Prebisch and Singer recommended that underdeveloped countries manufacture locally some of the products which they had previously imported from industrailised countries: import substitution. According to Prebisch such a strategy "would counteract the tendency towards the deterioration of the terms of trade by avoiding the allocation of additional productive resources to primary export activities and diverting them instead to industrial production" (Prebisch, 1984: 179).

Establishment of a local manufacturing industry, according to this view, could be achieved through various state interventions including targeted allocation of foreign currency for capital goods acquisition and industrial inputs, special subsidies for and protection of infant industries, and imposition of import quotas on consumer goods which are locally produced. For most African governments, ISI was adopted with several objectives in mind, including diversification of the economy, speeding up the process of industrialisation, and improving the balance of payments (BoP) situation. Since more of the imported consumer goods would be produced locally by promoting local industries employment would be created. It was also envisioned that promoting local industries would be a quicker way of importing technology from industrialised countries. Most importantly, ISI was seen by most African governments as a political strategy to reduce dependence of African economies on developed countries. This strategy envisioned a rapid growth of industrial activities in many countries, starting with light manufacturing such as the processing of agricultural products (including textiles, rubber and sisal), and subsequently moving into intermediate, and finally heavy duty, manufacturing of cars and other machinery. Some analysts have argued that "in most cases, import-substitution industrialisation was the only possible strategy, because initially the domestic market was the only market which could be secured, by state intervention" for industrialisation to occur (Sender and Smith, 1986: 72).

However, the performance of ISI in Africa was generally disappointing. Claude Ake (1981) identifies four major reasons which account for this failure. These include, that most government bureaucrats were naïve and did not understand properly the dynamics of such a development strategy; that such a strategy threatened the interests of foreign capital; that rampant rent-seeking and the appointment of inexperienced civil servants to run the state-owned enterprises made such ventures non-viable from the start; and that the politicisation of investment meant that economic considerations were sidelined. To these factors, Bade Onimode (1988) adds the small size of internal markets, concentration on the manufacturing of consumer goods (semi-luxury and luxury) over capital goods, and the heavy reliance on capital-intensive technology which was less suitable for African economies. Other reasons for the failure of ISI in Africa include the absence of what Hirschman (1958) referred to as "backward and forward linkages" in the economies. Overall, poor management, rent-seeking and shortage of capital – especially after the second oil shock – created problems for the local industries.

Of course ISI strategies were severely criticised by the governments of industrialised countries who saw protectionism as an affront to free trade. Ironically, most industrialised countries opposed this policy even though they have actually continued to adopt protectionist policies – especially against agricultural products from developing countries. As noted in Chapter 3, Robert McNamara in his *Nairobi Speech* identified the discriminatory trade barriers against poor countries as one of the challenges facing developing countries in their quest for growth and development.[21]

Despite the protests from industrialised countries, a number of African governments implemented ISI strategies during the 1960s and 1970s, and to start with there were a few success stories. Even analysts who were opposed to such ventures[22] acknowledged initial successes in local manufacturing and agro-processing in a number of Sub-Saharan Africa (SSA) countries such as Tanzania (sisal), Kenya (textiles), Ghana (cocoa processing), Zimbabwe and Zambia (cotton and textiles) (see Bates, 1981). ISI strategy was recommended on the basis that through such initiatives developing countries would retain a greater share of the value of commodities; they would absorb simple technology; and they would thereby reduce dependence on industrialised countries for manufactured products (Singer, 1984). Overall, the export promotion strategy which followed ISI also did little to bring about diversification of the economies, mainly because most of the manufactured goods produced in Africa faced steep competition from industrial countries that benefited from more sophisticated manufacturing capacity, technology and skill. This has remained the African story even today, as explained in Chapter 7.

Capitalism in Africa

Within PE traditions, the failure of Africa's economies to transform has been accounted for in terms of the stunted nature of capitalism that has evolved there. This has mainly been explained in reference to weak class formations which resulted in the failure to provide the dynamic forces for social, economic and political transformation. The absence of a clearly defined indigenous capitalist class has been seen to have limited the possibility of full-blown capitalism in Africa. The class formations thesis has been applied in both capitalist and socialist accounts, with the argument that a true capitalist class did not emerge in Africa to transform the pre-capitalist mode of production into a capitalist one, a process which would have released productive forces essential for a complete economic transformation. Neither did a distinct class of socialist leaders committed to the total transformation of society, emerge. Franz Fanon, for instance, argues that such a class in Africa did not emerge at all: what we saw was an "enlightened section of the new state" elites who are

> [neither] financiers nor industrial magnates ... The national bourgeoisie of underdeveloped countries is not engaged in production, nor in invention, nor building, nor labour; it is completely canalized into activities of the intermediary type. The Psychology of the national bourgeoisie is that of the businessman, not that of a captain of industry.
>
> (Fanon, 1963: 149–50)

For some analysts, as stated above, this condition means that while Africa relates to the capitalist world, it is not yet part of the capitalist system (see Saul and Leys, 1999).

However, some analysts dismiss this claim arguing that it is untrue to say that such a class did not emerge in post-colonial Africa. Sender and Smith (1986: 79) have argued that the "existence and importance" of a domestic bourgeois class has been underestimated in most analyses of capitalism in Africa, a phenomenon which has been attributed to a misconception that "a capitalist is a wealthy and educated employer who runs a large machine enterprise". Analysts who acknowledge the existence of an indigenous capitalist class, however, do admit that the class that emerged in Africa was not a true capitalist class in the sense that it was largely a class dependent on control of state power guaranteeing privileged access to state resources (Arrighi and Saul, 1968). According to this view, the pseudo-capitalist classes that emerged were not autonomous, they were appendages of international capital, without a clear ideology, with no distinct class consciousness and mission. Because of this, this class has not been able to play any important role in inducing the break from less productive to more productive social and economic relations – there has been a failure to unleash the transformative power of capitalism. The disarticulated class formation that emerged in Africa has been variously characterised as a bureaucratic elite, comprador bourgeoisie (Arrighi and Saul, 1968), bureaucratic bourgeoisie (Shiviji, 1976, Hyden, 1986), *kulak* or rural bourgeoisie (Berg, 1964), or an emerging bourgeois (Sender and Smith, 1986).

Although there are some analysts who argue that a distinct capitalist class emerged in Africa immediately after independence (see Iliffe, 1983; Sender and Smith, 1986), the common view has been that a true capitalist class has failed to emerge in Africa and that this is because capitalism failed to mature there (see Leys, 1996).[23] In this framework, entrenching of the capitalist mode of production is seen as the only hope for economic and social transformation in Africa, suggesting that this is the only way to create and sustain the productive forces and the new social relations necessary for social transformation to occur. Goran Hyden (1986), one of the proponents of this view, contends that capitalism has the greatest potential to effectively break the ties with pre-capitalist modes of production and release the productive forces in Africa. According to this view, the key lies in bringing the "uncaptured peasants" (who are the majority in Africa) under the capitalist mode of production. A similar argument is advanced by Kevin Cox and Rohit Negi, who argue that

> Capitalism *has assumed a stunted form over most of the continent.* This is due to the fact that for the most part the necessary conditions have been missing. There cannot be capitalism unless immediate producers are separated from the means of production and forced to sell their labour power for a wage.
> (Cox and Negi, 2010: 76, emphasis added)

Thus, it is asserted that only when peasant landowners are converted into agricultural or industrial workers that surplus value from the highly productive commercial agriculture and industrial sectors will be tapped to finance industrialisation and, subsequently, the transformation of the economy and society at large. The development of a local capitalist class is decisive in this process. While "international capital can only provide the systemic support that is necessary to reduce the influence of pre-capitalist formations" the "main thrust must be on the development of local capitalism whether in the rural or in the urban areas" (Hyden,

1983: 26). As long as the local capitalist class fails to emerge, Africa's growth and development prospects remain dull.

In recent debates around the Africa Rising narrative (ARN), there have been suggestions that the sustained economic growth over the past decade-and-a-half is due to the emergence of a class of African entrepreneurs bent on transforming the continent (Rotberg, 2013). Evidence of an emerging African entrepreneur class includes the deepening of the financial sector, the growing of capital markets from just eight stock exchanges in 2002 to 29 in 2012 (AfDB, 2013: 16). However, the nature and size of this new class of entrepreneurs is not well known, though it has been argued that the emerging African captains of industry are not dependent on state privileges as was the case during the 1970s and 1980s; the African capitalists are now able to survive on their own without relying on privileged access to state resources (Severino and Ray, 2011).

The uncaptured peasantry

Nonetheless, Africa still is predominantly characterised by a large subsistence sector where production and productivity are low. Under these conditions, it has been argued, Africa does not provide a suitable condition for the development of socialism "nor does it provide the fundamental class contradictions to produce socialist consciousness" (Hyden, 1983: 27). This is supported by the view that peasants have largely remained 'uncaptured' by virtue of their being independent producers. Under current circumstances accumulation from above or below is impossible, simply because there is little if any surplus value produced, and also because the means of capturing even the little that exists are non-existent. But if the peasants were integrated into the capitalist mode of production they would work either as commercial agricultural producers or wage labourers, and through these means surplus value would have been extracted to finance industrialisation. This is clearly stated in Hyden's response to critics who dismissed the notion of an uncaptured peasantry:

> My point is not that surplus appropriation and social differentiation are absent, as implied in this critique;[24] but rather that the peasant mode of production only permits a very limited form of accumulation that is not sufficient to enable those who extract this surplus to use it.
>
> (Hyden, 1986: 693)

A similar view was suggested by Geoffrey Kay (1975), who argued that the problem of development in Africa is not because of exploitation of Africans by capitalists, but because capitalism has not exploited the Africans enough to create surplus value. This view has been advanced by Leys as one of the explanations for the failure of development in Africa. In *The Rise and Fall of Development Theory*, Leys (1996) argues that the weak development of capitalism in Africa is responsible for its failed development because this essentially has meant that there was no mechanism for capital accumulation either from below or from above.

Analysts who advance this argument link it to Marx and Friedrich Engels' idea that capitalism has an incredible capacity to develop productive forces which can then transform the social order. In the *Communist Manifesto* the capitalist's ability to "create massive and colossal productive forces" was lauded (Marx and Engels, 1848: 7). However, these productive forces were only praised as a means to an end: the development of such productive forces would eventually generate contradictions between the proletariat (worker's class) and the bourgeoisie (capitalist class) such that the later becomes the 'sorcerer' who is unable to control his own spells.

There are several explanations for the failure to generate productive forces in Africa. The most common reason, as explained above, is that the class structure which evolved after independence was dominated by what has been referred to as 'the labour aristocracy of tropical Africa', a self-indulgent elite class (Arrighi and Saul, 1968). This labour aristocracy class failed to direct surplus resources from the subsistence economy towards industrial development. Instead, the extracted surplus was used on what has been termed 'discretionary consumption', which ignored investment in productive sectors. Giovanni Arrighi and John S. Saul (1968) argue that the self-professed African socialists failed to understand the problem posed by economic stratification, especially the colonial legacy of the rural-urban divide.

> There has really been little grasp, within the doctrine of African socialism, of such a form of inequality and the accompanying possibilities for exploitation by this labour aristocracy. The necessity of bridging the urban-rural gap is rarely given sufficient prominence.
>
> (Arrighi and Saul, 1968: 155)

Here again the importance of agriculture forms the basis for explaining Africa's inability to sustain economic growth and development. There is some suggestion in the broader literature that urban bias has left African economies untransformed, due to lack of capital investment in infrastructure. The urban group is seen as largely made up of working poor (see the next chapter) who often engage in self-employed income generating ventures as a last resort. These masses of urban poor are distinguished from a privileged cadre of workers whose salaries are ten times higher than peasant income. Because of the alliance between this group and the political elites, it is argued that policy has failed to address the issue of transforming society to ensure that the majority of people have sufficient income to meet basic needs.

Africa and the global capitalist economy

While there are some analysts who argue that any relationship with the capitalist world is bad for Africa, there are some PE analysts who have argued that in fact it is not Africa's relationship with the global economy, per se, which is the problem; rather it is the manner in which Africa is inserted into the global economy (Bush, 2008). Saul and Leys (1999) have argued, for instance, that the failure to transform the economic structure imposed by colonial rulers – who saw Africa as the source of primary goods – has been a source of disadvantage for the continent. The colonial production structure which imposed the growth of cash crops (mainly coffee, cocoa, tea, cotton, tobacco and sugar) on Africa, and the extraction of minerals, has meant that Africa has essentially remained the supplier of primary commodities to the global economy (see Rowden, 2013).

The problem with economies dependent on the export of primary commodities is (as we have seen in the analysis by Singer and Prebisch) that the price of these commodities is often vulnerable to volatility on the global commodity market and subject to the phenomenon of secular decline in the long-run, such that the resulting terms of trade are unfavourable to Africa in the long term. Although various studies and reports from the World Bank dispute the view that deterioration in terms of trade contributes significantly to Africa's poor economic growth experience (World Bank, 1983; 1989), the tendency for prices of primary commodities to decline has been observed for a long time (see Emmanuel, 1972). A study examining the impact of terms of trade on growth in Africa finds that they have had a negative impact on those African economies included in the study (Bleaney and Greenaway, 2001). In the case of SSA, the terms of trade index shows a declining trend for African exports over the period 1980–2001, as Figure 6.1 shows. While the regional figures shown hide the variations in the terms of trade at country level, the long-term trend in the price of commodities that the continent exports – relative to the price of imported manufactured goods – has been declining steadily.

Although some countries such as South Africa, Mauritius, Namibia, Tunisia and Egypt have a sizeable manufacturing sector, most of the countries in the region depend on primary product exports, mainly unprocessed natural resources such as oil, minerals and agricultural products (see Table 6.1). In some countries two or three commodities account for more than three-quarters of the total exports, as shown below.

In most of the petroleum exporting countries such as Chad, Nigeria, Sudan, Angola and Libya, crude oil accounts for more than 80 per cent of the total exports. It is also clear from Table 6.1 that the other non-oil exporting countries rely heavily on primary products – mainly agricultural products and mineral ores. The diversification index also suggests that little progress has been made, even in recent years, in terms of broadening the export base for most countries. This production and export structure is not only vulnerable to external price shocks, but puts most African countries at a disadvantage as far as the terms of trade over the long term is concerned. As noted in the next chapter, the activities in which most African countries are involved have low value added, resulting in a situation where an African country's share in any value chain is minute compared to other countries involved in high value-added activities.

The important point to this argument is that the declining terms of trade together with massive leakages of capital through various means has affected capital accumulation which, in turn, has blocked the process of industrialisation and infrastructure development in Africa. This has eventually resulted

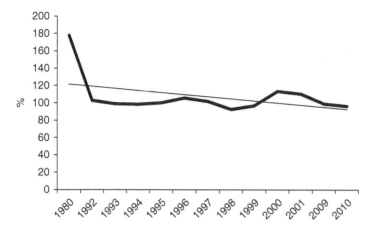

Figure 6.1. The trend in Africa's terms of trade (1980–2010)

Source: author, based on data from various years of the *Africa Development Indicators*.

Note: the base year is 1995. The figures for 2009 and 2010 are based on the unweighted mean of the 24 and 26 African countries, respectively, for which there were data.

in the failure of many countries to transform the production structure into a more diversified base with high value-addition activities. Africa's overreliance on agriculture and other primary commodities as the main source of foreign exchange has not only made many of its countries' external accounts vulnerable to the uncertainties arising from the volatility in price and demand for primary commodities, food security also becomes a persistent problem in some parts of the continent.[25]

Capital flight

Failure to enforce policies that prevent capital flight and other forms of illegal leakages of capital from the continent has meant that little reinvestment of capital generated from within Africa has taken place. If one looks at the 'known' levels of capital flight from SSA, there are clear signs that substantial amounts of money leak from the continent through clandestine acquisition of private assets, profit-taking, debt servicing, corruption,[26] and other means such as transfer pricing and the dubious invoicing of multinational corporations with subsidiary companies in Africa. A study examining the nature and level of capital flight trends between 1970 and 2000 in Africa estimates that an accumulated total of US$193 billion, in 1996 prices, leaked out of 25 heavily indebted poor countries over this period. If interest on the externalised resources is imputed, the total capital flight over the same period is estimated at US$285 billion (see Boyce and Ndikumana, 2000). New estimates covering the period between 1970 and 2004 put the figure at US$420 billion, and US$607 billion if the interest on the expatriated capital is added (Ndikumana and Boyce, 2008).

Table 6.1. Three major export products and diversification index for selected African countries

	Commodity 1	Share in total export (%)	Commodity 2	Share in total export (%)	Commodity 3	Share in total export (%)	Export diversification index
Angola	Petroleum oil	96.3	–	–	–	–	0.82
Burkina Faso	Cotton	52.1	Gold	19.9	Sesamum seed	9.1	0.72
Burundi	Coffee	76.1	Black tea	9.3	–	–	0.80
Chad	Petroleum oil	90.9	Oil (non-crude)	5.6	–	–	0.70
Congo Republic	Petroleum oil	87.8	–	–	–	–	0.82
Equatorial Guinea	Petroleum oil	72.7	Natural gas	22.2	Live goats	13.2	0.74
Gabon	Petroleum oil	69.9	Manganese	9.8	Logs/timber	7	0.85
Libya	Petroleum oil	79.3	Natural gas	9.1	Oil (refined)	4.8	0.82
Malawi	Tobacco	63	Dried legumes	8.8	Black tea (treated)	6.3	0.81
Niger	Uranium	70.5	Light oils	23.8	–	–	0.79
Nigeria	Petroleum oil	86.3	Natural gas	7.5	–	–	0.85
Seychelles	Tuna	59.2	Thunnus obesus	–	Skipjack	5.4	0.84
Sudan	Petroleum oil	91.3	–	–	–	–	0.74
Togo	Cocoa beans	47.1	Groundnut	8.3	Gold	7.7	0.71
Zambia	Copper	49.8	Copper anodes	16.5	Copper ores	8.3	0.86

Source: compiled by author, based on data from *African Development Indicator* (ADI, 2011).

Note: export diversification index is scaled from 0 (the least diversification of export) to 1 (the most diversified export). [–] = no data available.

The problem of capital flight from SSA is well known by politicians and international development agencies, although it has often been downplayed as legitimate 'profit-taking'. Sometimes it is argued that capital is externalised by Africans themselves, especially the 'native princes' and their networks. This view is clearly expressed by the former British secretary of state Lynda Chalker, who after acknowledging that 40 per cent of wealth created in Africa is expatriated, urged Africans to return the money: "If you can get your kith and kin to bring the funds back and have it invested in infrastructure, the economies of African countries would be much better than they are today" (cited in Ayittey, 2004). While a number of the 'native princes' have been involved in expatriating Africa's wealth, it is also clear that a large section of resources has been siphoned off through the activities of the multinational corporations based in industrialised economies, including Britain and the USA (UNECA-AU, 2012). Thus, the appeal to the African "kith and kin" to bring back the money should in fact be extended to the owners of the multinational corporations in developed countries who have been actively treating Africa as a workshop where you can make money, but keep it elsewhere.

A recent study on capital flight from South Africa shows that huge amounts of capital leave the country to more industrialised countries, and that the rate increased sharply following the liberalisation of financial and capital markets in 1996. The study estimates that capital flight increased from an annual average of 5.4 per cent of Gross Domestic Product (GDP) between 1980 and 1993 to an annual average of 9.2 per cent between 1994 and 2000. The rate then accelerated to an annual average of 12 per cent between 2001 and 2007, before jumping to a staggering 20 per cent of GDP in 2008 alone (see Ashman *et al.*, 2011).

According to a study by Paul Collier *et al.*, Africa's GDP per capita would have been 16 times greater if all the capital that has leaked since 1980 had stayed in the continent (see Ndikumana and Boyce, 2008). It is also estimated that Africa's capital flight is about three times the total debt that African countries owe the rest of the world (ibid.). Commenting on the levels of capital flight from Africa, Sam Ashman *et al.* (2011: 10) argue that "if only a quarter of the stock of its capital flight was repatriated to and invested in sub-Saharan Africa, the sub-continent would go from trailing to leading other developing regions in terms of domestic investments". The net effect of such a huge haemorrhage is a persistent shortage of investment capital which makes it difficult to build the sort of basic infrastructure on which economic growth and development can be sustained.

Challenges of structural transformation in Africa

As a result of massive outflows, Africa's fixed capital formation is the lowest of all the regions of the world, and this has serious implications for the transformation of the production structure. Given the high levels of capital flight being experienced in the continent, it is highly unlikely that countries there are using the windfall revenue generated by the recent high price of commodities to restructure their economies. For this reason Africa's relations with the rest of the world becomes an essential factor in understanding the continent's economic and development challenges; and the various PE perspectives that highlight these structural relations raise a fundamental issue as far as the African crisis is concerned.

Africa's relations with the rest of the world are crucial to understanding the challenges of diversification in the continent. In a paper proposing an alternative explanation and strategy to the World Bank's Structural Adjustment Policies (SAPs), the Economic Commission for Africa (UNECA, 1989) warns that growth will not be possible without a deliberate effort to transform the production structures of most African economies from their current heavy reliance on agriculture and extractive industries to a more diversified production structure. "Excessive outward orientation and dependence" were cited as the key characteristics of most African economies – which include features such as the predominance of subsistence activities, a disarticulated production base, weak inter-sectoral linkages, low productivity, dualism with a well-developed export sector *vis-à-vis* an underdeveloped subsistence sector, urban bias, and weak institutional capacity. The severe 'dependence' of African economies on one or two primary commodities, together with the 'extroverted structure' of these economies, was central in the report's diagnosis of the African development challenges.

> The weakness of the production base, the predominant exchange nature of the economy, and its openness, have perpetuated Africa's external dependence. One of the main features of the African 'economy' is the dominance of the external sector, which renders African economies highly susceptible to external shocks. In Africa, a few commodities often account for 80 percent of total export earnings and government revenue.
>
> (UNECA, 1989: 5)[27]

Although the UNECA report maintains that its "proposed framework is in sharp contrast to the models that underlie the orthodox stabilisation ... programmes" (UNECA, 1989: 28), some analysts have argued that the proposed UNECA alternative had many points of convergence with the SAPs, and that it was "flawed both in its analysis and prescriptions". However, the critics acknowledge that the UNECA strategy differs significantly from SAPs in its emphasis on the 'structural transformation' of African economies (see Ravenhill, 1993).

Nonetheless, the UNECA has, since the early 1980s, consistently maintained that the causes of Africa's economic and development challenges lie in the failure to transform the structures of the economies in the region. This is a view which has been repeated in most of the UNECA reports on Africa, including the *2011 Economic Report on Africa* (ECA, 2011b). In the *2012 Africa Report*, it is argued that even if most African countries have experienced positive growth of above 5 per cent per year since 2000, these gains would be hard to sustain without diversifying the economies of the continent. The report argues that most of the economies in the region remain heavily reliant on primary commodities – mainly agriculture and natural resources such as minerals and oil. Arguably, without structural transformation of their economies, most African countries will find it difficult to sustain economic growth over time and overcome developmental challenges, especially unemployment and poverty.[28] Focus on the extractive industries, especially minerals, without any intermediate value addition or beneficiation, presents major challenges for African economies on two specific fronts: lack of intermediate value addition makes it difficult to increase real wages and income for workers; and most importantly, export of raw mineral ores are more vulnerable to terms of trade deterioration, over time, compared to the export of semi-finished products (see UNECA, 2011a: 105).

This strong emphasis on the structural transformation of African economies is crucial given the fact that most countries in the region still have economic structures which are overly dependent on the export of one or two major primary commodities, and have tiny levels of manufacturing activity. Manufacturing in some countries constitutes only 5 per cent of GDP (see Chapter 3 and Chapter 7). In developmental terms such an economic structure presents a lot of challenges. Apart from the obvious one of severe risk to external shocks given the volatile nature of the demand and, consequently, the price of primary commodities, such structures make it difficult to sustain economic growth over a long time. Even if growth is recorded for a consecutive period of ten years and is supported by a sustained price for commodities on the global market, those prices may collapse in the eleventh or thirteenth year, reversing the growth momentum gathered in previous years. This has been the biggest challenge for most African economies, and this is largely to do with the nature of the production base of most economies in the continent. Second, with such an economic structure, growth in productivity often tends to occur in the tiny capital intensive extractive sectors which do not absorb more labour. The result of this type of growth is a combination of unemployment and growing inequality due to the fact that only a few employed in the capital intensive extractive industries benefit from growth (see UNECA-AU, 2008).

At this point the question that remains to be answered is why has there been no structural transformation over these years in Africa. This is a million dollar question, and the same as asking why there has not been sustained growth and development in the continent. As the discussion in the previous chapters suggests, different people will point to different factors to explain this. Some analysts have identified aid to be responsible for the lack of structural transformation in Africa, arguing that aid has focused on creating a regulatorily efficient environment for business instead of addressing the structural constraints (see Page, 2012). Recognising the importance of structural transformation and its elusive nature in Africa, it has now been suggested that genuine structural transformation can be brought about by a 'developmental state'. Although it is not clear how such states are to be established in Africa, its role is clearly elaborated. The envisioned role of a developmental state includes building infrastructure, providing incentives to increase productivity, design and implement development strategy and policies, and build capable, transparent and accountable institutions to manage the transformation process (UNECA, 2011a). Other analysts, though not using the language of a developmental state, see the state as indispensable in achieving structural transformation in Africa – arguing that history shows that "among successful transformers, the state has helped business meet its many challenges" (ACET, 2014: 6).

This chapter has analysed the political-economic accounts of Africa's economic growth and development challenges, focusing on the period prior to the current growth. The next chapter looks at the current growth episode in the context of the ARN.

Notes

1 NIE differs from the Old Institutional Economics (OIE). In NIE the firm is largely seen in terms of profit maximising through the reduction of transaction costs, while OIE sees the firm as a social institution which relies largely on "habit and traditions" or institutionalised rules. The views of the pioneers of the OIE school (Commons and Veblen) have survived to the present in the works of Hodgson and Lazonick (see Stein, 1994).

2 Some authors talk about the emergence of a 'new' political economy of development, and identify eclecticism (no dominant paradigm), empirical testing (validating theory through data analysis), comparative institutional analysis, and a case study approach as the key elements of the new PE (see Besley, 2007; Persson and Tabellini, 2000). However, it is not clear if this actually constitutes a new approach to political economy (PE); it seems more like the reassembly of the existing PE approaches.

3 For a classification of these different schools of thought, see Martinussen (1997: Chapters 4–7), who has made an estimable attempt.

4 Some of the proponents of dependency theory have been referred to as neo-Marxists, Trotskyists, neo-Trotskyists or Frankians, to distinguish them from faithful Marxist-Leninist followers.

5 This is distinguished from the 'Industrial Revolution', which involved the invention of machines used in the production of goods, especially manufactured goods. Commercial Revolution refers to the growth of trade and commerce as the main economic activity, and it took place almost two or three centuries before the Industrial Revolution.

6 In the Wallersteinian framework, Africa only becomes a peripheral region from about 1750; prior to that it was external to the world system (Wallerstein, 1976: 980).

7 This classification of Spain, Greece, Portugal, Ireland and Italy as semi-peripheral is not something that has emerged out of the Eurozone Crisis of 2011; these countries have not traditionally been seen as part of the North-Western European core.

8 Reference is made only to West Africa, and it is not clear what was happening to the rest of the continent. It seems that the assumption is that Europe only had contacts with West Africa because of its proximity, though also because of the shift of European activities from the Mediterranean to the Atlantic during the mercantilist period. If that is the case, it ignores European contact with Southern Africa – which started as early as 1652. Trade between Europe and the Cape was not only in slaves.

9 These have been described as non-essential goods, ones which a country could do without.

10 Martinussen (1997) argues that the structuralists, in their diverse forms, are often considered as "the forerunners to the neo-Marxist dependence theories" – mainly Frank, Cardos, Amin and, to a certain extent, Wallerstein. However, Frank, in his own autobiography, describes his work as a refutation of the structuralist, Keynesian, Marxist and modernisation theories of development (see Chew and Denemark, 1996).

11 Bleaney and Greenaway (2001) note that both Sing and Prebisch received little attention in the mainstream economic literature, although some economists teach the famous Prebisch-Sing hypothesis on terms of trade.

12 The other central claim made by development economics, according to Hirschman (1981), is the "rejection of monoeconomics"; the view that underdeveloped countries are the same as developed countries and that therefore the same economic tools and assumptions can be used to understand and explain their experiences.

13 The paper which resulted from this study was published in 1949 under the title, "Relative Prices of Exports and Imports of Underdeveloped Countries".

14 Evidence for the deterioration of terms of trade for later periods between developed and low-income countries has been provided in Singer's 1994 paper, which shows that the overall deterioration of terms of trade between 1957–1982 was 32 per cent; 45 per cent for agricultural products, 27 per cent for foodstuffs, 28 per cent for beverages, and 28 per cent for ores and metals.

15 Although free trade policies were widely adopted by the leading countries of the world after 1846, such policies lasted for a short period in most except England. For example, it is observed that the USA abandoned free trade only 20 years later, in 1861, with the Morrill Tariff; this was followed by France in 1871, Italy in 1877, Austria and Argentina in 1878, Canada in 1879, Australia in 1902 and Chile in 1916 (see Emmanuel, 1972: xiv). Various forums of the Doha Round Table negotiations only testify to the enduring practical difficulties (probably impossibilities) in implementing free trade among the nations of the world.

16 The prices of primary commodities, oil and minerals have been steadily rising since 2003, reaching their highest level since the 1980s in 2008 before the 2008–2009 financial crisis. This increase has largely been attributed to the China effect, which has seen increasing demand for raw materials, especially minerals.

17 The idea here is that factors are not competitive under conditions where they are assumed to be immobile; under such conditions, factors are, de facto, monopolistic. It is only competitive factor markets (mainly capital and labour, and to a lesser extent land and entrepreneurship), with total (or at least partial) factor mobility, that the factor share (e.g., the level of wages) would equalise between two nations. The absence of free mobility of factors between two countries would result in unequal rewarding of factors due to the difference in factor endowments. In Emmanuel's view this is what essentially leads to unequal exchange between two countries with different factor endowments (see also Bettelheim, 1972: 274).

18 Of course, Frank himself does not see his work falling within the Marxist tradition of thought, although there have been suggestions that debates about whether merchant capital and its consequent stages of exploitation (resulting mainly from exchange relations) does indeed constitute capitalism – i.e., capitalist social formation and the resultant class dynamics. Marx's ambiguity on this issue makes it possible for those on both sides of the debate to claim that they are both following his view (see Wallerstein, 1974a: 392; Femia, 1993). A similar debate surfaced between Maurice Dobb and Paul Sweezy during the 1950s, with some analysts arguing that Sweezy and Frank "better follow the spirit of Marx if not his letter", and that they bring us closer to "what actually happened and is happening than their opponents" (see Wallerstein, 1974a: 393).

19 Amin, for instance, argues that modes of productions are not "historical categories, in the sense of occurring in a necessary historical sequence" (1972: 107).

20 It is not very clear why Amin is referred to as a foreigner to Africa if he was born in Egypt. The probable explanation for this is that Egypt is not regarded as part of Africa, which is a common view for many commentators on Africa, including some international development agencies (as noted in Chapters 1 and 3).

21 In McNamara's view, "the problem is compounded by the delay of the wealthy nations in dismantling discriminatory trade barriers against the poor countries. Our studies

indicate, for example, that if the affluent nations were gradually to reduce their present protectionist trade restrictions against agricultural imports from the developing world, the poorer nations could, by 1980, increase their annual export earnings by at least $4 billion" (see McNamara, 1973). These practices have continued in the form of agricultural subsidies in the European Union (EU) and the USA despite the various trade arrangements with African countries, such as the Economic Partnerships Agreements (EPAs) for the EU and the African Growth Opportunity Act (AGOA) for the USA.

22 The criticism levelled against ISI was that privileged access to resources via the state, as well as the monopolistic and monopsonic nature of the firms that emerged, made these sectors uncompetitive, inefficient and corrupt. Eventually many collapsed. A strong criticism raised was that the money used to finance these inefficient firms or state corporations was taken from farmers through the National Marketing Boards (see Bates, 1981). At the heart of this is the general criticism that the state intervention inherent in ISI essentially means introducing inefficiency, corruption and all the other ills of the state in Africa.

23 This view is now changing, especially in the context of the ARN, which attributes the current episode of sustained growth in Africa to the emergence of a new generation of African entrepreneurs (Rotberg, 2013; Radelet, 2010).

24 Hyden was responding to Kasfir's critique of Hyden's idea of the uncaptured peasant in *Beyond Ujamaa in Tanzania: Underdevelopment and an Uncaptured Peasantry* (1980).

25 Countries in southern and eastern Africa are particularly vulnerable to severe drought and floods, which can affect economic performance if crops and other products are destroyed. Also, the shortage of food – which may necessitate importation of foodstuffs – would cause further strain on already stretched foreign reserves. In some instances this would mean diverting the little available foreign currency that there is from importing capital goods to importing food.

26 At the African Union (AU) conference on civil society in Addis Ababa in 2002, the former Nigerian president is reported to have estimated the money lost by African governments through corruption at US$140 billion (see Ayittey, 2004).

27 It is apparent that some of the theories discussed above influenced the thinking of the authors of this report. Though the report does not explicitly acknowledge its reliance on dependence, Marxist, neo-Marxist or structuralist views, the influence of such ideas is evident. Terms such as 'social organization of production', 'imitative modernization', 'social relations of production', 'differentiation', frequently used in the report, may be indicative of this, though this cannot be interpreted to mean that these ideas were uncritically applied to the African situation (as some commenters have claimed).

28 The World Bank's document on Africa's Development strategy also identifies lack of economic diversification as the main challenge that Africa is facing (see World Bank, 2011).

References

Africa Centre for Economic Transformation (ACET) (2014). *2014 African Transformation Report: Growth with Depth*. Accra: ACET.

African Development Bank (AfDB) (2013). "Annual Development Effectiveness Review 2013: Towards Sustainable Growth for Africa". Online, available at: www.afdb.org, accessed 23 October 2013.

Ake, Claude (1981). *A Political Economy of Africa*. Lagos: Longman Nigeria.

Alavi, Hamza (1982). "The Structure of Peripheral Capitalism" in H. Alavi and T. Shanin (eds) *Introduction to the Sociology of Development Societies*. New York: Monthly Review Press: 172–94.

Amin, Samir (1972). "Underdevelopment and Dependence in Black Africa: Historical Origin." *Journal of Peace Research*, Vol. 9, No. 2: 105–20.

Amin, Samir (1974a). *Accumulation on a World Scale*. New York: Monthly Review Press.

Amin, Samir (1974b). "Accumulation and Development: A Theoretical Model." *Review of African Political Economy*, No. 1: 9–26.

Amin, Samir (1990). *Delinking: Towards a Polycentric World*. London: Zed Books.

Arrighi, Giovanni and Saul, John S. (1968). "Socialism and Economic Development in Tropical Africa." *Journal of Modern African Studies*, Vol. 6, No. 2: 141–69.

Arrighi, Giovanni and Saul, John S. (1973). *Essays on the Political Economy of Africa*. New York: Monthly Review Press.

Ashman, Sam, Fine, Ben and Newman, Susan (2011). "Amnesty International? The Nature, Scale and Impact of Capital Flight from South Africa." *Journal of Southern African Studies*, Vol. 37. No. 1: 7–25.

Ayittey, George (2004). "NEPAD and Africa's Begging Bowl." *Global Dialogue*, Vol. 6, No. 3: 26–36.

Bates, Robert (1981). *Markets and States in Tropical Africa: The Political Basis of Agricultural Policies*. Berkeley: University of California Press.

Bayart, Francois (1993). *The State in Africa: The Politics of the Belly*. London: Longman.

Berg, Elliot J. (1964). "Socialism and Economic Development in Tropical Africa." *Quarterly Journal of Economics*, Vol. 78, No. 4: 549–73.

Besley, Timothy (2007). "The New Political Economy." *The Economic Journal*, Vol. 117, No. 524: F570-F587.

Bettelheim, Charles (1972). *Theoretical Comments by Charles Bettelheim in Emmanuel. "Unequal Exchange: A Study of the Imperialism of Trade*. New York/London: Monthly Review Press. Appendix 1: 271–322.

Bleaney, Michael and Greenaway, David (2001). "The Impact of Terms of Trade and Real Exchange Rate Volatility on Investment and Growth in Sub-Saharan Africa." *Journal of Development Economics*, Vol. 65: 491–500.

Boyce, James and Ndikumana, Leonce (2000). "Is Africa a Net Creditor? New Estimates of Capital Flight from Severely Indebted Sub-Saharan Countries 1970–1996." Research paper presented at the Political Economy Research Institute, University of Massachusetts.

Bush, Ray (2004). "Commissioning Africa for Globalisation: Blair's Project for the World Poor." *Global Dialogue*, Vol. 6, No. 3: 14–25.

Bush, Ray (2008). "Africa and Globalisation." *Soundings*, Issue 39: 20–31.

Cesaire, Amie [1955] (2000). *Discourse on Colonialism* (translated by Jason Pinkham). New York: Monthly Review Press.

Chabal, Patrick and Daloz, Jean-Pascal (1999). *Africa Works: Disorder as Political Instrument*. London: James Currey.

Chew, Sing and Denemark, Robert (1996). *The Underdevelopment of Development: Essays in Honour of Andre Gunder Frank*. Thousand Oaks: Sage Publications.

Cox, Kevin and Negi, Rohit (2010). "The State and the Question of Development in Sub-Saharan Africa." *Review of African Political Economy*, Vol. 37, No. 123: 71–85.

Emmanuel, Arghiri (1972). *Unequal Exchange: A Study of the Imperialism of Trade*. New York: Monthly Review Press.

Fanon, Franz (1963). *Wretched of the Earth*. New York: Groves Press.

Femia, Joseph (1993). *Marxism and Democracy*. Oxford: Oxford University Press.

Frank, Andre G. (1967). *Capitalism and Underdevelopment in Latin America: Historical Studies of Chile and Brazil*. New York: Monthly Review Press.

Frank, Andre G. (1970). "The Development of Underdevelopment" in R.I. Rhodes (ed.) *Imperialism and Underdevelopment*. New York: Monthly Review Press: 4–17.

Freund, Bill (2010). "The Social Context of African Economic Growth 1960–2008" in V. Padayachee (ed.) *The Political Economy of Africa*. London/NewYork: Routledge: 39–59.

Harvey, David (2000). *Spaces of Hope*. Edinburgh: Edinburgh University Press.

Hirschman, Albert (1958). *The Strategy of Economic Development*. New Haven: Yale University Press.

Hirschman, Albert (1981). *Essays in Trespassing: Economics to Politics and Beyond*. Cambridge: Cambridge University Press.

Hobsbawm, E. (1996). "The Future of the State." *Development and Change*, Vol. 27. No. 2: 267–78.

Hobson, John (1902). *Imperialism: A Study*. New York: James Pott & Co.

Hopkins, G.A. (1975). "On Importing Andre Gunder Frank into Africa." *African Economic History Review*, Vol. 2, No. 1: 13–21.

Hyden, Goran (1980). *Beyond Ujamaa in Tanzania: Underdevelopment and an Uncaptured Peasantry*. London: Heinemann.

Hyden, Goran (1983). *No Shortcuts to Progress: African Development Management in Perspective*. London/Nairobi: Heinemann.

Hyden, Goran (1986). "The Anomaly of the African Peasantry." *Development and Change*, Vol. 17, No. 3: 677–705.

Iliffe, John (1983). *The Emergence of African Capitalism*. Minneapolis: University of Minnesota Press.

Kay, Geoffrey (1975). *Development and Underdevelopment: A Marxist Analysis*. London: Macmillan.

Ki-Zerbo, Joseph (1994). "The Need for Creative Organisational Approaches" in M. Diouf and M. Mamdani (eds) *Academic Freedom in Africa*. Dakar: CODESRIA: 26–38.

Laclau, Ernesto (1971). "Feudalism and Capitalism in Latin America." *New Left Review*, 1/67. Online, available at: http://newleftreview.org/?view=816.

Leys, Colin (1977). "The 'Overdeveloped' Post Colonial State: A Re-Evaluation." *Review of African Political Economy*, No. 5: 39–48.

Leys, Colin (1996). *The Rise and Fall of Development Theory*. London: James Currey.

Mafeje, Archie (1994). "Beyond Academic Freedom: The Struggle for Authenticity in African Social Science Discourse" in M. Diouf and M. Mamdani (eds) *Academic Freedom in Africa*. Dakar: CODESRIA: 57–71.

Mamdani, Mahmood (1996). *Citizen and Subject: Contemporary Africa and the Legacy of Late Colonialism*. Princeton, NJ: Princeton University Press.

Martinussen, John (1997). *Society, State and Market: A Guide to Contemporary Theories of Development*. London: Zed Books.

Marx, Karl [1867] (1995). *Capital Volume 1* (Marx/Engels Internet Archive). Online, available at: www.marxists.org, accessed 18 February 2009.

Marx, Karl and Engels, Friedrich (1848). *Manifesto of the Communist Party. Marxist International Archives*. Online, available at: www.marxists.org, accessed 18 February 2009.

McNamara, R. (1973). *Nairobi Speech: Address to the Board of Governors by Robert S. McNamara, President of the World Bank Group*. Nairobi, Kenya. 24 September 1973. Online, available at: http://www.juerg-buergi.ch/Archiv/EntwicklungspolitikA/EntwicklungspolitikA/assets/ McNamara_Nairobi_speech.pdf, accessed 14 September 2012.

Mills, Greg (2011). *Why Africa is Poor: And What Africans Can Do about it*. Johannesburg: Penguin Books.

Mohan, Jitendra (1966). "Varieties of African Socialism" in R. Milliban and J. Sauville (eds) *The Socialist Register, 1966.* London: Merlin Press: 220–66.

Myrdal, Gunnar (1957). *Economic Theory and Under-developed Regions.* London: Duckworth.

Ndikumana, Leonce and Boyce, James (2008). "New Estimates of Capital Flight From Sub-Saharan African Countries: Linkages with External Borrowing and Policy Options." *Political Economy Research Institute (PERI) Working Paper Series,* No. 166.

Onimode, Bade (1988). *A Political Economy of the African Crisis.* London: Zed Books.

Page, John (2012). "Aid, Structural Change and the Private Sector in Africa." United Nations University (UNU)-World Institute for Development Economic Research (WIDER) Working Paper No. 2012/21. UNU-WIDER.

Persson, Torsten and Tabellini, Guido (2000). *Political Economics: Explaining Economic Policy.* Cambridge, MA: MIT Press.

Polanyi, Karl (1944). *The Great Transformation: The Political and Economic Origins of our Times.* Boston: Beacon Press.

Prebisch, Raul (1950). *The Economic Development of Latin America and its Principle Problems.* New York: United Nations Economic Commission for Latin America and Caribbean.

Prebisch, Raul (1984). "Five Stages in My Thinking on Development" in G.M. Meier (ed.) *Pioneers in Development.* New York/London: Oxford University Press: 175–204.

Radelet, Steven (2010). *Emerging Africa: How 17 Countries Are Leading the Way.* Washington DC: Brookings Institution Press.

Ravenhill (1993). "A Second Decade of Adjustment: Greater Complexity, Greater Uncertainty" in T. Callaghy and J. Ravenhill (eds.) *Hemmed In? Responses to Africa's Economic Decline.* New York: Columbia University Press. Chapter 1.

Rodney, Walter (1972). *How Europe Underdeveloped Africa.* Washington DC: Howard University Press.

Rotberg, Robert (2013). *Africa Emerges.* Cambridge: Polity Press.

Rowden, Rick (2013). "The Myth of Africa's Rise." Online, available at: http://www.twincities.com/ci_22327262/rick-rowden-myth-africas-rise, accessed 17 November 2013.

Saul, John and Leys, Colin (1999). "Sub-Saharan Africa in Global Capitalism." *Monthly Review,* Vol. 51, Issue 3: 5–24.

Sender, J. and Smith, A. (1986). *The Development of Capitalism in Africa.* London/New York: Methuen.

Severino, Jean-Michel and Ray, Oliver (2011). *Africa's Moment.* Cambridge: Polity Press.

Shivji, Issa (1976). *Class Struggles in Tanzania.* London: Heinemann.

Shivji, Issa (1990). "Tanzania: The Debate on Delinking" in A. Mahjoub (ed.) *Adjustment or Delinking? The African Experience.* London: Zed Books.

Singer, Hans W. (1950). "The Distribution of Gains Between Investing and Borrowing Countries." *American Economic Review,* Vol. 40, No. 2: 473–85.

Singer, Hans W. (1984). "The Terms of Trade Controversy and the Evolution of Soft Financing: Early Years in the UN" in G.M. Meier and D. Seers (eds) *Pioneers in Development.* Washington DC: The World Bank: 273–96.

Smith, Adam [1776] (2005). *The Wealth of Nations.* New York: Palgrave.

Stein, Howard (1994). "Theories of Institutions and Economic Reform in Africa." *World Development,* Vol. 22, No. 12: 1833–49.

Sweezy, Paul (1950). "The Transition for Feudalism to Capitalism." *Science and Society,* Vol. 14, No. 2: 134–57.

te Velde, Dirk Willem (2006). "Foreign Direct Investment and Development: An Historical Perspective." Background paper for World Economic and Social Survey for 2006. ODI (Commissioned by the UNCTAD).

United Nations Economic Commission for Africa (UNECA) (1989). *African Alternative Framework to Structural Adjustment Programmes for Socio-Economic Recovery and Transformation (AAF-SAP)*. Addis Ababa: UNECA.

United Nations Economic Commission for Africa (UNECA-AU) (2008). "Meeting Africa's New Development Challenges in the 21st Century: Issue Paper." First Joint Annual Meeting of the AU Conference of Ministers of Economy and Finance and UNECA Conference of African Ministers of Finance, Planning and Economic Development, 26–29 March 2008, Addis Ababa, Ethiopia.

United Nations Economic Commission for Africa (UNECA) (2011b). *Economic Report on Africa 2011: Governing Development in Africa*. Addis Ababa: UNECA.

United Nations Economic Commission for Africa (UNECA) (2011a). *Minerals and Africa's Development: The International Study Group Report on Africa's Mineral Regimes*. Addis Ababa: UNECA.

United Nations Economic Commission for Africa (ECA) (2012). *Economic Report on Africa: Unleashing Africa's Potential as a Pole of Global Growth*. Addis Ababa: UNECA.

Wallerstein, Immanuel (1974a). "The Rise and Future of the World Capitalist System: Concepts for Comparative Analysis." *Comparative Studies in Society and History*, Vol. 16, No. 4: 387–415.

Wallerstein, Immanuel (1974b). *The Modern World System: Capitalist Agriculture and the Origins of the European World-Economy in the Sixteenth Century*. New York: Academic Press.

Wallerstein, Immanuel (1976). "The Three Stages of African Involvement in the World Economy" in P. Gutkind and I. Wallerstein (eds) *The Political Economy of Contemporary Africa*. London: Sage: 30–57.

Wallerstein, Immanuel (1980). "Africa in a Capitalist World." *A Journal of Opinion*, Vol. 10, Nos 1–2: 21–31.

Williamson, Jeffrey (1995). "Globalisation, Convergence and History." National Bureau of Economic Research, Working Paper No. 5259.

World Bank (1983). *Sub-Saharan Africa: Progress Report on Development Prospects and Programmes*. New York: IBRD/World Bank.

World Bank (1989). *Sub-Saharan Africa: From Crisis to Sustainable Growth*. Washington DC: World Bank.

World Bank (2011). "Africa's Future and the World Bank's Support to it." The World Bank. Online, available at: http://www.worldbank.org/africastrategy, accessed 17 September 2011.

7 Africa Rising

Changing fortunes or another 'false start'?

Introduction

Most debates on Africa's economic growth and development experiences have focused on what some analysts are now referring to as the 'old Africa' (Rotberg, 2013); the Africa of erratic economic growth, low investment, negative global perception, life presidents, pervasive hopelessness, low self-confidence; the Africa of the 'Big Men', marginalised with poor future prospects. According to some analysts the 'old' Africa is now two decades behind us; what we are seeing today is the "new Africa", breaking "from the past and the beginnings of a wide-ranging economic, political and development turnaround dating back to the mid-1990s" (Radelet, 2010a: 13). While there have been controversies about the time when the alleged "new Africa" emerged, a popular narrative of an Africa that has turned a corner has imposed itself in international media and scholarly literature alike, especially post-2008–2009 global financial and economic crisis. Different commentators and observers are convinced that "Africa is at an auspicious moment in history" (AfDB/WEF, 2013: v); that it is "launching itself at full speed" like a meteor (Severino and Ray, 2011: 2).

These views, though challenged by many who do not believe that there is something fundamentally different occurring in Africa today (see Rickett, 2013, Rowden, 2013), have given rise to a new narrative – the Africa Rising narrative (ARN). Proponents of this view argue that the "evidence, big and small, is everywhere" (*The Economist*, 2014); that the difference between the 'old' and the 'new' Africa is

> like night and day: authoritarianism is giving way to accountability. Economic stagnation is turning to resurgence. And most important, despair is being replaced by hope – hope that people can live in peace with their neighbors, that parents can provide for their families, that children go to school and receive decent health care, and that people can speak their minds without fear.
>
> (Ellen Johnson Sirleaf, in Radelet, 2010a: 5)

In this narrative, stories that seek to relate the 'old' to the 'new' Africa are often dismissed as outdated and sterile debates, 'trapped by the evidence of the past'.

This chapter argues that while an account of Africa's growth and development experience is incomplete if the current dynamics are ignored, an African growth and development story delinked from past experiences is equally deficient. The new narrative, which is about three years old, is, in many ways, closely linked to the old one. The 'old' and the 'new' Africa are intricately linked such that driving a fissure between the two can lead to misrepresentation of the African experience, which has been one of the major causes of what some authors have called the worst tragedy of the twentieth century (see Chapter 4).

From a hopeless to a hopeful continent: changing fortunes or shifting perceptions?

In the last couple of years the tone and mood of mainstream media stories on Africa appear to have dramatically shifted. Just a decade ago, Africa made headline news in the same international media for being a place where famine, drought, malnutrition, HIV/AIDS, civil war, child soldiers, galloping inflation, overvalued domestic currencies, debt overhang, episodic economic growth, rogue politicians, failed states, slow demographic transition, illiteracy, high mortality rate, and weak economic and social infrastructure were prevalent (see *The Economist*, 2000). The list of such challenges, if put together on a string, could go round the Earth's circumference at the equator. Just a couple of years ago a former World Bank spokesperson for Africa, in a book meant to 'tell the truth about Africa', argued that had it not been "for their colourful national dress at international conferences, Africans would scarcely be noticed on the world stage", adding that "Africa … attracts adventurers, anthropologists, zoologists, missionaries, idealists, and some romantics rather than the down-to-earth people who make the world run" (Calderisi, 2006: 4–5). Not so long ago, many politicians, diplomats, journalists and academics were predicting that the African tragedy would become so bad in just a couple of years that Africans would be earnestly begging their former colonial masters to recolonise them (see Michaels, 1993), with some commentators suggesting that the best way to deal with the crisis in Africa would be to place African governments under some kind of trusteeship (Collier, 2006).

However, today it appears as though many commentators and observers are rapidly reassessing their positions, with some making a 180-degree turnaround. And the key question here is whether the fortunes of Africa are fundamentally changing to warrant this sudden turnaround that we have seen in the past three years, or whether this is mere media perception swinging in a different direction without anything substantive beneath it. The sudden change of tone, mood and direction of stories on Africa leaves one wondering whether they are reflecting the reality in Africa and not third-hand stories – just like those Africa map makers of earlier centuries (see Chapter 1). Because of the long practice of African stories being told by people who have never even been to the continent, it is understandable that critical observers insist on knowing the basis of these popular stories, including the ARN.

While some observers argue that nothing much has actually changed (Rowden, 2013), that it is the same 'old wine' packaged in 'new wine skins' – only this time by the Chinese (Lamido, 2013) – there are others who believe that Africa is experiencing a "golden interlude" with "true success stories, demonstrable improvements in governance and democracy, and a brighter outlook all around" (Rotberg, 2013: 2). It is now common to read stories like, "Economic growth rates are up nearly everywhere, poverty is dropping, and democracy seems to be stronger than ever before. Investors, who have usually ignored Africa as a marginal backwater, are now scouring for ways to capitalise on new opportunities" (Moss, 2011: 1). A growing number of analysts and commentators now believe that what we are seeing in Africa represents deep rooted fundamental changes in economic, political, social and leadership spheres, resulting in some sort of 'great transformation'. For some, this "turnaround is neither cyclical nor temporal. It is not just a blip on the screen, nor just a result of commodity prices. The revival is now 15 years in the making. It persisted through a global recession and falling prices in the late 1990s" (Radelet, 2010a: 15). Based on views like these, it has been argued that today Africa is "defying the usual pessimistic storylines of war, famine, stagnant economies, deepening poverty, destructive political leadership, [and] poor governance" (Radelet, 2010b: 88).

For the proponents of the ARN, it is no longer just African attire which is noticeable on the global stage, nor is Africa only attracting zoologists, anthropologists or romanticists; Africa has become "an investment destination of choice" (AfDB/WEF, 2013: v). Proponents of ARN now argue that the "wild swings in views of Africa" that we are seeing are not just the result of hype, but are a product of "real and dramatic changes" (Moss, 2011: 2). Some have observed that "Hardly a week goes by without an African investors' conference or growth summit" taking place in Africa or elsewhere in the world (Deverajan and Fengler, 2012: 1). Apparently, Africa seems to capture the attention of not just the media and romanticists, but scholars and big investors alike:

> within the last year, Africa was able to gain increasing attention, not just in the media but also from large think tanks, research institutes, ... and even from big global investors. For the first time ..., conservative institutional investors and pension funds are starting to explore the opportunities on the continent.
>
> (Ernst & Young, 2011: 18)

Proponents of the ARN cite several factors, including the dynamic demographic profile, rapidly growing market size, improving political and economic governance, penetration of communication technology (especially mobile technology), low levels of foreign debt, steadily rising investment and economic activities, and the emergence of a new crop of leaders and entrepreneurs – whom some authors are referring to as the 'cheetah generation'[1] – as evidence of a real turnaround. For example, it is reported that "In 2012 ... net private capital flows to the region increased by 3.3 percent to a record $54.4 billion notwithstanding the 8.8 percent decline in capital flows to developing countries" (World Bank, 2013). A report from the World Bank asserts that Gross Domestic Product (GDP) per capita stopped declining at the turn of the twenty-first century, and by 2014 real GDP recovered to its 1976 peak (World Bank, 2014). But critics have described this new narrative as a myth, dismissing it as a "flight of fancy" (Somerville, 2013).

While the Afro-pessimist narrative still looms large, this new ARN seems to be drowning any vestiges of Afro-cynicism and is winning converts among a wide range of sceptics – including even the most unflinching detractors who just a few years earlier declared Africa a hopeless continent with irrepressible 'natural' inclinations towards failure and chaos. Because of its popularity, the ARN has created some kind of social media hype, spearheaded by business consulting firms and major media houses. As a result of the hype created by the ARN, Afro-cynics are now finding it difficult to maintain their positions. To defend the Afro-pessimist view it is no longer just a matter of showing a picture of a starving child in Somalia, or a nine-year-old boy brandishing an automatic rifle in the Central African Republic. In other words, the stereotypes are coming under serious scrutiny by many who follow the African story (Radelet, 2010b).

Although this is not the first time that a large number of independent African countries have experienced growth rates of above 5 per cent for a decade (see Lawrence, 2010; Appendix III) and a positive anticipation of the times to come, the new narrative is asserting an Africa that is breaking with the past; an Africa that is unstoppably shifting scale and direction. For example, it is becoming increasingly common in the media, as well as in academic literature, to come across statements such as "Africa is ... changing scale and direction at a dizzying pace" (Severino and Ray, 2011: 2). Some analysts have even gone to the extent of suggesting that the current changes taking place in Africa are unstoppable; there are deeply rooted forces "irresistibly propelling Africa from the status of a mere object to that of an independent subject of public policy and international relations" (Severino and Ray, 2011: 262).

A quick glance at the numerous media stories and scholarly literature on Africa in the past few years, especially after the 2008–2009 global financial and economic crisis,[2] confirms this rapidly shifting perception, tone and mood about the continent among many journalists, academics, researchers, investors and donors. That said, there are still many observers who are not convinced that this is a real turnaround. The positive mood in the ARN is reflected in the metaphors, idioms and images used, including the "Africa Rising" terminology itself (Mahajan 2009, *The Economist*, 2012; 2013), "The Fastest Billion" (Robertson *et al.*, 2012), "The Rise of the Phoenix" (KPMG, 2013), "Africa's Moment" (Serverino and Ray, 2011), "Africa Emerges" (Rotberg, 2013; KPMG, 2013), "African Growth Miracle" (Young, 2012), "The African Meteor" (Rotberg, 2013), "Lions on the Move" (MGI, 2010), "The Awakening Giant" (*The Economist*, 2014), the "African Lions"[3] and the "Lions Go Digital" (MGI, 2013), "an African economic renaissance" (AfDB/WEF, 2013), and "African Take off" (Perry, 2012).

These images entered into the narrative during and after the 2008–2009 global financial and economic crisis. What sparked this upsurge of positive portraits of Africa was the fact that many analysts and casual observers had expected the growth episode in most African economies, which began towards the end of the 1990s, to vanish into thin air as had been the case in the past. But most economies in Africa, though growth rates fell, were resilient and weathered the crisis unexpectedly well with an average growth rate of about 3 per cent in 2009, and rebounding to more than 5 per cent in 2010 and 2011. In countries such as Nigeria, Ethiopia, Chad, Rwanda, Mozambique and Tanzania, GDP growth even during the crisis period was above 6 per cent. This resilient growth in most economies caught many analysts – who were prophesying the fulfilment of the commodity 'super cycle' – by surprise (see Brixiova and Ndikumana, 2011). The dynamism of the commodity super cycle has continued, widely attributed to the 'China effect' (see UNCTAD, 2013b). This 'China effect' has maintained the economic buoyancy that the ARN seems to be capturing in the above images and metaphors. However, some analysts within the ARN contend that the current growth episode is not just about high prices and demand for commodities; the source of growth involves a broader set of variables including improved governance, accountability, leadership, entrepreneurial skills, etc. (see Radelet, 2010a).

Coming to terms with the 'old' and the 'new' Africa

Broadly, there are three discernable views in the Africa Rising discourse. There is one view that sees the current dynamism as an unprecedented opportunity for rapid, broad transformation in Africa, with a good prospect of accelerating economic growth and development. The other view remains cynical about any prospect for the emergence of Africa from the galleys of chaos and failure. Between these two extremes is a view that straddles a cautious middle lane, neither dismissing the current dynamism nor celebrating it just yet. However, many commentators have now come to believe that there has been something unique occurring in the continent in the past decade. For the ARN proponents, the signs of a rising Africa are plain to those who want to see them:

> It can be seen along the streets … It is evident in the expanding airports and flight paths … It can be seen in the extraordinarily rapid growth of banking, cell phones, automobiles, and consumer goods. It is right there in plain sight as you walk through the streets of Africa.
>
> (Mahajan, 2009: 24)

But understanding and explaining these current developments in Africa has also proved to be tricky, largely because of the nature of the changes occurring in the continent, and partly because many analysts have become accustomed to an Africa defined by failure and disorder. Negotiating the transition from old portraits of Africa to an Africa with a positive outlook is unsettling for both cynics and optimists. For the cynics, it is hard to accommodate the idea that Africa is changing positively, while for the optimists the thought of an Africa 'on the move' overwhelms them to the point that they seem to overlook some of the enduring challenges that the continent is still facing.

While various sections of the international media are strongly asserting the discourse of a rising Africa, explaining what this means on the ground is proving to be elusive, especially if the current dynamism is delinked from past experiences. As illustrated in the preceding chapters, understanding and explaining economic growth and development experiences in Africa has been murky, and more of this is to be expected today when irresistable changes are said to be taking place (Severino and Ray, 2011). As one would expect, views about what exactly is happening in Africa today are diverse and contested. Perhaps the divergent stories emerging about Africa are a healthy sign in as far as this forces observers and commentators to reflect more critically on the African experiences.

Arguably, the most appropriate background to reflect on the current economic growth and development experience in the continent should be the continent's past experience. As illustrated in the preceding chapters, explaining the growth experience in Africa has been as elusive as growth itself, and often a daunting task – the protracted search for meaning has driven some analysts to the threshold of discovering a new branch of economics, what Ben Fine (2010) calls the 'economics of poverty' or what can be referred to as *Afronomics*. To appreciate Africa's current economic growth dynamics it is essential to see Africa's current dynamism in the context of the past growth experience. While it is essential to avoid being 'trapped' by history, it is equally dangerous to dismiss history as if it is something not connected to what is happening now. Dismissing past experiences as outdated and sterile (see Severino and Ray, 2011) can lead to misconstrued analysis, premature celebration, and, inevitably, a misleading prognosis and projection. As some analysts have observed, "a proper understanding of the problems requires both contemporary and historical accounts of the transformation of institutions, structures and policies in Africa" (Stein, 2003: 153). The very notion of a rising or emerging Africa is meaningless if one takes it out of the context of the past experience. In a fundamental way the past and the present are inextricably linked, to the point that the present is often meaningless without the past.

Undoubtedly, African stories did not start with the current wave of economic dynamism; the 1960s were a period of sustained economic growth with countries such as Cote d'Ivoire, Botswana, Togo, Mauritania and Gabon recording an average annual GDP growth rate of more than 5 per cent for the entire decade (see Appendix III) – which generated great expectations for economic, political and social transformation (see Lawrence, 2010; Doornbos, 1990). While the current economic growth episode is widely seen to be different[4] from what has been referred to as "Africa's false start" (Dumont, 1966), there are lessons one can draw from the past experience to understand the current developments in the continent better. Whereas the dangers of dwelling too much on the past are that one may freeze the present in that past – as is evident among some of the staunch Afro-pessimists who dismiss any notion of positive change in the continent – the present can also be liberated by knowledge and awareness of the past.

The genesis of the Africa Rising narrative

It is difficult to pin down a date when the ARN emerged from a background of several centuries of negative images, stories and portraits of Africa (see Chapter 1). The common portrait of Africa in the international media, even at the turn of the new millennium, has been a gloomy one:

> At the end of the 20th century, we are repeatedly reminded, Africa is a nightmarish world where chaos reigns. Poverty and corruption rule. War, famine and pestilence pay repeated calls. The land, air, water are raped, fouled, polluted. Every nation's hand is out, begging aid from distrustful donors.
>
> (McGeary and Michaels, [1998] 2001)

In the quest to explain the causes of Africa's poor economic growth and development performance, many eminent economists during the 1990s spent thousands of hours sifting through the statistical databases for clues to what they saw as the African malaise, often depicted in terms of the Africa dummy.

> But a decade of statistical analysis and bitter academic debates [has] not managed to get to the root of the 'African dummy' variable … Like tarot cards … the databases have been far from eloquent on this enigma, supplying in each case contradictory findings, circular arguments, and a chaos of truism.
>
> (Severino and Ray, 2011: 56)

Drawing from the notion of Africa being a 'nightmarish' place, international journalists, academic researchers, policymakers, donors and tourists alike, even within the continent, saw no prospect for progress, no potential for transformation. Some analysts assigned themselves the duty of reminding the rest of the world that anyone searching for order, peace, sustainable growth, social stability, broad-based development, and the rule of law and democracy in Africa, was bound to be terribly disappointed – chaos, disorder, underground networks, patrimony, hunger and dictatorship were the order of the day (Chabal and Daloz, 1999), leading to the widely but tacitly held view that Africa should not be taken seriously.

The opinion that Africa should not be taken seriously had become a popular belief by the end of the 1990s, and this has often been reflected in the way that donors have interacted with Africa and Africans. One American blogger (in response to Bill Clinton's speech during his visit to Africa in 2000, during which Clinton urged his audience: "We should not ask what are we going to do *for* Africa, but rather what are we going to do *with* Africa?"), argued that the only constructive way of dealing *with* Africa would be to evacuate everyone from the continent, distribute Africans elsewhere, and then turn Africa into an industrial and agricultural zone for the world. In response to this proposal one of the followers of the blog replied to the effect that evacuating people from Africa would not be necessary – if HIV/AIDS did not do the job in the next decade or so, then civil wars and famine would.

African renaissance in the midst of doom and gloom

If the images and perceptions of Africa were so negative just a couple of years ago, what accounts for the dramatic change in perception and portraits of Africa in the international media and academic literature over the last five years? Is it just mere hype created by some international media houses? In other words, what reasons do the proponents of the ARN offer for this sudden swing in the tone, mood and genre of stories and images of Africa? Before discussing the reasons offered for this shift, it is important to remember that, even at the height of what was widely seen as the African crisis, not everyone saw Africa as a land infected with irretrievable proclivities towards disorder, chaos, instability, hopelessness, fragility, corruption and dependency. There were some lonely and isolated African voices, even at the height of the economic and social crunch, insisting that Africa's moment was on the horizon; that the time for Africa had come. One clear example of this is former South African president Thabo Mbeki (he was deputy president at the time), who in his effort to counter the disheartening waves of Afro-pessimism (even among African leaders themselves), boldly talked about the "moment for Africa". In his address at the Corporate Council on Africa Summit in 1997 in Virginia, USA, Mbeki brazenly proclaimed: "Those who have eyes to see, let them see. The African renaissance is upon us. As we peer through the looking glass darkly, this may not be obvious. But it is upon us" (Chikane *et al.*, 1998: 201).

Mbeki's view of an emerging Africa was later converted into the Africa Renaissance Project which was instrumental in the transformation of the Organisation of African Unity (OAU) into the African Union (AU) in 2001–2002, as well as the creation of the New Partnership for African Development (NEPAD) agency. At this time, the notion of an African rebirth was indeed a lonely voice in the vast wilderness of Afro-pessimism and Africa bashing. The few who asserted an African renaissance during the 1990s were not taken seriously; many were dismissed as people living in Disneyland.

Whether Mbeki's words anticipated the current narrative is another matter; what seems obvious is that while at that time the Africa rebirth narrative was widely snubbed, today it has become fashionable to talk about a new Africa, the Africa that has broken with its past, the Africa that is relaunching itself like a meteor, the Africa in 'five-gear speed'. For example, in March 2013, a special report by *The Economist* painted "a picture at odds with Western images of Africa", arguing that Africa has made "huge leaps". In a similar fashion, a report by the McKinsey Global Institute (MGI, 2010) talks of a rapidly changing Africa which no one had anticipated just three years earlier.

Other than Mbeki's African renaissance drive, *Time Magazine* in 1998 hinted at the notion of a new Africa and, in fact, coined the phrase "Africa Rising". It published an article in 1998 (and republished it in 2001) written by Johanna

McGeary and Marguerite Michaels, entitled "Africa Rising", in which the authors, though they agreed with the popular international view that suffering and hopelessness characterised the continent, argued that a new Africa, a new optimism, was budding in the depths of despair and bleakness. "Hope is Africa's rarest commodity. Yet buried though it is amid the despair that haunts the continent, there is more optimism today than in decades" (McGeary and Michaels, [1998] 2001). They argued that while the stereotypical pictures of Africa were true in some places, it was

> no longer the whole picture. Academics, diplomats and bankers who do business there talk seriously these days about an African renaissance. A grand word, it turns out, for the slow, fragile, difficult changes that are giving the continent a second chance. Out of sight of our narrow focus on disaster, another *Africa is rising*, an Africa that works.
>
> (McGeary and Michaels, [1998] 2001, emphasis added)

The authors of the article gave many reasons why they were convinced that there was something distinctively new occurring in Africa. These ranged from the demise of apartheid, the inspirational leadership of Nelson Mandela, the rise of the new African leadership, and the ditching of Marxism and socialism by African governments in favour of the embryonic democracies that could be seen to be budding in many African countries. One thing which was quite obvious to the authors was that there was something new coming out of Africa:

> What's new is how some nations are figuring out ways to harness their natural and human resources into working models of development, even while others cannot. What's new is the astonishing extent to which ordinary Africans are searching out their own paths to progress.
>
> (McGeary and Michaels, [1998] 2001)

Like Mbeki's assertion of an African rebirth in the midst of the lost decades of the 1980s and 1990s, the story in this article was largely ignored even within Africa, with popular debates and the international media paying no attention to it. Even today, when people talk about a rising Africa, no reference is made to these earlier stories of hope in the midst of gloom and doom. But does this tell another story about how Africa easily slips through the clouded prisms of media and scholarship; a story of how, because of the blinkers of Afro-pessimism, we fail to notice the small stories of progress; our eyes peering through the clouded dark glass of centuries of Africa bashing only allow us to see the imperfect images of ourselves? Could the blinkers of Afro-pessimism and Eurocentricism account for the persistent elusiveness in explaining Africa's economic growth and development experiences? Conversely, are the blinkers of Afro-optimism making us fail to grasp what is currently going on in Africa? In the exhilaration of the Africa Rising hype there is often a temptation to forget that for more than two-thirds of Africans nothing, really, has changed. They may have access to mobile phone banking, but they have nothing to bank; they may hear of an Africa Rising, but wonder where this is happening.

Critics have suggested that *Time Magazine*'s main motive for publishing such stories was not that they were concerned with painting a positive picture of Africa; rather, it was to better the bottom line by telling a story about Africa that was contrary to the routine offering. Motives for doing something are difficult to pin down, but what is clear in this case is that this story, in 1998, was barely noticed by the mainstream media, or by seasoned scholars and experts on Africa. This may be an indication that the idea of an Africa Rising was instinctively brushed aside, reflecting the dominant approach to and perception of Africa. About a decade later the same phrase is used, and it seems to have fired up sympathisers and cynics alike (see Rickett, 2013).

The ARN pedigree

The ARN seems to have been kindled by myriad media stories, all traceable back to *The Economist*'s December 2011 article which reported the impressive growth recorded by African countries since the late 1990s. According to this article

> Over the past decade six of the world's ten fastest-growing countries were African. In eight of the past ten years, Africa has grown faster than East Asia … Even allowing for the knock-on effect of the northern hemisphere's slow-down, the IMF expects Africa to grow by 6% this year.
>
> (*The Economist*, 2011)

This story was followed by many related articles including the *Time Magazine* one, in 2012, that reported impressive progress and a positive prospect for Africa (Perry, 2012). Most of the stories that depict a rising Africa – whether through social, print or electronic media – refer to these two articles as being the origin of the ARN. But these stories were preceded by the MGI story in 2010 which talked about "Lions on the Move", reporting that households with discretionary income in Africa would increase by 50 per cent in the next 10 years (MGI, 2010). However, the MGI article did not receive much attention in the media and in public discussion; it was *The Economist*'s story of 2011 that received widespread attention and that is widely cited in the Africa Rising debate.

The Economist article, however, cautions against wholesale optimism, arguing that things are still "bleak in much of the continent": famine and drought persists, kleptocratic states in Angola and Equatorial Guinea, Ethiopia and Rwanda are still "noxious", elections in countries such as Congo are shoddy, countries like South Africa have been tainted with corruption, and Zimbabwe remains a "scar on the conscience of the rest of southern Africa". Yet "against that depressingly familiar backdrop, some fundamental numbers are moving in the right direction. Africa's enthusiasm for technology is boosting growth. It has more than 600m mobile-phone users – more than America or Europe" (*The Economist*, 2011).

Time Magazine agrees, projecting a continent full of hope, a continent on an irresistible trajectory of change for the better. "Africa is in the midst of a historic transition, and during the next few decades hundreds of millions of Africans will likely be lifted out of poverty … So tantalizing is the new hope across Africa, it infects even the most sceptical", argues Alex Perry (2012), the author of the *Time Magazine* article. Like the editor of *The Economist*, Perry cautions against both unflinching Afro-pessimism and unwarranted Afro-optimism. "But if Afro-pessimism is outdated, undiluted Afro-optimism is premature", he argues (Perry, 2012).

The pillars of ARN

The demographic tsunami

Other than these media stories, there has been scholarly work carried out that discusses the current dynamism in Africa. Notable is Jean-Michel Severino and Oliver Ray's (2011) *Africa's Moment*, which argues that the most important challenge for those who care about Africa is to understand the current forces at work in its new momentum. They argue that failure to properly understand the forces behind Africa's current economic, social and political dynamism make it difficult for the continent to seize the moment. Regrettably, the authors argue, "we do not understand Africa and are blind to the extraordinary forces currently at play there". A multitude of books, models and formulae produced over the decades talk about "yesterday's Africa", and the views contained in such books are outdated and will not help us "make sense of the events that are shaking the continent and transforming it before our eyes" (Severino and Ray, 2011: 1). Apart from dismissing the old (outdated) narratives, the authors argue that something not seen before is happening in Africa, but we do not properly grasp it because we are trapped in the "evidence of the past":

> The moment has come to understand the consequences of these transformations of seismic intensity – for Africa itself, its neighbours and the rest of the world. What we can perceive, examining both present and future, is the strategic re-emergence of Africa, with both the risks and opportunities this involves.
>
> (Severino and Ray, 2011: 3)

According to the authors, if there is a single factor that captures the core of the current momentum in Africa today it is what they refer to as the "demographic earthquake" which, in their view, is reshaping the continent and its societies. This demographic earthquake is seen in this analysis as the engine driving everything else including the alleged improving political governance and leadership, economic performance, policy environment, the impact of the mobile communications revolution, increasing foreign investment and the emergence of a new crop of African entrepreneurs. The authors argue that past social transformations everywhere else in the world have been driven by some demographic tsunami of sorts.

> As elsewhere on the planet and at other periods of history, this process of human concentration ... automatically generates substantial gains in productivity ... and thus a certain tempo of economic growth. It is not just people who see their productivity shoot up: public policy also becomes more effective.
>
> (Severino and Ray, 2011: 84–5)

Surprisingly, while there are many authors who are now pointing to the demographic dynamics as a force for Africa's current and future economic growth, some others see the slow demographic transition in Africa as one of the factors accounting for poor economic performance, as noted in Chapter 4. Other analysts see the issue of a high population growth rate as both a challenge and an opportunity; a factor that might have a negative impact, or that might positively spur the current momentum (Rotberg, 2013). Robert Rotberg (2013) also focuses mainly on the "rapidly swelling middle class", which is seen as an irresistible force for demanding and creating accountable, transparent and participatory structures of governance.

Africa's golden interlude?

Rotberg's *Africa Emerges* (2013: 2) talks about a *new Africa* that has "begun to banish the misery (and miserable public relations) of the past". Like Severino and Ray (2011), Rotberg (2013) talks about a continent that is decisively on the move for the better:

> Sub-Saharan Africa is no longer a troubled 'dark continent.' Most of its countries are now enjoying significant economic growth and political progress. The new Africa has begun to banish the miseries of the past, and appears ready to play an important role in world affairs.
>
> (Rotberg, 2013: 2)

While Rotberg (2013) identifies myriad challenges on the continent, he argues that Africa is experiencing a "golden interlude", driven mainly by a new generation of leaders, a strong emphasis on improved governance, accountability and transparency, and the growth in public demand for meaningful popular participation in the running of its constituent countries. Three main reasons are offered to account for this golden interlude: the demographic surge, the improving quality of governance, and the improving calibre of African leaders and leadership. Interestingly, commodity prices in this account do not feature prominently – they are only mentioned in passing.

The main argument that Rotberg makes in the book is that while there are numerous signs that Africa is "emerging" (by which the author means Africa is "catching up with progress and modernity"), there are innumerable challenges which African countries have to address in order to sustain the current momentum. This work, which is described by the author as "squarely about the onrush of positive change south of the Sahara amid consummate challenges and opportunities for growth", is an example of someone who is struggling to strike a balance between the optimism generated by the ARN and the pessimism of the Africa bashing stories. Thus, Rotberg does not only focus on the "heady" opportunities in the seemingly emerging sub-continent, he also talks about the "the remaining obstacles and possible stumbling points of [the] coming decades" (Rotberg, (2013: 5).

The cheetah generation and the ARN

A similar work is Steven Radelet's 2010 book, *Emerging Africa*, which talks about an Africa that is fundamentally changing, although he restricts this to the 17 nations[5] which he calls the "emerging countries". He argues that the turnaround that we are seeing in Africa "reflects much more fundamental changes taking place in the political, economic, and social spheres of these countries" (Radelet, 2010a: 15). Among the factors that account for the current momentum in Africa are five forces of change which are under way, namely: the spread of democratic and accountable government, prudent economic policy and management, debt cancellation, the spread of technology, and the emergence of the new generation of leaders (Radelet, 2010a: 15). Like Rotberg (2013), Radelet (2010a: 12) is also aware of the many challenges but believes that "there are good reasons to be optimistic that most of the emerging countries will continue their progress and sustain solid economic growth, poverty reduction, and stronger governance". He dismisses high commodity prices as the main driver of the current economic momentum in Africa, arguing that this is too simplistic; there are more fundamental processes under way which are interacting to create the turnaround.

When a billion Africans go shopping!

Related to the above work is Vijay Mahajan's (2009) *Africa Rising* book, which focuses mainly on profiling the potential market that the growing population in Africa (with a growing income) presents. Mahajan's main argument is that Africa is a force to reckon with in terms of its market size when the one billion Africans go shopping. This is an analysis that is largely influenced by market research approaches and it seems to be targeted at convincing potential investors in Africa to see the market prospects that the continent offers. Several stories have been presented to support this view, including the relocation of the Coca-Cola headquarters from Windsor in the UK to Johannesburg (Mahajan, 2009: 12).

The bottom billion becomes the fastest billion

Another recent book that portrays a rising Africa is *The Fastest Billion* (Robertson *et al.*, 2012: 3). In the book the authors argue that "after decades of genuine struggle, Africa's time has arrived and its people are crying out to be recognised". The main sources of the current momentum cited in the book are services, construction and infrastructure. This analysis leans more on the convergence hypothesis, arguing that low-income countries in Africa will grow much faster and catch up with the developed countries; the reasoning being that as technology filters and diffuses to African countries, they will effectively reap a technological dividend since the cost of technology for latecomers is subsidised by the pioneers. It is for this reason that the "bottom billion" is now imposing itself as the "fastest billion".

It is not possible to tell how much of the scholarly work on this issue has been a result of the hype created by the ARN. From evidence presented in these works it appears as if they were meant to repair Africa's tainted PR, without spending much time on understanding what it actually means for Africa to rise. So far the evidence presented to support the view that Africa is rising is restricted to economic indicators of increasing GDP and GDP per capita, and political governance measurements such as the Polity IV and Freedom House indices. Evidence about the quality of life in Africa, as well as figures on poverty and inequality, have been largely glossed over in the narrative. While there is some clear pattern of improvement in most economic variables, it is not clear if all Africans are indeed participating, contributing and, most importantly, sharing in this reported turn of fortunes. As illustrated later (pp. 248–49), available evidence suggests that more than two-thirds of Africans remain outside the circuit of growth that the ARN is capturing.

The past in the present?

There are several commentaries, tweets, blogs, what's ups, podcasts, and LinkedIn and You Tube stories linked to the ARN. While the notion of a rising Africa can be traced back to *Time Magazine*'s 1998 article (McGeary and Michaels, [1998] 2001), the story of Africa on the move has gained more public currency in the post-2008–2009 financial and economic crisis period. Even though indicators of economic growth started to improve for most countries towards the end of the 1990s, many journalists, academics, development agents, donors, media analysts, commentators and researchers adopted a 'wait and see' approach given the episodic nature of Africa's economic growth in the past. By 2008, although most economies had experienced ten or more years of sustained growth, analysts were, at best, cautious (and sometimes suspicious) of this growth, with some arguing that, just as in the past, the African growth would fizzle out.[6] For instance, Jorge Arbache and John Page (2009), while acknowledging that there had been sustained acceleration in income per capita and GDP growth rates, argued that this growth was still fragile because investment and institutions remained weak. Some analysts view the recent positive growth in Africa as a passing episode related to the current commodity 'super cycle', arguing that there is nothing different from what we have seen in Africa before (Rickett, 2013).

During the 2008–2009 financial and economic crisis most analysts remained uncertain about whether the growth in Africa was going to rebound afterwards, with some anticipating that the growth experienced in the previous decade would be followed by a prolonged period of deceleration and decline – as had been the experience of the past. But when most African economies recovered to their pre-crisis growth rates in 2011 – growing at an average of 4.5 per cent, with the International Monetary Fund's (IMF's) October 2013 *Economic Outlook on Africa* projecting over 6 per cent in 2012 (IMF, 2013) – many critics began to revise their positions and many of them began to confirm that this latest growth dynamic was on a different trajectory from the episodic growth seen in the past (Brixiova and Ndikumana, 2011). This view was reinforced by Pascal Fletcher's (2011) articles for the press agency Reuters, the *Time Magazine* story in 2012 (Perry, 2012), and follow-up articles by *The Economist* in 2012 and 2013. Thus far the focus within the ARN has been on celebrating the idea that the "fundamental numbers are beginning to move in the right direction", while critics are holding fast to the past in the present (*The Economist*, 2014).

The tale of the African middle class

One of the commonly cited reasons for asserting that Africa is rising is the view that Africa's demographic profile presents a force for generating not just economic growth, but also political and social change. Expressed differently by different analysts, the demographic dividend is widely believed to be a crucial factor in explaining the current momentum, whether one looks at things from the supply side end of the equation in terms of the abundant and young (though maybe not so skilled) labour force, or the demand side in terms of market size. What seems popular in this narrative is the idea of the growing market size of Africa – when the one billion Africans go shopping (see Mahajan, 2009). In some quarters this market size has been expressed in terms of the size of the middle class in Africa, particularly the increase in the number of African households with discretionary income. Findings from a study conducted by the African Development Bank (AfDB) on the size and trend in the middle class in Africa reinforced the Africa Rising story, especially among business houses which interpreted this expanding middle class as a burgeoning market for their goods and services. In the AfDB study it was reported that in 2010, 34 per cent (350 million) of Africans lived in households which were classified as 'middle class'. A middle class household for the purposes of the study was defined as one with a daily per capita income of between US$2–US$20 (AfDB, 2011).[7] There have been several other attempts to measure the size of the middle class in Africa (see MGI, 2010), and they all suggest that this section of the African population is expanding rapidly. To an entrepreneur sitting in Abuja, Nairobi, Johannesburg, London, Mumbai, Brasilia or Beijing, a population of 350 million people with discretionary expenditure means an attractive investment window. Thus, the story of a growing African middle class provides a different spin to the investment calculus, with most investors rushing to carve out a sizeable share of this seemingly fast-expanding market.

ARN and the bottom line

Several business consulting firms – including Renaissance Capital, KPMG, Ernst & Young, and Deloitte – are using figures on African households with disposable income to attract business investment into the continent. They argue that Africa offers a bigger market than Europe and one which is expected to be bigger than Asia by the year 2020 (Robertson *et al.*, 2012). For instance, MGI (2010) says: "The number of households with discretionary income is projected to rise by 50 per cent over the next 10 years, reaching 128 million. By 2030, the continent's top 18 cities could have combined spending power of $1.3 trillion." Companies offering business services to investors are using these numbers to market the continent, as well as make their own business services attractive to would-be investors. Some investors are persuaded by the idea that, "Early entry into African economies provides opportunities to create markets, establish brands, shape industrial structures, influence customer preferences, and establish long-term relationships" (MGI, 2010).

In this sense, the ARN is not just an Afro-optimistic frenzy; it is also about the bottom line for businesses, and this largely accounts for the growing popularity of this narrative within international media houses both in and outside Africa. Broadly, the middle class is seen as a key factor in the rise of Africa, though not just from an economic point of view as a source of demand for goods and services. It is also seen as crucial in advancing social progress, political transformation and improvement in governance by promoting accountable and transparent government (Ncube and Shimeles, 2012). Thus, proponents of the ARN see growth of a middle class as a fundamental force for transforming Africa.

Critics of the Africa Rising narrative

Critics of the ARN have, however, cautioned against the hype generated by the current growth episode in Africa. Some critics believe that this is just an "insidious little fiction manufactured by global corporate finance" (see Rickett, 2013). Some have observed that there is nothing in Africa's rising that has not been seen before; the only difference is that China is now doing the same thing that the colonialists have been doing for the past century. Parselelo Kantai, for example, argues that

> What is happening on the continent economically is a new era of massive resource extraction, catalyzed mostly by Chinese domestic demands. And because it is almost exclusively extraction without on-site value addition, it's a process where the continent's elites, the Chinese and Westerners, are the only people who benefit. I don't see why it shouldn't be called by its real name: the Second Scramble for Africa.
>
> (cited in Rickett, 2013)

Similarly, the former Nigerian Central Bank governor, Sanusi Lamido, argues that nothing seems to have changed in terms of Africa's relations with other players like China:

> So China take our primary goods and sells us manufactured ones. This was also the essence of colonialism. The British went to Africa and India to

secure raw materials and markets. Africa is now willingly opening itself up to a new form of imperialism.

(Lamido, 2013)

Other critics have argued that the ARN has no roots; that the structural foundations on which the current growth is based are fragile and unsustainable, and Africa needs to change this if it is to genuinely rise: "Despite the important gains in services industries and per capita incomes, Africa is still not rising, and services alone will not create enough jobs to absorb the millions of unemployed youth in Africa's growing urban areas" (Rowden, 2013). This view is supported by findings from other studies which show that the structural base of the economies in Africa remain weak, as evidenced by indicators such as the manufacturing-to-GDP ratio, the ratio of agriculture labour, and the ratio of commodities in total exports – which have barely changed since the 1970s (see AfDB/WEF, 2013: 41). Critics of the ARN have thus suggested that instead of being pacified by these numbers "steps must be taken to revise WTO [World Trade Organization] agreements and the many trade agreements and bilateral investment treaties currently being negotiated so that Africa has the freedom to adopt the industrial policies it needs in order to make genuine progress" (Rowden, 2013). A number of commentators critical of the excitement created by the ARN hype have argued that there has been no country in the history of the world that has developed on the basis of services.

Other critics of the ARN have pointed out that often its proponents fail to realise that Africa's current growth is primarily driven by high commodity prices, with little growth coming from agriculture – where the majority of the people work. Most economies have a narrow tax base supported by the commodity extraction sectors, making them more vulnerable to commodity price shocks (Somerville, 2013). Still other critics have argued that there is actually nothing to be excited about since current African income levels are comparable to pre-industrial Europe, with similar institutional constraints that need to be overcome for countries to embark on a path towards mature open economies (Broadberry and Gardner, 2013). The issue of institutional weakness as a constraint to sustainable growth has also been raised by Arbache and Page (2009) and by Daron Acemoglu and James Robinson (2010), who argue that claims of institutional reforms contributing to current growth in Africa are not supported by empirical evidence.

The evidence

Overall, evidence on either side of the ARN has been thin. For the ARN proponents, some of the factors most widely cited include, as we have seen earlier, Africa's demographic profile, the increasing rate of investment, sustained annual growth, improved governance, the spread of democratic reforms (which has been referred to by some analysts as the 'democratic boom'), better policy implementation and management of economies, massive debt relief, the information and communications technology (ICT) revolution (particularly mobile technology), a steadily growing middle class, a gradually budding generation of African entrepreneurs (not depending on privileged access to state power and resources, see Rotberg, 2013), a sustained period of peace and stability in most countries, increasingly active citizenry and civil society organisations demanding account-ability and transparency from public and private sector office bearers, and the emergence of a new generation of political leaders willing to listen to the people and protect basic human rights. The ditching of socialist policies that were wide-spread on the continent prior to the end of the Cold War is also mentioned as one of a long list of factors (Severino and Ray, 2011).

> Africa owes its takeoff to a variety of accelerators, nearly all of them external and occurring in the past 10 years: billions of dollars in aid, especially to fight HIV/AIDS and malaria; tens of billions of dollars in foreign-debt cancella-tions; a concurrent interest in Africa's natural resources, led by China.
>
> (Perry, 2012)

Mobile technology is mentioned by many commentators, although the actual contribution to GDP growth by mobile usage in Africa has not yet been estimated. Some estimates, however, put the internet's contribution to GDP (the iGDP) at just 1.1 per cent (see MGI, 2013). The argument is that mobile usage makes up for the poor communications infrastructure – roads, transport, banking facilities – making it a lot easier for information and services to flow between users, leading to enhanced levels of exchange in these economies. Different figures for mobile penetration are cited, and there are huge variations between countries, though on average the number of mobile subscribers jumped from just over 30 per thousand in 2000 to 212 per thousand in 2007 (AfDB/AU/UNECA, 2009: 59).

Several other indicators, such as the fall in infant mortality rates and maternal deaths, and declining HIV/AIDS infection rates, are also mentioned as positive signs of Africa's turnaround.

Economic indicators

Other indicators also suggest that there has been progress when compared to the past. In terms of economic growth indicators (GDP and GDP per capita), avail-able evidence points to a sustained improvement on past experiences, although the credibility of the data has been questioned by some analysts.[8] As Figure 7.1 shows, GDP and GDP per capita both grew sustainably up to 2007, and then declined in 2008 and 2009, but recovered to positive growth in 2010. The overall trend for these two indicators has been positive, and the projection is that this is likely to continue in the next couple of years (see IMF, 2013). Although these aggregate figure do not tell us about the growth disparities between and within countries, it is evident that, unlike in previous periods, the majority of coun-tries experienced positive growth, with some – such as Nigeria, Mozambique, Ethiopia, Rwanda and Angola – recording an annual average GDP growth rate of over 7 per cent over the 2000–2010 period (see Appendix III). Comparing the 1990–1999 to the 2000–2010 period, only two countries (Guinea and Zimbabwe)

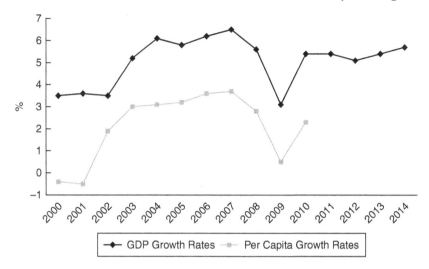

Figure 7.1. GDP and GDP per capita growth for Africa (2000–2014)

Source: author, based on data from the *African Development Indicators* (2005–2012) and *Regional Economic Outlook* (IMF, 2008; 2013).

Note: figures from 2011 onwards are only for Sub-Saharan Africa (excludes North Africa) and figures for 2013 and 2014 are estimates.

recorded negative average per capita growth rates in the later period compared to 25 countries in the 1990–1999 period. In terms of GDP growth, similar trends are reported in the data with only one country reporting negative growth in the 2000–2010 period – compared to 19 countries in the 1990–1999 period. Thus, it is the fewer number of negative growth episodes in the recent period that accounts for an overall upward movement in African economic performance (Arbache and Page, 2009).

This upward trend seems to be confirmed by other macroeconomic indicators such as inflation, interest rates, fiscal balance, exchange rates, the external account, external debt, and others, as Table 7.1 shows.

Table 7.1 shows a remarkable reduction in the debt burden around 2005–2006, as well as a substantial increase in foreign direct investments (FDI) around 2008–2009. While this hides some variations between countries, it does show a positive trend for the continent as a whole. In more recent years, remittances have overtaken aid and FDI.

Other indicators such as net primary school enrolment and access to water show steady improvements between 1990 and 2010, as Table 7.2 suggests.

However, these aggregate numbers do not give us the whole story about what is going on in the continent. There are other crucial numbers that should accompany the above figures to begin to get a clear sense of the dynamics in the continent. Unfortunately, on key issues such as national savings, fixed capital formation, and agriculture productivity there has been little progress,

Table 7.1. Selected macroeconomic indicators for Africa (2000–2011)

	2000	2001	2002	2003	2004	2005	2006	2007	2008	2009	2010	2011
GDP/capita (US$, current)	684	680	663	801	954	1,094	1,236	1,404	1,604	1,478	1,669	1,792
GDP/capita (US$, constant)	684	680	693	714	791	816	846	877	901	905	926	..
Real GDP (billions US$, constant)	567.5	587.9	608.3	633.2	696.6	735.8	780.1	827.3	869.6	893.9	935.7	..
GDP (billions US$, current)	567.5	568.3	581.2	688.7	833.1	976.5	1,123.6	1,308.7	1,565.3	1,477.1	1,705	..
Debt to GDP ratio	54.5	52.4	49.3	44.5	43.1	33.7	25.2	23.6	19.7	23.8	21.4	21.3
Debit service to export ratio	15.4	..	..	..	11.1	12.1	12.3	15.8	7	4.7	..	..
Current account balance (GDP %)*	0.7	-0.9	-2.3	-2	-1.5	-0.4	0.5	4.5	3.9	-1.5	0.5	1.3
ODA (billions US$)		16.8	21.4	27.4	30	35.8	44.6	39.5	45.2	47.8	48	51.3
ODA (US$/capita)	18.4	20	26	27.6	29	30.8	37	43.9	39.7	42.2	42.1	..
FDI (billions US$)	..	20	14.6	18.2	17.4	30.5	36.8	51.5	57.8	52.6	43.1	42.7
FDI (US$/capita)	11.1	..	17.1	16.6	21.3	20	32	48	55	59.1	50.5	..
Remittance (billions US$)	..	12.1	12.8	15.4	19.5	33.7	37.7	44.9	49.7	45.4	52.3	56.9
Reserve cover (months)*	..	..	..	..	4.3	4.7	5.6	5.8	6.1	6.7	4.2	4.5
Inflation rate (%)	10.3	8.7	8.3	8.9	8.9	7.5	8.8	8.7	15	9.2	7.2	10.1

Source: author, based on data from *African Development Indicators* (various years), *African Statistical Year Book 2012* and the *African Economic Outlook 2013*.

Notes: [FDI] = foreign direct investments, [ODA] = official development assistance, [*] = figures for Sub-Saharan African countries only, [..] = no data available. Constant US$ are in 2000 prices.

Table 7.2. Basic social indicators for Africa (1990–2010)

	1990	2000	2010
Population (million)	631.6	819.9	1,020.7
EAP (million)	263.9	310.1	381.7
Real GDP/capita (constant US$)	727	712	935
Real GDP (constant US$, millions)	452,854	657,068	885,365
Net primary enrolment (%)	59	85	85.7
Net secondary enrolment (%)	30	35.4	36
Pupil to teacher ratio	..	41	45.7
Access to clean water (%)	56	59	66

Source: author, based on data from *African Development Indicators* (2005–2012/2013).

Note: [EAP] = economically active population.

Table 7.3. Africa's savings, capital formation, investment ratios, value added (1980–2010, %)

	1980	1990	2004	2005	2006	2007	2008	2009	2010
Domestic savings	24.2	18.8	21.1	22.1	23.8	24	24.4	19.3	20.7
Fixed capital formation	24.5	21.1	18.4	19.2	20.2	22.1	23.6	23.9	21
Investments	24.3	18.7	18.4	19.2	20.2	22.1	23.5	23.8	23.1
Agriculture (value added)	17.3	18.1	15	14.3	14	13.6	11.7	12.9	11.5
Industry (value added)	39.1	33.2	36	37.2	38	37.5	38	34.9	35.4
Services (value added)	44.2	48.8	48.9	48.5	48.1	49	49.5	52.5	53.1

Source: author, based on data from *African Development Indicators* (2012/2013).

as Table 7.3 shows, and this needs to be taken into account for a better picture of the full story. Even though FDI flows have recovered in the post-2008–2009 crisis, most of these investments are going into extractive industries with little effect in terms of transforming the structure of the economies concerned (Page, 2012).

If we look at domestic savings and fixed capital formation, the current figures are below 1980 levels. Capital formation in Africa has mostly been below its potential due to colonial economic machination; this problem has continued and is worsening, as evidenced from level of capital flight (see Table 7.4).

If one considers the 2005–2010 period, total resource inflows (FDI and official development assistance, ODA) are one-third less than the total capital outflow. Even if capital flows into the continent are reported to have increased significantly in the last decade (see World Bank, 2014), the net flow is always small, and recent estimates suggest that most countries now have a negative net international investment position (NIIP, see Hou *et al.*, 2013). These figures underrepresent the actual outflow because large sums of money leak from the continent undetected (Boyce and Ndikumana, 2012).

Table 7.4. Capital flight from SSA (1970–2010)

Capital flight 1970–2010		Capital inflows (billions US$)				Capital outflows (billions US$)			Net flow
Period	Billions US$	Period	FDI	ODA	Total FDI and ODA	Net transfer on debt	Total capital flight	Outflow as % of FDI and ODA	
1970–1974	28.3	1970–1979	23.3	63.3	86.6	81.3	116.9	134.9	-34.9
1975–1979	88.6								
1980–1984	66.8	1980–1989	18.7	132.6	151.3	62.1	205.4	135.8	-35.8
1985–1989	138.6								
1990–1994	107.5	1990–1999	53.7	181.1	234.8	-20.1	138.4	58.9	42.1
1995–1999	30.9								
2000–2004	151.1	2000–2010	210.4	282.5	492.9	5.4	353.5	71.7	28.3
2005–2010	202.4	1970–2010	306.4	659.5	965.9	128.6	814.5	84.3	15.7

Source: author, based on data from Boyce and Ndikumana (2012).

Note: capital inflow excludes portfolio, bond and remittance flows, but these have only become significant sources of capital into Africa since 2006 (see AfDB/OECD/UNDP/UNECA, 2013). The figures in this table are for 33 Sub-Saharan Africa (SSA) countries.

What is even more worrying is the sectoral distribution of GDP. It is apparent that growth in value added is occurring in industry and services, which account for an increasingly smaller proportion of the workforce. This is an indication of the lack of a transformation, which has been a perennial challenge as far as economic growth and development in Africa is concerned. Productivity, especially of labour, diversification, competitiveness and improved human capital have remained weak, reflecting the lack of structural transformation needed to achieve sustained growth (see ACET, 2014). Productivity growth in agriculture, where the majority of people work, has actually been falling over the years. What this suggests is that the majority of people are not taking part in generating the growing output and, hence, are not sharing in the growth that is being experienced in the continent. This scenario makes it difficult for growth to be sustainable when almost 70 per cent of the population is not participating meaningfully. Although proponents of the ARN talk of the "opportunity to end poverty and embrace shared prosperity", the available evidence suggests that finding a way to share this growth is possibly one of the biggest challenges that Africa is facing today (AfDB, 2013: v). Growth seems to be concentrated within the commodity and services sectors, with little or no linkage to the rest of the economy – thereby creating two *Africas*: the new and rising, and the old and stagnant. And this is one of the reasons why, even if growth has been robust over the past decade-and-a-half, there has been little effect on poverty and inequality in most African countries (Dulani *et al.*, 2013).

Creating bridges between the old and new 'Africas' is fundamental in setting Africa on a sustainable path to inclusive and shared prosperity. This is a challenge which, in the old narrative, has been expressed in terms of diversifying or transforming African economies to create backward and forward linkages, thereby generating capacity to use human and natural resources more effectively. The presence of two 'Africas' largely reflects a failure to address the structural problems inherent in most African economies, as argued in preceding chapters. A good example is the century-long concern that most African countries are heavily dependent on primary commodity exports in which only a handful of the labour force meaningfully participates. Challenges of diversifying the economy to provide a strong base for sustained growth have not been addressed, and this has been acknowledged even by those who support the new narrative (see AfDB/WEF, 2013). As Table 7.5 shows, the manufacturing sector accounts for only a tiny section of the exports of most African countries. The larger share of export earnings for most countries in Sub-Saharan Africa (SSA) still comes from agriculture, where productivity is actually declining. In countries such as Benin, Burundi, Burkina Faso, Ethiopia, Ghana, Malawi, Sierra Leone, Tanzania and Uganda, three-quarters of export earnings comes from agricultural commodities.

For another set of countries such as Cameroon, Mozambique, Niger, Nigeria, Angola, Chad, Sudan and Zambia, their export earnings are mainly from either oil or metals and ores. For instance, oil accounts for 87 per cent of Nigeria's exports and 91.3 per cent of Sudan's; coffee and tea account for 85 per cent of Burundi's exports; uranium and oil account for over 93 per cent of Niger's; and copper accounts for over 70 per cent of Zambia's exports (World Bank, 2011).

Table 7.5. The composition of exports for selected SSA countries (2000–2005, %)

	Manufacturing	Agricultural commodities	Other
Benin	12.8	85.8	1.4
Burundi	6.2	91.0	2.8
Burkina Faso	8.0	88.8	3.2
Cameroon	3.3	30.1	66.6
Côte d'Ivoire	20.0	65.0	15.0
Ethiopia	11.4	87.9	0.7
Ghana	12.1	82.1	5.8
Kenya	21.1	51.7	27.2
Madagascar	22.5	66.9	10.6
Malawi	16.3	83.3	0.4
Mali	54.3	31.9	13.8
Mozambique	7.0	15.5	77.5
Niger	7.9	34.0	58.1
Rwanda	10.3	59.6	30.1
Sierra Leone	7.5	92.4	0.1
Sudan	0.7	11.6	87.7
Tanzania	14.4	73.4	12.2
Togo	58.1	30.4	11.5
Uganda	17.0	75.6	7.4
Zambia	8.8	28.8	62.4

Source: author, based on data from *African Development Indicators* (World Bank, 2008).

Note: the 'Other' category includes ores, minerals and fuel (mainly oil), and services.

As many analysts have noted, economies with this sort of production structure remain very vulnerable to commodity price volatility, a point that critics of the ARN have rightly highlighted (Rowden, 2013). From this perspective, it is clear that the current sustained growth being experienced in Africa remains fragile as long as the economic structures are not transformed, and there is little evidence suggesting that the windfall revenue from high commodity prices are being used to restructure the production base of these economies.

A similar picture emerges when we look at the employment structure. Table 7.6 shows that a number of countries still have more than two-thirds of the labour force employed in agriculture, and more than 90 per cent of these are involved in subsistence agriculture. There has been little change in this situation over the past decade in many countries (ILO, 2012).

A 2012 International Labour Organisation (ILO) report (2012) suggested that in 2010 an average of 63 per cent of the total labour force in Africa was employed in agriculture, mainly in subsistence farming with very low, irregular wages/income and no social protection of any kind. While the proportion of the agricultural labour force in some countries is slowly declining, the proportion

Table 7.6. Agricultural share in labour force for selected African countries (2000–2010)

	2000	2005	2010
Burkina Faso	..	84	66.9
Nigeria	..	59.9	59.8
Morocco	47.9	46.5	40.9
Cape Verde	22.2	29.7	13.5
Senegal	55.7	52.9	49.5
Ethiopia	77.7	77.7	
Mauritius	11.6	9.8	8.1
Tanzania	77.7	69.8	71.3
Uganda	92	74	68
Zambia	77.7	69.8	71.3
Namibia	25.6	25.9	15.6
South Africa	..	6.4	4.9

Source: author, based on data from ILO (2012).
Note: [..] = no data available.

involved in low wage, low value added activities is extremely high. Such figures also exclude people in informal urban employment where most 'workers' receive irregular wages and incomes – often below the minimum living wage[9] (Fox *et al.*, 2013). In most cases this amounts to inefficient use of human resources given that most of these workers are grossly under-employed. If Africa is to reap a demographic dividend, as some analysts have suggested it will (Severino and Ray, 2011), these long-term issues of human capital development and utilisation must be addressed urgently.

The desperate condition of most people engaged in low wage, low productive activity is revealed by the unusually large proportion of working poor. Even at the low figure of US$1 per day per capita, most countries have more than two-thirds of their labour force subsisting below this threshold (see Table 7.7).

At US$2 per day the proportion of working poor, even in middle-income countries such as Namibia and Botswana, is distressingly high. Challenges of human capital development and utilisation are also evident when we compare Africa with other regions. Table 7.8 also suggests that in Africa tertiary education enrolments are the lowest in the world, and there has been no progress in the last decade in this regard even though the continent has experienced sustained economic growth.

The picture on research and development (R&D) also reveals a massive challenge that Africa has to confront if it is to benefit from the demographic comparative advantage which it is expected to enjoy in the next few decades. Competitiveness in African economies can be achieved by developing a relatively advanced pool of skills in the labour force, and this requires raising education enrolment ratios, particularly at secondary and tertiary level, as well investment in R&D. Existing evidence suggests that very little progress is being

Table 7.7. The ratio of working poor in selected African countries (2009)

Country	Working poor at US$1 or less (%)	Working poor at US$2 or less (%)
Botswana	47.4	82.6
Burundi	63.1	95.0
Central African Republic	80.8	94.4
Ghana	54.8	89.7
Lesotho	63.4	87.7
Madagascar	73.6	94.4
Malawi	49.4	89.9
Mali	82.8	95.0
Mozambique	44.4	90.9
Namibia	58.2	83.1
Niger	74.1	95.0
Nigeria	79.9	94.5
Uganda	89.0	95.0
Zambia	79.9	95.0
Zimbabwe	67.3	91.5

Source: ILO (2010). The ILO report uses the US$1 per day per capita figure as its basis for defining the working poor.

Table 7.8. Human capital and research investment in comparative terms

Region	Tertiary education enrolment ratio (%)		Region	Research as % of GDP	% Share in global research GDP
	1999	2009			
Middle East and North Africa	18	22	Oceania	2.2	1.8
East Asia and Pacific	14	28	Asia	1.6	33
Latin America and Caribbean	20	37	North America	2.7	32.7
North America and Western Europe	60	72	Latin America and Caribbean	0.7	3.1
South Asia	7	12	Europe	1.8	28.5
Sub-Saharan Africa	4	5	Africa	0.4	0.9

Source: author, based on data from UNCTAD (2013).

made in this direction, and concrete plans to grow a sizeable pool of labour with the sort of middle-level skills necessary to attract significant manufacturing companies is not yet on the agenda.

The scenario of a large section of the population working in agriculture, with low and irregular income, is a reflection of the fundamental structural problems in most African economies. On average, 60 per cent of the labour

Table 7.9. Growth, poverty and inequality trends in Africa's fastest growing economies

Country	Mean GDP growth, 2001–2010 (%)	Survey year	Headcount (%)	Poverty gap (%)	Poverty severity (%)	Gini index (%)
Angola*	11.1	2008	43.4	16.5	8.2	42.7
		2000	54.3	29.9	20.5	58.6
Chad*	7.9	2002	61.9	25.6	13.5	39.8
Ethiopia*	8.4	2010	30.7	8.2	3.1	33.6
		2005	38.9	9.6	3.3	29.8
Mozambique*	7.9	2007	59.6	25.1	13.7	45.7
		2002	74.7	35.4	20.5	47.1
Nigeria*	8.9	2011	54.4	21.8	11.5	39.8
		2009	67.9	33.7	20.6	48.8
		2003	63.1	28.7	16.6	42.9
Rwanda*	7.6	2010	63.2	26.6	14	50.8
		2005	72.1	34.8	20.5	53.1
		2000	74.6	36.8	22	51.5
Ghana**	5.6	2005	28.6	9.9	4.8	42.8
		1998	39.1	14.4	6.9	40.7
Tanzania**	6.8	2007	67.9	28.1	14.8	37.6
		2000	84.6	41.6	24.4	34.6
Zambia**	5.4	2010	74.5	41.9	27.7	57.5
		2006	68.5	37	23.9	54.6
		2004	64.3	32.8	20.8	50.7

Source: *African Development Indicators* (World Bank, 2006); *African Statistical Year Book* (AfDB/AU/UNECA, 2013) and PovcalNet (World Bank, 2012).

Notes: [*] = the six fastest growing economies in Africa in the period 2001–2010. [**] = countries projected to be among the ten fastest growing economies in the period 2011–2015. Chad only has data for 2002. Headcount is the ratio of the population below a specified poverty line.

force is engaged in agricultural production, another 18 per cent in domestic work (largely unpaid family work), those in waged employment account for about 16 per cent, with the unemployed making up 6 per cent (Fox *et al.*, 2013). Additionally, the value added growth in sectors where most people work is either stagnant or declining, suggesting that current growth is being generated by a small section of formal waged workers in services and the extractive industries – sectors which on average account for less than 15 per cent of the total labour force (ILO, 2012).

With such an economic structure it becomes difficult to address the crucial issues of poverty reduction, inequality and sustainable growth. If we look at the fastest growing economies in Africa it is evident that the majority of these have not been able to reduce poverty or inequality, as Table 7.9 shows.

In countries like Zambia the poverty headcount is increasing at a time when their economies are reporting sustained growth. For Africa as a whole, "Despite the continent's growth turnaround and progress in the fight against poverty during the last decade, poverty in Africa remains unacceptably high, and the pace of reduction unacceptably slow. Almost one out of every two Africans lives in extreme poverty today" (World Bank, 2013: 14).

Thus, if Africa is rising, there are strong indications that it is rising with only 20 per cent of its population. The remaining 80 per cent who are not meaningfully taking part in the take-off are effectively left on the runway watching a lucky few who have managed to board the "African meteor". The key question is whether the rising African meteor will remain airborne when the majority of the population is being left behind. The biggest challenge in this regard is to ensure that more and more people get on board, participating and sharing meaningfully in the growth. As some analysts have noted, recording GDP growth rates of above 5 per cent was probably the easiest task that African leaders faced; the more difficult challenge is to sustain this growth and ensure that more and more people are participating in and contributing to it (Deverajan and Fengler, 2012). While the progress that Africa has made must be acknowledged, there are lots of challenges that need to be taken into account before we can begin celebrating the 'Africa moment'.

Notes

1　This refers to mostly younger Africans from different walks of life who are asserting themselves in business, government and social sector leadership. This term also refers to the general African populace that is becoming more educated, aware and assertive of their rights, demanding transparency, accountability and inclusive politics (see Ayittey, 2005).

2　There were strong fears during the 2008–2009 financial and economic crisis that the crisis was going to reverse the growth momentum in Africa. But the post-crisis resurgence of many African economies (with average GDP recovering from a meagre 2.5 per cent in 2009 to 5.2 per cent in 2010) changed the view of many, including some staunch Afro-pessimists (Brixiova and Ndikumana, 2011).

3　The significance of the 'Lion' metaphor, as opposed to the 'Tiger' (as in the Asian Tigers: originally Hong Kong, Singapore, South Korea and Taiwan) is not clear in the usage, although there is a sense in which the difference in the metaphor is meant to convey the difference in the actual economic dynamism. The Lion metaphor may suggest stronger but slower growth when compared to the Tiger – and of course the Asian Tigers grew at much faster rates than we have seen in Africa thus far.

4　For example, Radelet (2010b: 97–8) argues that the current economic momentum in Africa is different from the 1960s and early 1970s in two respects. First, *more* economies are growing now than was the case in the 1960s and 1970s. Second, the current dynamic has already surpassed the 1960s in terms of its duration, and it also seems to be built on "stronger foundations … starting with more accountable and democratic governance".

5　The 17 countries referred to as "emerging" include: Botswana, Burkina Faso, Cape Verde, Ethiopia, Ghana, Lesotho, Mali, Mauritius, Mozambique, Namibia, Rwanda, Sao Tome and Principe, Seychelles, South Africa, Tanzania, Uganda and Zambia. It is not clear however, if transparent and accountable governance have taken root in all these countries. The basis for selecting these countries was that they maintained a GDP per capita growth rate of 2 per cent between 1996 and 2008 (see Radelet, 2010a; 2010b).

6 *The Economist* (2014) reports that renowned African political economist, Thandika Mkandawire, as well as Princeton professor of economics, Dan Rodrik, are convinced that this growth will fizzle out.

7 This definition of a middle class has been criticised by some analysts who argue that the parameters used by the AfDB are too low when compared to the standards used by the United Nations – which uses a figure of a daily per capita income of between US$10–US$100. The AfDB defended its position saying that the US$2–US$20 per day per capita was appropriate for Africa's cost of living (see Akwagyiram, 2013). If we use the US$10–US$100 criterion, it becomes apparent that only 9 per cent (or 78 million) of Africans fall into this income bracket. If we further reduce the lower threshold to US$4–US$100, fewer than 15 per cent of African households meet this criterion (AfDB, 2013).

8 Both Jerven (2013) and Deverajan and Fengler (2012) have raised concerns and doubts about the credibility of national accounts data in Africa. Data challenges in Africa have been acknowledged by many analysts and organisations, including the IMF (see IMF, 2013). The IMF has now started reporting the data capability index for African countries.

9 The ILO labour force survey counts everyone who carried out some employed work during the reference period, although employment is then classified into various categories. But the headline figures often quoted in the media do not make the distinction.

References

Acemoglu, D. and Robinson, J. (2010). "Why Is Africa Poor?" *Economic History of Development Regions*, Vol. 25, No. 1: 21–50.

African Development Bank (AfDB) (2012). *African Statistical Year Book 2012*. Tunis: AfDB, African Union Commission and UNECA.

Africa Centre for Economic Transformation (ACET) (2014). *2014 African Transformation Report: Growth with Depth*. Accra: ACET.

African Development Bank (AfDB) (2011). "The Middle Class Pyramid: Dynamics of the Middle Class in Africa." Market Brief, 20 April 2011. Online, available at: www.afdb.org, accessed 12 February 2012.

African Development Bank (AfDB) (2013). "Annual Development Effectiveness Review 2013: Towards Sustainable Growth for Africa." Online, available at: www.afdb.org, accessed 23 October 2013.

African Development Bank/African Union/Economic Commission for Africa (AfDB/ AU/UNECA) (2009). *African Statistical Year Book*. Addis Ababa/Tunis: AfDB/AU/ UNECA.

African Development Bank/OECD Development Centre/United Nations Development Programme/Economic Commission for Africa (AfDB/OECD/UNDP/UNECA) (2013). "African Economic Outlook 2013." Online, available at: www.africaneconomicoutlook.org, accessed 2 July 2014.

African Development Bank/World Economic Forum (AfDB/WEF) (2013). *The African Competitive Report*. Geneva: World Economic Forum.

Akwagyiram, Alexis (2013). "Africa Rising – Who Benefits?" British Broadcasting Corporation (BBC) Africa. 18 June 2013. Online, available at: http://www.bbc.co.uk/news/world-africa-22847118, accessed 12 November 2013.

Arbache, Jorge S. and Page, John (2009). "How Fragile is Africa's Recent Growth?" *Journal of African Economies*, Vol. 19, No. 1: 1–24. Online, available at:

http://siteresources.worldbank.org/INTPOVCALNET/Resources/Global_Poverty_
Update_2012_02-29-12.pdf, accessed 13 May 2013.

Ayittey, George (2005). *Africa Unchained: The Blueprint for Africa's Future.* New York:
Palgrave Macmillan.

Boyce, J. and Ndikumana, L. (2012). "Capital Flight From Sub-Saharan African Countries:
Updated Estimates, 1970–2010." Political Economy Research Institute, research report.
University of Massachusetts, Amherst.

Brixiova, Zuzana and Ndikumana, Leonce (2011). "Supporting Africa's Post-crisis Growth:
The Role of Macroeconomic Policy." *Political Economy Research Institute (PERI) Working
Paper*, No. 54. University of Massachusetts, Amherst.

Broadberry, Stephen and Gardner, Leigh (2013). "Africa's Growth Prospect in a European
Mirror: A Historical Perspective." Competitive Advantage in the Global Economy
(CAGE), Chatham House Paper Series No. 5. Online, available at: http://www.warwick.
ac.uk/go/cage, accessed 15 December 2013.

Calderisi, Robert (2006). *The Trouble with Africa: Why Foreign Aid Isn't Working.* New
Haven/London: Yale University Press.

Chabal, Patrick and Daloz, Jean-Pascal (1999). *Africa Works: Disorder as Political Instrument.*
London: James Currey.

Chikane, F.W., Esterhuyse, M., Langa, V., Mavimbela, V. and Pahad, E. (1998). *Africa: The
Time Has Come – Selected Speeches of Thabo Mbeki.* Cape Town/Johannesburg: Tafelberg
& Mafube.

Collier, Paul (2006). "African Growth: Why a Big Push?" *Journal of African Economies*,
Vol. 00, AERC Supplement 2: 188–211.

Deverajan, Shanatyanan and Fengler, Wolfgang (2012). "Is Africa's Recent Economic
Growth Sustainable?" French Institute for International Relations (IFRI) Policy Note.
Online, available at: http://www.ifri.org/?page=contribution-detail&id=7349, accessed
28 November 2013.

Doornbos, Martin (1990). "The African State in Academic Debate: Retrospect and
Prospect." *Journal of Modern African Studies*, Vol. 28, No. 2: 179–98.

Dulani, Boniface, Mattes, Robert and Logan, Carolyn (2013). "After a Decade of Growth
in Africa, Little Change in Poverty at the Grassroots." Afro-Barometer Policy Brief,
No. 1.

Dumont, Rene (1966). *False Start in Africa* (translated by Phylis Nauts Ott). London:
Andre Deutsch.

The Economist (2000). "Hopeless Africa." 11 May 2000. Online, available at: http://www.
economist.com/node/333429, accessed 18 September 2011.

The Economist (2011). "Africa Rising: The Hopeful Continent." 3 December 2011.
Online, available at: http://www.economist.com/node/21541015, accessed 3 October
2012.

The Economist (2012). "Representative Government is Still on the March in Africa,
Despite Recent Hiccups." 31 March 2012.

The Economist (2013). "African Lives Have Already Greatly Improved Over the Past
Decade, Says Oliver August. The Next Ten Years Will Be Even Better." 2 March 2013.
Online, available at: http://www.economist.com/printededition2013-03-03, accessed
18 November 2013.

The Economist (2014). "An Awakening Giant: Manufacturing in Africa." 8 February
2014.

Ernst & Young (2011). *It's Time for Africa: Africa Attractiveness Survey*. Midrand: Ernst & Young.

Fine, Ben (2010). "From the Political Economy of Development to Development Economics: Implications for Africa" in V. Padayachee (ed.) *The Political Economy of Africa*. London/NewYork: Routledge: 60–82.

Fletcher, Pascal (2011). "African 'Lions' Can Still Rise – IMF and World Bank." Reuters, 23 September 2011. Online, available at: http://www.reuters.com/article/2011/09/23/africa-economy-idUSS1E78I1O32011092, accessed 12 September 2012.

Fox, L., Haines, C. Munoz, J.H. and Thomas, A. (2013). "Africa's Got Work to Do: Employment Prospects in the New Century." IMF Working Paper, No. 13/201.

Hou, Z., Keane, J., Kennan, J., Massa, I. and te Velde, D.W. (2013). "The Changing Nature of Private Capital Flows to Sub-Saharan Africa." Shockwatch Bulletin Working Paper 376. London: Overseas Development Institute.

International Labour Organisation (ILO) (2010). KILMnet (Beta Version) online database. Online, available at: http://kilm.ilo.org/kilmnet, accessed 3 June 2010.

International Labour Organisation (ILO) (2012). *Decent Work in Africa: A First Assessment Based on National Sources*. Rome: ILO.

International Monetary Fund (IMF) (2008). *Regional Economic Outlook October 2008: Sub-Saharan Africa*. Washington DC: IMF.

International Monetary Fund (IMF) (2013). *Regional Economic Outlook October 2013: Sub-Saharan Africa – Keeping Pace*. Washington DC: IMF.

Jerven, Morten (2013). "Comparability of GDP Estimates in Sub-Saharan Africa: The Effect of Revision in Sources and Methods Since Structural Adjustment." *Review of Income and Wealth*, Vol. DOI: 10.1111/roiw. 12006, 201.

KPMG (2013). *The African Emergence: The Rise of the Phoenix*. Johannesburg: KPMG. Online, available at: http://www.kpmg.com/Africa/en/IssuesAndInsights/Articles-Publications/Documents/African%20Emergence-Rise%20of%20the%20phoenix%20 2013.pdf, accessed 6 August 2013.

Lamido, Sanusi (2013). "Africa Must Get Real about Chinese Ties." NiraLand, 19 March 2013. Online, available at: http://www.nairaland.com/1230001/sanusi-lamido-sanusi-africa-must, accessed 8 November 2013.

Lawrence, Peter (2010). "The African Tragedy: International and National Roots" in V. Padayachee (ed.) *The Political Economy of Africa*. London/NewYork: Routledge: 19–38.

Mahajan, Vijay (2009). *Africa Rising: How 900 Million Africa Consumers Offer More than You Think*. New Jersey: Wharton School Publishing.

McGeary, Johanna and Michaels, Marguerite [1998] (2001). "Africa Rising." *Time Magazine*. Online, available at: http://content.time.com/time/magazine/article/0,9171,138851,00. html, accessed 3 December 2013.

McKinsey Global Institute (MGI) (2010). "Lions on the Move: The Progress and Potential of African Economies." McKinsey Global Institute/McKinsey & Company, June 2010. Online, available at: http://www.mckinsey.com/insights/africa/lions_on_the_move?p=1, accessed 23 November 2013.

McKinsey Global Institute (MGI) (2013). "Lions Go Digital: The Internet's Transformative Potential in Africa." November 2013 report. Online, available at: www.mckinsey.com, accessed 4 December 2013.

Michaels, Marguerite (1993). "Retreat from Africa." *Foreign Affairs*, Vol. 72, No. 1: 93–108.

Moss, Todd (2011). *African Development: Making Sense of the Issues and Actors.* Boulder: Lynne Rienner.

Ncube, Mthuli and Shimeles, Abebe (2012). "The Making of the Middle Class in Africa." African Development Bank. Online, available at: www.afdb.org, accessed 17 November 2013.

Page, John (2012). "Aid, Structural Change and the Private Sector in Africa." United Nations University (UNU)-World Institute for Development Economic Research (WIDER) Working Paper No. 2012/21. UNU-WIDER.

Perry, Alex (2012). "Africa Rising." *Time Magazine*, 3 December 2012. Online, available at: http://content.time.com/time/magazine/article/0,9171,2129831,00.html, accessed 18 November 2013.

Radelet, Steven (2010a). *Emerging Africa: How 17 Countries Are Leading the Way.* Washington DC: Brookings Institution Press.

Radelet, Steven (2010b). "Success Stories from 'Emerging Africa'. " *Journal of Democracy*, Vol. 21, No. 4: 87–101.

Rickett, Oscar (2013). "Is This the Century of Africa's Rise?" posted 22 January 2013. Online, available at: http://www.vice.com/read/is-this-the-century-of-africas-rise-1, accessed 18 September 2013.

Robertson, C., Mhango, Y. and Moran, M. (2012). *The Fastest Billion: The Story Behind Africa's Economic Revolution.* London: Renaissance Capital.

Rotberg, Robert (2013). *Africa Emerges.* Cambridge: Polity Press.

Rowden, Rick (2013). "The Myth of Africa's Rise." Online, available at: http://www.twincities.com/ci_22327262/rick-rowden-myth-africas-rise, accessed 12 November 2013.

Severino, Jean-Michel and Ray, Oliver (2011). *Africa's Moment.* Cambridge: Polity Press.

Somerville, Keith (2013). "Africa Emerges – But from What and into What? A Triumph of Hope Over Experience in Robert Rotberg's New Assessment of the Continent." African Arguments, 4 September 2013. Online, available at: http://africanarguments.org/2013/09/04/africa-emerges-, accessed 18 November 2013.

Stein, Howard (2003). "Rethinking African Development" in H. Chang (ed.) *Rethinking Development Economics.* London: Anthem Press: 153–78.

United Nations Conference on Trade and Development (UNCTAD) (2013a). *Economic Development in Africa Report 2013.* New York/Geneva: UNCTAD.

United Nations Conference on Trade and Development (UNCTAD) (2013b). *Trade and Development Report 2013.* New York/Geneva: UNCTAD.

World Bank (2006). *African Development Indicators 2006.* Washington DC: World Bank.

World Bank (2008). *African Development Indicators 2008.* Washington DC: World Bank.

World Bank (2011). *African Development Indicators 2011.* Washington DC: World Bank.

World Bank (2012). "PovcalNet: An Online Poverty Analysis Tool." Online, available at: http://iresearch.worldbank.org/PovcalNet/index.htm, accessed 13 May 2013.

World Bank (2013). "Africa Pulse Rate: An Analysis of Issues Shaping Africa's Economic Future." October. Vol. 8. Online, available at: http://www.worldbank.org/content/dam/Worldbank/document/Africa/Report/Africas-Pulse-brochure_Vol8.pdf, accessed 13 February 2014.

World Bank (2014). "Africa Pulse Rate: An Analysis of Issues Shaping Africa's Economic Future." April 2014. Vol. 9. Online, available at: http://www.worldbank.org/content/dam/Worldbank/document/Africa/Report/Africas-Pulse-brochure_Vol9.pdf, accessed 24 June 2014.

Young, Alwyn (2012). "The African Growth Miracle." *Journal of Political Economy*, Vol. 120, No. 4: 696–739.

8 African intellectuals and the African growth and development challenges

Introduction

Intellectuals (especially, organic intellectuals[1] in the Gramscian sense) constitute an important 'layer' of civil society[2] and ought to play a crucial role (as the 'organising element') in defining and influencing national consciousness, struggles, and the formation of popular culture. Whether intellectuals play this role in society depends on a number of factors, some of which will be discussed in the course of this chapter. One of the key factors that influences the role intellectuals play in society is the group's consciousness of its sense of a clearly defined mission in relation to the broader society. A blurred sense of mission in relation to broader society often leads to fragmentation and weak relations between various elements of that society, including the state and markets. Figure 8.1 shows the graphical relationship between state, civil society and markets, highlighting the idea that both state and markets are 'embedded' in *society*, of which intellectuals are an integral part.

This view of society is more prominent in the Polanyian conception of the different elements of society. In this view, the market (economy) as well as the 'political society' (the state, in the Gramscian view) are embedded in society; society is not embedded in the market as implied by the notion of a 'market society'. Conceived in this way, civil society is a far-reaching relational space with diverse entities including political parties, professional associations, independent media, voluntary non-profit making organisations, trade unions, student movements, different religious groupings, peasants, academia, social movements, etc. In both the Polanyian and Gramscian conception there is a unique attention given to "the role of intellectuals in elaborating popular consciousness, and connecting it to vistas of national and global history" (Burawoy, 2003: 207).

As may be evident in Figure 8.1, intellectuals are one among the many components of civil society. However, intellectuals by the nature of their work and position in society are expected to play an important role in the production and organisation of ideas (knowledge), including ideas about economic growth and development.[3] Intellectuals are particularly central in the Gramscian view of civil society, which is seen as a constructed hegemonic space where struggles between the different components of society occur. In this contested space, intellectuals

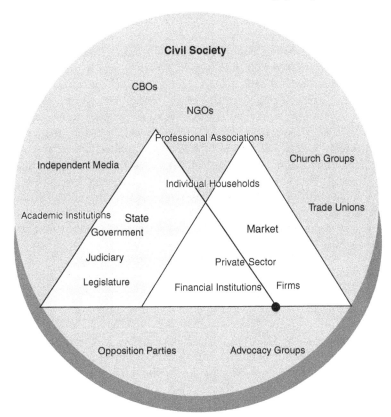

Figure 8.1. Civil society, the state and the economy
Source: adapted by author from Offenheiser and Holcombe (2003: 279).

are expected to play the role of articulating ideas in support of the contesting elements. In the case of organic intellectuals, they assign themselves the responsibility of articulating the aspirations of, and providing cohesion among, the masses, the working poor and the large pool of unemployed to which they are an integral part or organically bound.

The term 'intellectuals' is here used in a broad sense to include thinkers from a diverse section of civil society, ranging from opposition party leaders through social and student movements to members of professional associations.

The role of African intellectuals in Africa

There have been persistent debates in Africa about whether there has ever been a 'mass of intellectuals' of 'an organic kind' directing and providing a cohesive and organising force, articulating the appropriate ideology, and with a strong connection to the peasantry and working poor. Some analysts have argued that there has been no mass formation of intellectuals of an 'organic' kind in Africa; a few individual organic intellectuals have appeared here and there, but they have remained small in number and are often marginalised, especially after the fall-out with nationalist leaders during the 1970s. Various explanations for the low number of organic intellectuals in Africa have been offered, including the argument that the nature of education that most Africans receive makes them alien to their own culture, people and various social strata (see Armah, 2010, Brown, 2006). Other analysts have attributed what they see as the absence of organic intellectuals in Africa to the view that African intellectuals often strive towards the Western model of intellectualism, which makes it difficult for them to relate to the African masses and the African challenges (see Fanon, 1963, Ekeh, 1975). Some critics have gone even further to suggest that most African intellectuals will be more at home in Europe or North America than in their respective African communities, and that because of this they tend to disengage from active society (Calderisi, 2006).

The African intellectual in context

In the debates about the African intellectual/scholar, it is important to see him/her as a product of the dynamic African context, a context which should be the object of his or her inquiry. Thus the African intellectual, when reflecting on economic growth and development experiences in the continent, is seeking to make sense of that which he or she is part of – not as a 'participant observer', for he or she is both an actor and an observer, but as an 'auto ethnographer' for the lack of a better term (see Anyidoho, 2006). Being both (an observer and an observed) can be a source of great advantage, but also challenging. Thus, in discussing the African intellectual's role, the context matters:

> we should not forget that the underdevelopment of our countries is the necessary background, an inescapable and ubiquitous condition of our reality, operating like a vast osmotic medium or, ... like a pervasive magnetic field that polarizes all our problems, imposing a direction on all their component elements.
>
> (Ki-Zerbo, 1994: 29)

This "magnetic field" or "osmotic medium" is both the topic of inquiry, but also forms an important part of the inquirer. However, it is essential to note that the African intelligentsia, as would be expected, is not a homogenous stratum operating within a single paradigm or with the same worldview. As may be evident in the preceding chapters, different African scholars and intellectuals operate from different perspectives, and often provide diverse explanations for the continent's growth and development experiences – explanations which often conflict and are frequently 'spiced up' with the aromatics of the disciplines in which the individual is schooled. This diversity of viewpoints is not a unique feature of African intellectuals and scholars; it constitutes the essence of a genuine intellectual undertaking everywhere. Thus, it is a major affront to the African scholar/intellectual to assert that they have a tendency towards "an excess of analytical conformism", and that they are quick to brand anything critical as racist, imperialist, neo-colonial and chauvinistic (Chabal and Daloz, 1999: 128–9). The dilemma of the African intellectual is that she/he has been criticised from within as a shameless "intellectual imitator and disciple of the West" (Mazrui, 1994: 119), and from without as a bad student who has been largely unsuccessful in learning the art of critical thinking and rigorous research in mainstream disciplines (see Robertson, 1985).

African intellectuals and civil society

In some debates the African intellectual is sometimes portrayed as a thinker in the process of *becoming*. For some critics, as we shall see, this is the basis for denying the existence of African intellectuals, while some generous commentators render the African intellectual triflingly visible. There are several arguments advanced to explain the 'in-the-making' status ascribed to African scholars. These include the idea that African states are not formally instituted; because of this they tend to be very pervasive or overextended such that there is little space which would otherwise be the free realm of the primordial society. It is thus argued that because of the overextended nature of African states it is difficult for civil society in Africa to flourish; civil society is suffocated by the corpulent state. For some critics the very idea of civil society in Africa is questionable. They argue that the

> notion of civil society would only apply if it could be shown that there were meaningful institutional separations between a well organised civil society and a relatively autonomous bureaucratic state. Instead, what we observe in Black Africa is constant inter-penetration, or straddling of the one by the other.
>
> (Chabal and Daloz, 1999: 17)

Given this, it is argued, civil society as an analytical concept is only a residual term.

A related argument with regard to the state of civil society in Africa is that the weak development of capitalism in the continent has affected the formation of distinct social classes which could have been instrumental in articulating a genuine *etat civille*, that is distinct from the *etat politique*. Instead, it is contended, what we have seen is an inarticulate social formation which has been structurally weak, and often absorbed by or identical to the political elite and state bureaucrats (see Leys, 1976). There is also the argument that because of the repressive nature of the African leviathan, civil rights (the right to freedom of expression, freedom of association, freedom of assembly and freedom of movement), the prerequisite for a flourishing civil society, are often trampled on through various means including draconian legislation (such as the infamous Maintenance of Public Order Act, and Information Bill, etc.). This has served to silence those critical of the state by either elimination or imprisonment. Given this context the type of intellectual expected is one who is severely constrained; indeed some analysts observe that this situation has been worsened by decades of weak economic and development performance.

Who is an African intellectual?

Given the disagreement about whether there are any African intellectuals, this chapter adopts the criterion used by the "Africa's 100 Best Books of the 20th Century" initiative, which defined an African author as "someone either born in Africa or who became a citizen of an African country" (*African Studies*, 2002).[4] Adopting this approach makes it possible to include African scholars who were born on the continent but who have since moved to other continents, as well as those who were born elsewhere but have moved to the African continent and become citizens of any of its 54 countries. This approach also makes it possible to include African diaspora scholars and intellectuals. In this framework there are many who do not fit the definition but have contributed immensely to African scholarship, and to African economic growth and development scholarship in particular. To distinguish the scholars of Africa who have in the past, or are currently, working on African themes, from African scholars, the former are often referred to (or see themselves) as 'Africanist' (see Mkandawire, 1997; Martin and West, 1995; Bates *et al.*, 1993, Chabal, 1991, Momoh, 2003). While this classification (African-Africanist) is widely used, it is also important to note that many scholars often do not see themselves either as African or Africanist intellectuals/scholars; they frequently see themselves in terms of their disciplinary orientation or educational/occupational/professional backgrounds as anthropologists, journalists, development economists, geographers, sociologists, historians, civil engineers, philosophers, lawyers or bone surgeons (see Hodder-Williams, 1986: 596). Regrettably, these professional and occupational precincts have evolved into higher and more enduring walls than the Berlin Wall, aggravating the challenge of creating "intellectual communities" in Africa (Ki-Zerbo, 1994).

Politics of recognition

A discussion of African scholarship in the context of Africa's economic growth and development experience is crucial for three reasons. First, for reasons related to the nature and structure of global knowledge production itself, there has been a tendency to ignore and sometimes doubt the existence of African scholars and their contributions to understanding the African economic growth and development experience. This has been captured well in what sounds like an autobiographical portrait of African intellectuals/scholars:

> Let me also state that if at times I sound querulous and too insistent on declaring our existence, it is partly because others have chosen to obliterate

us either by studied silence about our existence or by declaring that we simply do not exist.

(Mkandawire, 1997: 16)

If one accepts the observation that there have been 'deliberate attempts' to render African scholarship invisible, a discussion about African intellectuals cannot
take for granted either the existence or non-existence of African scholarship.
Under these circumstances it becomes imperative that such a discussion, at least,
provides some concrete evidence in support of either of the two positions. For
those who subscribe to the *existence* thesis, it is important to demonstrate the
existence of such scholarship; while for those who take the *non-existence* thesis,
it is equally imperative to present some evidence to illustrate the non-existence
of African scholarship.

The second reason why it is important to discuss African scholarship is that a
general account of scholarship on Africa often paints a picture of domination of
the field by Africanist scholars. So to make African scholarship visible (i.e., not
in competition with others who study Africa) requires that African scholarship
be distinguished from other types. Further, to the extent that African scholarship
faces unique challenges (as elaborated earlier), it is necessary to consider African
scholarship on its own – not only in an historical context but also in a contemporary one – so as to gain insight into what this type of scholarship has, and has
not, contributed to our understanding of African societies.

Third, a discussion of African scholarship becomes crucial given the view that
there has been a double deficit as far as understanding Africa's economic growth
and development challenges is concerned. While it has been observed that general scholarship on Africa receives much less recognition in the social science
disciplines, it is not only research by African scholars which is sidelined but the
entire study of the continent as an area of study (Bates *et al.*, 1993; Melber, 2009);
the African scholar is almost invisible within the sidelined study field of Africa.
For example, a

> well-known French Africanist concluded … that there was only one intel-
> lectual in the whole of Black Africa … in light of such remarks … we feel
> that the invisibility of African scholarship has gone on for so long that we
> are inclined to attribute it to deliberate attempts to render it invisible.

(Mkandawire, 1997: 16)

In this sense, African scholarship suffers from being sidelined at two levels: at
the level of the disciplines as well as at the level of the general African scholarship. In addition to the politics of invisibility, African scholars find themselves
waging battles not only against the menacing Leviathan, but also against those
who control the means of production and the circulation of knowledge, with
the former declaring African scholarship as either irrelevant or reactionary, and
contributing little to national development. The latter group, meanwhile, brand
African scholarship as "lacking rigor" or overly descriptive, with no theoretical

grounding. In this case the African intellectual/scholar is found to be fighting on two fronts: "institutionally against the authoritarian state and intellectually against domineering western paradigms" (Zeleza, 2003b: 158).

African intellectuals and social change

With regard to economic growth and development scholarship on Africa, many African scholars and intellectuals have contributed to the pool of ideas which exist on this topic – as may be evident in the preceding chapters. A distinction, however, is often made between the influence of African scholars and the academic research work of Africans on economic and development policy in Africa. While many African intellectuals and scholars may have written and published their views and findings, they may not have had considerable influence over what came to be the dominant economic development policy or strategy. The reasons for this are discussed later in the chapter. For now, it suffices to note that African scholarship on this topic has stressed different perspectives, influenced largely by the dominant ideology adopted by a particular African state.

Distinguishing political from economic change, some analysts have argued that while African intellectuals and scholars may have contributed immensely to political change and development, they have done little to effect economic change in post-colonial Africa (Mazrui, 2006). With regard to political change, African intellectuals and scholars played a significant role, including the mobilisation of the African population during the liberation struggle as well the creation of unified nations from the fragmented colonial administrative structures (see Ajayi, 1982). In this sense African intellectuals were truly 'organic', providing ideological and organisational leadership to the liberation movements, as well as helping define the struggle itself. Many African political leaders (most of whom were intellectuals) – including Leopold Senghor (Senegal), Nnamdi Azikwe (Nigeria), Julius Nyerere (Tanzania), Sekou Toure (Equatorial Guinea), Kwame Nkrumah (Ghana), Amilcar Cabral (Guinea-Bissau), Tsiranana (Madagascar), Gamal Abdel Nasser (Egypt), Hastings Kamuzu Banda (Malawi), Amar Ouzegane (Algeria), Jomo Kenyatta (Kenya), Kenneth Kaunda (Zambia), Robert Mugabe (Zimbabwe), Patrice Lumumba (former Zaire), Nelson Mandela (South Africa), and many more – contributed to the political transformation from colonial/apartheid rule to independent/majority rule.

What distinguishes these African leaders is not that they were all liberation struggle activists (nationalists), or that all except two became president/prime minister of their respective countries. What unifies them is that they have all been agents of not only political change, but also social, and to a certain extent, economic, change. Though most of them became authoritarian leaders, highly intolerant of opposing or differing views, they all had a vision about how their respective societies were to overcome the structural barriers imposed by colonial rule, and a vision for establishing multiracial, multicultural societies in which all people had an equal prospect of fulfilling their human potential. These were not intellectuals or leaders because of their educational achievements, but because of their role and ideas about social change – particularly the ending of minority colonial rule and the inauguration of majority self-rule. While not every one of them developed super-strategies or grand theories of economic growth and development, all had a passion for transforming the colonial into a post-colonial political, social and economic order, with the aim of improving the living conditions of their people (Mohan, 1966). It is probably unfair to argue that for most of these African leaders economic growth and development was not on the agenda from the beginning. While it is true to say that little economic transformation actually occurred following the independence of many of these countries, most had a vision (and devised strategies to that effect) to transform the colonial economic structure into one that provided opportunities to the broader society (see Mkandawire, 2003).

The nationalist project and Africa's development

Contrary to the view that development in terms of improving the living conditions of the majority of the people had never been on the nationalists' agenda (see Ajayi, 1982; Bayart, 1993; Ake, 1996), one of the priorities of the nationalist project was improving the living conditions of the people, especially in the rural areas as one analysts observes:

> the argument that 'development' was externally imposed … [is] … misinformed and … insulting to the many African leaders and intellectuals … It is quite clear from nationalist historiography that development – the eradication of the 'unholy trinity of ignorance, poverty and disease' – was a central component of the nationalist agenda.
>
> (Mkandawire, 2003)

The claim that the nationalists were only preoccupied with overthrowing the colonial regime; that economic development was either absent or that "it was low on their list of priorities" (Ajayi, 1982: 2), is an unfair indictment on the African nationalists. For example, in *I speak of Freedom* (Nkrumah, 1961) as well as in *Consciencism* (Nkrumah, [1961] 1972), and other works, Kwame Nkrumah conveys a sense of the urgency to improve the well-being of the people. It was not just liberation from political bondage, but economic, social, cultural and religious freedom which the nationalists envisioned (see Biney, 2008). Similar strong emphasis on lifting the masses from dire poverty can be found in the writings of other African leaders immediately after independence. "We are at war. TANU [the Tanganyika African National Union] is involved in a war against poverty and oppression in our country; the struggle is aimed at moving the people of Tanzania (and the people of Africa as a whole) from a state of poverty to a state of prosperity" (*Arusha Declaration*, 1967). The awareness and intention to improve the well-being of the majority of the people, who in many countries at the time of independence (even at the moment) happened to be living in rural areas, is evident in statements such as, "in the period ahead we must concentrate and direct our efforts to those projects and areas which are likely to bring maximum benefit to the greatest of people in rural areas. In other words comrades, from now on, our priority is rural development" (Kaunda, 1969: 20).

Although critics often dismiss such statements as the mere politicking or populism that is typical of nationalist/socialist propaganda (Ayittey, 2004), one has to distinguish between having a vision and a strategy, and implementing them. The literature on early post-colonial Africa amply demonstrates the intent, at least, among African political leaders to achieve economic growth and development as part of the process of nation-building. Although most of the visions were framed in the popular term 'catching up', influenced by the modernisation paradigm (Nabudere, 1997), these were views (viable or not) created by African thinkers reflecting on and thinking about both the material and social conditions in which they found themselves. As Thanidka Mkandawire (2003) has noted, while it may be true that economic growth and development concerns were somehow sidetracked or derailed along the way, the idea, the thinking, and the intentions were there at the beginning.

The arguments that all the ideas produced by these African thinkers were merely the recycling of foreign ones, and that these projects had little relevance in Africa (Bayart, 1993) should be evaluated in the context of the African leaders themselves, demonstrates a rejection of "both Western Capitalism and Eastern Communism" and choosing an alternative middle way (see Mohan, 1966: 229). The whole notion of *African socialism*, as noted earlier, was a loud cry to let the world know that 'we' are not just grafters or peddlers of other people's ideas; we are able to reflect on our own situation and come up with our own solutions relevant to the realities in which we live. This is especially evident in Senghor: "We have chosen democratic socialism and have turned our backs on capitalism, which depends upon the exploitation of man by man, and on Communism, which ignores liberty and espouses atheism" (cited in Mohan, 1966: 229). This was partly the practical demonstration of the essence of independence; the freedom to think, choose, plan independently and implement the planned measures without having to have them approved by someone else. Thus, it is equally problematic to categorise the nationalists as being against colonial rule but in favour of the colonisers' ideals, institutions and way of life (Ekeh, 1975).

Of course democratic socialism did not flourish anywhere in the continent, and neither did socialism – as noted in the preceding chapter. While one cannot deny the influence of Marxism or the modernisation theory on some thinkers, it is an exaggeration to claim that they simply grafted foreign ideas on to African conditions. Such views often reinforce the racist view that Africans are incapable of reflecting on their own conditions or devising ways to address the challenges they face.[5] Some of these leaders actually developed what in their view were unique models of development. Famous among them are Nyerere's philosophy of *Ujamaa*, Kaunda's *Humanism*, and Naser's *Arab Socialism*. Through such ideas, African political leaders communicated their thinking, vision and plans for their own societies.

Pan-Africanism and Africa's development

Linked to the idea of economic growth and development in Africa in the early post-colonial days was the imperative of uniting the African continent and diaspora in terms of the pan-African movement, something the early African political intellectuals advocated. For Nkrumah, the independence of individual African countries meant little as long as there were others that were still under colonial rule. The need a consolidated political and economic African voice was noted earlier as an essential requirement for making the continent's independence meaningful.

> We need the strength of our combined numbers and resources to protect ourselves from the very positive dangers of returning colonialism in disguised forms. We need it to combat the entrenched forces dividing our continent and still holding back millions of our brothers. We need it to secure total African liberation.
>
> (Nkrumah, 1961: 27)

Similar views can be found in the *Arusha Declaration* (1967), which asserted that Tanzania could not be free until the rest of Africa was also.

This strong sense of unity and integration – which was later re-emphasised in the Lagos Plan of Action (LPA) of 1980, and more concretely in the Abuja Treaty of 1991 – was a practical response to the realities of the global economy and politics. The idea of a single continent was probably more strongly articulated by African leaders than anyone else, although it has failed to materialise into any concrete form (see Ayittey, 2004).[6] The creation of Regional Economic Communities (RECs),[7] however, has not helped much to realise the dream of a unified Africa in the fight against the challenges of poverty, illiteracy, disease, corruption, repression and inequality. With the persisting crisis of governance in the Eurozone area, a region that many African leaders see as the perfect example of what a unified Africa should emulate (together with the brutal killing of 'brother leader' *Muammar Gaddafi*), the aspiration for a unified Africa has been dealt a serious blow. Though not much has been achieved in this regard, the desires and intentions for a unified Africa among some African leaders have been clear.

The scholarly intellectuals of Africa

Other than the political intellectuals discussed above, there have been other African thinkers and writers who have expressed their views about development in general and economic growth in particular. It is not possible here to discuss the ideas or contributions of each; rather an attempt is made to present some of the ideas which have influenced scholarly understanding of the economic and development challenges that the continent has been facing. As indicated earlier, since the existence of African intellectuals is questioned (and often rendered invisible) by some analysts and commentators, this discussion is an affirmation that African intellectuals do not just exist, but that they have, in various ways and at various times, been thinking about the condition in Africa, and many have expressed their views about the situation.

In discussing the African intellectuals in this category I will limit the discussion to those scholars who have expressed their ideas either in literary works, art, in the media, or as part of scholarly work. This is done not to exclude the non-published African intellectuals, who are sometimes referred to as the "sage philosophers" (see Hountondji, 1996). It is the case that not including the unpublished African thinkers, though a widely adopted approach, is biased towards the literate type of intellectual, with a heavy leaning towards the scholarly type. A typical example of this bias is reported by Mamadou Diouf in his discussion of the conceptualisation of intellectuals in Senegal. He observes that although the concept of intellectuals in Senegal is more elastic, there is a widely held view that an "intellectual is expected to hold a university degree, and to be a practicing academic specialist in some recognised discipline" (Diouf, 1994: 214). A similar observation is made by Mkandawire (1995), who reports that there is a a widespread tendency to define an intellectual as a person with a formal (usually university) education. Unfortunately, the discussion that follows will be limited to African scholars involved in the production of knowledge for the practical reason that the ideas of other intellectuals may not be known to the intellectual community in Africa, thereby making them difficult to discuss.

In his discussion of African intellectuals, Mkandawire (1995) talks about three generations, starting from the post-World War Two period through to the time when he was writing in the mid-1990s. Table 8.1 summarises the key features of each generation.

In proposing this typology of African intellectuals, Mkandawire (1995) is well aware of the broad generalisations this involves. For example, the distinguishing features of the three generations may not be as sharply drawn as this typology suggests. What is more, African intellectuals, even if we restrict the term to academic intellectuals, appeared well before the "cold war airlifts of African students especially to the United States" (Mkandawire, 1995: 75). Several Africans attended Western universities (mainly French, American and British universities) way before the end of World War Two. Well-known examples include the first Nigerian president, Azikwe, who in 1925 went to the USA and later graduated with an advanced degree in political science from Lincoln University in 1933, and in 1937 published *Renascent Africa*, which contained his ideas about Pan-Africanism. Other examples of pre-World War Two African intellectuals include Banda (former president of Malawi), who studied in the USA at the Wilberforce Academy in Ohio and graduated as a bachelor of medicine in 1937 from Meharry Medical College in Tennessee; and Nkrumah, who graduated as a master of science in education and as a master of arts in philosophy from the University of Pennsylvania in 1942. I am sure there are many more African intellectuals of this era who are not widely know. Thus, what Mkandawire refers to as the first generation could actually be the second or third generation of African scholars. Nonetheless such a typology is essential to the understanding of the

Table 8.1. Generations of African intellectuals

1st Generation	2nd Generation	3rd Generation
Trained abroad, majority came back home	Trained abroad, majority did not come back	Trained locally, under sev2re economic conditions
Core to the indigenisation programme	Involved in first wave of African brain drain2	Keen to go abroad, but little international exposure
Sympathetic to nationalist developmentalism	Faced stiff competition for promotions	Face the tragedy of identity crisis for universities
Internationally recognised	Experienced state-intellectual animosity and political repression	Subjected to 'rates of return' arguments (funding cuts)
Strong anti-neo-colonial, keen on debunking (neo-) colonialist views	Relatively mobile, ready to look for greener pastures	Less marketable internationally and not known outside Africa
Reactive to non-African scholars	Experienced purging of intellectuals by authoritarian regimes	Little familiarity with theoretical debates abroad and tend to be overly descriptive
Exclusively external explanations for Africa's crisis	Training did not equip them well to work in the African context	Offer internal explanations of the African crisis
Set up Pan-African research networks (e.g., CODESRIA and AAPS, SAPES, OSERIA)	Did not worry about reproduction of intellectuals	Organise strikes over conditions of services and academic freedom
Trained under Cold War politics	Keen on doing consultancy work	Proactive rather than reactive in discussing Africa

Source: author, based on Mkandawire (1995).

Note: AAPS is the African Association of Political Sciences, SAPES is the Southern Africa Political Economy Series and OSERIA is the Organization for Social Sciences Research in East and Southern Africa.

broader context in which African scholarship is located, and in identifying some of the challenges peculiar to the evolution of African scholarship.

The nationalists and Africa's intellectuals

What is interesting from the above typology is the observation that during the liberation struggle and the short period following independence, most African intellectuals and scholars supported and worked closely with the nationalist leaders on various projects, including nation-building and development projects. This is an observation which is widely noted in the literature on African intellectuals (see Ki-Zerbo, 1994; Mazrui, 1994; Williams, 2000; Zeleza, 2003a). During this period, which has been referred to as the "age of euphoria", the first generation of post-colonial African academic intellectuals collaborated with the nationalists in their quest to deal with the unholy trinity of hunger, ignorance and disease as a practical expression of *freeing* the people – an expression of total independence. In a way, during this period there was some sort of common ground forged between intellectuals in general and the nationalists, resulting in a relatively amicable relationship between the two. Many intellectuals were appointed to key positions within government. Indeed a number of African intellectuals became the "bourgeoisie of the diploma to the boot", sometimes serving as crucial allies of the state (see Mkandawire, 2003).

While it is largely true that African intellectuals provided the theoretical backing for the post-independence grand nationalist projects (William, 2000), this cooperation and affirmation quickly disappeared during the 1970s. This was for a number of reasons, including the apparent failure of the nationalist project as evidenced by repression, nationalist chauvinism and authoritarianism. What sparked the falling-out was the discrediting of the modernisation approach that many nationalists had bought into. By the end of the 1970s the optimism of the 1960s and early 1970s had dissipated, "transformed into 'Afro-pessimism' during the decades of the 1980s and 1990s" (Biney, 2008: 132) – which led to the rupture of the intellectual-nationalist alliance. Prior to this rupture the terms of association between the two had been largely based on mutual understanding, rather than the form of co-option which became the *modus operandi* in later years.

The contribution of most African intellectuals during this period of 'euphoria', however, was largely administrative; most African scholars returning from abroad played an important role in the formulation and implementation of the indigenisation policies which most African governments adopted. Their contributions in terms of development policy and theory was largely within a nationalist framework of nation-building and fast-track industrialisation. Most of the development strategies were contained in the national development plans, and many intellectuals identified with the objectives contained in them. As a result they willingly collaborated in such projects as administrators or policy advisors.

There are several reasons that account for the rupture of the alliance between the nationalists and the intellectuals. During the period referred to as the 'second generation' of African intellectuals in the above typology, most became targets of the military and one-party state regimes that had come to power in many countries. During this period African intellectuals were isolated or targeted for persecution, especially those who were critical of the repressive regimes; many were simply ignored as reactionary agents of the neo-colonialists. The first report on the *State of Academic Freedom in Africa* published by Council for the Development of Social Research in Africa (CODESRIA) in 1995 highlights the souring relationship between state officials and African intellectuals (Sall, 1995). Country briefs from Algeria, Cote d'Ivoire, Nigeria, Kenya, Cameroon, Congo, Egypt, Guinea, Sudan and the Democratic Republic of the Congo (DRC) all illustrate deterioration of the once amicable relationship. A report from Cote d'Ivoire captures the nature of the state-intellectual tension:

> On two occasions, in May 1980 and April 1981, a lecturer of the faculty of law was arrested by order of the political authorities (the Ministers and

the DI of Higher Education) and the police authorities (National Security), respectively, for statements made during a programme on national radio (stance taken on the Ivorianisation of senior officials) and concerning the contents of his lectures. He was accused of seeking to propagate Marxism. The second time, he was arrested in the middle of one of his lectures at the university.

(Dehni-Segui, 1996: 72)

Such tensions were to become characteristic for subsequent generations of African scholars and intellectuals. Various reasons have been advanced to account for the deterioration in the relationship, ranging from the nature of the authoritarian rule adopted by many African leaders shortly after independence (see William, 2000), to the collapse of the nationalist project which led many intellectuals to lose faith in the state, to incompatibility between the nationalist resolve to achieve national unity *at any cost* and the intellectuals' demands for freedom of expression and association as prerequisites for a successful intellectual project. In some countries tensions between the nationalists and the intellectuals surfaced early, as is evident in Nkrumah's statement: "We do not intend to sit idly by and see these institutions which are supported by millions of pounds produced out of the sweat and toil of common people continue to be centres of anti-government activities" (cited in Mkandawire, 2003). In some cases politicians prescribed regime loyalty as a necessary feature of African universities and intellectuals:

We want the university college to cease being an alien institution and to take on the character of a Ghanaian University, loyally serving the interest of the nation ... If reforms do not come from within, we intend to impose them from outside, and no ... cry for academic freedom ... is going to restrain us.

(Nkrumah, cited in Mkandawire, 2003)

Looking back, the alliance between African intellectuals and the nationalists was an uneasy one from the beginning given the radical nature of the nationalist project, on the one hand, and the necessity for freedom of expression and opinion as the hallmark of the intellectual project, on the other. Freedom of expression and the liberty to think critically and independently did not sit well with the nationalist ideology of unity at any cost or, at worst, conformism. Evidently, within the nationalist project the universities and intellectuals were expected to support the state's programmes and policies. Any expression of a different view was interpreted as being unpatriotic, pro-colonialist, Westernised, and, in some cases, anti-government.

This was accompanied by the then growing hostilities of the ruling African elites towards the universities, which they saw as centres of opposition to their predatory rule, [where] centres of resistance had to be destroyed as focal points of progressive thought and activism.

(Mbeki, 2010)

The growing tension between African governments and African academic intellectuals increased during the 1980s when the World Bank and the International Monetary Fund (IMF) forced many governments to cut funding to universities. However, this tension, as noted above, had surfaced earlier.

In a fundamental way the strong ideological inclination and charismatic personality of most of the first presidents of independent African countries made it difficult for pluralistic views and critical engagements to flourish. Most of the ideologies developed after independence – Ujamaa, Humanism, Consciencism, or 'Authenticity' – were adopted and implemented with little consultation. These were ideas formulated by the leaders, perhaps after discussion among the inner circles of the ruling parties where dissent was implicitly prohibited. As authoritarianism spread, most intellectuals began to feel that what was being witnessed was actually a betrayal of the idea of freedom which the independence and liberation struggle had been based upon (Mafeje, 1994). This feeling of betrayal was heightened by widespread reports of corruption and elitism during the late 1960s and early 1970s, and gave rise to *coup d'etats* in countries such as Ghana (1966), Nigeria (1966), Togo (1963), Uganda (1971), and Ethiopia (1974), among many others.

While they were criticised for being unpatriotic, African academic intellectuals accused their African leaders of betraying the values and objectives of the liberation struggle for narrow party and personal interests (see Mkandawire, 2003). Deteriorating material conditions, together with the increasing marginalisation of those intellectuals who were critical of state inefficiencies and corruption, further intensified the tensions. In some countries this resulted in the persecution and secrete elimination of critical voices. This all served to render impossible the contribution of African intellectuals to official economic growth and development policies; most African scholars were not consulted or engaged by bureaucrats or politicians. From the Ivorian experience it has been observed that "it did not take long, however, for those [intellectuals] who had been purged to be liberated, and then rehabilitated with grand ceremonies in 1970–71, after accepting various material compensation" (Bayart, 1993:184). But the general trend, even before the onset of Structural Adjustment Programmes (SAPs) (which hijacked the policy space), had been the marginalisation of African intellectuals by most governments.

In the face of conciliatory approaches from governments, however, many academic intellectuals resisted 'rehabilitation' and 'material compensation', and maintained critical positions, especially during the SAPs era. Most, however, redirected their criticism at the World Bank and the IMF for misguiding development in Africa (see Lancaster, 1997). But some crafty African leaders devised various means – ranging from 'oiling' the hands of some intellectuals, to open threats – in order to keep intellectuals from questioning, and thereby undermining, their regimes, especially in those countries where intellectuals had grown in number and were a formidable force such as was the case in Cote d'Ivoire during the Houphouet-Boigny rule.[8]

African intellectuals and the African crisis

Despite the onslaught by the repressive regimes, a number of African intellectuals have been engaging not just in knowledge production through research and publication, but also in public debates. In the area of economic growth and development theory, it is interesting to note that many African intellectuals, from many different disciplines and backgrounds, have participated in conducting research and publishing their findings. Critical views on the economic and development crisis in Africa have also come from authors in the literary tradition who have used their creative abilities to communicate their observations and understanding of the crisis and its impact on Africa. One example of this is Chinua Achebe's (1987) *Anthills of the Savannah*. In this story the writer describes a state ruled by a young and inexperienced army officer who appoints his fellow inexperienced army staff to key positions in government. Characteristic of this government are: civil servants who have been given positions because they are friends to "His Excellence, the Head of State" (the 'Big Man'); and members of the executive council being 'yes men' (they cannot say anything contrary to the Big Man's viewpoint). There is also an absence of a national vision to act as a guide for government efforts. Interestingly, there is a professor (i.e., an academic) who is very close to His Excellence and who serves as personal advisor to the Big Man.[9]

The author's message is that the outcome of such a government is obvious: no development (in fact, in the story, conditions on the ground get worse by the day), the state coffers being looted, and all those connected to the 'Big Man' enjoying impunity for any illegal activity – be it drug trafficking, murder, corruption or rape – as long as they remain loyal to His Excellence. Other observations that Achebe brings out in the story include the elimination of opponents, the arbitrary nature of appointment to office, the suppression of all freedoms including the freedom of assembly, and, above all, the strong desire of His Excellence to remain in power at any cost. Through the main character Ikem, the argument advanced is that the main cause of the crisis in Africa is bad leadership; for things to improve Africa needs good leadership. This is one view expressed by one African intellectual. In this view, the hope is that once the leadership issue is 'sorted', improvement in the living conditions of the people will follow.

Another example from the literary archive is *Petals of Blood* by Ngugi wa Thiong'o (1977). Unlike Achebe, Ngugi borrows from the Marxist view of society to explain the causes of underdevelopment in Africa. At the core of the story is the idea that Africa had a half-revolution which saw the overthrow of colonial rule by peasants and workers, but that this revolution failed to break from the imperial chains of capitalism. In other words, Africa has been politically liberated, but has economically remained in chains. Although the story is critical of capitalism for being responsible for the fictitious nation of Ilmorog's underdevelopment, it is also critical of the local political elites (personified by Nderi, a member of parliament) for their subservient relations with international capital – and therefore for facilitating the exploitation of African people. In Ngugi's view, the building of infrastructure such as roads is not primarily intended for the benefit of the local people, but to enable the local elites, together with their foreign counterparts, to export raw materials to Western countries.

In *Petals of Blood* the problem identified is capitalism, and the solution proposed is to mobilise peasants and workers to complete the revolution by breaking from the enslaving chains of capitalism. In this case, development is only seen as possible in Africa following a peasants' and workers' revolution. Interestingly, peasants are given a role to play in the overthrow of capitalism – not just the proletariat. Of course a revolution championed by workers in Africa would appear to be a far-fetched dream given the fact that wage labourers (the real proletariat) form only a tiny section of the population (see Fox *et al.*, 2013). Most of the possible protagonists of the revolution (the peasants) are not *doubly* free in the Marxian sense of being "freed from the means of production" and "free" to offer their labour in exchange for wages (as opposed to being coerced, or slave labourers). However, the workers and peasants' revolution seems to have been overtaken by events at the beginning of the 1980s when a more vicious form of capitalism was forcefully entrenched in the continent, and against which both workers and peasants had no time to mobilise. They were all treated to a kind of "shock therapy", from which they have probably not yet recovered. Those who have jobs and belong to trade unions are not interested in the revolution any more; instead they are "more interested in securing better working conditions than advocating for a socialist revolution" (Okolo, 2006: 38).

In both stories mentioned above we have two African intellectuals reflecting on conditions in the continent, and as a result of such reflections, views are offered on what is perceived to have gone wrong and what can be done to correct it. These views may not have been listened to by those in power, and neither have they influenced development theory and policy, but they have, nevertheless, been expressed. There are many more examples of authors using fictional narratives and characters to present their own interpretations and understandings of various aspects of the 'real' world – Wole Soyinka's *Play of the Giants*; Achebe's *A Man of the People*; Dambudzo Marechra's *House of Hunger*; Mariama Ba's *Une si longue letter*. Such literary works have, in fact, led African scholarship in providing a commentary about, a critique of, and proposals for, social change.[10] The list of such intellectuals includes authors such as Chiek Anta Diop, Bernard Dadie, Rene Depestre, Franz Fanon, Keita Fodedba, Camara Laye and Ferdinand Oyono (see Mudimbe, 1988: 85). Examples in anthropology include: A. Ajisafe's *The Laws and Customs of the Yoruba People*; J.B. Danquah's *Akan Laws and Customs* and *The Akan Doctrines of God*; D. Delobus's *Les Secrete des Sorciers Noirs*; M. Quenum's *Au Pay des Fons: Us et Coutumes du Dahomey*; Jomo Kennyatta's *Facing Mount Kenya*; and F.M. Deng's *Tradition and Modernisation: A Challenge for Law Among the Dinka of Sudan*.

Early examples of African scholarship in the field of political studies include: K. Busa's *The Position of the Chief in Modern Political System of Ashanti*; P. Hazoume's *Le Pacte du Sang au Dahomey*; W.E. Graft-Johnson's *Towards Nationhood in West Africa*; Azikiwe's *Renascent Africa*; Nkrumah's *Towards*

Colonial Freedom; Amie Cesaire's *Discourssur le Colonialisme*; and Mamdani's *Citizen and Subject*.

In historical studies, leading African scholarship includes Joseph Ki-Zerbo's *Histoire de l'Afrique Noire*; J.C. de Graft Johnson's *African Glory: The Story of Vanished Negro Civilisation*; and Chiekh Anta Diop's *Nations Negres et Cultures*. In philosophy, V.Y. Mudimbe's *The Invention of Africa*; Steve Biko's *I Write What I like*; Paulin Hountondji's *Sur la Philosophie Africaine*; Kwesi Wiredu's *Philosophy and an African Culture*; Kwame Gyekye's *African Philosophical Thought*; Aphiah Kwame's *In My Father's House*; and Achille Mbembe's *On the Post Colony*.

In political economy and development studies, key early African scholarship includes Samir Amin's several works, Walter Rodney's *How Europe Underdeveloped Africa*; Claude Ake's *A Political Economy of Africa*; Isa Shivji's *Class Struggle in Tanzania*; C. Kamau's "Localising Capitalism"; Peter Ayang-Nyongo's "Liberal Models of Capitalist Development in Africa" and *Development of Agrarian Capitalism in Ivory Coast*.

In the area of economics, and development economics in particular, few scholarly works authored by Africans are cited in the published literature on Africa. For example, in a chapter reviewing the discipline of economics and African studies, Paul Collier only mentions the research studies initiated by Benno Ndulu at the University of Dar es Salaam – which investigated whether a reduction in public investment leads to the increase in private investment through the "crowding out" process (see Collier, 1993: 64). However, towards the end of the chapter the work of Ademola Simon Oyejide and Ade Ajayi at the University of Ibadan, Elbadawi at the World Bank, and Samuel Wangwe at the University of Dar es Salaam, are mentioned. But we know that there are many African development economists and practitioners who have been working on and writing about Africa's economic condition since the early 1970s. These became more prominent during the 1990s as the economic crisis deepened. Leading examples include the work of African economists at the Economic Commission for Africa (UNECA), and, more recently, research work conducted in more than 20 African countries coordinated by the African Economic Research Consortium (AERC) under the project title "Explaining African Economic Growth Performance".[11]

Hegemony of the disciplines

Although a number of African scholars have been involved in conducting research and the production of knowledge on Africa, as the preceding section suggests, there are still questions about whether 'original' academic intellectuals or thinkers exist in Africa. Those who acknowledge their existence end their acknowledgement with, "but these are not original thinkers". This allegation is especially levelled against African scholars from the non-fiction/non-creative disciplines, with critics arguing that most African scholars have not been original enough within the framework of their particular disciplines; they have often been accused of misunderstanding the Western paradigms that they have sprinkled over their studies of Africa (see Zeleza, 2003b). In the case of the development discourse, African scholars reacted to these views by highlighting the fact that the concept of development was a post-World War Two construct used by the West to justify its political, economic, cultural and intellectual dominance; that development was a project which entrenched the dominance of the West over the rest of the underdeveloped world. It is for this reason that some African scholars have suggested that for the

> crisis of Africa to be tackled, the European and now jointly Western grip on the continent must be brought to an end. To achieve this, the African people must be brought to the centre of their own transformation through their own perceptions of the path and direction of the transformation.
>
> (Nabudere, 2006: 48)

Reflecting on the crisis of development in underdeveloped regions of the world during the 1980s and 1990s, some analysts went as far as suggesting that in a post-development period, development itself has largely been exposed as a mere delusion, reflected especially in the Third World in its failure to live up to its promise (see Escobar, 1995). While the post-modern, post-industrial and post-development critiques may be justified in their affront at the universal, unilinear, evolutionary and Eurocentric models of socio-economic and political change, their *subversive* approach renders them more susceptible to populist capture, easily seized upon to advance goals diametrically opposed to their objective of promoting pluralism and diversity of view. This is probably why post-development ideas have had little influence on the ground among practitioners and theorists of development, most of whom are either unaware of, or disinterested in, the post-development ideolgy (see Gardner and Lewis, 1996).

Within African intellectual circles the struggle against the universalist approach, based on Eurocentric paradigms, has often translated into the fight for recognition and sometimes acceptance in the traditional disciplines. The emphatic assertion of the non-existence of African intellectuals, as noted by Mkandawire (1997), is not just about African intellectuals being rendered invisible or existing on the margins – it touches on the uneven structure of knowledge production and the resulting power relations between African scholars and the disciplines (Bates *et al.*, 1993). The challenge at the heart of this struggle is the tension which arises in the quest to purge the domineering impact of Eurocentricism, and the danger of falling into the sort of cultural relativism which ignores the existence of common problems and the possible solidarities that this can engender. An example of this tension is evident in Mudimbe (1988), who in trying to respond to the allegation that African intellectuals have not been original – that they have been regurgitating Western ideas which they dress in African clothes – goes to the extreme of denying that Western scholars (such as Jean-Paul Sartre or Fernad Braudel) had little or no influence on African thinkers like Ki-Zerbo, Cabral, Cesaire, and others. This approach, which often finds solace in cultural relativism, views African intellectuals as locked in a hegemonic dichotomy in which they are always at a disadvantage in relation to their Western counterparts, whether in African studies or in the traditional disciplines (Mazrui, 1994).

In the context of a colonial period which cannot be unmade, the debate about the originality of African scholarship need not be couched in terms of who influenced whom, and when. The central issue should be about whether the African intellectual is able to reflect on the African condition using tools which help in understanding these conditions more meaningfully. Admittedly this ability to transcend paradigmatic constraints beyond their European or American context is one of the biggest challenges most African intellectuals face, particularly in the conventional disciplines. In this regard the focus should not be on "how the study of Africa has shaped the disciplines" (Bates *et al.*, 1993), but rather how the disciplines have shaped how we view and study Africa. Well-intended efforts to render African studies politically appealing often invert the question by focusing on the contributions that the study of Africa makes to the disciplines, which in a way overlooks the harm that the disciplines may have inflicted on the study of Africa and Africans (see Momoh, 2003). For example, justifying the study of Africa on the grounds that "the inhabitants of Africa number among the poorest and the least powerful members of human society'" (Momoh, 2003: xiii), hides the subtle powerplay involved and may fail to ask the right questions. Primarily, this obscures the possibility of asking whether the way Africa has been studied and understood has contributed to *making* Africans the poorest members of the human community. Such questions are precluded under the assumption that the disciplines always bring salvation to Africa. For some analysts "Africa is poor because it is rich and Africa is portrayed as a poor continent so that Africans will continue to be hapless and hopeless about Africa" (Momoh, 2003: 34). Inverting the question leads to putting the well-being of the disciplines before that of the people who the disciplines should be seeking to understand, and perhaps assist.

When looking at the disciplines it becomes evident that those which have allowed African scholars to reflect more creatively on their African conditions – such as the arts and the humanities – have made huge strides in reflecting an African worldview; it is in these areas of study where African scholars and the production of knowledge on Africa stands out. A good example is the creative arts. Any list of literary works on Africa is dominated by African writers and scholars. The very opposite is true for non-fiction disciplines, especially the social and natural sciences. One is at pains to find African scholars on the reference list, even on an African topic. For example, out of a list of more than 270 bibliographical entries of anthropological researchers on Africa, only six are African.[12] While this may be due to bias in the selection of publications that the author included, the sheer gap between African and Africanist scholars is a matter of concern for those who take African intellectuals seriously (see Mkandawire, 1997; Zeleza, 2003b). The list for economics, political science, and even history, produces a similar result. On the relation between African and Africanist scholars, it has been observed that

> The works of African-based scholars are … rarely cited in Africanist literature … [they] are routinely denied access to journals and edited volumes, usually with the vacuous … explanation that *they* are too busy trying to make

a living and ... have little time to engage in the serious business of reflection and intellectual production.

(Martin and West, 1995: 26)

Certainly there are many reasons one can cite to explain this, but it also shows that there are relatively low numbers of African scholars being published compared to their non-African counterparts. This has often given rise to the notion that African scholars do not actually exist. A.F. Robertson offers his own explanation as to why African scholars are not getting published:

They complain of lack of funds, heavy administrative burdens ... inadequate publishing opportunities. But what is more obviously missing is an active community of scholars, capable of sustaining and reproducing itself ... I have been unable to think of an authentic intellectual style or tradition ... which has emanated from within Africa.

(Robertson, 1985: 258)

In the context of African intellectuals and the African economic growth challenges, the main concern is not just about the visibility (or invisibility) of African intellectuals through knowledge production and research projects, but more about knowledge being produced, and its relevance to Africa. The tension between relevance and recognition is often couched in the dictum "publish or perish" (see Nyamnjoh, 2004). It is here that the temptation to produce for the sake of production, to produce knowledge in order to avoid 'perishing', should be resisted because it directs intellectual energies in the continent down avenues which may have nothing to do with contributing to Africa's progress even though the knowledge produced may be contributing to improving the image of the discipline or institution. As some African scholars have observed, "Unlike our so-called 'African specialists', we do not merely wish to research and write just for the sake of writing or to be historians for the sake of being historians. We wish to consciously and actively use our historical knowledge for the liberation of our people" (Maina and Kinyatti, 1971, cited in Campbell, 2008: 150).

The African intellectual community

As noted earlier, when discussing African intellectuals it is important to note that this is not a homogeneous group of people with a well-defined, agreed on mission; it is a heterogeneous group made up of members with different views, ideological orientations, education, training and convictions. These are scholars who are engaged in thinking about Africa in their different countries, and who rarely share views except via each other's publications – which often they are unable to access. Although there have been several initiatives to encourage African intellectuals to get to know each other since the fifth Pan-African Scholars meeting in Manchester (1945),[13] few gatherings have been convened since. Early initiatives include the Representative Government and National

Progress, held at the then University College of Ibadan in Nigeria in 1959 (see Ajayi, 1982). Later initiatives include the Kampala Symposium, which culminated in the *Kampala Declaration on Academic Freedom* to promote the consciousness of African and diaspora intellectuals as a community reflecting on common challenges and aspirations. At the political level the first meeting for African intellectuals was held in 1996 in Dakar, Senegal, followed by a conference organised by the African Union (AU) in 2004, again in Dakar, to provide a platform for promoting interaction.[14]

Within the African intellectual community it is amazing how little each knows about the work of another; not because of any malicious or deliberate disinterest, but rather because the avenues through which their work might be shared are limited. Accessing international or African journals requires a subscription, and if the university or institution is unable to subscribe (which is often the case), very few African intellectuals subscribe on an individual basis. The end result is that the ideas of other African scholars become difficult to access. Research work conducted by students and staff at one African university is often inaccessible to students and staff at another because there is no effective way of bulk-sharing information and knowledge. Even with the advance of technology, which makes it possible to gain electronic access to most publications and research studies (online access), access for many African scholars to a wide range of scholarly work is still a problem, leading to a situation in which *African* scholars have "the latest data but outdated references" and *Africanist* scholars have the latest bibliography but old data (Mkandawire, 1997: 30). The problem of access becomes even more pronounced when one considers the diverse English, French and Portuguese colonial heritage of Africa. The work of most African scholars writing in French or Portuguese is inaccessible to many English-speaking African scholars, and vice versa. Only a small section of translated work is accessible between scholars operating in different colonial languages. This hideous legacy of Africa's history, which has been branded "linguistic neo-colonialism" (see Mazrui, 1994), adds to the constraints faced by African scholars and intellectuals, and is a persisting barrier to creating African intellectual communities.

The problem of access to published scholarly work by Africans also manifests itself in the fact that in the writings of African scholars, references to fellow African authors on the relevant topic are often very few – again not because of any deliberate intention to undervalue each other's work, but simply because very few *know* about each other's work, sometimes even within the same university. This also applies to the course material recommended for students. In some universities students are not prescribed materials by African scholars under the pretension that "Africa has no intelligentsia worth reading" (Mamdani, 1998). I have several times heard colleagues teaching in African universities say that "there are no suitable works by African scholars in this field". This has often meant that Africa is studied through the prism of non-African scholars. In this regard the recommendations that "we need to make greater effort to know each other's work on Africa" (Mkandawire, 1997: 34), as well as the call to create an "intellectual community" (Ki-Zerbo, 1994: 33), are relevant.

Further, and as hinted at above, most African intellectuals are spread throughout the disciplines; many identify themselves primarily as historians, sociologists, engineers, psychologists, economists, political scientists, philosophers, linguists, anthropologists, journalists, African writers, and so on, and not as African intellectual scholars (see Hodder-Williams, 1986). In some instances these disciplinary curtains act as barriers to forging collaborative work even within closely related fields of study. Thus, the sense of facing a common challenge, of contributing to the building of an effective understanding and representation of Africa, is dissipated such that issues surrounding Africa's development continue to be approached from within the narrow prism of each individual discipline. Scholars, even within the same university – by virtue of belonging to different disciplines – relate to each other at arm's length on scholarly matters, especially in those 'guarded disciplines' with strict gate-keeping rules.

Nonetheless, African scholars, in as much as they are not a homogenous group, do not share and need not have the same viewpoint about economic and development challenges in Africa. Contrary to claims that Africans tend to maintain the "artificial consensus" which makes critical engagement through debate unpleasant (see Chabal and Daloz, 1999), there have been robust and sometimes vicious debates about Africa's economic and development crisis among African scholars. Heated debates between Archie Mafeje and Wole Soyinka and Ali Mazrui,[15] between Dani Nabudere and Issa Shivji,[16] between Paul Zeleza and Achille Mbembe[17] and Bernard Mangubane,[18] are some examples of this.

To think that African intellectuals maintain 'artificial consensus' on issues as complex as economic growth and development is the highest form of disregard that one can have for any group of independently thinking human beings, let alone intellectuals and scholars. Differences in opinion and approach are to be expected, and there is nothing wrong with African intellectuals having divergent views. The problem arises when one group of African or non-African scholars claims monopoly over knowledge production and consequently takes a hegemonic posture in explaining and understanding Africa (see Ngugi, 1985).

Similarly, African intellectuals and their views about Africa's economic growth and development crisis are not static; they change over time along with changing circumstances and changes in the dominant ideologies (see Zeleza 2004; Bates *et al.*, 1993). As noted earlier, during the early days of independence – when nationalism and developmentalism were the dominant ideologies – most African and non-African intellectuals found such ideas very attractive and so they not only provided theoretical support for them, they participated actively: some of them in key positions as advisors to policymakers.[19]

Challenges for African intellectuals

A discussion of African intellectuals and their contribution to the understanding of the African growth experience is incomplete without setting a context in which they work. Here I will restrict the discussion to the academic branch of the African intelligentsia in order to provide concrete examples. One of the outstanding features of the context in which most African intellectuals have been operating since the 1980s is that of declining resources – both in terms of remuneration as well as the resources required to carry out effective academic work. This is important because it negatively impacts on the ability of intellectuals to contribute to the economic growth and development discourse through knowledge production. As Mkandawire (1995) observes, prior to the 1980s the first generation of African intellectuals worked in an environment where resources were available; many, though, were more preoccupied with national development issues. However, the economic decline, which started during the mid-1970s and had its negative impact during the 1980s, worsened further with the introduction of SAPs. This resulted in declining resources being allocated to universities, and a deterioration of teaching facilities. Working conditions for staff and students have been very poor ever since then.

> The economic crisis which made the 1980s a lost decade for Africa, led to a decline in the pay and conditions of teachers as well as students. Teachers' real salaries decreased steeply and probably more than that of other workers. In many countries, salaries were very irregularly paid or not paid at all. Working conditions for teachers deteriorated severely and teachers' status in society compared badly with ten years earlier … Teaching facilities including laboratories and libraries were deplorable.
>
> (UNESCO/BREDA, 1995, cited in Sall, 1995: 1)

Such conditions affect the productivity of African scholars, and, most importantly, divert their energies into other activities such as consultancy – which became a big income-earning venture for some academics on the continent during the 1980s and 1990s (see Ake, 1994). Writing in the mid-1990s, Mahmood Mamdani makes this observation:

> During the early days at the University of Dar es Salaam (1973–79) … we used our modest salaries and informal networks to do field work. But all that changed as structural adjustment programmes [SAPs] dramatically undercut our real income and forced us to become truly market responsive. I have to admit that only research grants – at first a small grant from IDRC on the commercialisation of agriculture, later a more generous 'reflections on development' grant from Rockfeller/CODESRIA – saved me from having to double as a Kampala taxi driver to ensure enough income for a decent living.
>
> (Mamdani, 1996: ix)

In the 1995 *State of Academic Freedom in Africa Report* by CODESRIA, it was stated that some salaries for academic staff were as low as US$100 per month (see Sall, 1995: 7). The Nigerian case study presented in the same report showed that the average salary for a senior lecturer declined from US$2,000 per month in 1982 to US$62.80 per month in 1994 (see Mustapha, 1995). Although there have been few studies into the working conditions for academics, and the condition of learning and teaching facilities, it is unlikely that the situation has changed much for the better. A 2006 study conducted in five African universities (Universities of Botswana, Ghana, Ibadan, Makerere and KwaZulu-Natal) found that dissatisfaction with salary packages was one of the key factors undermining the commitment of academics across all institutions of higher education, leading to a high rate of staff turnover. Although basic pre-tax salaries have increased compared to the 1990s, salaries in some universities were as low as US$410 per month (2005) for a senior lecturer.[20]

Marginalisation

The other challenge that most African intellectuals face is the fact that most of them, ever since the nationalist-intellectual fall-out of the 1970s and 1980s, are marginalised from many processes in society. It has been observed that this marginalisation of African intellectuals deepened with the introduction of SAPs for the simple reason that there was no policy space left, even for the state bureaucrats tasked with following the prescriptions of the World Bank and the IMF (Mkandawire, 2003, Owusu, 2003). The effect of SAPs was not just that they cut the state's allocation to universities (jusified on the 'rates of social return argument'), they also increased the alienation felt by academics, and effectively prevented them from participating and contributing to governance and development issues (Mafeje, 1994, Ake, 1994). All the answers and all the development strategies were henceforth to be provided by experts from Washington DC.

The immediate response from African scholars throughout the continent was to oppose and criticise the measures, not for self-serving purposes, but on account of their different understanding and interpretation of the crisis itself (see Chapter 3). One common criticism was that states in Africa had submitted to a process that led to the abandonment of the nationalist vision articulated at independence. Most intellectuals viewed SAPs as anti-developmental and a continuation of colonialism (see Kapur *et al.*, 1997).

The state, in response to such criticism, began to question the relevance of the work that universities were carrying out. A common state criticism of African academics was that they had failed to transform universities into centres where graduates were prepared to work in African conditions; universities were accused of producing students who were only capable of working in Europe or America (see Mazrui, 1994). It was not only the curriculum which was under attack, "African academic research appeared to the state functionaries 'irrelevant', either because it was not applied research, or because African intellectuals were adversarial ... or because they blindly followed Western research themes that did not address local conditions" (Zeleza, 2004: 48).

African intellectuals in some instances were even accused of being "comprador intelligentsia" because of their inclination towards the Western-style of life (see Mkandawire, 2003). Some critics questioned the validity and competence of research conducted by African scholars. The result of these accusations and counter-accusations was a complete marginalisation of local intellectuals and scholars. This was partly driven by the donor agencies – who brought in their own researchers or, in most cases, contracted those same scholars ignored by the state, to conduct the research. Some analysts have observed that during the 1980s and 1990s, "African governments could only access African intellectuals through donor-contracted reports" (Mkandawire, 2003).

Identity crisis

The other challenge which many African intellectuals have faced is the so-called 'identity crisis'. This relates mainly to the idea that when African universities were set up at independence, they were given the task of supplying manpower to carry out the nationalists' post-colonial developmental project. It has been argued that most universities accomplished this mission successfully during the 1970s, such that by the 1980s, since most African economies were not growing enough to accommodate more skilled labour, universities needed a new mission (Mkandawire, 1997; 2003, Zeleza, 2004). This 'identity crisis' is related to the role of the universities and academics in a context in which their contribution to society was not clearly visible. Some have even argued that university education is simply contributing to growing unemployment by producing unemployable graduates. To a certain extent this is a narrow argument since it reduces the university to a skilled labour supplying machine when in fact a university serves many purposes in society besides training and issuing degrees (see World Bank, 2000; Tettey, 2006).

African and Africanist scholars

Another area of concern raised is the relationship between African scholars and their Africanist counterparts. In this regard, concerns (raised mainly by African scholars) include the fact that most Africanists have been acting as gatekeepers of knowledge production on Africa, negatively affecting even the assessment of work carried out by Africans for publication or research grants. Other related concerns are that African scholarship is detached and not often empirically grounded; that there is an asymmetrical division of labour whereby the Africanist "carries out the conceptual work, designs fieldwork programmes for African researchers who conduct the interviews, fill in the forms etc."; that there is deliberate failure on the part of Africanists to acknowledge the work of African scholars by citing the latter's work; and that there is a negative portrayal of Africa by most Africanists (see Mkandawire, 1997: 26ff). This has always put the African in a subservient position, reinforcing the claims that African academic intellectuals cannot do research. In all of these arguments, African intellectuals' contribution to the understanding of the development and economic experience in Africa tends to be downplayed.

The debate about understanding Africa's growth and development experience requires different views, all of which may contribute to putting together the pieces of the African economic growth and development puzzle. Knowledge hegemony – whether by Africanists or Africans – does harm to the development project in the continent not just in terms of the poor economic performance, but also in terms of contributing to a deficiency in the understanding of this performance. Hence, explaining and understanding Africa should not be the monopoly of any single group; anyone should be able to study Africa and present his or her views based on the information gathered. When all is said and done, we are still facing a knowledge crisis on Africa – which remains a key hindrance to the continent's development – and in this regard the words of Cabral are still relevant today:

> the crisis of African revolution … is not a crisis of growth, but mainly a crisis of knowledge. In too many cases, the struggle for liberation and our plans for the future are not only without a theoretical base, but are also more or less cut off from the concrete situation in which we are working.
>
> (Cabral, cited in Arrighi and Saul, 1973: 7)

The pressure is on African intellectuals/scholars to account for their role in understanding and explaining the African experience and how to respond to the challenges.

Notes

1 Organic intellectuals are distinguished from traditional intellectuals, with the latter largely detached from the masses while the former are seen as deeply engaged with everyday struggles in society (see Gramsci, (1970).

2 Here the term civil society is used in the broader Polanyian sense of an *active society* as well as the Gramscian sense of a *regulated society*, referring to the *space* which is distinct from both the market (for Polanyi) and the state (for Gramsci), and yet subsumes and transcends both realms (see Burawoy, 2003).

3 It has been suggested that although Polanyi and Gramsci's theories come from different perspectives and lineages, their views converge in their "divergent rejection of classical Marxism" (see Burawoy, 2003: 208).

4 This was an initiative of the Zimbabwe International Book Fair (ZIBF) in 1998. The objective of the project was "to celebrate the achievements of African writers over the last century … and above all to increase awareness and knowledge of books and writing by African authors". The project was motivated by the fact that many Africans scholars have written and published widely on diverse topics, and in various forms, styles and languages; but that their work remains largely "unknown and uncelebrated". Books written by Africans (as defined) were nominated, and from a list of 1,521 a total of 500 books were shortlisted – 100 were eventually picked out in 2002 by a panel of 16 African scholars sitting in Accra, Ghana.

5 There are many examples in the past of authors, mainly of the Western tradition, who have expressed suspicion about the African's ability to think. Influential writers such as Immanuel Kant, Georg F.W. Hegel, David Hume, Thomas Jefferson and Arnold Toynbee have at various times expressed such views (see Chapter 1).

6 Since the LPA in 1980, and in recent years, African unity has been featuring strongly on the continent's agenda and in the debate in favour of integration of the continent. This debate picked up momentum at the conference held in the Libyan resort town

of Sirte in 1999, with United States of Africa proposals strongly advocated by the late Libyan leader, Muammar Gaddafi. The transformation of the Organisation of African Unity (OAU) into the African Union (AU) in 2001 has been seen as a strong move towards "an integrated, prosperous, equitable and well governed and peaceful United States of Africa, effectively managed by its own citizens and representing a creative dynamic force in the international arena" (see the Pan-African Parliament website at: www.pan-african-parliament.org).

7 The seven RECs are South Africa Development Community (SADC), East African Community (EAC), Economic Community of West African States (ECOWAS), Common Market for Eastern and Southern Africa (COMESA), Community of Sahel-Saharan States (CEN-SAD), Economic Community of Central Africa States, Arab Maghreb Union and Intergovernmental Authority on Development (IGAD).

8 It is argued that "One of Houphouet-Boigny's main worries seems to have been how to maintain his guardianship of the intellectuals, in order to avoid the development of a 'learned neo-bourgoisie' and to prevent them from questioning the post-war pre-eminence of his faction, which had been gained since the Second World War" (Bayart, 1993: 183).

9 This is a case of an academic intellectual who has been 'rehabilitated' and integrated into the system, and they no longer play the role of being a voice of reason and discipline.

10 Among the 100 books selected by "Africa's 100 Best Books of the 20th Century" initiative, only about a quarter (26) are classified as non-fiction/scholarly; the rest (74) are classified as literature and creative writing. Authors of fiction have been highly critical of colonialism as well as the condition of economic and social development in post-colonial Africa. In this sense African writers of fiction have played a critical role not just in the liberation of the African people from Eurocentrism, but also in supporting the current struggles of the African peoples (see Okolo, 2006).

11 For details on specific country studies, see Ndulu *et al.*, 2008. Studies conducted include: Ali and Elbadawi (Sudan), Doumbouya and Camara (Guinea), Gouge and Evlo (Togo), Mamadou and Yakoubou (Niger), Iyoha and Oriakhi (Nigeria), Kasekende and Antingi-Ego (Uganda), Kobou and Njinkeu (Cameroon), Mwega and Nungu (Kenya), Nkurunziza and Ngaruko (Burundi), Fosu and Ndiaye (Senegal), Davies (Sierra Leone), and Aryeetey and Fosu (Ghana).

12 These are Oppong (1981), Obbo (1975), Deng (1971), Danquah (1958), Busia (1951) and Wilson (1952, 1957, 1959 and 1981) (see Moore, 1993).

13 This was a Anglophone Pan-African Congress organised by George Padmore and Kwame Nkrumah in Manchester, and attended by many African intellectuals and diaspora – including William E. DuBois and Amy A. Garvey.

14 The AU conference hosted 700 African and diaspora intellectuals, and was also attended by several African heads of state including the host Abdoulaye Wade (Senegal), as well as Thabo Mbeki (South Africa), Yoweri Museveni (Uganda), Pedro Pires (Cape Verde), Amadou Toumani Toure (Mali), Muammar Gaddafi (Libya, via video conference) and Alpha Oumar Konare (chairman of AU at that time); see the *Report of the First Conference of Intellectuals of Africa and the Diaspora* (2004). This is the first meeting at which African political leaders seemed to show interest in the views of African intellectuals. Both Wade and Mbeki urged the gathered intellectuals to help address challenges that the continent faced. As usual, at the end of the conference several recommendations were made but nothing has been heard of them since.

15 These were a series of sometimes acrimonious exchanges between, in particular, Mafeje and Mazrui regarding the latter's idea of "self-colonization". The debate with Soyinka was about Mazrui's notion of Africa having a "triple heritage" that is Islamic, African and Western (see CODESRIA Bulletin, Nos 3 and 4).

16 Nabudere's critique of Shivji's *Class Struggle in Tanzania* (1976).
17 Zeleza's response to Mbembe's "Getting out of the Ghetto: The Challenge of Internationalization".
18 This is a debate between Mangubane, and Epstein and Mitchell. The debate was about the latter's claim that European clothes, occupations, education and incomes were key indicators of social change or acculturation among the urban settlers in Africa (see Mangubane, 1972, with responses from Epstein and Mitchell, and others).
19 A key example of this is the intellectuals' support for Nyerere's socialist views during the early days. A number of Tanzanian and Africanist scholars from within the University of Dar es Salaam supported Nyerere and the policies he adopted (Williams, 2000, Arrighi and Saul, 1968). However, not all intellectuals supported the stated policies in Tanzania. For example, Shivji has been very critical of state bureaucrats and the policies they have adopted (see Shivji's *Class Struggle in Tanzania*, 1976).
20 The 2005 basic salary for a senior lecturer at the University of Botswana was US$3,590 per month, compared to US$588 at Makerere, US$410 at the University of Ghana and US$756 at the University of Ibadan. However, the study notes that while the basic salary in other universities appears low, actual income is much higher when other benefits such as accommodation and allowances are added (see Tettey, 2006: 39).

References

Achebe, Chinua (1987). *Anthills of the Savannah*. London: Heinemann.
African Studies (2002). "Africa's 100 Best Books of the 20th Century." Online, available at: http://library.columbia.edu/locations/global/virtual-libraries/african_studies/books.html, accessed 4 January 2011.
Ajayi, Ade J.F (1982). "Expectations of Independence." *Daedalus*, Vol. 111, No. 2: 1–9.
Ake, Claude (1994). "Academic Freedom and Material Base" in M. Diouf and M. Mamdani (eds) *Academic Freedom in Africa*. Dakar: CODESRIA: 17–25.
Ake, Claude (1996). *Democracy and Development in Africa*. Washington DC: The Brookings Institution.
Anyidoho, Nana A. (2006). "Identity and Knowledge Production in the Fourth Generation" in B. Beckman and G. Adeoti (eds) *Intellectuals and African Development: Pretension and Resistance in African Politics*. Dakar: CODESRIA: 156–69.
Armah, A. Kwei (2010). "Remembering the Dismembered Continent." *New African*, 1 March.
Arrighi, Giovanni and Saul, John S. (1973). *Essays on the Political Economy of Africa*. New York: Monthly Review Press.
Arrighi, Giovanni and Saul, John (1968). "Socialism and Economic Development in Tropical Africa." *Journal of Modern African Studies*, Vol. 6, No. 2: 141–69.
Arusha Declaration (1967). 5 February 1967. Online, available at: http://www.marxists.org/subject/africa/nyerere/1967/arusha-declaration.htm, accessed 11 May 2010.
Ayittey, George (2004). "NEPAD and Africa's Begging Bowl." *Global Dialogue*, Vol. 6, No. 3: 26–36.
Azikiwe, Nnamdi [1937] (1968). *Renascent Africa*. London: Routledge.
Bates, Robert, Mudimbe, V.Y. and O'Barr, Jean (1993). "Introduction" in R. Bates, V.Y. Mudimbe and J. O'Barr (eds) *Africa and the Disciplines: The Contribution of Research in Africa to the Social Sciences and Humanities*. Chicago/London: University of Chicago Press. Chapter 1.

Bayart, Francois (1993). *The State in Africa: The Politics of the Belly.* London: Longman.

Beckman, B. and Adeoti, G. (2006). "Introduction" in B. Beckman and G. Adeoti (eds) *Intellectuals and African Development: Pretension and Resistance in African Politics.* Dakar: CODESRIA: 1–10.

Biney, Ama (2008). "The Legacy of Kwame Nkrumah in Retrospect." *Journal of Pan African Studies,* Vol. 2, No. 3: 129–59.

Brown, Michael B. (2006). *Africa's Choices: After Thirty Years of the World Bank.* London: Pluto Press.

Burawoy, Michael (2003). "For a Sociological Marxism: The Complementary Convergence of Antonio Gramsci and Karl Polanyi." *Politics & Society,* Vol. 31, No. 2: 193–261.

Calderisi, Robert (2006). *The Trouble with Africa: Why Foreign Aid Isn't Working.* New Haven/London: Yale University Press.

Campbell, Horace (2008). "Ethics and the Enterprise of Studying Africa." *African Studies Review,* Vol. 51, No. 3: 149–55.

Chabal, Patrick (1991). "African, Africanist and the African Crisis." *African Journal of the International African Institute,* Vol. 61, No. 4: 530–2.

Chabal, Patrick and Daloz, Jean-Pascal (1999). *Africa Works: Disorder as Political Instrument.* London: James Currey.

CODESRIA (2008). Archie Mafeje Debates in the CODESRIA Bulletin. CODESRIA Bulletin Nos 3 and 4: 59–113.

Collier, Paul (1993). "Africa and the Study of Economics" in R. Bates, V.Y. Mudimbe and J. O'Barr (eds) *Africa and the Disciplines: The Contribution of Research in Africa to the Social Sciences and Humanities.* Chicago/London: University of Chicago Press: 58–82.

Dehni-Segui, Rene (1996). "Academic Freedom and University Autonomy in Cote d'Ivoire" in E. Sall (ed.) *The State of Academic Freedom in Africa Report.* Dakar: CODESRIA: 58–80.

Diouf, Mamadou (1994). "Intellectuals and the State in Senegal: The Search for a Paradigm" in M. Diouf and M. Mamdani (eds) *Academic Freedom in Africa.* Dakar: CODESRIA: 213–46.

Ekeh, Peter (1975). "Colonialism and the Two Publics in Africa: A Theoretical Statement." *Comparative Studies in Society and History,* Vol. 17, No. 1: 91–112.

Escobar, Arturo (1995). *The Making and Unmaking of the Third World.* Princeton, NJ: Princeton University Press.

Fanon, Franz (1963). *Wretched of the Earth.* New York: Groves Press.

Fox, L., Haines, C. Munoz, J.H. and Thomas, A. (2013). "Africa's Got Work to Do: Employment Prospects in the New Century." IMF Working Paper, No. 13/201.

Gardner, Katy and Lewis, David (1996). *Anthropology, Development and the Post-Modern Challenge.* London: Pluto Press.

Gramsci, Antonio (1970). *Selections from the Prison Notebooks.* London: Lawrence & Wishart.

Hodder-Williams, Richard (1986). "African Studies: Back to the Future." *African Affairs,* Vol. 85, No. 341: 593–604.

Hountondji, Paulin (1996). *African Philosophy: Myth and Reality* (English translation by Henri Evans, 2nd edition). Bloomington: Indiana University Press.

Kapur, Devesh, Lewis, John and Webb, Richard (1997). *The World Bank: Its First Half Century,* Vol. 1. Washington DC: The Brookings Institution.

Kaunda, Kenneth (1969). *Towards Complete Independence*. Lusaka: Zambian Information Services.

Ki-Zerbo, Joseph (1994). "The Need for Creative Organisational Approaches" in M. Diouf and M. Mamdani (eds) *Academic Freedom in Africa*. Dakar: CODESRIA: 26–38.

Lancaster, Carol (1997). "The World Bank in Africa Since the 1980s: The Politics of Structural Adjustment Lending" in D. Kapur, J. Lewis and R. Webb (eds) *The World Bank: Its First Half Century*. Washington: The Brookings Institution. Chapter 5: 161–94.

Leys, Colin (1976). "The 'Overdeveloped' Post Colonial State: A Re-Evaluation." *Review of African Political Economy*, No. 5: 39–48.

Mafeje, Archie (1994). "African Intellectuals: An Inquiry into their Genesis and Social Options" in M. Diouf and M. Mamdani (eds) *Academic Freedom in Africa*. Dakar: CODESRIA: 193–211.

Mamdani, Mahmood (1996). *Citizen and Subject: Contemporary Africa and the Legacy of Late Colonialism*. Princeton, NJ: Princeton University Press.

Mamdani, Mahmood (1998). "Is African Studies to be Turned into a New Home for Bantu Education at UCT?" Text of remarks by Professor Mahmood Mamdani at the seminar on the Africa Core of the Foundation Course for the Faculty of Social Sciences and Humanities, University of Cape Town, 22 April 1998. Online, available at: http://www.hartford-hwp.com/archives/30/136.html, accessed 29 February 2012.

Mangubane, Bernard (1972). "A Critical Look at Indices Used in the Study of Social Change in Colonial Africa." *Current Anthropology*, Vol. 12, Nos 4–5: 419–45.

Martin, William and West, Michael (1995). "The Decline of the Africanists' Africa and the Rise of New Africa." *Journal of Opinion*, Vol. 23, No. 1: 24–6.

Mazrui, Ali (2006). "The Role of Academics in Political and Economic Revival: Uganda in a Comparative Perspective." Paper delivered at the 40th anniversary of the establishment of Makerere University, Kampala, Uganda.

Mazrui, Ali (2008). "Self-colonisation and the Search for Pax Africana: A Rejoinder." CODESRIA Bulletins 3 and 4. Dakar: CODESRIA.

Mbeki, Thabo (2010). "The Role of Africa's Student Leaders in Developing the African Continent." Address by former president of South Africa, Thabo Mbeki, at the African Student Leaders Summit Meeting held at the University of Cape Town, 6 September 2010.

Mbembe, Achille (1999). "Getting Out of the Ghetto: The Challenge of Internationalization" in CODESRIA Bulletin Nos 3 and 4: 3.

Melber, Hennings (2009). "The Relevance of African Studies." *Wiener Zeitschrift fur Afrikastudien*, Vol. 16, No. 9: 183–200.

Mkandawire, Thanidka (1995). "The Three Generations of African Academics: A Note." *Transformation*, Vol. 28: 75–83.

Mkandawire, Thandika (1997). "The Social Sciences in Africa: Breaking Local Barriers and Negotiating International Presence." *African Studies Review*, Vol. 40, No. 2: 15–36.

Mkandawire, Thandika (2003). "African Intellectuals and Nationalism." Paper presented at the conference on the 30th anniversary of CODESRIA, Dakar, Senegal.

Mohan, Jitendra (1966). "Varieties of African Socialism" in R. Milliban and J. Sauville (eds) *The Socialist Register, 1966*. London: Merlin Press: 220–66.

Momoh, Abubakar (2003). "Does Pan-Africanism Have a Future in Africa? In Search of the Ideational Basis of Afro-Pessimism." *African Journal of Political Science*, Vol. 8, No. 1: 31–57.

Moore, Sally F. (1993). "Changing Perspectives on a Changing Africa: The Work of Anthropology" in R. Bates, V. Y. Mudimbe and J. O'Barr (eds) *Africa and the Disciplines: The Contribution of Research in African to the Social Sciences and Humanities.* Chicago/ London: University of Chicago Press: Chapter 3.

Mudimbe, V.Y. (1988). *The Invention of Africa, Gnosis, Philosophy and the Order of Knowledge.* Bloomington and Indianapolis: Indiana University Press.

Mustapha, Abdul R. (1995). "The State of Academic Freedom in Nigeria" in E. Sall (ed.) *The State of Academic Freedom in Africa Report.* Dakar: CODESRIA: 103–20.

Nabudere, Dani (1997). "Beyond Modernisation and Development, or Why the Poor Reject Development." *Human Geography,* Vol. 79, No. 4: 205–15.

Nabudere, Dani (2006). "Development Theories, Knowledge Production and Emanicipatory Practice" in V. Padayach (ed.) *The Development Decade? Economic and Social Change in South Africa 1994–2004.* Pretoria: HSRC Press: 33–52.

Ndulu, B., O'Connell, S. Azam, J.-P. Bates, R.H. Fosu, A.K. Gunning J.W. and Njinkeu, D. (2008). "Introduction" in *The Political Economy of Economic Growth in Africa 1960– 2000* (Vols 1 and 2: Country Case Studies). Cambridge: Cambridge University Press.

Ngugi wa Thiong'o (1977). *Petals of Blood.* Ibadan: Heinemann.

Ngugi wa Thiong'o (1985). "The Commitment of the Intellectuals." *Review of African Political Economy,* No. 32: 18–24.

Nkrumah, Kwame (1961). *I Speak of Freedom: A Statement of an African Ideology.* London: Heinemann.

Nkrumah, Kwame [1961] (1972). *Consciencism: Philosophy and Ideology for Decolonisation.* New York: Monthly Review Press.

Nyamnjoh, Francis (2004). "From Publish or Perish to Publish and Perish: What 'Africa's 100 Best Books' Tell Us About Publishing Africa." *Journal of Asian and African Studies,* Vol. 39, No. 5: 331–55.

Offenheiser, Raymond and Holcombe, Susan (2003). "Challenges and Opportunities in Implementing a Rights-Based Approach to Development: An Oxfam American Perspective." *Non-Profit and Volutnary Sector Quarterly,* Vol. 32, No. 2: 268–306.

Okolo, M.S.C. (2006) "Re-establishing the Basis of Social Order in Africa: A Reflection on Achebe's Reformist Agenda and Ngugi's Marxist Aesthetics" in B. Beckman and G. Adeoti (eds) *Intellectuals and African Development: Pretension and Resistance in African Politics.* Dakar: CODESRIA: 11–26.

Owusu, Francis (2003). "Pragmatism and the Gradual Shift from Dependency to Neoliberalism: The World Bank, African Leaders and Development Policy in Africa." *World Development,* Vol. 31, No. 10: 1655–72.

Robertson, A.F. (1985). "Doing Research in Africa." *African Affairs,* Vol. 84, No. 335: 279–90.

Sall, Ebraime (1995). "Introduction" in E. Sall (ed.) *The State of Academic Freedom in Africa Report.* Dakar: CODESRIA.

Shivji, Issa (1976). *Class Struggle in Tanzania.* London: Heinemann.

Tettey, Wisdom (2006). "Staff Retention in African Universities: Elements of a Sustainable Strategy." Study commissioned by the World Bank. Online, available at: www.worldbank.org, accessed 29 February 2012.

Williams, Adebayo (2000). "Intellectuals and Governance" in G. Hyden, D. Olowu and H. Okhoth-Ogendo (eds) *African Perspectives on Governance.* Asmara: Africa World Press: 295–318.

World Bank (2000). *Higher Education In Developing Countries: Peril or Promise.* Report of the Task Force on Higher Education and Society. New York: World Bank.

Zeleza, Paul (2003a). "Academic Freedom in the Neoliberal Order: Government, Globalisation, Governance and Gender." Journal of High Education in Africa (JHEA), Vol. 1, No. 1: 149–94.

Zeleza, Paul (2003b). *Rethinking Africa's Globalisation*. Trenton, NJ: Africa World Press.

Zeleza, Paul (2004). "Neoliberalism and Academic Freedom" in P.T. Zeleza and A. Olukoshi, *African Universities in the Twenty-First Century*. Dakar: CODESRIA: 42–68.

Appendices

In most reports by the World Bank and the IMF, the five North African countries are reported separately from the rest of Africa. In Appendices I, II and III below they are each included in their own right in view of the discussion of what constitutes Africa in Chapter 1.

Appendix I. Africa's decadal mean GDP per capita growth rates (1961–2012, %)

Country	1961–1970	1971–1980	1981–1990	1991–2000	2001–2010	2011–12
Algeria	1.8	3.4	−0.2	−0.2	2.4	0.2
Angola	..	..	0.3	−1.6	7.8	2.1
Benin	1.2	0.3	0.3	1.1	0.7	1.6
Botswana	5.7	11.1	7.4	2.5	2.8	4.2
Burkina Faso	1.4	1.4	1.0	2.5	2.9	3.8
Burundi	2.5	0.6	1.4	−3.6	0.0	0.8
Cameroon	−0.2	3.9	0.5	−1.3	0.7	1.7
Cape Verde	..	..	3.7	9.0	5.4	2.8
Central African Rep.	..	−0.9	−1.3	−1.0	2.6	4.0
Chad	−0.9	−3.9	2.7	−0.8	7.3	1.4
Comoros	..	..	0.2	−1.3	−0.5	0.1
Congo, Dem. Rep.	0.6	−2.2	−1.9	−8.2	2.0	4.1
Congo, Republic.	1.4	3.5	2.2	−1.2	1.9	0.9
Cote d'Ivoire	4.5	0.8	−3.0	−0.5	−0.5	0.1
Djibouti	..	..	..	−3.7	1.5	..
Egypt, Arab Republic	0.4	4.4	3.1	2.6	3.1	0.1
Equatorial Guinea	..	..	−1.1	17.3	12.9	0.9
Eritrea	..	..	0.0	3.6	−2.7	4.4
Ethiopia	..	..	−0.7	−0.2	5.8	7.1
Gabon	5.2	7.0	−0.5	−0.8	−0.4	3.8
Gambia	0.9	1.9	−0.6	0.3	0.7	−2.7
Ghana	0.4	−1.7	−0.8	1.7	3.2	9.0

Appendix I (cont.)

Country	1961–1970	1971–1980	1981–1990	1991–2000	2001–2010	2011–12
Guinea	..	..	0.3	0.1	0.4	1.3
Guinea-Bissau	0.0	−0.5	2.9	−1.2	0.4	−3.3
Kenya	1.3	4.3	0.4	−1.0	1.4	1.7
Lesotho	3.2	5.5	1.8	2.3	3.2	2.8
Liberia	2.5	−1.0	−10.3	4.3	5.2	6.6
Libya	..	..	..	0.2	2.5	..
Madagascar	0.4	−1.8	−2.2	−1.3	−0.2	−0.3
Malawi	2.2	2.9	−1.9	1.9	0.1	0.2
Mali	0.6	2.5	−0.9	1.5	2.8	−1.8
Mauritania	5.4	−1.1	−1.1	0.0	2.1	3.1
Mauritius	..	−0.3	5.1	4.1	3.0	3.1
Morocco	2.8	2.9	1.7	1.0	3.9	0.7
Mozambique	..	..	−0.6	2.5	4.9	4.7
Namibia	..	..	−2.1	1.2	3.2	3.5
Niger	0.1	−1.2	−2.7	−1.6	0.8	2.6
Nigeria	2.8	2.1	−3.1	−0.6	6.4	2.8
Rwanda	0.4	2.3	−1.3	1.2	5.3	5.1
Sao Tome and Principe	..	..	0.0	0.0	1.6	1.7
Senegal	−0.9	−1.0	−0.4	0.3	1.3	−0.2
Seychelles	1.2	6.1	2.8	3.1	1.1	6.3
Sierra Leone	2.6	0.0	−1.4	−2.6	3.2	8.5
Somalia	..	..	..	..	..	..
South Africa	3.5	1.1	−0.9	−0.4	2.1	1.6
South Sudan	..	..	..	..	..	−26.3
Sudan	−1.1	0.6	−0.3	2.6	3.4	3.3
Swaziland	..	3.2	5.6	0.8	1.1	−2.1
Tanzania	..	..	0.4	0.1	4.0	3.5
Togo	5.3	1.8	−2.2	0.0	−0.4	2.5
Tunisia	1.3	5.1	1.1	3.1	3.5	−0.1
Uganda	..	..	..	3.1	3.9	1.6
Zambia	0.8	−1.9	−1.8	−1.7	2.8	3.7
Zimbabwe	3.0	−0.1	0.8	0.1	−5.0	4.9

Source: author, based on World Bank Data (http://databank.worldbank.org/data).

Note: [..] = no data. Figures for 2011 and 2012 are estimates and forecast rates respectively.

Appendix II. Africa's decadal mean GDP per capita (US$, current prices, 1960–2012)

Country	1961–1970	1971–1980	1981–1990	1991–2000	2001–2010	2011	2012
Algeria	246.95	1,062.47	2,399.10	1,612.78	3,123.49	5,271.59	3,547.70
Angola	..	..	493.5	570.1	2,397.4	5,159.2	5,482.4
Benin	107.7	218.8	312.2	356.7	556.6	745.9	751.9
Botswana	87.5	503.6	1,482.4	2,943.4	4,926.7	7,697.4	7,238.0
Burkina Faso	80.8	167.8	263.0	248.7	421.9	649.9	651.7
Burundi	65.1	127.3	223.3	153.9	154.2	246.9	251.0
Cameroon	143.9	401.9	899.9	747.1	927.4	1,204.7	1,166.9
Cape Verde	..	47.2	599.9	1,321.1	2,553.6	3,801.4	3,695.4
Central African Republic	92.8	210.9	368.8	332.3	365.4	498.8	482.7
Chad	123.7	196.8	215.3	222.2	602.0	1,006.3	1,035.3
Comoros	..	39.4	419.4	485.7	649.4	871.7	830.5
Congo, Dem. Rep.	236.1	447.4	316.0	162.3	150.7	245.6	261.8
Congo, Rep.	178.4	486.7	1,049.9	864.8	1,863.1	3,414.1	3,153.7
Cote d'Ivoire	227.0	707.3	835.5	777.8	980.2	1,241.6	1,244.0
Djibouti	..	..	382.33	745.55	621.82	..	..
Egypt, Arab Republic	164.31	315.33	654.75	1,055.03	1,695.18	2,972.58	3,256.01
Equatorial Guinea	156.4	251.6	193.1	845.3	1,2642.6	2,3473.4	2,4035.7
Eritrea	..	..	..	156.7	246.5	439.5	504.3
Ethiopia	..	..	225.0	152.9	201.2	334.7	454.8
Gabon	439.6	3,056.9	4,560.7	4,569.1	6,637.3	1,1768.6	1,1256.5
Gambia	53.8	232.5	306.3	719.5	489.2	517.8	506.6
Ghana	227.3	309.2	374.5	384.5	757.7	1,594.0	1,604.9
Guinea	..	..	204.6	444.7	372.4	454.0	491.8
Guinea-Bissau	11.5	134.6	182.8	220.3	420.4	595.8	494.3
Kenya	115.8	275.1	358.3	366.9	590.2	800.0	942.5
Lesotho	57.1	158.1	253.8	439.8	693.2	1,243.9	1,193.0
Liberia	189.7	344.0	387.9	117.1	203.8	376.9	413.8
Libya	..	..	678.55	6,316.46	7,614.49	..	..
Madagascar	150.7	292.9	301.7	247.7	336.2	457.2	447.4
Malawi	56.7	127.5	171.7	184.4	249.9	363.6	268.1
Mali	23.5	148.1	223.6	273.7	486.9	740.5	699.3
Mauritania	161.1	339.3	464.8	585.0	767.8	1,154.1	1,106.1
Mauritius	..	522.1	1,537.5	3,406.5	5,621.1	8,748.1	8,119.5
Morocco	204.9	546.4	772.8	1 218.5	2 119.62	3 044.10	2 002.33
Mozambique	..	29.0	248.9	191.4	318.8	511.3	565.2
Namibia	..	214.1	1,573.3	1,941.8	3,443.8	5,692.2	5,785.7
Niger	157.5	249.3	292.5	209.8	272.4	388.3	394.8
Nigeria	120.3	460.5	395.6	273.8	967.5	2,518.6	2,722.3
Rwanda	45.4	135.3	298.3	250.4	325.7	570.2	619.9
Sao Tome and Principe	..	..	..	55.0	829.3	1,355.4	1,400.3
Senegal	255.6	426.5	594.3	580.5	800.9	1,083.3	1,023.3
Seychelles	317.0	1,064.2	3,209.5	6,793.3	10,151.4	12,289.3	12,782.7

Appendix II (cont.)

Country	1961–1970	1971–1980	1981–1990	1991–2000	2001–2010	2011	2012
Sierra Leone	155.3	248.9	255.5	195.2	351.8	501.0	634.9
Somalia	80.1	127.3	143.0	..	..	..	..
South Africa	592.6	1,559.3	2,950.1	3,435.0	4,809.5	7,789.9	7,351.8
South Sudan	..	..	..	..	444.6	1844.3	943.0
Sudan	125.6	318.3	562.8	358.5	829.0	1,537.6	1,580.0
Swaziland	179.7	541.5	820.7	1,522.6	2,237.2	3,274.4	3,041.9
Tanzania	..	..	57.5	223.7	399.1	530.4	608.7
Togo	108.1	258.6	319.8	328.8	397.9	569.5	574.1
Tunisia	230.46	783.53	1,256.11	2,028.51	3,370.41	4,350.33	4,236.79
Uganda	98.3	183.3	253.8	234.3	341.2	440.8	551.2
Zambia	315.5	520.1	453.1	373.5	747.3	1,408.6	1,462.9
Zimbabwe	301.2	646.8	830.2	626.2	463.5	663.6	714.2

Source: author, based on World Bank Data (http://databank.worldbank.org/data).
Note: [..] = no data. Figures for 2011 and 2012 are estimates and forecast rates respectively.

Appendix III.   Africa's mean decadal GDP growth rates (1960–2012, %)

Country	1961–1970	1971–1980	1981–1990	1990–2000	2001–2010	2011	2012
Algeria	4.6	0.0	2.8	1.6	3.7	3	3.4
Angola	..	6.4	4.2	1	3.7	8.1	7.2
Benin	3.0	0.0	3.1	4.5	3.8	3.5	3.8
Botswana	8.7	2.8	11.5	5.3	4	5.8	5.1
Burkina Faso	3.0	15.2	3.7	5.1	5.8	6.4	6.7
Burundi	4.8	3.3	4.3	−1.4	3.5	4.1	4.3
Cameroon	2.2	2.4	4	0.4	3.2	4.6	4.8
Cape Verde	..	6.8	6.4	5.2	6.2	4.8	4.9
Central African Republic	2.0	0.0	0.9	1.3	1.3	3.8	4
Chad	1.0	1.3	5.4	2.2	8.7	..	..
Comoros	..	−1.8	2.7	1.6	1.9	2.5	3.5
Congo, Dem. Rep.	3.3	0.0	1.8	−5.5	5.6	6.6	8.2
Congo, Rep.	4.2	0.5	6.8	0.8	4.5	4.7	5.6
Cote d'Ivoire	8.9	6.6	−0.2	2.6	1	8.2	7
Djibouti	0.0	5.5	..	−2	4	..	..
Egypt, Arab Rep.	5.4	0.0	5.9	4.3	5	2.4	3.2
Equatorial Guinea	0.0	6.7	0.9	20.2	14.4	..	..
Eritrea	..	..	..	8.1	3.9	..	..
Ethiopia	..	..	2.4	2.7	8.9	7.8	7.5
Gabon	6.9	0.0	1.9	2.5	2.4	4.7	3.5
Gambia	1.8	9.2	3.9	3.1	3.4	3.9	10.7
Ghana	3.0	5.0	2	4.3	6.3	7.5	7.8

Appendix III (cont.)

Country	1961–1970	1971–1980	1981–1990	1990–2000	2001–2010	2011	2012
Guinea	..	0.5	4.5	4.3	2.6	4.8	5
Guinea-Bissau	..	..	2.9	2	2.5	−2.8	3
Kenya	4.7	1.3	4.2	2.2	4.4	4.3	4.9
Lesotho	5.2	8.2	2.1	4.1	3.8	4.3	5.2
Liberia	4.9	8.0	−4.5	1.2	6	..	..
Libya	..	1.9	..	..	5.4	..	..
Madagascar	3.0	..	0.4	1.6	3.3	2.2	4.5
Malawi	4.8	1.1	1.7	4.1	5.1	4.1	5.4
Mali	1.0	6.2	0.6	3.6	5.1	−1.5	3.5
Mauritania	8.5	4.2	2.2	2.6	5.6	4.8	5.2
Mauritius	..	1.8	4.3	5.2	3.9	3.3	3.6
Morocco	5.0	0.4	3.9	2.8	4.8	3	4.4
Mozambique	..	5.2	0.4	5.5	7.5	7.5	8
Namibia	..	..	1.1	4.1	4.9	4.2	4.3
Niger	2.9	..	0	1.9	4.2	12	6.8
Nigeria	5.1	1.6	0.9	3.1	6.8	6.5	6.6
Rwanda	3.0	6.2	3.2	2.1	7.9	7.7	7.5
Sao Tome and Principe	..	5.6	..	..	..	..	..
Senegal	2.0	0.0	2.4	2.7	4.1	3.7	4.8
Seychelles	3.8	1.8	2.1	4.9	2.9	3.3	4.2
Sierra Leone	4.3	8.1	1.1	−4.3	6.6	25	11.1
Somalia	..	2.3	..	..	..	..	..
South Africa	6.0	0.0	2.2	1.4	3.7	2.4	2.7
South Sudan	..	..	..	..	..	−2	11
Sudan	1.7	3.7	3.4	4.4	7.1	3	3.2
Swaziland	0.0	3.8	8.6	3.7	2.4	−2	1
Tanzania	0.0	6.4	3.8	3.3	7	6.5	6.8
Togo	8.4	0.0	2.6	2.6	2.6	4	4.4
Tunisia	4.8	4.4	3.6	5.1	4.4	2.4	3.2
Uganda	0.0	7.5	3	7.1	7.7	3.4	6.2
Zambia	3.9	0.0	1.4	0.4	5.7	6.7	7.1
Zimbabwe	6.5	1.5	5.2	2.6	−5.1	5	6
Sub-Saharan Africa	**5.0**	**0.0**	**2.2**	**2.1**	**4.9**	**4.6**	**4.9**

Source: author, based on World Bank Data (http://databank.worldbank.org/data).

Note: [..] = no data. Figures for 2011 and 2012 are estimates and forecast rates respectively.

Index